FROM ANCIENT TO MODERN
ARCHAEOLOGY AND AESTHETICS

Edited by Jennifer Y. Chi and Pedro Azara

Including contributions by Jennifer Y. Chi, Pedro Azara, Marc Marín, William B. Hafford, Richard L. Zettler, Holly Pittman, Naomi F. Miller, Kim Benzel, Jack D. M. Green, Jean M. Evans, and Clemens Reichel

Published by the Institute for the Study of the Ancient World at New York University and by Princeton University Press on the occasion of the exhibition *From Ancient to Modern: Archaeology and Aesthetics*, at the Institute for the Study of the Ancient World, February 12–June 7, 2015

Institute for the Study of the Ancient World
New York University
15 E. 84th Street, New York, NY 10028
isaw.nyu.edu

Princeton University Press
41 William Street, Princeton, NJ 08540
press.princeton.edu

This exhibition has been organized by the Institute for the Study of the Ancient World at New York University in collaboration with the University of Pennsylvania Museum of Archaeology and Anthropology.

Managing Editors: Jennifer Babcock, Roberta Casagrande-Kim

Copy Editor: Mary Cason

Design: CoDe. New York Inc., Mischa Leiner

Color Separations and Printing: Professional Graphics Inc., Rockford, IL

The book was set in Berthold Akzidenz Grotesk and printed on Hanno Art Silk.

Library of Congress Control Number: 201495684

ISBN: 978-0-691-16646-9

Printed in the USA

Institute for the Study of the Ancient World
at New York University
February 12, 2015–June 7, 2015

Published by
Institute for the Study of the Ancient World
at New York University

Princeton University Press
Princeton and Oxford

This exhibition and its accompanying catalogue were made possible
by the generous support of the David Berg Foundation, Agnes Gund,
the Tianaderrah Foundation, Hicham and Dina Aboutaam, Fred and
Diana Elghanayan, and the Leon Levy Foundation.

Contents

The Penn Museum is delighted to lend some of the most important pieces from its Near Eastern collections to *From Ancient to Modern: Archaeology and Aesthetics* at the Institute for the Study of the Ancient World.

Sir Leonard Woolley's finds at the ancient city of Ur, in southern Iraq, rank as one of the most important collections of material in the archaeology of the ancient world, and the most famous among them are the burials that are collectively known as the Royal Tombs of Ur. There, in an unprecedented and so far unrivaled discovery, Woolley excavated a series of burial chambers, some of which contained as many as sixty-eight individuals and large amounts of golden objects and other grave goods. While some of these individuals are of high status—presumably members of one or more royal families—the majority are the ladies-in-waiting and palace guards who accompanied their kings and queens into the afterlife.

Among the material included in *Archaeology and Aesthetics* is one of the most spectacular sets of personal adornment from the graves—the beaded "cloak" and golden headdress of Queen Puabi—as well as a selection of representative rings and other accoutrements. The importance of the ISAW exhibition, however, lies not only in the objects themselves, but in its emphasis on the ways that they have been received, reconstructed, and contextualized, and to this end we are no less delighted to be able to offer select items from Woolley's notes, contemporary publications, and subsequent research carried out at the Penn Museum since the excavation of the royal tombs in 1925–26. We are also pleased that through the joint Penn Museum and British Museum collaborative project entitled *Ur of the Chaldees: A Virtual Vision of Woolley's Excavations*, with lead sponsorship from the Leon Levy Foundation, all of Woolley's field notes, along with images and catalogue information, will soon be made publicly available through a web resource.

The participation of Penn Museum experts, particularly Holly Pittman, Ph.D., and Richard L. Zettler, Ph.D., as well as archivist Alex Pezzati, in the planning of *Archaeology and Aesthetics* is also particularly timely for us as we enter an intensive phase of research, planning, and design of our own in service of a dramatic reinstallation of the Penn Museum's Ancient Near East galleries. Puabi's cloak and headdress will be among the iconic items from our collections spotlighted and contextualized in this reinstallation.

We congratulate the ISAW team on the vision and implementation of this fascinating show and look forward to many future collaborations with our near neighbor.

Julian Siggers
Williams Director
University of Pennsylvania Museum of Archaeology and Anthropology

From Ancient to Modern: Archaeology and Aesthetics brings ISAW's exhibition program to a new level of intellectual exploration with an examination of the complex process through which archaeological artifacts are transformed into works of art. Presenting more than fifty outstanding Early Mesopotamian objects side by side with illuminating documents, photographs, drawings, and other archival material, *Archaeology and Aesthetics* reveals the roles of archaeologists, art historians, journalists, museum curators, and conservators in constructing identities for ancient artifacts that not only resonated with Western popular and artistic culture, but also placed many of these extraordinary finds within the scholarly discourse on Western art history. In another first for our institution, the exhibition includes modern and contemporary art, documenting the evolving influence that many of these objects, and the way they were presented, had and continue to have on artists of our time. The combination of such diverse material creates an unprecedented and multilayered view of such famous sites as Ur in Sumer, Kafajah in the Diyala region, and Kish on the Euphrates River, and, importantly, illustrates the ongoing life of ancient objects, be they utilitarian, religious, or magical.

We are enormously grateful to the University of Pennsylvania Museum of Archaeology and Anthropology, our main collaborator in this exhibition project. This team, lead by Julian Siggers, Williams Director, provided critical curatorial support, as well as unprecedented loans from their world-famous collection of material from Ur, including that related to the legendary Queen Puabi. The Oriental Institute, in Chicago, also played a key role, with support given throughout the entire project by Director Gil Stein and Chief Curator Jack Green, who generously provided loans from the museum's spectacular collection of Sumerian sculpture, and opened the doors to its rich archive. Special thanks also go to the Field Museum for providing seminal loans and expertise.

At ISAW, the curatorial team was lead by our Exhibitions Director and Chief Curator, Jennifer Chi, and Pedro Azara, Professor of Aesthetics and the Theory of Art at the Polytechnic University of Catalonia. It is this type of cross-collaboration that ISAW embraces, as it allows innovative and thought-provoking interpretations of what is now considered iconic material. The exhibitions team again provided the consistent and admirable support that was required to complete one of our most complicated exhibitions.

Finally, I would like to express my thanks to this exhibition's funders, who had the vision to see the importance of connecting the ancient to the modern. We thank the David Berg Foundation, Agnes Gund, the Tianaderrah Foundation, Hicham and Dina Aboutaam, and Fred and Diana Elghanayan for their generous support, and the Leon Levy Foundation for making this exhibition possible.

Roger S. Bagnall
Leon Levy Director
Institute for the Study of the Ancient World

Acknowledgments

From Ancient to Modern: Archaeology and Aesthetics displays a series of spectacular Early Mesopotamian objects alongside rich documentation, opening a window onto the transformation of an archaeological object into a work of art. This transformation raises fundamental and critical questions: What biographies were initially given to these objects by their discoverers? How were these objects filtered through the eyes and voices of the press to be seen for the first time by the public? How were the objects' biographies affected by or reflective of the tastes of the time? How were the items presented in museums and received by artists of the period? And finally, how do they continue to influence artistic production today, even though their origins date back to well over five millennia? Our goal is to illustrate that these biographies do not begin and end in antiquity, or even upon the discovery of the objects through modern-day excavation, but continue to be written through scholarly inquiry and reconsideration, through museum displays and the relationships they create for the viewer, and through the ways in which they inspire artists of our time. The discovery of an object in the modern trench is in fact the starting point for a multiplicity of approaches, each creating a better understanding of the ancient piece.

The preparation of this exhibition involved the participation of many individuals and institutions. My collaboration with Pedro Azara, Professor of Aesthetics and the Theory of Art at the Polytechnic University of Catalonia, had its inception early in the new year of 2011, when he made a special visit to ISAW to introduce himself and express his admiration for its exhibition program. *From Ancient to Modern: Archaeology and Aesthetics* emerged from the creative dialogue that ensued that cold winter's day, drawing on Pedro's more than twenty years of experience curating critically acclaimed exhibitions. I am grateful for the spirit of scholarly partnership that has informed every aspect of our relationship as cocurators, and now as colleagues and friends.

Pedro and I would first and foremost like to recognize the work of Zainab Bahrani, Edith Porada Professor of Ancient Near Eastern Art and Archaeology at Columbia University, and Jean Evans, Research Associate at the Oriental Institute at the University of Chicago. The recent writing of both Bahrani's *The Infinite Image: Art, Time and the Aesthetic Dimension in Antiquity* and Evans's *The Lives of Sumerian Sculpture: An Archaeology of the Early Dynastic Temple* were seminal in our research, and provided us with an intellectual structure for framing the exhibition narrative. They have pushed our knowledge of Mesopotamian aesthetics to a whole new level, providing curators, such as Pedro and myself, with a new way of looking at Early Mesopotamian art.

I must express enormous gratitude to ISAW's partner institution, the University of Pennsylvania Museum of Archaeology and Anthropology. When I first approached Julian Siggers, Williams Director, with the idea of highlighting the excavations at Ur through the site's spectacular finds as well as the rich archival material related to it, he readily embraced the project. Julian had the vision to understand why it was critical to include the extraordinary objects associated with the legendary Queen Puabi, paving the way to new views of this important but elusive Sumerian figure. With such significant loans from both the permanent and archival collections, there was a myriad of details to be considered, and I am indebted to Stephen J. Tinney, Deputy Director and Chief Curator, who provided a consistent voice of guidance and support, and to James Mathieu, Chief of Staff to the Williams Director and Head of Collections, who facilitated the many visits made by Pedro, me, and the ISAW exhibitions team to research the material. The rigorous study of Puabi and her related items could not have been completed without the guidance and passion of the Penn Museum's curatorial team. The group was led by Richard Zettler, Department Chair of Near Eastern Languages and Civilizations and Associate Curator-in-Charge of the Near East Section, along with Holly Pittman, Bok Family Professor in the Humanities in the Department of Art History, Curator of the Near East Section, and a member of ISAW's Advisory Committee. Both Richard and Holly provided great insight into the material from Ur, contributed thought-provoking catalogue essays, and participated in all of our exhibition design discussions, enhancing the content of this project. Alessandro Pezzati, Senior Archivist, and Eric Schnittke, Assistant Archivist, welcomed the ISAW team on many occasions to view the archival material and aided in our selection and presentation.

Also at the Penn Museum, I am grateful to Lynn Grant, Head Conservator, for her guidance around complex issues of display. Katherine Blanchard, Fowler/Van Santvoord Keeper of Collections, was exceptionally helpful with initial planning, facilitating visits to storerooms, and providing expert knowledge of the objects. Anne Brancati, Registrar for Loans, worked closely and enthusiastically with the ISAW team on all aspects of the loan process. Robert Thurlow, Registrar for Traveling Exhibitions, provided essential support. William Brad Hafford, Leon Levy Foundation Project Manager for the Ur Digitization Project, offered a wealth of information on the archival material and coauthored an informative essay with Richard Zettler. Naomi Miller, Consulting Scholar for the Near East Section, coauthored an article with Holly Pittman, adding essential content. I am indebted to this talented team and hope that this is the first of many rich collaborations with ISAW.

The Oriental Institute at the University of Chicago, led by Gil Stein, has also played an important role in the development of *From Ancient to Modern*. Gil has been wonderfully hospitable and energetically facilitated his institution's collaboration with ISAW. It has been a pleasure to work with Jack Green, Chief Curator of the Oriental Institute Museum, whose enthusiasm, knowledge, and professionalism greatly informed our decision-making process. His assistance with the selection of Sumerian sculpture from the museum's world-renowned collection was invaluable. He, along with Jean Evans, Research Associate, contributed a stimulating article to the catalogue. Kiersten Neumann, Curatorial Assistant, helped with the planning and the dissemination of information. John Larson, Archivist, provided insight and support into the Oriental Institute's exceptional archival material. In addition, I thank the conservation and preparation team of Laura D'Alessandro, Conservator, Alison Whyte, Associate Conservator, Helen McDonald, Registrar, and Erik Lindahl, Preparator.

I am grateful to Clemens Reichel, Associate Curator at the Royal Ontario Museum and Assistant Professor in the Department of Near and Middle Eastern Civilizations at the University of Toronto, who wrote an informative article on the Diyala-region excavations and project.

At the Field Museum, I would like to thank the curatorial and archival teams of William A. Parkinson, Curator of European Mediterranean Archaeology; James Phillips, Curator of North Africa and the Near East; Karen Wilson, Kish Project Coordinator; Armand Esai, Museum Archivist; and Nina Cummings, Photo Archivist. All warmly welcomed Pedro and me during our initial research trip, not only opening the doors of storage rooms but also offering their expertise. Angie Morrow, Head Registrar, provided support, advice, and enthusiasm throughout the planning phase of the exhibition.

At the Metropolitan Museum of Art, I want to express my deep gratitude to my colleagues in the Ancient Near Eastern Department. Joan Aruz, Curator-in-Charge, recognized the importance of the Tel Asmar statuette loan and did not hesitate to facilitate the loan request. Kim Benzel, Associate Curator, provided exceptional support to ISAW's in-house team, fielding questions about Puabi and Ur in general and writing a thoughtful essay on the meaning behind technique in Puabi's ensemble. Tim Healing, Senior Administrator, helped facilitate the loan request of archival material, along with Daira Szostak, Graduate Summer Intern. Emily Foss, Registrar, facilitated the object loans.

The Birmingham Art Gallery and Museum loaned several Mary Louise Baker watercolors that enhance the archival section in our Puabi display. I would like to thank Adam Jaffer, Curator of World Cultures, Helen Olivers, Loan Registrar, and Domniki Papadimitriou, Picture Librarian, for making these loans a reality.

At the British Museum, Jonathan Tubb, Keeper of the Middle Eastern Department, and Sarah Collins, Assistant Keeper, were generous with the loan of two original Woolley notebooks. Planning was overseen by Dean Baylis, Senior Administrator and Loan Coordinator.

In a first for ISAW's exhibition program, we have installed a series of modern and contemporary works of art. There were several institutions and a private collection that made our desire a reality. Fayez and Susan Sarofim lent their extraordinary Willem de Kooning painting, allowing ISAW to discuss the seminal connection between Sumerian sculpture and the artist's *Woman* series. I would like to thank ISAW Friend Frances Marzio for graciously facilitating this request. I am grateful for the loan of a work by de Kooning from the Brooklyn Museum, where Arnold Lehman, Shelby White and Leon Levy Director, and Kevin Stayton, Chief Curator, both embraced this exhibition project.

From Ancient to Modern has been able to explore the work of Henry Moore and his interest in Sumerian sculpture thanks to two institutions. The Henry Moore Foundation lent an important sculpture, and I am grateful to Sebastiano Barassi, Chief Curator; Theodora Georgiou, Registrar; Sophie Orton, Curatorial Assistant; Rosie Bass, Personal Assistant to the Senior Curator of Collections and Exhibitions; and Emily Unthank, Archive Image and Licence Coordinator. At the Sainsbury Center for Visual Arts, I would like to thank Paul Greenhalgh, Director, Joanna Foyster, Registrar, and Maria Ledinskaya, Assistant Conservator, for their openness and assistance with the loan of another sculpture by Moore.

A series of Alberto Giacometti drawings was lent by the Fondation Alberto and Annette Giacometti, and I thank Catherine Grenier, Director, and Alban Chaine, Registrar, for their assistance.

Father Pius-Ramón Tagan, Head of the Scriptorium Biblicum et Orientale at the Montserrat Abbey, generously provided hundreds of unpublished photographs taken by Father Bonaventura Ubach during his many journeys to the Middle East. Angels Ruis, Head Librarian, facilitated the loans.

The goal of the exhibition—a confrontation between Sumerian and modern and contemporary art—would have been meaningless without the contribution of living artists who have looked to Sumerian art as a starting point for their exploration of the contemporary geopolitical situation. I am extremely grateful to Michael Rakowitz, whose work Pedro first saw at Documenta 13 in Kassel in 2012. Pedro and I then viewed more of his work the following year at the Museum of Contemporary Art in Chicago, in *The Way of the Shovel: On the Archaeological Imaginary in Art*, an enlightening exhibition about what archaeological knowledge and processes bring to our understanding of the world and of ourselves. Michael accepted our invitation to meet and discuss the possibility of working together, resulting in an exceptionally fruitful collaboration. I am grateful to the Lombard Freid Gallery, which represents the artist in New York, for the loan of his seminal work, *The Invisible Enemy Should Not Exist*. Jane Lombard, Partner, and Lea Freid, Partner, understood the importance of Michael's work to this exhibition and graciously facilitated the loan. Alia Fattouh, Director, oversaw a myriad of details. I am thankful to Rebecca Ashby-Colón, Gallery Assistant, and Cameron Crawford, for their help.

Pedro discovered the fascinating work of Jananne al-Ani at the Venice Biennale in 2011. The artist uses images from family albums and of cultural heritage to create complex and subtle pieces that express the intimate loss caused by both Gulf Wars. Thanks to her suggestion and to the enthusiasm of the Imperial War Museum in London, Kathleen Palmer, Head of Art, and Sara Bevan, Curator, were extremely helpful in securing the important loan of Jananne's *Untitled May 1991 [Gulf War Work]*.

It is hard for me to express my gratitude to the permanent team at ISAW. Its members are an exceptionally talented group, passionate about their chosen areas of expertise and a joy to work with. Amanda Dietz, Senior Exhibition Associate, Angela Nacol, Exhibitions Registrar and Installation Manager, Jennifer Babcock, Curatorial Post-Doctoral Associate, Roberta Casagrande-Kim, Curatorial Post-Doctoral Associate, and Narges Bayani, Curatorial and Production Assistant, all enlightened this project with their dedicated efforts and knowledge. Marc Marín, with endless enthusiasm, worked closely with Pedro in the selection of material to be displayed and on the exhibition design, and coauthored an article. He brought a new and fresh view to our work, which was inspiring. I thank Joan Borrell for the magnificent interpretation of a Sumerian hymn. Mischa Leiner, Principal of CoDe. New York Inc., pushed our institutional boundaries for exhibition and catalogue design in a manner that was both respectful and forward thinking, and I thank him for the always vibrant and creative dialogue. Marianne Hoag, Lighting Designer, again made our gallery space luminous, creating the dramatic atmosphere we had hoped for. Scott Hoefer produced beautiful casework. Lucy O'Brien represented the exhibition perfectly to the media. Mary Cason, our trusted editor, edited the text.

Finally, this exhibition would not have been possible without ISAW's donors, who recognized the importance of connecting past to present and present to past. I thank the David Berg Foundation, Agnes Gund, the Tianaderrah Foundation, Fred and Diana Elghanayan, Hicham and Dina Aboutaam, Frances Marzio, Vartan and Clare R. Gregorian, the Carnegie Corporation of New York, and of course our main funders, the Leon Levy Foundation. I am grateful for your visionary support.

Jennifer Y. Chi
Exhibitions Director and Chief Curator, Institute for the Study of the Ancient World

From Ancient to Modern: A Chronology

ANCIENT PERIODIZATION

6000–3800 BCE **Ubaid Period**
5500 BCE Foundation of Ur

3100–2900 BCE **Jemdet Nasr Period**
Kish's earliest recognizable settlement
Eshnunna's earliest occupation (modern Tell Asmar)
Tell Agrab: earliest excavated remains
Khafajah or Khafaje: earliest excavated remains

2900–2650 BCE **Early Dynastic I–II Periods**

2650–2350 BCE **Early Dynastic III**

2350–2150 BC **Akkadian Period**

2100–2000 BC **Ur III Period**
2500–2100 BCE Royal Cemetery at Ur
2500–2400 BCE Early Dynastic royal tombs at Ur (PG 789 and PG 800)
2400–2300 BCE Cemetery A at Kish

MODERN PERIODIZATION

1920	Iraq, previously part of the Ottoman Empire, becomes a British Mandate under the Colonial Office. Monarchy is established the following year at the Cairo Conference, attended by Winston Churchill, T. H. Lawrence, and Gertrude Bell.
Circa 1920	Paul Poiret, known as the "King of Fashion," mixes modernism with orientalism when designing Art Deco headdresses.
1922–34	Archaeological mission at Ur (Iraq)
1923–33	Archaeological mission at Kish (Iraq)
1927–28	Discovery of Queen Puabi's tomb at Ur
1927–37	Alberto Giacometti draws Gudea and Gudea-period sculptures at the Louvre Museum in Paris.
1929	Georges Contenau writes "L'art sumérien: Les conventions de la statuaire," on Sumerian sculpture as art.
1929	Carl Einstein publishes *Aphorismes méthodiques*, on how to evaluate African objects as art.
1929–31	Henry Moore's sculpture inspired by Sumerian art is on view at the British Museum in London.
1930–38	Archaeological mission at the Diyala Valley (Iraq)
1931	Greta Garbo stars as Mata Hari in the eponymous George Fitzmaurice film.
1933	Discovery of the Tell Asmar hoard (Diyala Valley, Iraq)
1934	Jurgis Baltrušaitis publishes *Art sumérien, art roman*, on the influence of Sumerian art on Romanesque art.
1935	Christan Zervos publishes *L'art de la Mésopotamie*.

1936	Agatha Christie publishes *Murder in Mesopotamia*, based on her experience at the archaeological mission in Ur. Katharine Woolley inspired the main female protagonist.
1950–54	Willem de Kooning produces his *Woman* series, inspired in part by a Sumerian worshiper statue at the Metropolitan Museum of Art in New York.
1951	Poet Charles Olson publishes an essay on Sumerian art, "The Gate and the Center."
1991	Jananne al-Ani creates a photographic installation on the loss of Iraqi heritage, *Untitled (Gulf War Series)*.
2003–11	In the Second Gulf War, an international coalition invades and occupies Iraq. During the hostilities, the upper part of the Kish ziggurat is heavily damaged as are the Ur tombs. The National Museum of Iraq in Baghdad is looted April 10–12, 2003, with 15,000 items damaged or robbed. Since then roughly 7,500 artifacts have been retrieved, but the Museum, currently under renovation, remains closed to the public.
2007	Michael Rakowitz creates a sculptural installation on the looting of the National Museum of Iraq, *The Invisible Enemy Should Not Exist*.

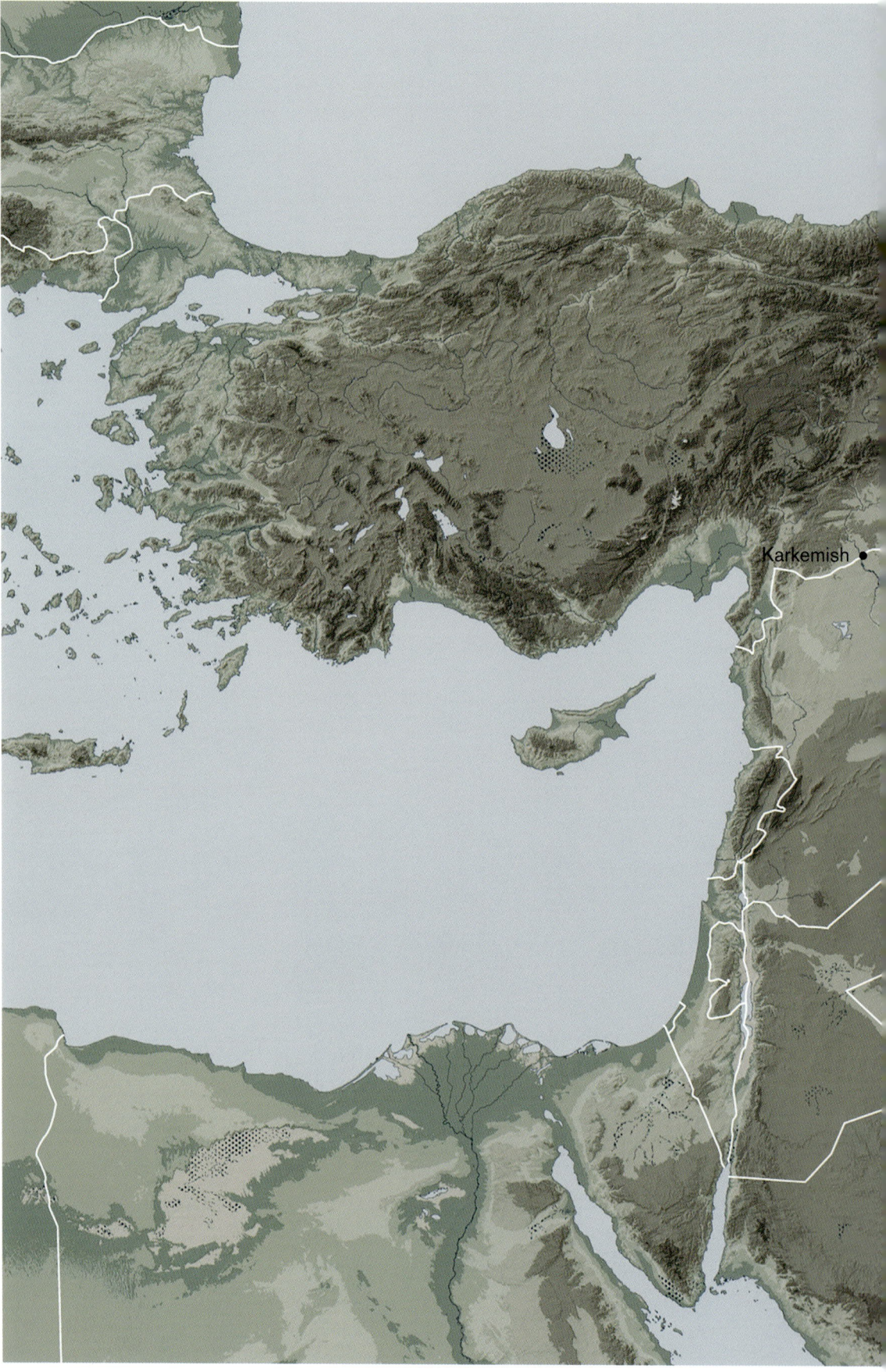

Karkemish •

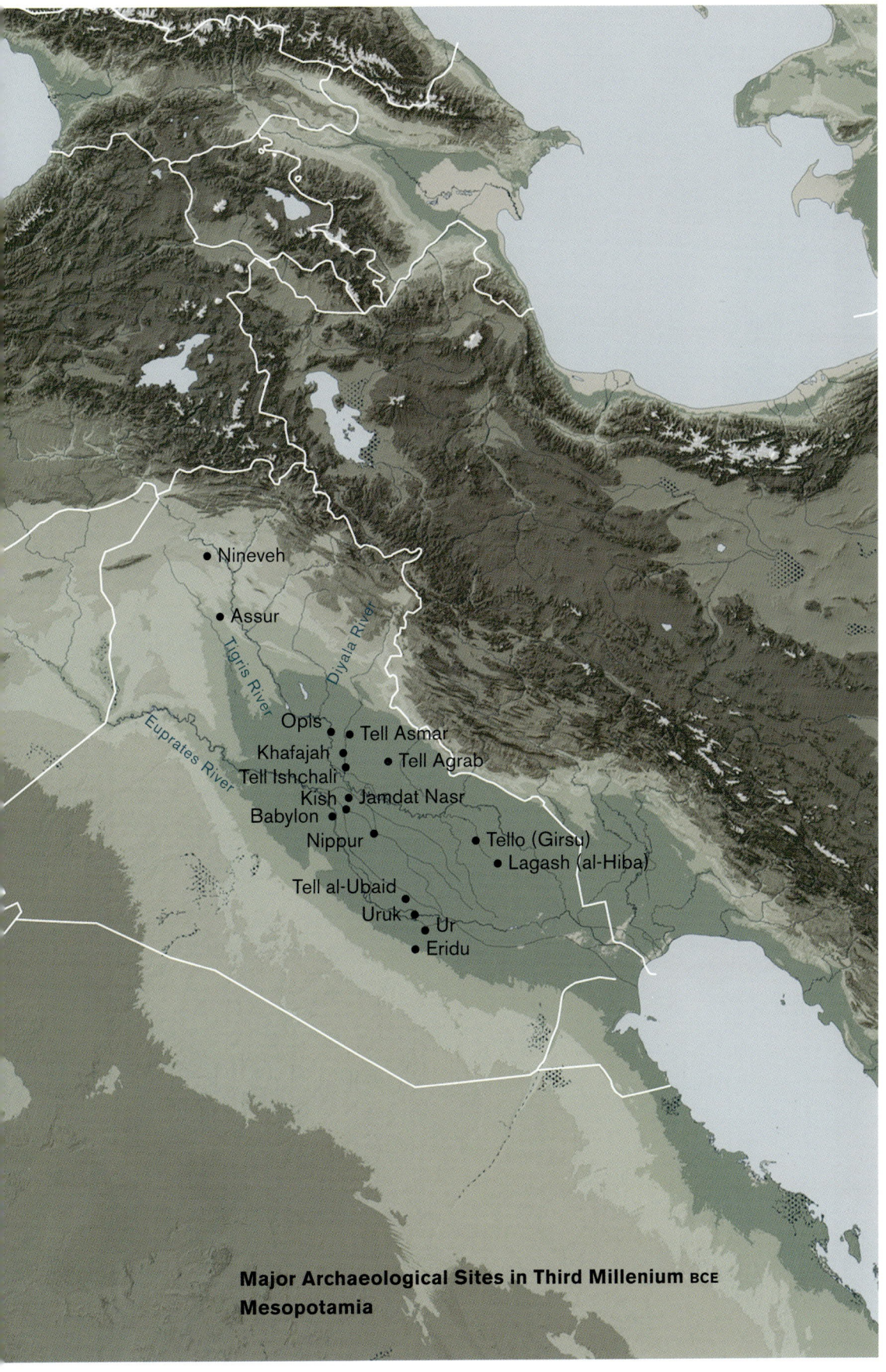

Major Archaeological Sites in Third Millenium BCE **Mesopotamia**

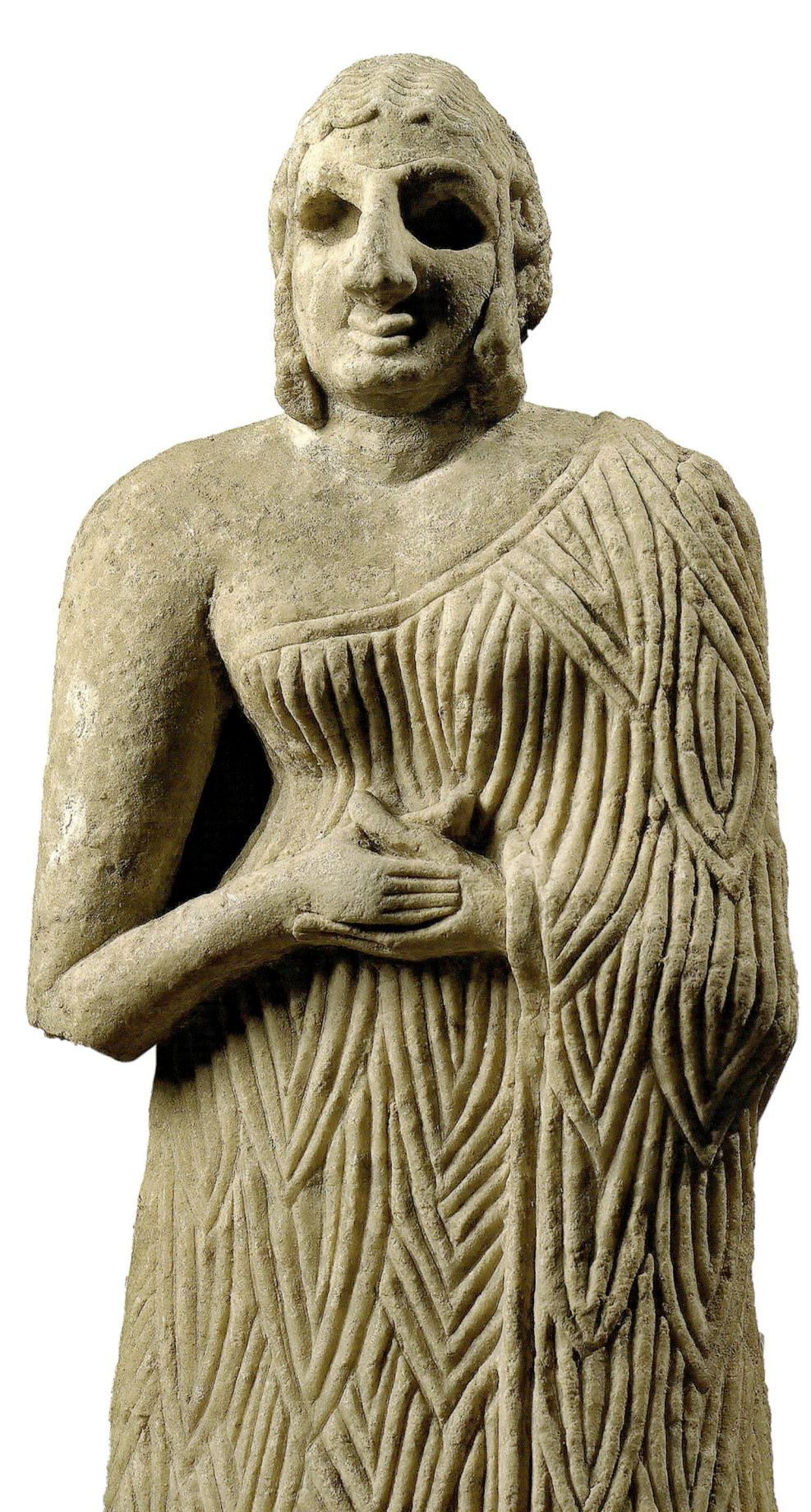

Glam-UR-ous:
The Art of Archaeology and Aesthetics

Jennifer Y. Chi and Pedro Azara

Introduction

How does an "archaeological object" become a work of art? How do practices such as excavation, reconstruction, study, and display transform and transfigure an archaeological object—be it utilitarian, sacred, or magical—into a work of art that is then displayed for the pleasure of the senses and the mind? *From Ancient to Modern: Archaeology and Aesthetics* takes a critical look at these questions to illustrate the multiple layers of meaning that a single object can acquire over the course of its existence—from its creation to its final archaeological context, its discovery, and finally its interpretation and cultural use by modern artists and scholars alike.

In many senses archaeology deals with the deepest layers of culture, demonstrating that history comprises multiple levels of human intervention. Archaeology exposes the past and at the same time reveals how far away it is. As an approach archaeology reveals the distance between us and those who lived long ago, and seeks reasons for humankind's behavior and ways of perceiving the world. By looking so closely at the past, archaeology allows us to be present in our world, and helps to legitimize our actions and beliefs.

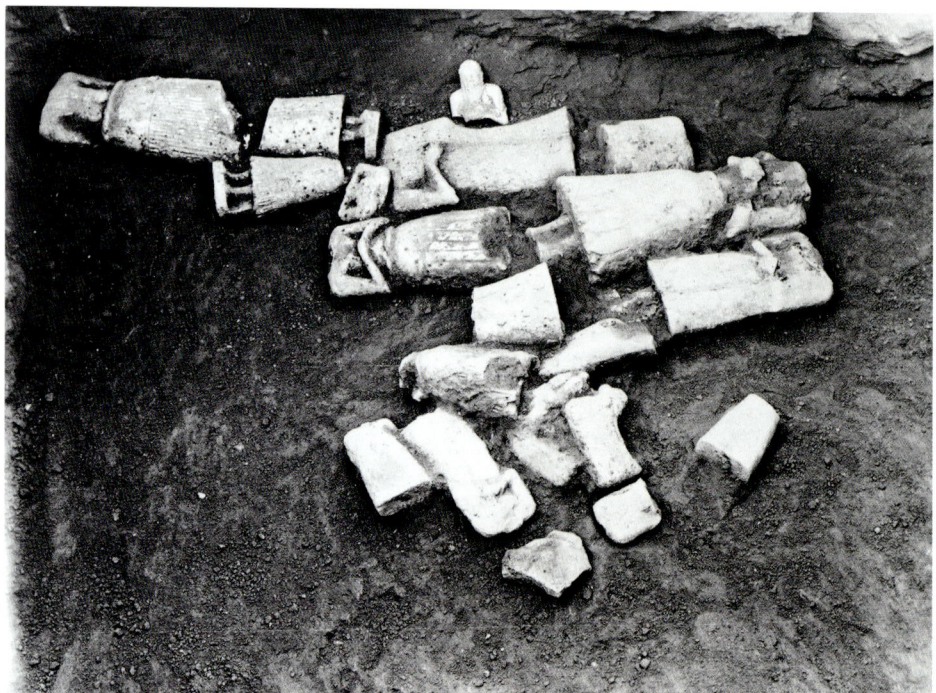

1-1. Statues in situ, Locus: Q42:7, Khafajah. Photograph, 1933–34. OIM: Kh. IV. 135. Expedition of the Oriental Institute, 1930–37. Checklist no. 1.

1-2. Standing Male Figure. Gypsum, alabaster, shell, black limestone, bitumen, Eshnunna (Tell Asmar), ca. 2900–2600 BCE. MMA: 40.156. Fletcher Fund, 1940. Checklist no. 140.

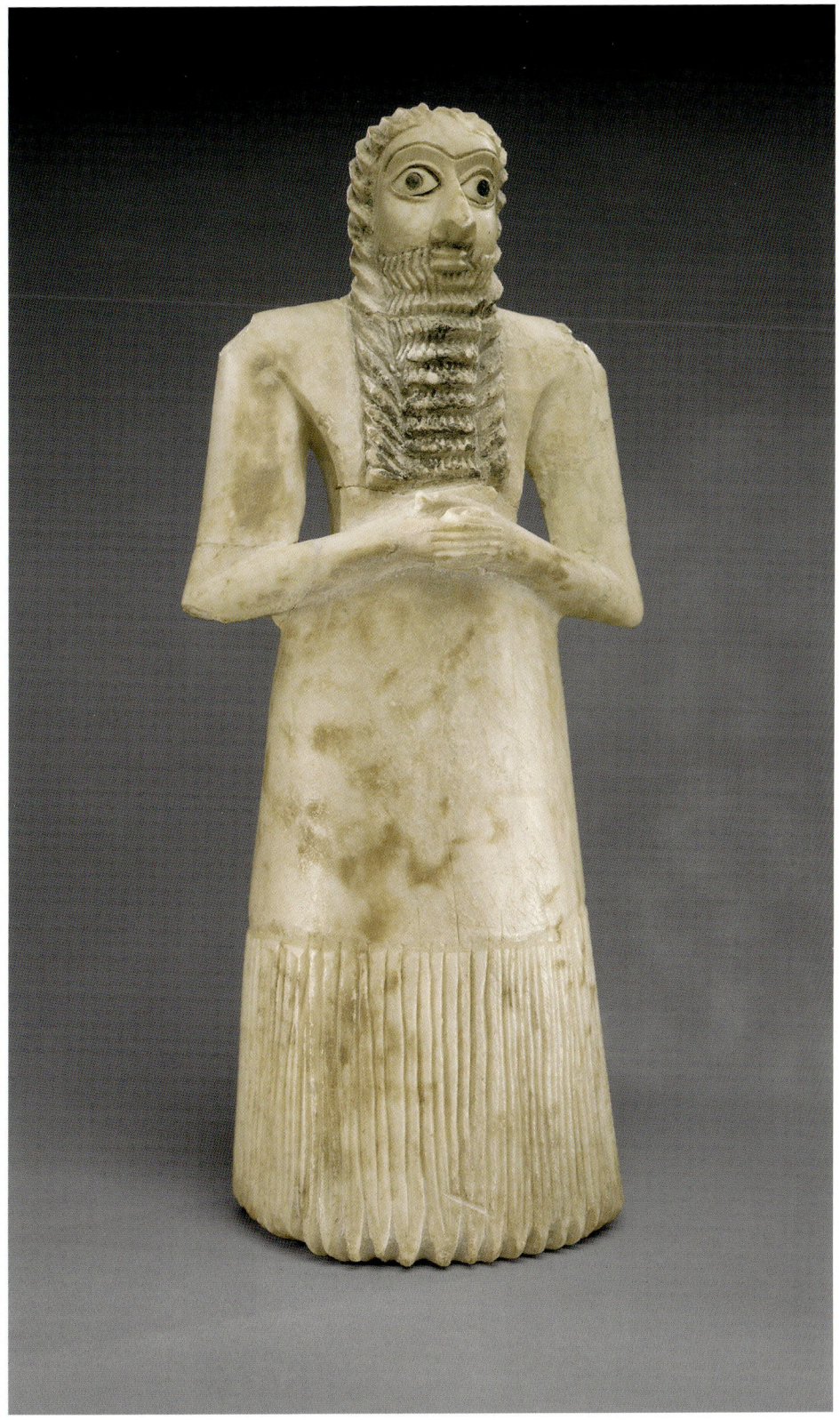

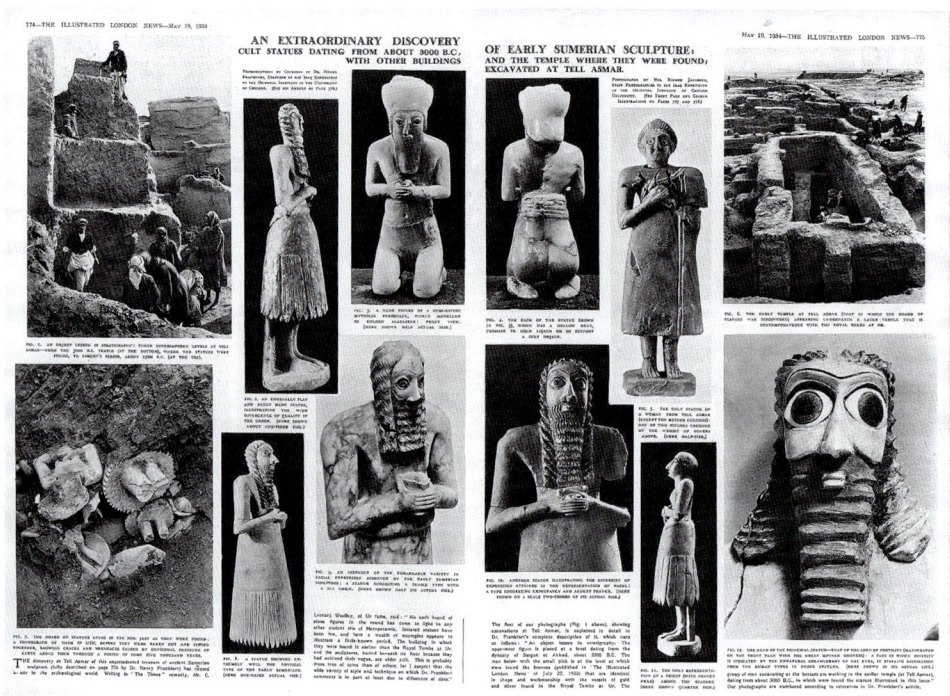

1–3. "An Extraordinary Discovery of Early Sumerian Sculpture." *Illustrated London News*, May 19, 1934, 774–75. MMA: Ane.ILN.4. Courtesy of the Department of Ancient Near Eastern Art. Checklist no. 23.

Archaeology and archaeologists also search for meaning. When an object is first discovered, it exists primarily as something from the past, disconnected from us, buried in the ground and in our minds (fig. 1–1). The next step in the process is to find a reason for the object's existence. What does it tell us about the past, the present, or ourselves? Attempting to answer these questions is in many ways the most subjective part of an archaeological approach. The meaning ingrained in an archaeological item can belong to the object, it can be assigned, or it can even be imposed.

The disciplines of aesthetics and art history focus primarily on works of art, posing the critical and primary question of why a particular object stimulates our senses. Aesthetics allow us to contemplate both our inner and our outer worlds, and how a work of art relates to these two complex spaces—spaces that are embedded with a multiplicity of influences, whether individual or cultural. Aesthetics infuse a work of art with meaning and allow the viewer to analyse or criticize it (fig. 1–2). By relating aesthetically to objects, we, as spectators, judge them as or transform them into objects—or images—with meaning, into windows to the world or to ourselves.

While these two fields at first seem mutually exclusive, both approaches are used in making an archaeological object into a work of art. To show this intersection, *Archaeology and Aesthetics* is the first U.S. exhibition to include a fascinating mixture

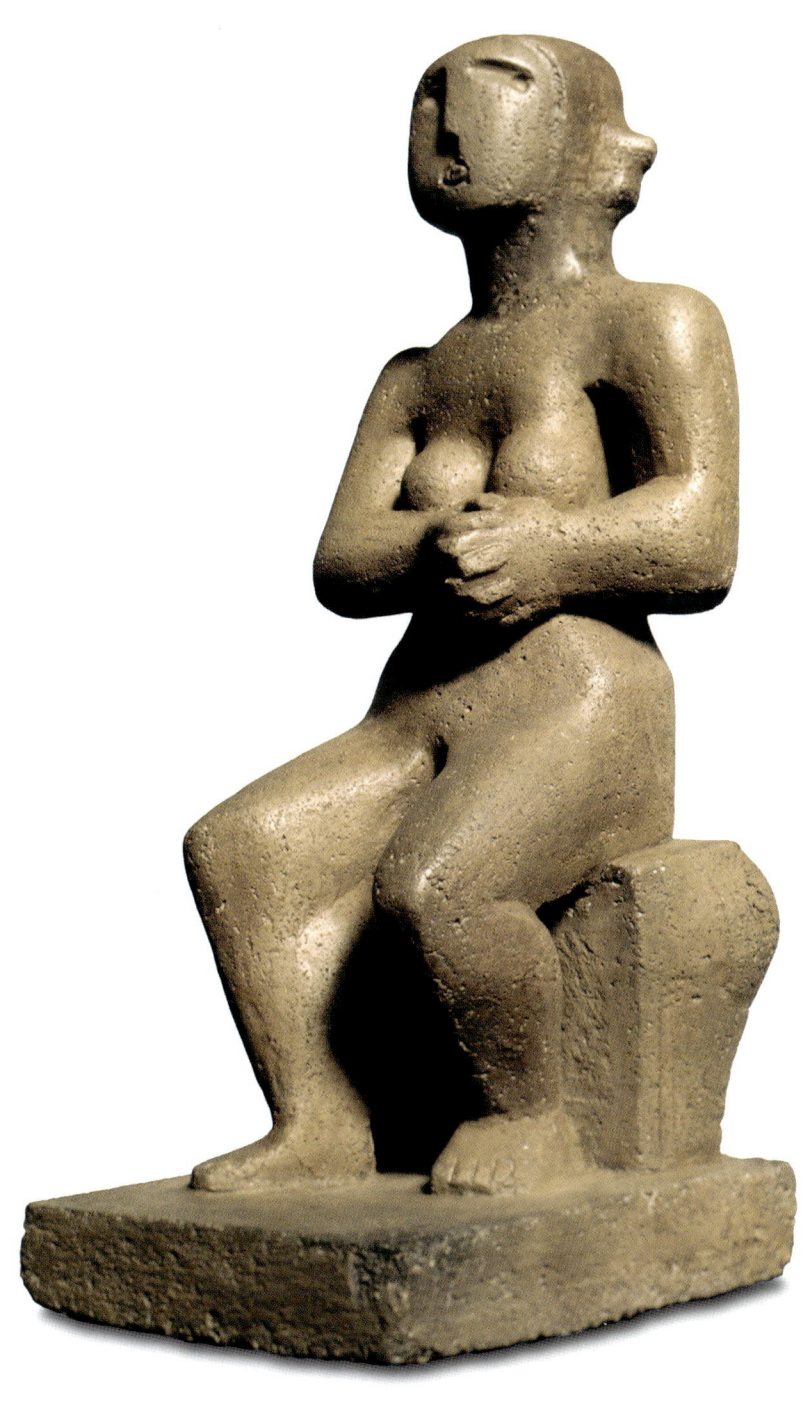

1–4. Henry Moore. *Seated Figure*. Cast concrete, 1929. HMF: LH 65. Gift of Irina Moore. Checklist no. 147.

of Early Mesopotamian art from iconic archaeological sites, as well as a rich grouping of archival material (fig. 1–3), alongside modern and contemporary works of art.

Archaeology and Aesthetics presents the "biography" of objects, illustrating their discovery and transformation, be it into a virtuoso work of art, a cultural symbol, or a popular icon. The exhibition begins at the point of an object's discovery, looking at it from an archival as well as a historiographic perspective. We examine how it was first presented to both a scholarly and a larger general audience, and trace how this perspective influenced the object's place in our understanding of the history of art, and in our modern aesthetic consciousness. To illustrate this latter process, the exhibition includes a selection of modern and contemporary artworks that explore the subject of the reappearance and reconstruction of the past. Artists such as the British sculptor Henry Moore (fig. 1–4) viewed Sumerian art as a powerful expression of original but lost artistic energies, and some of their works directly reflect Sumerian material. This essay begins first with a presentation of the ancient and archival material and is followed by a discussion of our selection of modern and contemporary artworks.

Ur and Puabi: Myth and Reality

The first exploration of the Sumerian site of Ur began in the mid-nineteenth century. On behalf of the British Museum, J. E. Taylor, the British vice-consul in Basra, excavated extensively at the site, and his finds suggested that further excavation would be fruitful. R. Campbell-Thompson in 1918 and H. R. Hall in 1919 were both commissioned by the British Museum to reinstate excavations.[1] However, full exploration of the site did not commence until 1922, when a joint British Museum and University of Pennsylvania team under the direction of an independent British archaeologist, Charles Leonard Woolley, arrived at the site (fig. 1–5).[2] Woolley had worked at the Ashmolean Museum with Sir Arthur Evans, the excavator of such legendary Bronze Age sites as Troy, Knossos, and Mycenae. Woolley had also excavated at Corbridge and in Nubia, as well as with T. H. Lawrence at Karkemish, before moving on to Ur, where the mission continued until 1934.

Woolley's assistant from 1925–31 was the young archaeologist Max Mallowan, whom the novelist Agatha Christie would marry after meeting him on the site in 1930. Christie described life at the mission and the strong personality of Woolley's wife, Katharine, through the character of Louise Leidner in *Murder in Mesopotamia,* a riveting crime novel published in 1936 that is now a valuable resource in understanding the social organization of the complex mission house of Ur (fig. 1–6). Katharine Woolley, through her fictional character, was described as brilliant, capricious, and annoying—the pivotal figure around which tensions and relations among the members were woven. The novel was also the first to offer accurate and intelligent views on how an archaeological mission worked. It could at times be a complex structure, located in a remote and not

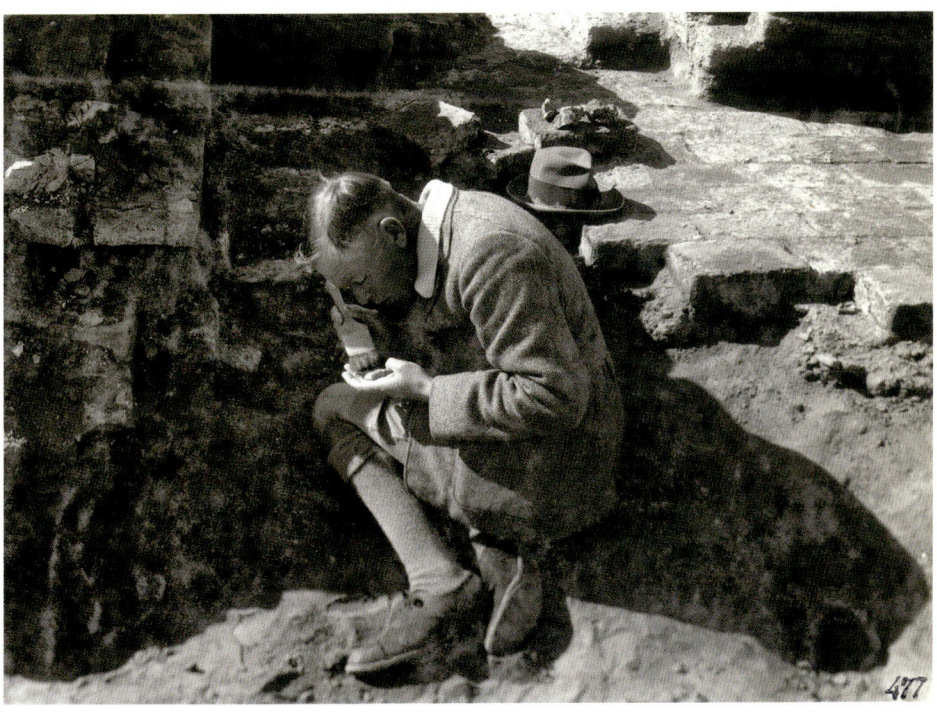

1–5. Leonard Woolley brushing an artifact, Ur. Photograph, ca. 1925. Courtesy of the University of Pennsylvania Museum of Archaeology and Anthropology. Checklist no. 75.

always friendly place, closed like a monastery, where egos were normally repressed but could sometimes explode, as the novel brilliantly explores.

Another notable on the site was the epigrapher Father Léon Legrain, who attended to the second reconstruction of Puabi's dress, shown at the University of Pennsylvania Museum of Archaeology and Anthropology in 1929 (fig. 1–7). He disagreed with Katharine Woolley's molded head of Queen Puabi and her reconstruction of the head-dress, and chose to fabricate a second mannequin and a new display for her accoutre-ments. This would be the first reevaluation of how the jewelry should be presented to the public, an issue that continues to perplex and fascinate scholars today.

One of the more interesting social facts about the Ur mission was the relationship between Leonard Woolley and his wife, Katharine Keeling Woolley (fig. 1–8), whom he had met in Oxford. When she first arrived at the site on the invitation of Woolley, she was a widow—or, as Woolley described her, a woman "who was not looking for a hus-band"—and worked on an all-male team of archaeologists in the middle of the desert.[3] A letter from the director of the University of Pennsylvania Museum to Woolley indi-cates that he was afraid of a puritan reaction by potential wealthy donors to Katharine's presence at the site. However, it is clear from the beginning that she was useful,

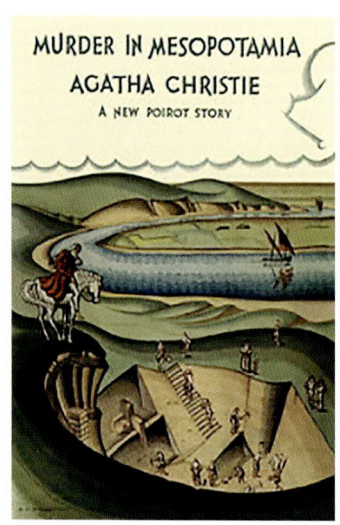

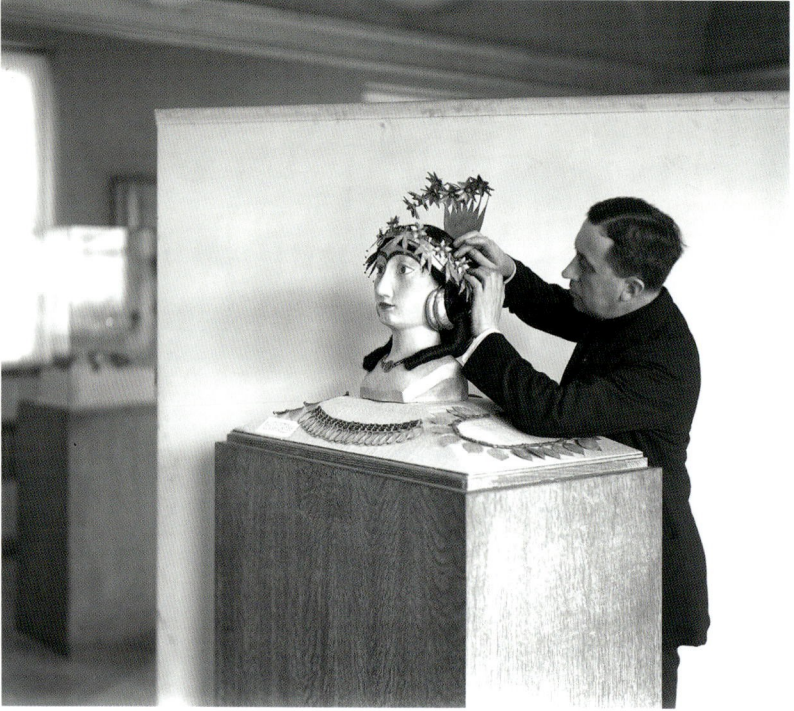

1–6. Agatha Christie. *Murder in Mesopotamia.* Facsimile dust jacket of the 1936 Collins Edition.

1–7. Léon Legrain adjusting Puabi's headdress. Photograph, 1929. Courtesy of the University of Pennsylvania Museum of Archaeology and Anthropology. Checklist no. 101.

drawing many of the finds, acting as a guide to rich North American visitors, as well as performing such menial duties as cleaning the mission house and keeping the young archaeologists "up to standard" (whatever that might have been), according to Leonard Woolley.[4] After their wedding in 1928, Katharine Woolley received a higher salary than Max Mallowan, which did not please Agatha Christie.[5]

The work undertaken during this fourteen-year period was stunning both in terms of the extraordinary finds and the extent of the city that the team was able to excavate. At its height the mission included hundreds of workmen, allowing for huge sectors of Ur to be uncovered in rapid fashion. Without question, the site's most famous find was an extremely large cemetery consisting of roughly two thousand tombs of varying date. Sixteen of these were differentiated from the rest by their architecture, the richness of their grave goods, and the existence of human sacrifice. Woolley immediately described and promoted the graves as "royal" and as rivaling the discovery of King Tutankhamun's tomb in Egypt, which had been unearthed by Howard Carter in 1922.[6]

At the center of *Archaeology and Aesthetics* is the Royal Tomb of Queen Puabi.[7] Her name, written on a seal found there in what has been read as two cuneiform signs, was first read as Shub-ab, but later also read in Akkadian as Puabi, or "word or mouth of the father." Her undisturbed and expansive tomb (4.35 by 2.8 m), numbered as PG 800 by Woolley, contained extraordinarily rich finds. Jewelry made of gold and semiprecious stones was worn by the deceased and included a complicated headdress all of gold and a heavy "cloak" of beads ending in an ornate belt (see fig. 5–1). Surrounding Puabi were musical instruments, including a lyre, and three more persons described as attendants, who had been deliberately killed.[8]

Most of the jewelry adorning Queen Puabi was found in a condition that rendered reconstruction of the individual elements into their original form challenging (fig. 1–9). Strings had vanished and semiprecious beads lay scattered around her outline. The colorful patterns of a few necklaces and bracelets could be identified, but in some cases excavators found simple masses of beads.

Various members of the team soon began to undertake hypothetical reconstructions of the queen's headdress, "diadem," cuffs, necklaces, and beaded cloak, some of which are now recognized as inaccurate. These inaccuracies are best exemplified by Puabi's so-called diadem, which scholars at the University of Pennsylvania—where many of the discoveries from her tomb are now housed—have recently deconstructed and reinstalled in a manner that this team believes more closely reflects its original use and intention.[9] When Puabi's tomb was unearthed, thousands of lapis lazuli beads as well as a variety and abundance of gold pendants were discovered (see fig. 1–9). In their reconstructions, could Woolley or any of the other team members have had contemporary fashions in mind, or at least have been subconsciously influenced by these fashions? Indeed, Woolley's final reconstruction was a flat band-like diadem with hanging pendants,

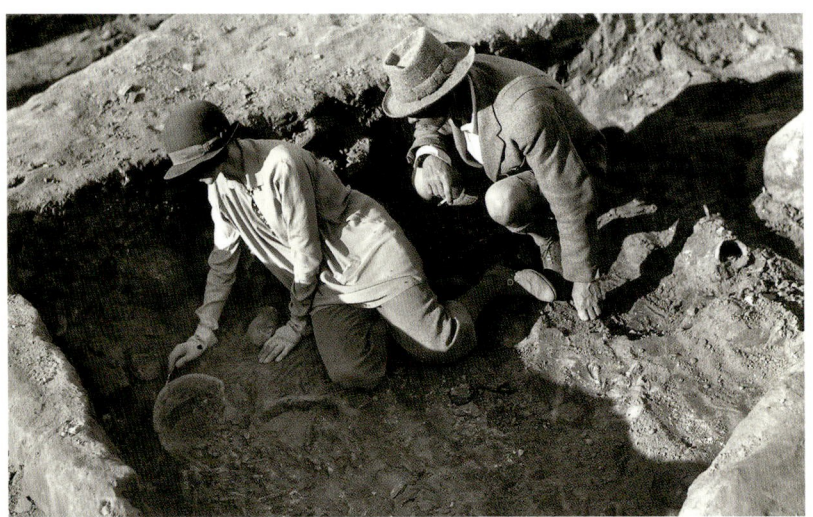

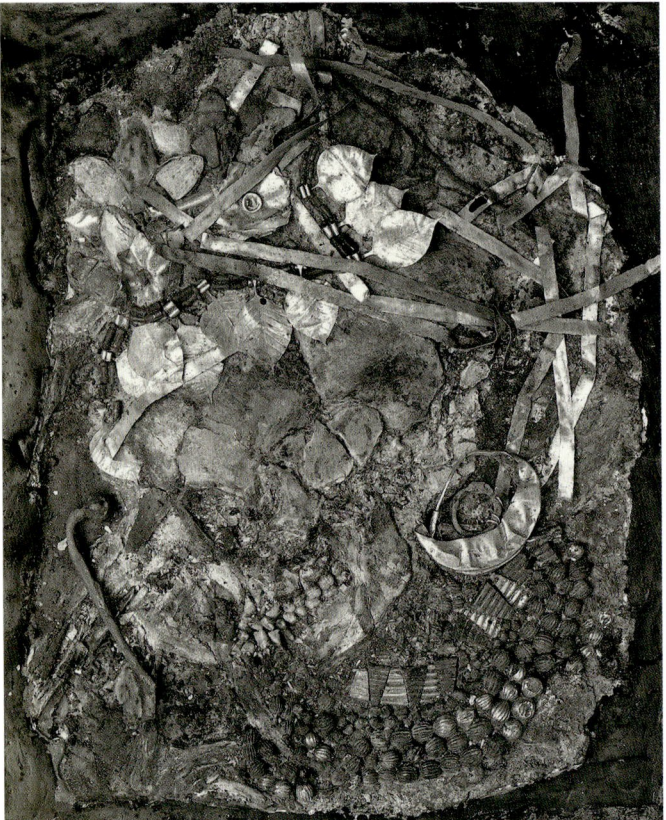

1-8. Leonard Woolley and Katharine Woolley excavating. Photograph, 1927–28. Penn Museum: 1587. Courtesy of the University of Pennsylvania Museum of Archaeology and Anthropology.

1-9. Puabi's headdress, pins, and jewelry in situ, PG 800. Photograph, 1927–28. Penn Museum: 1336. Courtesy of the University of Pennsylvania Museum of Archaeology and Anthropology.

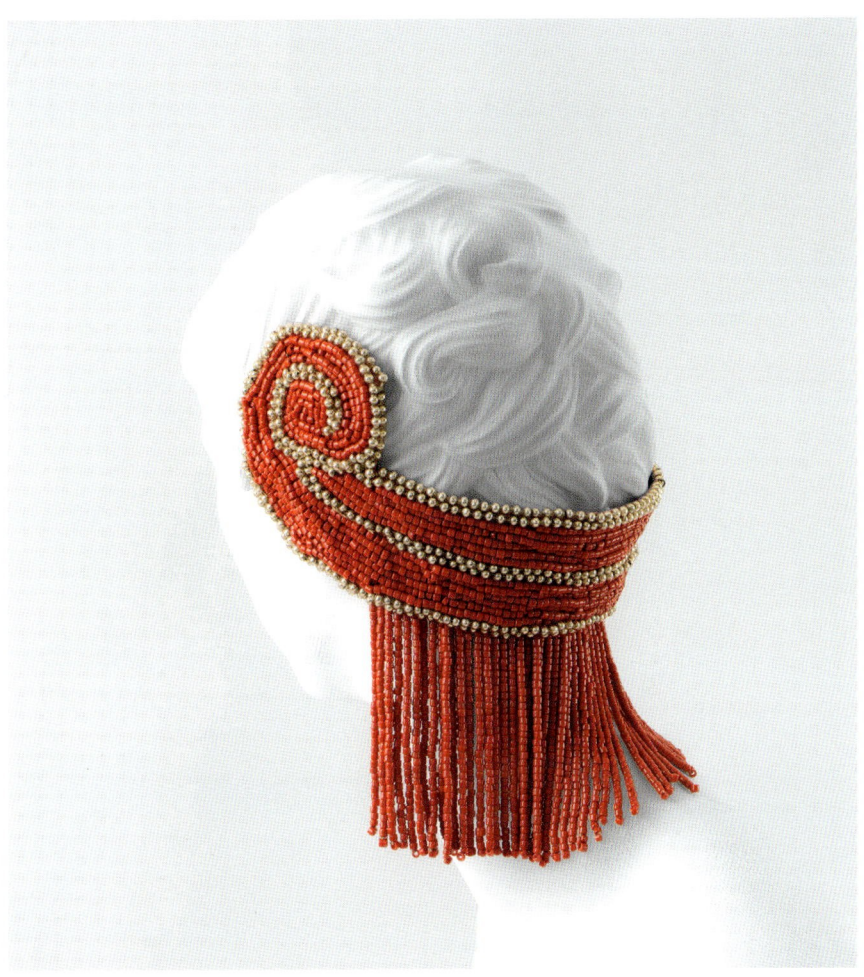

1–10. Paul Poiret. *Headdress.* Cotton, metal, ceramic, L. 32.4 cm. MMA: 2005.206. Gerson and Judith Leiber Foundation Fund, 2005.

uncannily reminiscent of diadems created by contemporary fashion houses. In the 1920s simple band-like diadems as well as elaborate headdresses were very stylish among the affluent. As diadems could also signify royalty, and Puabi was thought to be a queen, a diadem would have been a logical attribute.

From photographs as well as archival imagery, we know that Katherine Woolley was a follower of fashion. She was always unexpectedly well dressed on the excavation site, wearing carefully ironed, drop-waist dresses and fashionable hats, all of which looked as if they had just been purchased from a high-end shop. It may be possible that the Woolleys used the form of a contemporary headdress, similar to that of one designed by Paul Poiret, a leading French fashion designer during the first two decades of the twentieth century, as their conscious or subconscious inspiration (fig. 1–10).

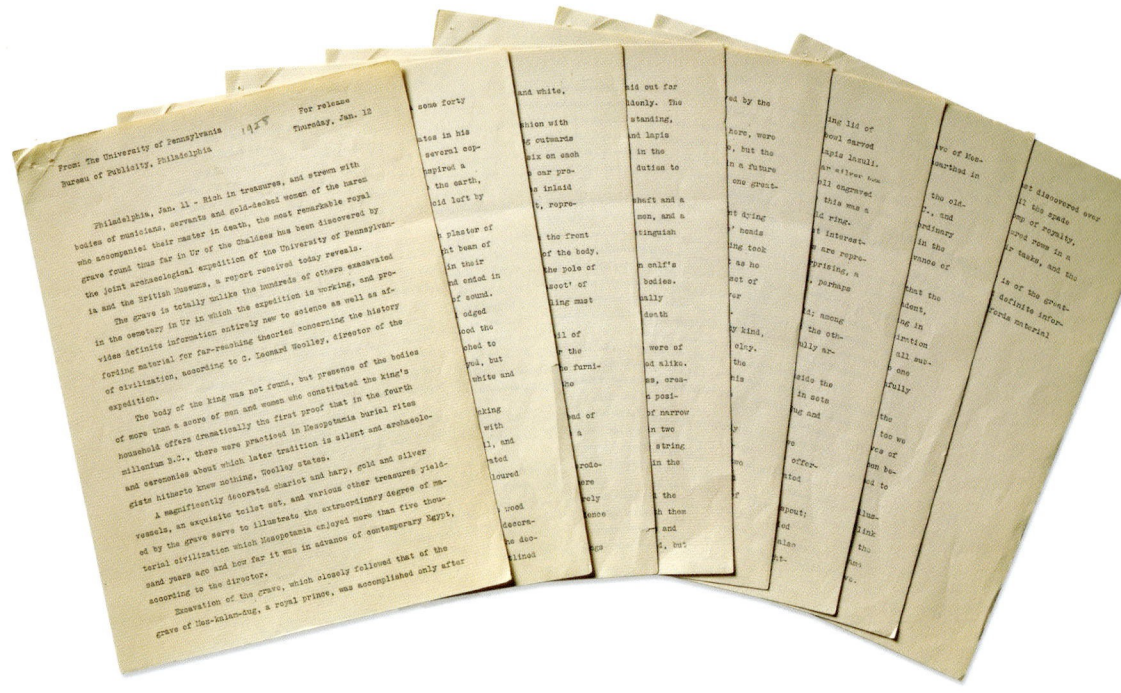

1–11. Press release from the Bureau of Publicity, University of Pennsylvania, Philadelphia, January 12, 1928. Courtesy of the University of Pennsylvania Museum of Archaeology and Anthropology. Checklist no. 83.

The discovery of Puabi's tomb set off intense media interest in the site, interest that was supported and even prompted by Woolley. Although archaeologists have published their discoveries more or less regularly since the mid-nineteenth century, it was not until the first part of the twentieth century that finds were announced to general-interest publications. By the 1920s popular news on archaeology focused not on stratigraphy but instead on spectacular finds, as well as on sensationalized descriptions of the cultures that produced them. For example, Howard Carter, the excavator of Tutankhamun's tomb, used the press to the significant benefit of the site in order to promote his Egyptian discoveries to an international audience, thereby launching Egyptomania throughout Europe and America.[10] Woolley followed the same strategy immediately after the first discoveries in Ur, spending extensive time writing detailed press releases that were meant to attract the general reader (fig. 1–11). The words were simple, the titles flashy. His deliberate intention is evident in the fact that he even discussed with the University of Pennsylvania and the British Museum when, where, and how to announce future extraordinary findings so that they could reach the broadest audience.[11] Using these releases, newspapers printed spectacularly written articles, produced as centerfolds with sensationalized titles such as "Evidence that the Queen

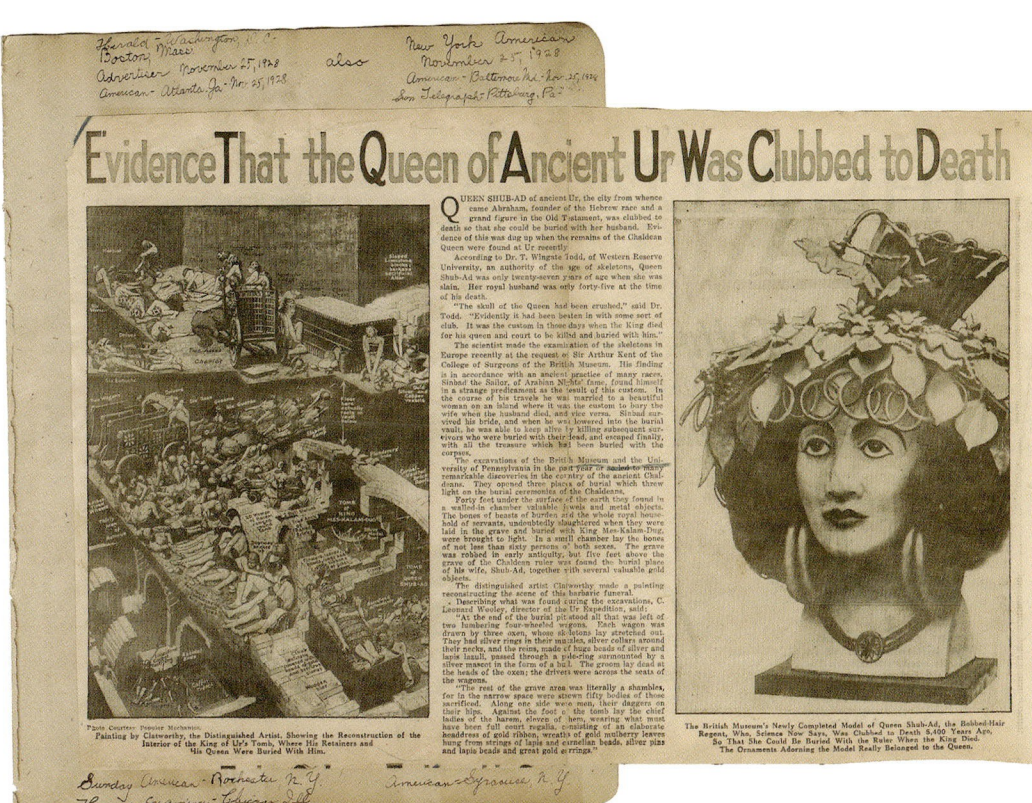

1–12. "Evidence that the Queen of Ancient Ur Was Clubbed to Death." *Washington (DC) Herald*, November 25, 1928. Courtesy of the University of Pennsylvania Museum of Archaeology and Anthropology. Checklist no. 96.

of Ancient Ur Was Clubbed to Death" and "Ancient Queen Used Rouge and Lipstick" (fig. 1–12).[12] When viewed together the articles clearly show a tension between wanting to relate Puabi to a modern understanding of royal behavior and accepting the evidence of what was perceived as the violent, almost savage death of those interred with her; such human sacrifice must have been shocking to the modern, Western viewer. It is almost as if audiences had trouble coping with the fact that such a clearly elite woman could be found in such a brutal final context, even in the ancient past.

The Diyala Valley: Archaeology Finds Aesthetics

The finds from North American and British archaeological missions during this period can certainly be described as having their own character. While Ur delivered the most elaborate and impressive Sumerian jewelry, the Diyala Valley became known for its exceptional repertoire of sculpture. As a corpus these statuettes are now considered the aesthetic and technical paradigms of Sumerian sculpture, and scholars continue to reconsider their value to and meaning for third-millennium culture (figs. 1–13a, b).

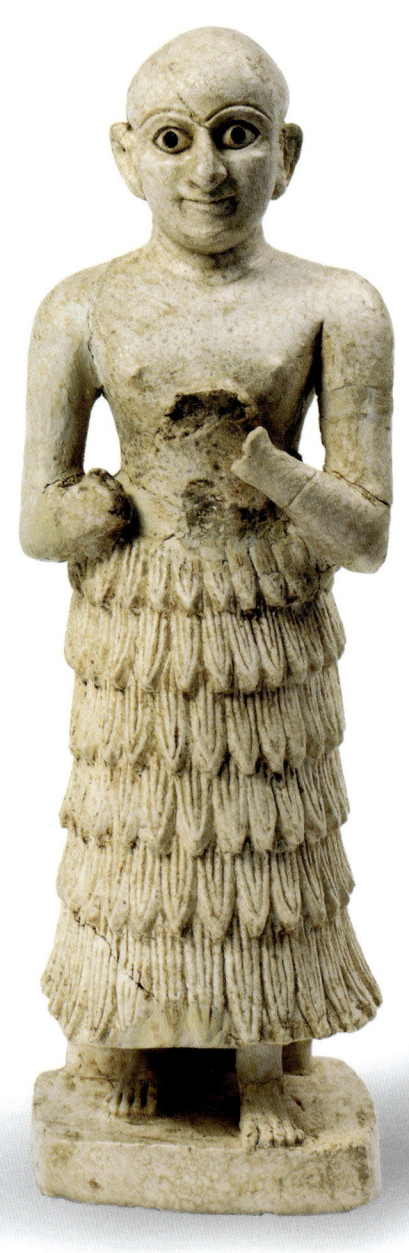

1-13a, b. Standing Male Figure. Alabaster, shell, lapis lazuli, Khafajah (Nintu Temple), Early Dynastic II (ca. 2650–2550 BCE). Penn Museum: 37-15-28. Khafaje Expedition. Checklist no. 49.

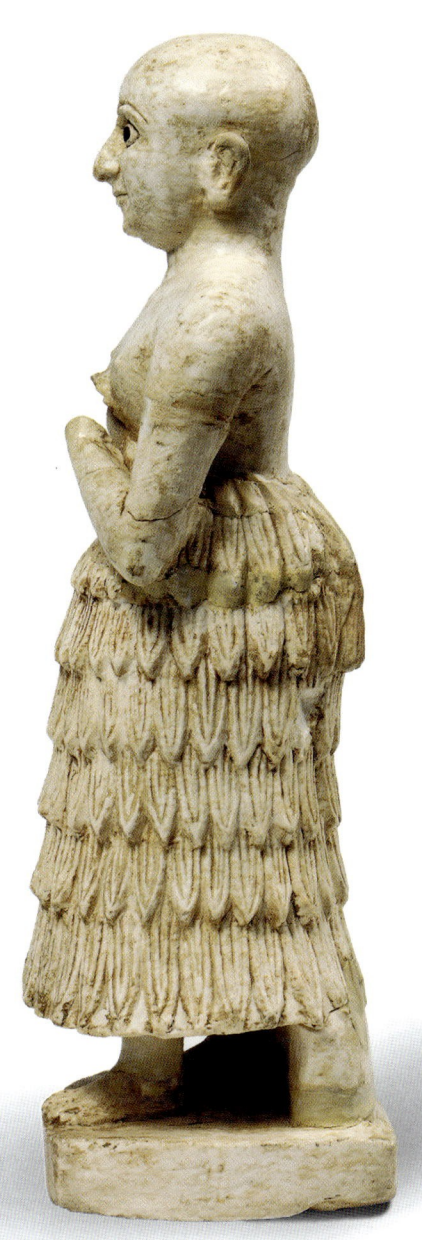

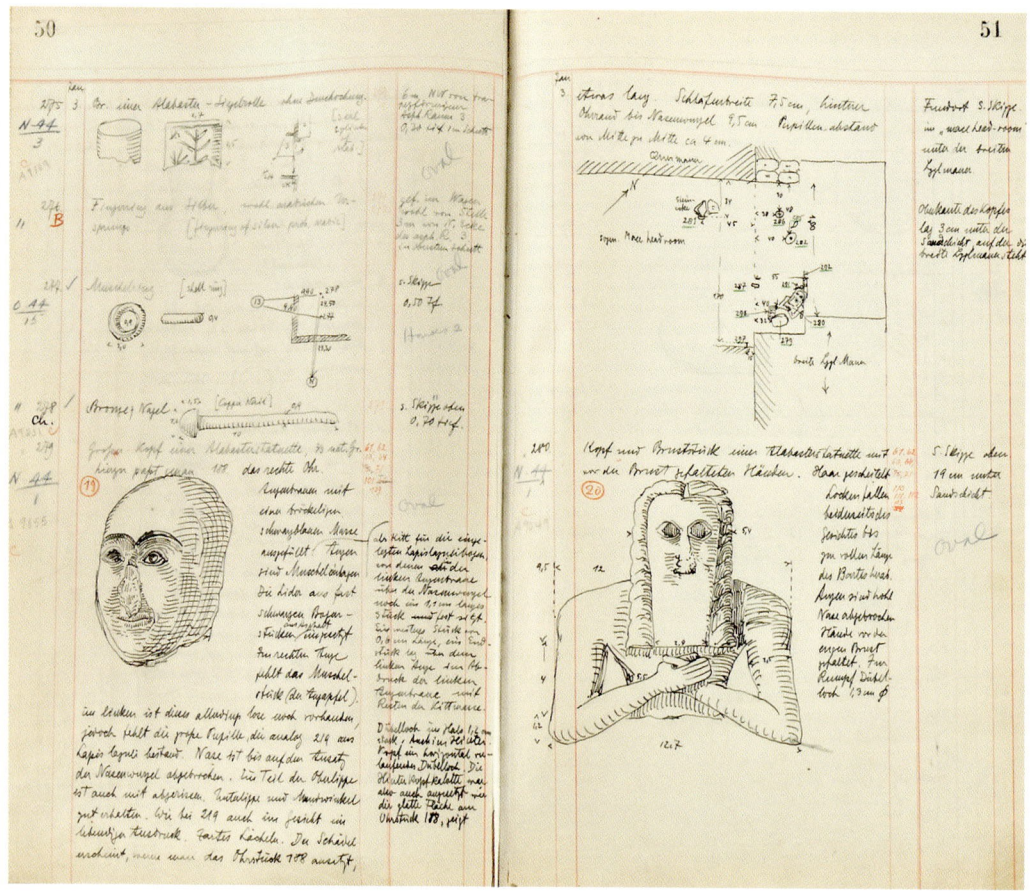

1–14. Field register of objects showing pages 50–51. Khafajah, November 1930–March 1932. Pages 50–51. Courtesy of the Oriental Institute of the University of Chicago. Checklist no. 39.

Diyala is the name of a river originating in the Zagros Mountains, running chiefly through eastern Iraq and flowing into the Tigris. Four main archaeological sites have been excavated: Tell Agrab, Tell Asmar, Ishchali, and Khafaje. Supported by the Oriental Institute of the University of Chicago, these missions began in 1930 and continued through 1937, followed by short interventions run jointly by the Oriental Institute and the University of Pennsylvania.[13] The area was far from known Sumerian sites, which were located in or near the southern marshes of the Tigris and the Euphrates rivers (including Ur, Uruk, Tello, and Eridu). A sudden flow of antiquities in the souks of Baghdad in the 1920s, objects that were considered authentic and known to come from sites near Baghdad, showed that the Sumerian culture reached farther north than expected.

All four missions were led by Henri Frankfort, a Classical art historian and an archaeologist who was also a specialist in Ancient Egyptian culture, and the author of the seminal and still relevant publication *The Art and Architecture of the Ancient Orient*.[14] Renowned Sumerologists such as the epigraphist and poet Thorkild Jacobsen[15]—whose

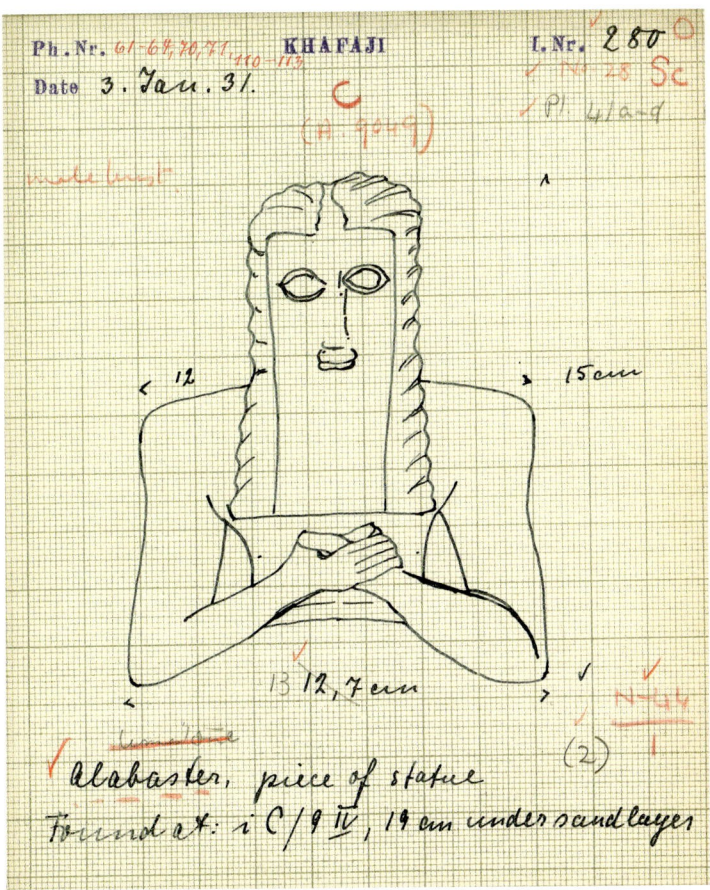

1–15. Field card, top half of a male figure, Khafajah, January 3, 1931. OI: 280 158. Courtesy of the Oriental Institute of the University of Chicago. Checklist no. 32.

work illustrated that Sumerian "poetry" could be appreciated by modern readers—also participated in the Diyala mission. In Frankfort's nine publications, both architecture and sculpture were presented as relevant "arts."

The archival material chosen for the exhibition reflects the scholarly, meticulous, and clearly aesthetic approach to excavation and documentation at Diyala, an approach that may have been advanced by Frankfort's gifts of organization and interpretation of material. Field registers meticulously record each object's find spot and are also regularly punctuated by fine drawings of objects (fig. 1–14). Carefully drawn images of objects on field cards show sculptures thoughtfully placed in the white space of each page, almost like fine-art drawings, with short descriptions placed toward the corners in order to balance the impact of the image (fig. 1–15). In a way, these drawings can be appreciated simply for their artistry. The first photographs taken of finds also have an artistic quality, again as if these objects were considered as works of art. Many photographs show objects from several different angles and not only provide valuable

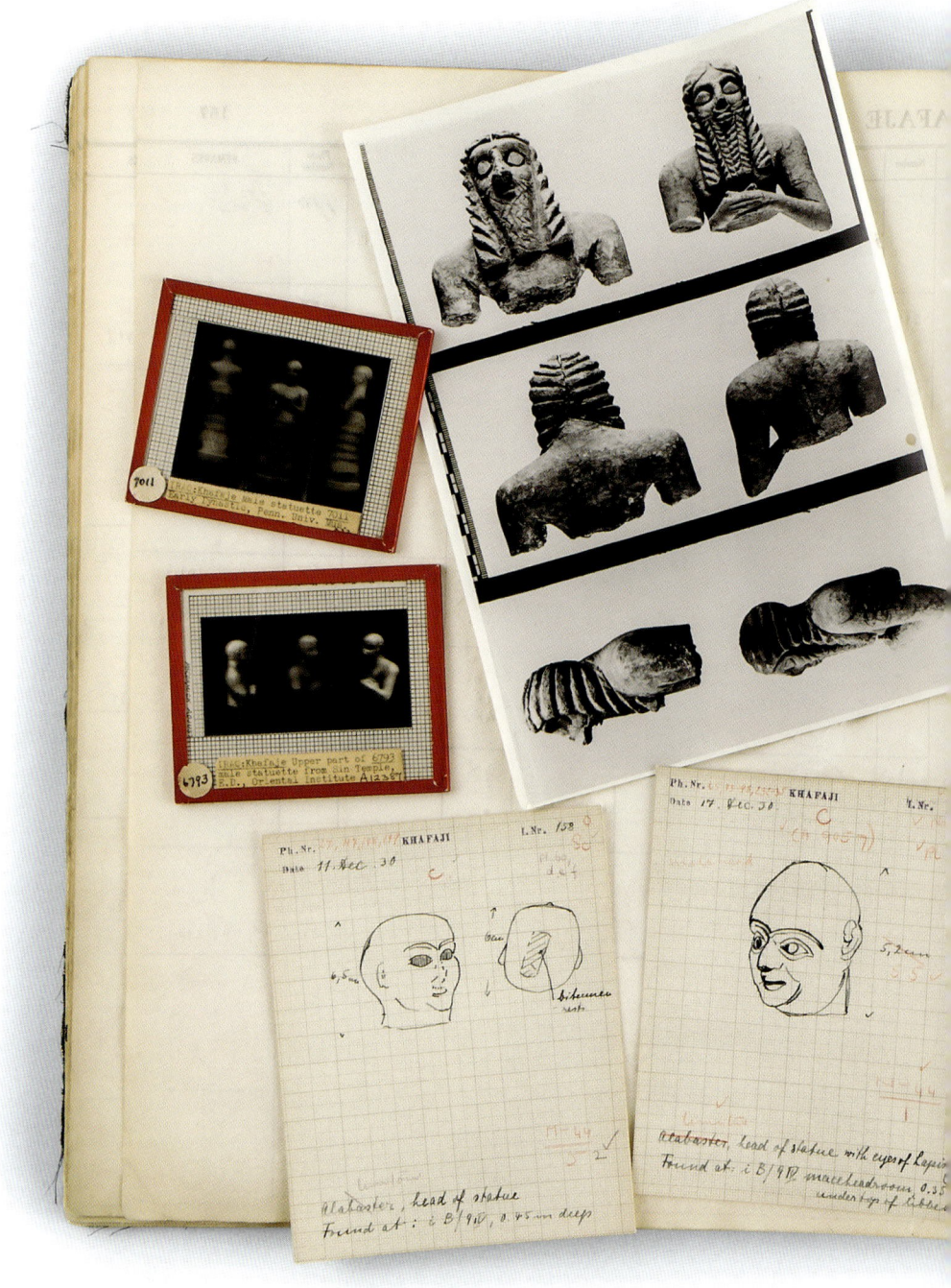

1–16. Field register of objects, two field cards, five slides of ancient artifacts and field shots, and two photographs of ancient artifacts. Khafajah, 1930–31. Courtesy of the Oriental Institute of the University of Chicago. Checklist nos. 9, 13, 27, 28, 39.

ate	Number	DESCRIPTION	Material	Size (Centimetres)	Provenance	Photo Number	REMARKS
31ˢᵗ	292	blackpainted head female head	limestone	3.6 × 3.0 × 5.4	Q-42 7 (5) 39-03 IV	166 202	Suz IX fr 39-03 C (H 12376)
"	293	female head	limestone	7.4 × 5.5 × 6.4	" 39-03 52-19	160 201	B
"	294	black female head	"	9.7 4.0 7.5	" Sm-IX 39-03	159. 195 201 261	B
"	295	rest of body found later bust of man	limestone	8.7 9.7 3.7	" 39-03 Sm-IX	193 241	Sc
"	296	back of man's head	"	5.0 × 4.2			
"	297	man's head	"	3.3 2.4 2.4			
"	298	man's head	"				
"	299	man's head					

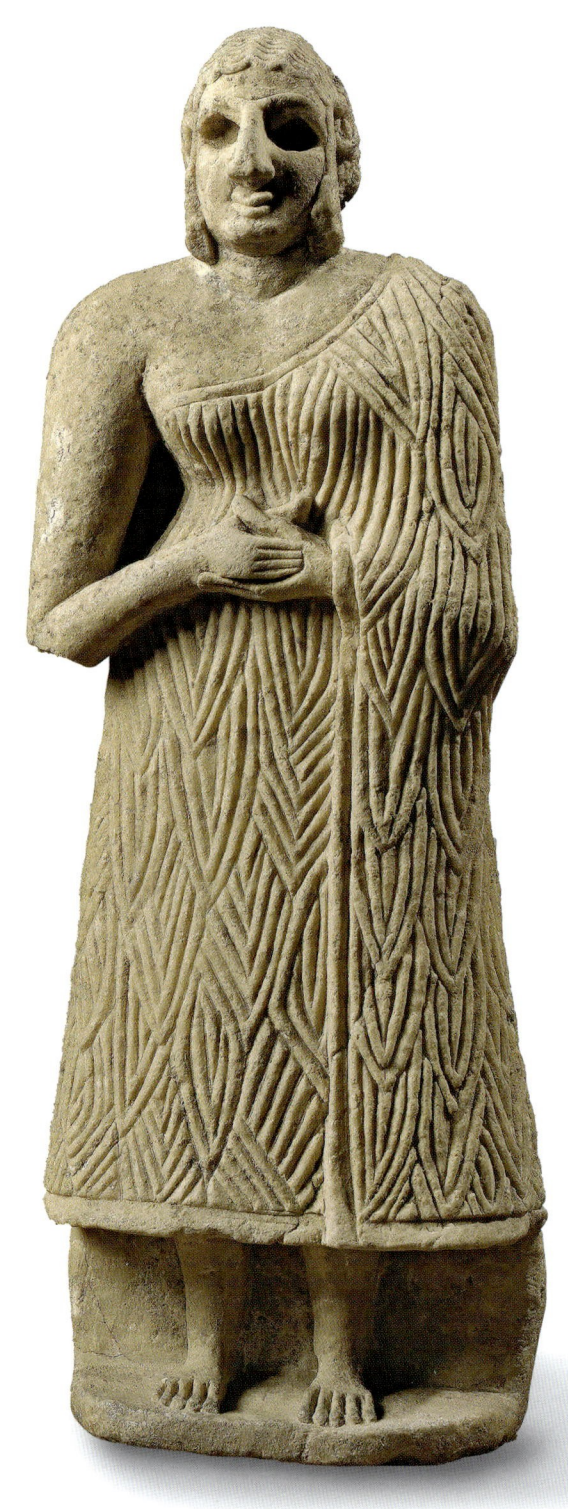

1–17. Standing Female Figure. Gypsum, Diyala, ca. 2700–2500 BCE. Private Collection, USA. Checklist no. 48.

documentation of what the material looked like after it was first cleaned, but also artistically embrace the three-dimensional quality of the material (fig. 1–16). When viewed as a group, the Diyala photographs have an immediacy similar to that of 1930s documentary photography that captured difficult living conditions after the Crash. Some of these Diyala photographs were used to illustrate books that Frankfort wrote on the aesthetic qualities of Sumerian sculpture.[16] Thanks to the austere isolation created by dark backdrops in these images, the sculptures can be appreciated as free-standing objects, separate from the influence of the architecture—temples, palaces, and tombs—to which they were originally attached. The photographs of the Diyala Valley were the means by which Sumerian archaeological finds were transformed into timeless works of art.

The large number of statuettes found also allowed scholars to identify certain main types: the now iconic standing, bearded male "worshipers" with their hands clasped in front of them and wearing long skirts; standing female figures in the same pose with varying hairstyles and dress (fig. 1–17); and male figures seated on large rectangular boxes. The majority were found buried in the Abu Temple at Tell Asmar, and in the Nintu Temple at Khafajah—hence, the term "worshiper"—and were soon considered the first sculptures in the history of Western art. In Frankfort's *Art and Architecture of the Ancient Orient*, however, and in many of his other texts, the context is omitted, and the sculptures are described as representing the origin of sculptural art. "Instead of sharply contrasting, clearly articulated masses," Frankfort wrote, "we see fluid transitions and infinitely modulated surfaces. Instead of abstract shapes, we see a detailed rendering of the physical peculiarities of the model. By a new and subtle treatment of the surfaces…the Early Dynastic sculptors, having followed abstraction to its utmost limits, began to explore the possibilities offered by the opposite approach."[17] Leading art historians defined the works as "primitive," connecting them to a world that was not yet rational.[18] However, because they were related to magical or superstitious thoughts, the objects were not judged as true works of art, since within the terms of mid-twentieth-century aesthetics, disinterested creations—as defined by Kant—could not exist. But Frankfort, who became director of the Warburg Institute of London after the Second World War, helped to give a new meaning to the word "primitive," one that removed any pejorative connotations. Now the term could describe art that was different, but not inferior, incomplete, or basic. So-called primitive images, such as Sumerian sculptures, communicated an understanding of human beings and their position between the visible and invisible worlds, rendering these images as sensible as any work of art. Influenced by the art historian Aby Warburg—who interpreted images as a way to express the pathos, or expressions, that characterize and shape human lives—Frankfort wrote that "the fundamental difference between the attitude of modern and ancient man as regards the surrounding world is this: for modern, scientific man the phenomenal world is primarily an 'It'; for ancient—and also the primitive—man it is a 'Thou.'"[19] These ancient sculptures were "works of art" and presented a starting point for Western interest in the human form.

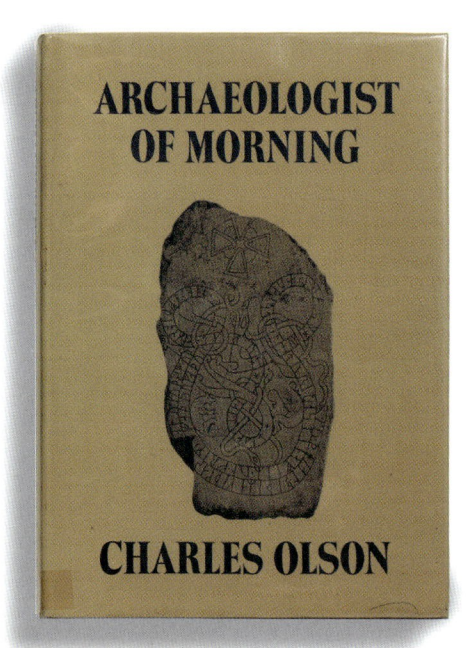

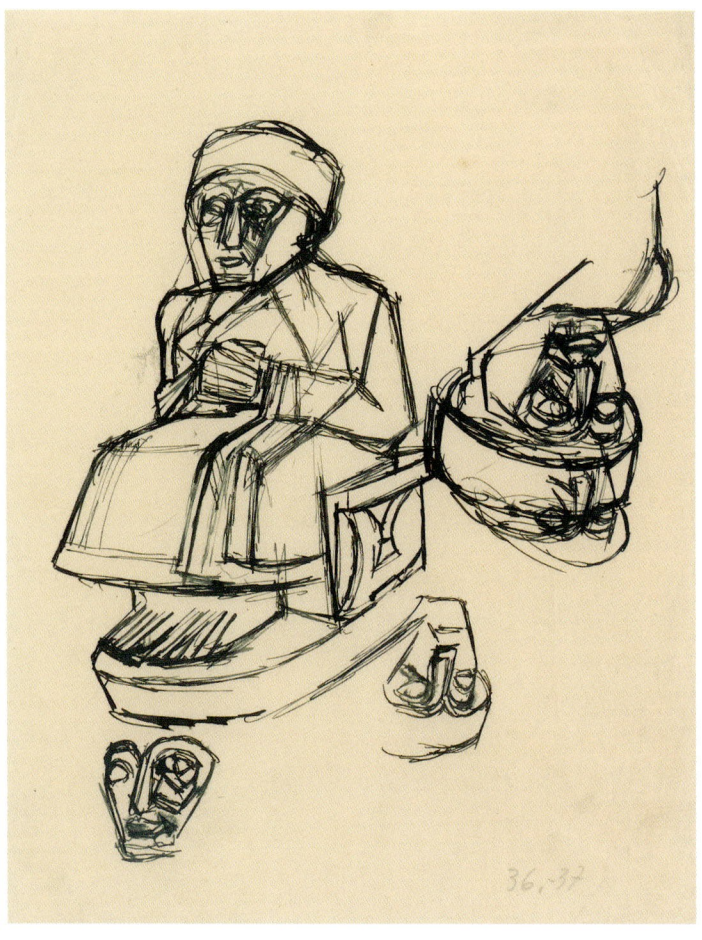

36.37

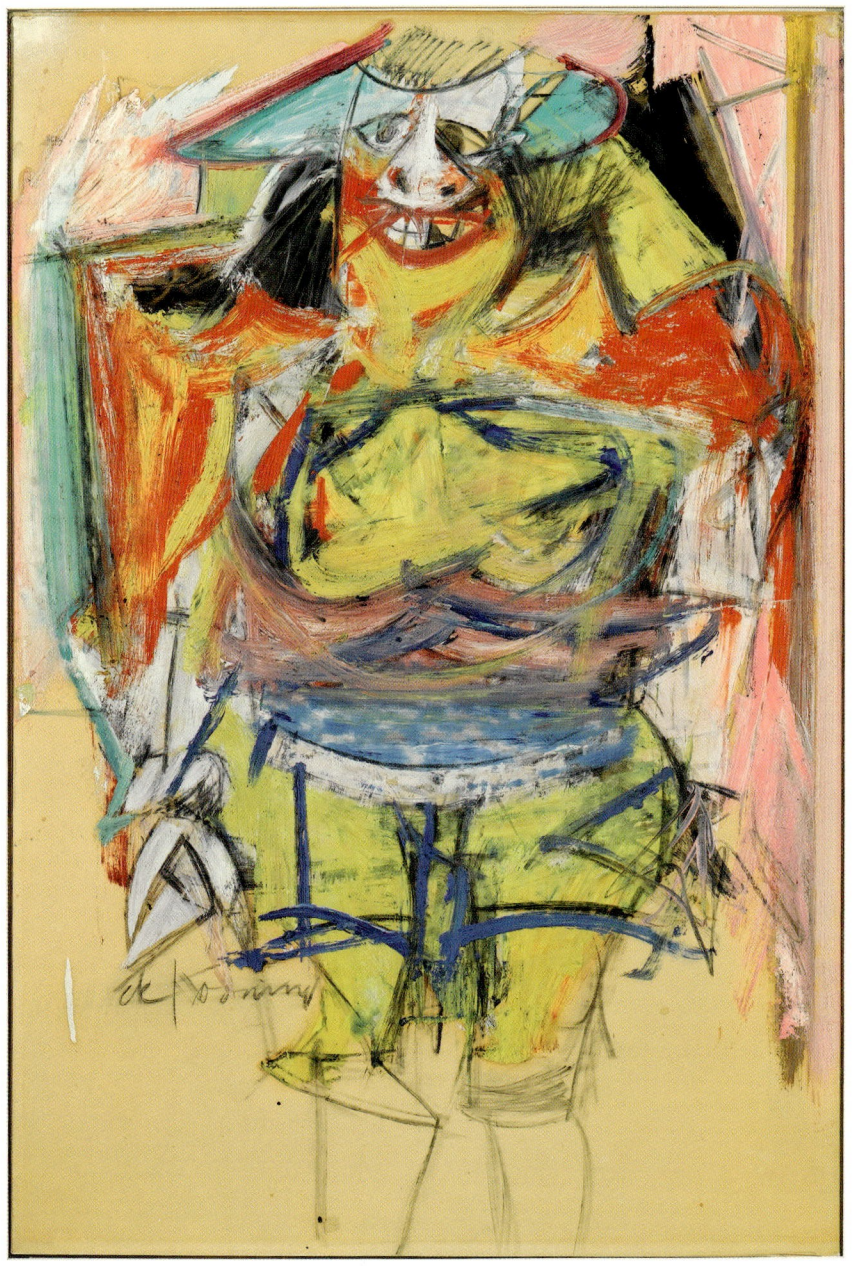

1–18. Charles Olson. *Archaeologist of Morning*. London, 1970. Private Collection, USA. Checklist no. 180.

1–19. Alberto Giacometti. *Seated Gudea: After a Sumerian Sculpture*. Ink on paper. GF: 1994-0704. Courtesy of the Alberto Giacometti Estate. Checklist no. 143.

1–20. Willem de Kooning. *Woman*. Oil on paper board. 1953–54. TBM: 57.124. Gift of Mr. and Mrs. Alastair B. Martin, the Guennol Collection. Checklist no. 142.

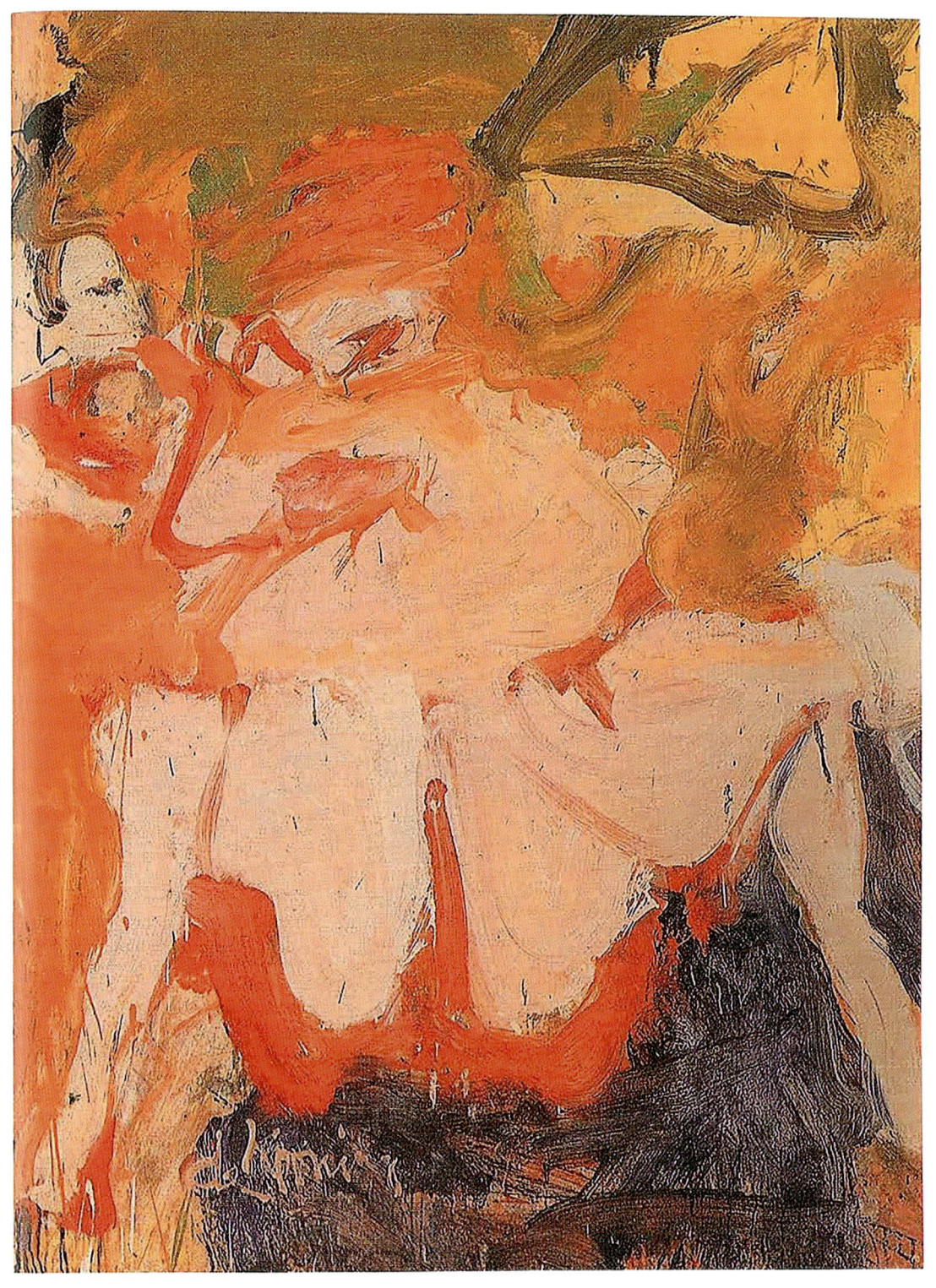

1–21. Willem De Kooning. *Woman on a Sign II*. Oil on paper mounted on canvas. 1967. The Fayez Sarofim Collection. Checklist no. 141.

It is within this context that the sculptures' first and ongoing exhibition in museums must be understood. For example, at the Chicago's World Fair of 1933–34, known as "A Century of Progress," five statuettes were on view in a museum vitrine and described as "the oldest ever found in Asia."[20] In both temporary and permanent installations, Sumerian sculptures were and continue to be presented as works of art.

From Ancient to Modern and Beyond

Modern artists also began responding to Sumerian art soon after the material made its way into public display. The discovery and exhibition of "primitive" artifacts in the early twentieth century—due to the efforts of Western colonial powers in Africa, Asia, and Oceania—and a revitalized interest in the "pre-Classical" arts of Europe led artists such as Braque and Picasso to present the vital structures and shapes of the world without reproducing their appearance, resulting in Cubism and other artistic movements.

New visions of the inner and outer worlds were translated into new shapes and compositions and entered the world of art at the end of the 1920s. Sumerian anthropomorphic figurines, such as the Diyala statuettes on display in this exhibition, were considered the first artistic manifestation of the human figure. On view in some museums throughout Europe and America, they fascinated Surrealists before the Second World War, including Alberto Giacometti, Georges Bataille, Henry Moore, and Barbara Hepworth, and artists and poets in the 1950s, including Willem de Kooning, David Smith, and Charles Olson (fig. 1–18).[21] These painters, sculptors, and writers saw in Sumerian art and poetry the translation of original energies and values that had been lost. A new path for the history of art was being opened.

Both Giacometti and Moore, who began their artistic careers in the 1920s, are represented in this exhibition.[22] For them the discovery of Sumerian sculpture was a revelation, and they felt that something essential to the understanding of human life was revealed by these objects. Giacometti, in response, created a series of drawings that embraced the image of Gudea, emphasizing the geometric patterns that structured the sculpture (fig. 1–19). After breaking with his academic training, Moore found Sumerian sculpture to be the simplicity and expression of life (see fig. 1–4), "with no decorative trimmings, which are the sign of decadence, of flagging inspiration," as he wrote in his 1935 review of Christian Zervos's book *L'art de la Mésopotamie*, one of the first publications on Sumerian "art" considered as art.[23] Moore was fascinated too by the relation he discovered in Sumerian statuettes between the head and the clasped hands, which, although small, held for him "a wealth of meaning." In his view these austere heads and hands were a sign of true humanity.

The painter Willem de Kooning is also known to have looked at the Tell Asmar statuettes for inspiration. Between 1950 and 1953, he produced six large, seminal female

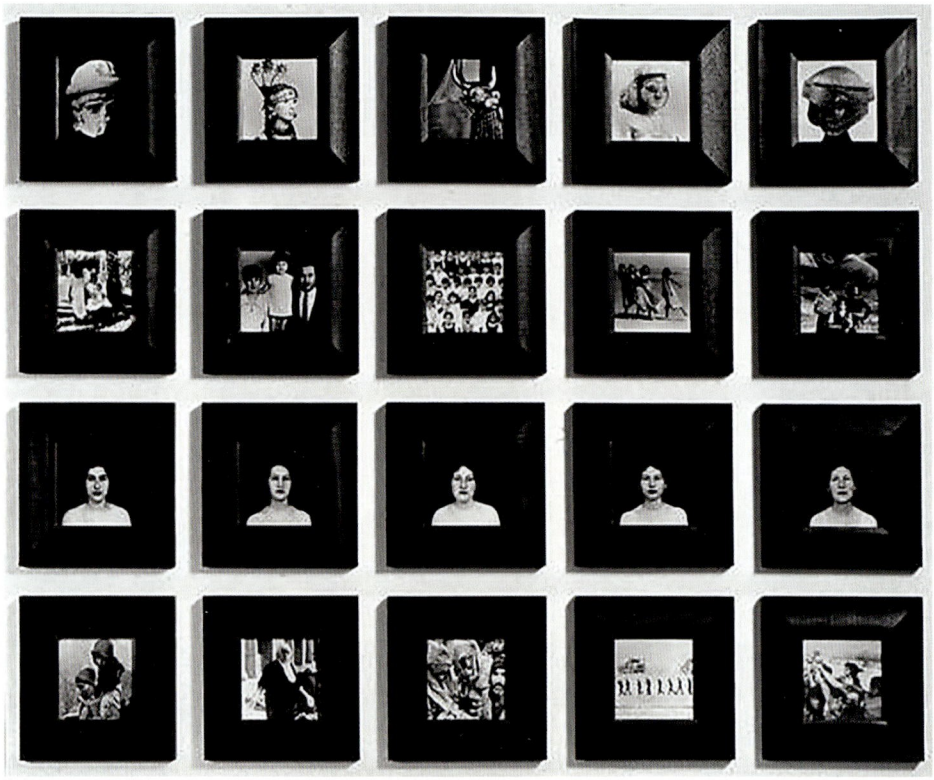

1–22. Jananne al-Ani. *Untitled May 1991 [Gulf War Work]*. Silver gelatin print on paper. IWM: 16417. Courtesy of the artist. Checklist no. 178.

paintings (as well as complementary series of color drawings and engravings), known as the *Woman* series, that are seen as opening the doors to Abstract Expressionism. Abstract they are not, but instead recognizable grotesque female images submerged in a rain of short intense brushstrokes, as if defining and destroying the bodies. Significant in the present context, many show a strong frontality and have the wide, staring, hypnotic eyes that are so intimately connected with Sumerian sculpture (figs. 1–20, 1–21).[24]

Past as Present and Present as Past
Since the 1950s artists have continued their fascination with Sumerian art. The loss and destruction of Mesopotamian art and architecture during recent invasions in the Near East and current civil wars have poignantly alerted contemporary artists such as the Iraqi-Irish Jananne al-Ani and Michael Rakowitz, who is of Jewish-Iraqi heritage, that an erasure of human memory is occurring in the region, an erasure that apparently will not stop until it destroys the land, its historical monuments, and its inhabitants and their riches.

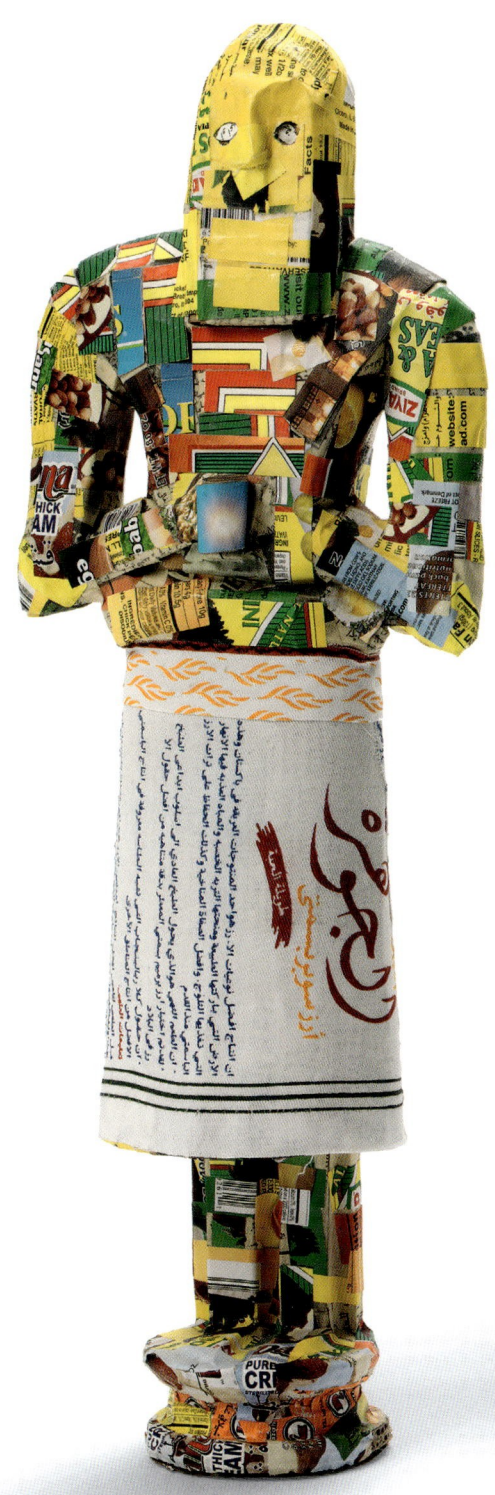

1–23. Michael Rakowitz. *Bearded male with skirt holding Vase (IM19753)*. Middle Eastern packaging and newspapers, glue. Courtesy of the artist and Lombard Freid Gallery: 8046. Checklist no. 151.

Currently living in London, al-Ani in her work deals partly with Westerners' biased image of Near Eastern human geography as well as the loss of memories of the historic past through destruction propelled by humankind itself. *Shadow Sites II* is an extraordinary video installation illustrating that the desert, an icon of Near Eastern spaces both dreamed and feared by Westerner travelers, is not in fact a desert.[25] Subtle layers of past and present—archaeological structures, agricultural interventions, military camps, roads, and landing fields—remain, revealing that deserts have been and are populated, and thus sites where traces of human beings are registered, places of memories.

Untitled May 1991 [Gulf War Work], also by al-Ani, and on view in this exhibition, is a collection of black-and-white photographs related to the artist's memories, as well as those of people living in Iraq, that illustrate why it is important to feel attachment to one's land and to what is being lost and destroyed by the incessant series of wars that have plagued the Near East since the 1980s (fig. 1–22). Among these images are family portraits that trace ties and losses, including Sumerian artifacts that may seem exotic to the Westerner but that are clearly familiar to people who have roots in Near Eastern culture. Overall, the series exposes the insidious effect that war and its destruction can have on families and their memories, gone forever.

In the same vein, Rakowitz's art comments on the current destruction of history reaching deeply into the past. His family fled Iraq in the 1940s, and the embattled country and its perception in Western countries is a main focus of Rakowitz's art. *The Invisible Enemy Should Not Exist (Recovered, Missing, Stolen)* shows life-size reproductions of Mesopotamian artifacts (primarily sculptures) made of cheap, mass-produced Iraqi materials, displayed on a sinuous table that evokes a path (fig. 1–23).[26] This allusion is not gratuitous. The title of the installation is a translation of the name of the Babylonian processional way that in ancient times led to the temples; in Rakowitz's installation it drives us only to the loss of part of the collection of the National Museum of Iraq in Baghdad, left unprotected from pillage during the Second Gulf War and the invasion of Iraq in 2003. The reproductions show some of the temporarily or still-missing masterpieces. Made with boxes of everyday Iraqi products that can be bought in markets and shops in Baghdad, Rakowitz's sculptures symbolize the disposable condition of these manufactured items, thrown away after use, just as Sumerian artifacts were treated as trash—through cupidity and ignorance—by robbers and invaders. The work symbolizes ignorance of the past, and the recognition and acceptance of the "other" that affects our modern culture.

Conclusion

By exhibiting archaeological objects alongside archival material (letters, pictures, documentaries, notebooks and field records, press clippings, and publications) and modern and contemporary works of art, we hope to convey that these things are not substantially different,[27] but rather ontologically identical. Documents show how an archaeological find has been received and promoted, allow a find to become a work of art, illuminate the way an archaeological object has been transfigured into an aesthetic object, and stand as proof that this transubstantiation has taken place. In some cases an archaeological find was accompanied by documents in a deliberate attempt to create a certain modern image of the object, with the desired result that the discovered object was actually accepted as a work of art. The ontological metamorphosis is complete when an artist interprets an archaeological item and produces his or her own work of art, which is either superficially or essentially similar to the ancient item. This process has enlarged the worlds of archaeology and aesthetics. It has also given new meaning to certain ancient objects, making them more complex and more intriguing, and breathing continuous life into them.

From Ancient to Modern: Archaeology and Aesthetics suggests the vital and complex role that personalities, and their desire for the promotion of archaeological material in an international context, have played in the conversion of specific objects into works of art. It also offers information about the discovery, presentation, and interpretation of archaeological finds in order to allow the viewer to judge them by his or her own standards. Some art theorists argue that a true work of art has enough power or magic to communicate the embodied message to anyone who is looking or listening to it,[28] while others assert that we cannot evaluate a work of art if we know nothing of its history or agenda.[29] We agree that a work of art cannot be perceived and evaluated without knowledge of its past and the story it tells. This exhibition and the catalogue that accompanies it communicate information about the exhibited archaeological material and the history of its promotion and reception, a history that explains how and why these items have entered the world of art, to which at first they did not and could not belong. The exhibition invites us to look at these archaeological finds with new eyes. Just as they are transformed by our perception, may we be able to bear their scrutinizing eyes, which change us too by letting us discover a new world and new meanings for already known worlds.

Endnotes

1   For a full discussion of the early excavation of Ur, see Zettler 1998. See also Emberling 2010; Kuklick 1996; Bernardhsson 2005.

2   For the full ten volumes of Woolley's reports on the Ur excavations, see Woolley 1927–76. For a summary, see Woolley 1954.

3   Woolley, at Oxford, to G. B. Gordon, in Philadelphia, Aug. 8, 1926, cited in Pedro Azara, "La arqueóloga y la moral de la tropa," in Azara 2012: 317.

4   Ibid.

5   Ur, Iraq Expedition Records, Correspondence, Exp. V, Jan.–July, 1927, UPennMuseum Archives, Philadelphia.

6   For a discussion and analysis of Puabi's jewelry, see Benzel in this volume.

7   "Are we right then in calling these royal graves and their occupants Kings and Queens?... Dr. H. R. Hall said...the finds [at Ur] could only be compared with Schliemann's at Mycenae in wealth of gold; and their completeness rivalled the funerary outfit of Tutankhamen." Woolley 1928: 425.

8   For a full discussion of Puabi's tomb, see Zettler and Hafford in this volume. See also Zettler 1998; Reade 2003.

9   Miller 2013. See also the essay by Pittman and Miller in this volume for an alternative view of the diadem.

10 Egyptomania—that is, public infatuation, especially in France, with Egyptian sites and finds, increased by traveling exhibitions of original funerary offerings, or copies, from Tutankhamun's tomb—has itself become an issue in the exhibition world. See, among others, Brier 2013; Collins and McNamara 2014. For a full discussion of the press surrounding Ur, see Azara and Marín in this volume.

11 Frederick G. Kenyon, at the British Museum (to unknown recipient), about publicity of the finds, Jan. 5, 1928; Kenyon to Mrs. McHugh, Jan. 17, 1928, Ur, Iraq Expedition Records, Correspondence, Exp. V, Jan.–July, 1927, UPennMuseum Archives, Philadelphia.

12 Among the publications that featured the news were the *Washington (DC) Herald*, Nov. 25, 1928, and the *Rochester (NY) Times-Union*, Nov. 8, 1929.

13 A complete bibliography on the Diyala Valley archaeological missions has been prepared by the Diyala Project, which is led by a team of scholars at the Oriental Institute; see https://oi.uchicago.edu/research/projects/diyala/bibliography. See also Frankfort 1939 and 1943. See also Reichel in this volume.

14 Frankfort 1954.

15 Jacobsen 1987.

16 Frankfort 1939 and 1943.

17 Frankfort 1954: 28.

18   For a discussion of primitivism and its use in the study of Sumerian sculptures, see Evans and Green in this volume.

19   Frankfort and Groenewegen-Frankfort 1946: 4.

20   The title of a black-and-white photograph of the showcase holding the Diyala worshiper statues, in the Social Science Hall at the 1934 Chicago World's Fair, appears in "Images of Progress: Views from A Century of Progress International Exposition, 1933–1934," *A Century of Progress Records, 1927–1952*, University of Illinois at Chicago Library, Special Collections and University Archives, COP_17_0003_00087_002, http://collections.carli.illinois.edu/cdm4/item_viewer.php?CISOROOT=/uic_cop&CISOPTR=590&CISOBOX=1&REC=5.

21   See Wood 2003. The recent work of Zainab Bahrani investigates the influence of Sumerian art on Giacometti and Moore (Bahrani 2014: chap. 1, esp. 16–27). Her work was seminal in our thinking around these two artists and around modern perspectives on Sumerian art in general. Alice Correia, cat. entry for Henry Moore's *Half-Figure* (1932), in *The Camden Town Group in Context*, ed. Helena Bonett, Ysanne Holt, and Jennifer Mundy, 2012. The North American draftsman and sculptor David Smith was inspired by the way scenes engraved in Sumerian cylinder seals are displayed. See Robert Taplin, "David Smith: Toward Volume," *Art in America*, April 2002, 119. See also Charles Olson, "The Gate and the Center (1951)," in *Collected Prose*, ed. Donald Allen and Benjamin Friedlander (Berkeley: University of California Press, 1997), 168–73.

22   Evans 2012a: 66–67; Bahrani 2014: 15–48.

23   Henry Moore, "Mesopotamian Art," *The Listener*, June 5, 2005, quoted in *Henry Moore: Writings and Conversations,* ed. Alan Wilkinson (Berkeley: University of California Press, 2002), 100. See also Rubin 1984, the catalogue for the exhibition *"Primitivism" in 20th Century Art: Affinity of the Tribal and the Modern*, at the Museum of Modern Art, New York. The show was much criticized; see, for example, Danto 1987, and Morphy and Perkins 2005.

24   *Willem De Kooning: Works, Writings, Interviews*, with text by Sally Yard (Barcelona: La Polígrafa, 2007); Sally Yard, *Willem De Kooning: The First Twenty-Six Years in New York* (New York: Garland, 1986).

25   Lazaar 2011.

26   Roelstraete 2014: 186–95.

27   Rancière 2011.

28   Didi-Huberman 1992.

29   While Danto (1981) considers the viewer as the subject, Didi-Huberman (1992) fully credits the work of art for transforming us into a viewer. We cease to be blind after confrontation with the work, which acts as an illumination. Our eyes open to the world, and we are able to see what it means through art's sensible shapes. The power of images to choose their viewers and to offer them humanity by allowing them to look, as described by Didi-Huberman, is the fundamental premise of the Byzantine theology of divine images. While Didi-Huberman's theory of art analyzes the relationship between a work of art and the viewer awakened by it, Gell (1998) considers that a fetish, such as a Sumerian worshiper statue, is a living being able to exert a powerful influence not only on one person but on a group, whose vision of the world is altered by the object, by the belief in its illusory—but felt as real—power.

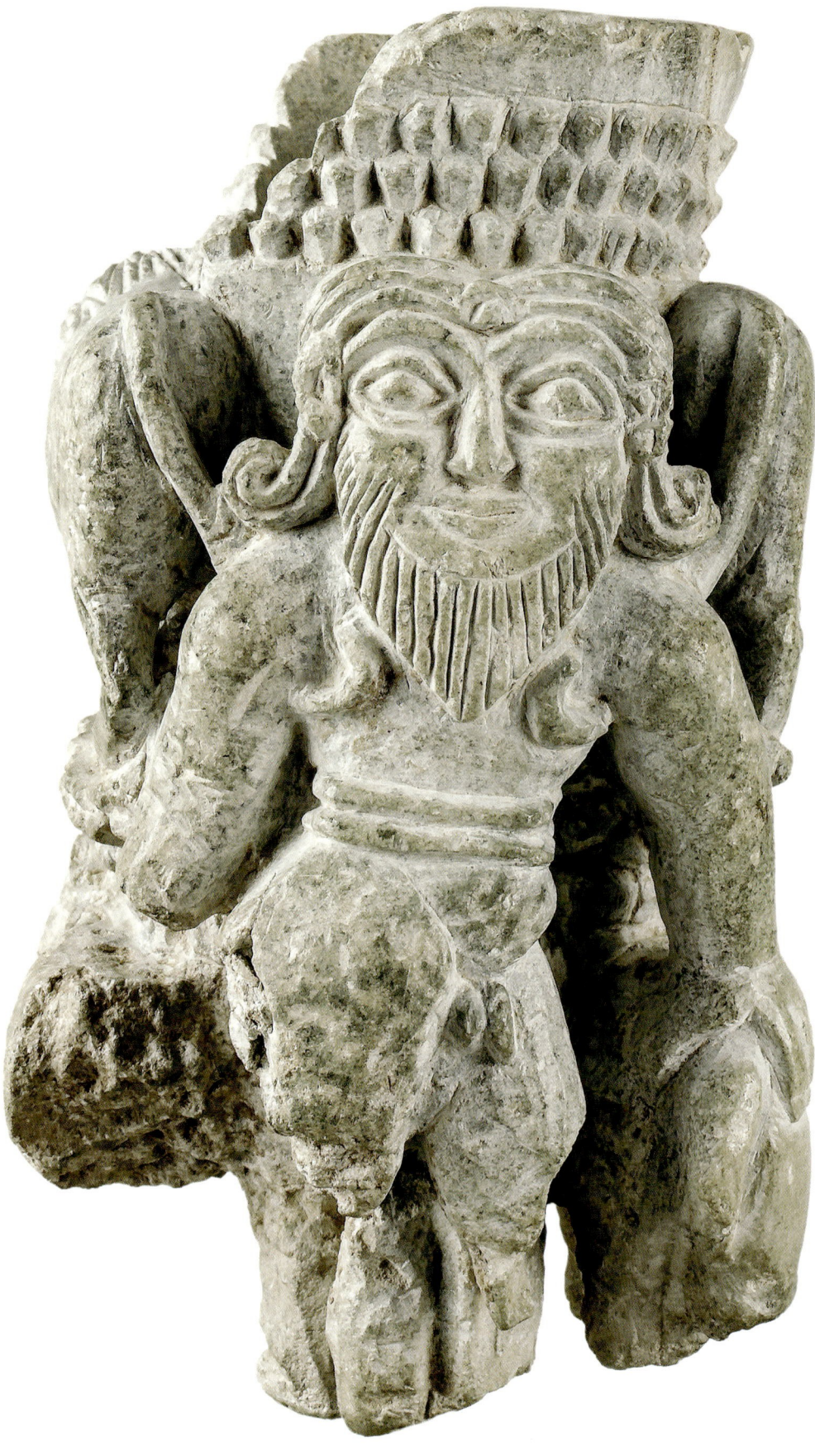

The Golden Image of Archaeology before the Second World War

Pedro Azara and Marc Marín

"When the artifacts are found
chiselled out, cleaned up and looked at again
as things of beauty

they are not lost

(never were lost)

what do we recognize?"[1]

The 2006 opening in Paris of the Musée du Quai Branly, which holds the world's largest collection of artifacts from "primitive cultures," followed years of acerbic discussion in French academia. This huge institution, designed by the French architect Jean Nouvel, is located in the heart of Paris, an urban area limited by strict building restrictions on the banks of the river Seine, almost facing the Eiffel Tower. The Musée du Quai Branly was called at first the Musée des Arts Premiers, a name that can be understood as "Museum of the First Arts" but also as "Museum of the Fundamental Arts." Its holdings were drawn from the collections of the Musée National des Arts d'Afrique et d'Océanie, established for the 1931 Colonial Exhibition in Paris to exhibit artifacts from the French colonies around the world, and from the Musée de l'Homme, a collection of prehistoric finds and "tribal" artifacts.

The Musée du Quai Branly currently holds pre-Columbian, African, and Oceanic artifacts, in addition to some Asian objects. There are no European collections, either ancient or modern. These belong to the Louvre, which is considered an "art" museum—in spite of its collections of ancient and medieval objects that were produced not as works of art but for practical or religious reasons. Like the Musée Guimet, which holds most of the Asian collections in Paris, the Musée du Quai Branly is deemed an ethnographic museum.

The Musée du Quai Branly was established and built in accord with a presidential decree. However, its creation was preceded by years of discussion regarding its rationale, with the name of the institution as well as the focus of its collections heavily criticized. What is meant by the "first arts?" Those from Paleolithic or Neolithic times or cultures? Certainly not, since some of the objects in the collection were handcrafted in the twentieth century and might logically fall within the purview of the Musée d'Art de la Ville de Paris or the Centre Pompidou. Some of the artifacts exhibited at the Musée du Quai Branly are ancient, older than those shown in the Louvre, and thus archaeological material. But the Louvre also holds archaeological finds. In fact, the criteria for division of archaeological material between the two museums is geographical. The Louvre retains Western "art" as well as "Islamic" examples, but only works of fine art and decorative arts. This choice implies that non-European and many non-Islamic works are not aesthetic but rather ethnographic objects. Moreover, the collecting focus of the various institutions suggests that all "first" or "primitive" arts originated outside of Western cultures. These criteria and assumptions are also now followed in Barcelona at the Museu de Cultures del Món (Museum of World Cultures), which opened at the end of 2014 and exhibits material from the "colonial" worlds, especially Spanish. Meanwhile, Western archaeological material and "the primitives"—that is, late medieval art as understood in the history of Western art—are shown either in the Museu d'Arqueologia de Catalunya or at the Museu Nacional d'Art de Catalunya, both of which are considered repositories of fine art rather than collections of tools or fetishes. From the examples of these museums' collecting policies, we can infer that artifacts from Mesopotamia are commonly perceived as belonging to the realm of art, in spite of having been created or handcrafted at the "dawn of history," or even before the time of writing. What does this mean and imply?

Mesopotamia "Discovered," or How the West "Found" It

Western historians discovered Mesopotamia at a relatively late date. The first journeys to the East after the fall of the Roman Empire began during the ninth century with Muslim geographers from the Córdoba caliphate (which ruled the Iberian Peninsula and part of North Africa) on their way to Mecca.[2] Later, in the twelfth century, Christian adventurers explored the Holy Land and reached Mesopotamia. However, none of these journeys visited Sumerian sites in the south of Mesopotamia, as they were largely unknown—being absent from the Bible, the Quran, and Herodotus's written texts. Only Babylonian and Assyrian capitals, which had substantial ruins, had been identified, thanks to written records. Before the nineteenth century Western knowledge of antiquity comprised primarily Egyptian, Greek, and Roman cultures, although there was also limited understanding of the art of Babylon, Assyria, and Persia. Continuous and extended visits, along with initial excavations, began with Ottoman and Western "archaeologists" in the early nineteenth century. Again, northern and central Mesopotamia were the first lands to be explored before interest in the south began in the mid-1850s.

The Ottoman Empire posed a problem for certain Western countries in terms of Westerners' journeys to the East. Colonies in India and the Far East were difficult to reach due to limitations imposed on Western travelers by Ottoman administrations. However, during the Crimean War of 1853–56, Western troops were sent to Turkey to ensure Ottoman control, thus guaranteeing uninterrupted travel from the port of Basra to India. Western troops stationed in Turkey after the war offered an excellent opportunity to explore Assyrian capitals mentioned in the Bible. When conflict erupted between the Ottoman and the Persian empires just after the Crimean war, Western troops this time acted in favor of Persia to avoid an expansion of Ottoman power. Once more, troops remained after the war, in Mesopotamia, and explorations began (fig. 2–1).

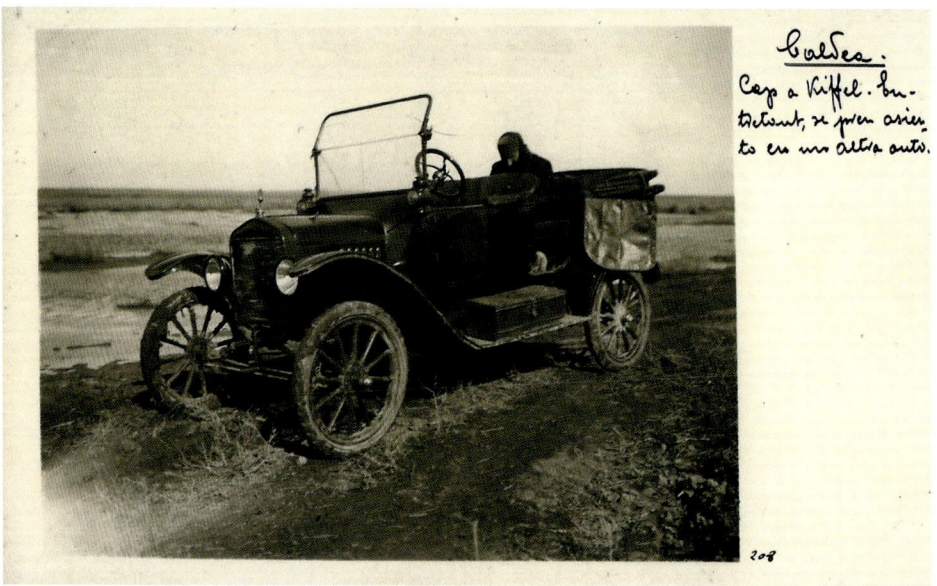

2-1. Father Bonaventura Ubach traveling to Kiffel, Mesopotamia. Photograph, 1922–23. Monserrat: 2. Courtesy of the Monserrat Abbey.

But why is there a relationship between members of the military and archaeologists? The answer is explained in this excerpt from the 1927 report of the Ur excavations:

> In the year 1839–40 the hostilities that threatened to break out between Persia and Turkey owing to frontier disputes were avoided by the mediation of the Governments of Great Britain and Russia, with the result that commissioners nominated by the four Powers assembled a Commission to delimitate the disputed boundary. Colonel Williams, R.A. [later, Sir W. F. Williams, the famous defender of Kars during the Crimean War] was the British representative, and to his staff a geologist was appointed, Mr [later, Sir] William Kennett Loftus, F.G.S. The Commission started out on its work in the year 1849, proceeding southwards by way of the Tigris and Mosul to Baghdad, and thence via Hillah, Diwaniyah, and the Lower Euphrates to Basrah, on its journey to the southern end of the boundary in Arabistan. During the journey, Mr. Loftus, who was keenly interested in the ancient remains along the route, took careful notes of the chief ruined sites, such as Niniveh, Babylon, Nuffar [Nippur], Warka [Erech], and tell-Muqayyar [Ur], and on arrival at Muhammarah he obtained leave from Colonel Williams to return to Warka and dig there on a small scale. The result of this, the first excavation in southern Babylonia, were to be sent to the British Museum, and they are there now, the kernel of our early Babylonian collections.[3]

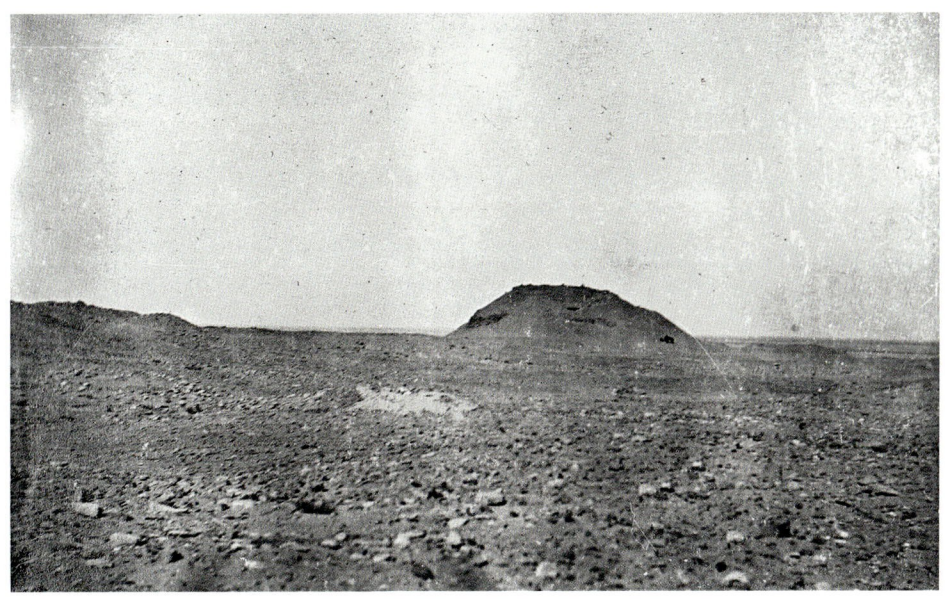

2-2. Gertrude Bell's view of the Ziggurat at Ur before the arrival of the Woolley archaeological mission. Photograph, 1916–17. GBA: W_078. Courtesy of the Gertrude Bell Archive.

Thus, most of the first archaeologists in this region were also military men.[4] As such, they believed that land should be controlled in order to obtain benefits. The land did not belong to the local, indigenous populations, but rather to the people who governed and studied it; and the same held true for the ancient objects that were unearthed there. This perspective took two directions: horizontal, symbolizing control across the land, and vertical, indicating that those at the top of the hierarchy had the right to inhabit, control, and exploit the land. Significantly, military maps and aerial photographs were made available for archaeological missions. With the use of military capabilities, trenches were opened by "natives" subject to Westerners. Minds—ideas, plans, interpretations—were proper to the foreign (soon to be colonial) powers; work, to the local inhabitants. Some of the laborers were in fact prisoners, as was the case with excavations by H. R. Hall in Eridu, undertaken with the help of seventy Turkish prisoners of war.[5] War was thereby a benefit for archaeology, as Hall and Charles Leonard Woolley wrote: "It is curious that the first excavations of the British Museum on this site [Ur] should have taken place during the Crimean War, and the next during the Great War of 1914–18. In each case war gave an opportunity to archaeology."[6] (The irony of this argument was perhaps not evident eighty-five years ago.) The common vocabulary of war and archaeology is an unexpected but clear signal of the ties between the two: "campaign" and "mission" are terms that belong to both fields. Archaeological missions took advantage of the occupation ensuing from war, and quickly began to discover items to fill the newly founded public and private museums in Europe and the United States that were financing the excavations. As Hall wrote:

> In 1918 the Trustees of the British Museum desired to take advantage of the British military occupation of Iraq to resume their long interrupted work at Muqayyar.... [T]he Director, Sir F. G. Kenyon, arranged with the military authorities for the transference to archaeological work from the Intelligence section of the army of Capt. R. C. Thompson.... I was similarly transferred from the Intelligence branch of the army in England to Mesopotamia in order to carry on the work begun by him, and on arrival was attached by Sir (then Lieut.-Col.) A. T. Wilson to the Political Service for archaeological duty.[7]

In an explicit letter, Kenyon wrote to G. B. Gordon, director of the Museum of Archaeology and Anthropology of the University of Pennsylvania, that "Colonel Lawrence [a well-known English spy, military man and archaeologist] was digging for us [the British Museum] at Carchemish."[8]

In spite of the Englishwoman Gertrude Bell's defense of Iraqi interests (fig. 2–2), the relationship between Iraqis and Western archaeologists was not an easy one. Not only was southern Iraq unstable—rebel tribes were constantly on the move, and attacks to the missions necessitated armed guards—but the tone used by some archaeologists denoted a certain disregard for Iraqi curators.[9] The expression "native director of antiquities" was written, we suspect, with contempt, by S. Langdon to E. T. Leeds, keeper of the Ashmolean Museum in Oxford, in January 1929.[10]

At Ur, or Carter vs. Woolley

Finds in Mesopotamia were viewed within the context of previous and simultaneous missions in Egypt. The Egyptologist Howard Carter discovered the Tutankhamun tomb in early 1923. Press coverage was widespread, as was the ensuing public fame of the discoveries. Ancient Egypt played a leading role within the Western imagination, and the press considered Egyptian finds highly newsworthy. Large Assyrian and neo-Assyrian stone statues had been recovered in northern Iraq in the nineteenth century, but there had been no golden treasures to fascinate the public. Tutankhamun and the glittering finds of his tomb were almost certainly in every archaeologist's mind while excavating in Mesopotamia. A 1927 letter from the Ur mission noted that "it is impossible nowadays to speak of 'rich tombs' without evoking a memory of the marvellous treasures of Tutankhamen."[11]

In the early 1920s missions also began in Mesopotamia—in Ur, Kish, and the Diyala Valley north of Baghdad (including Tell Asmar and Khafajah; figs. 2–3, 2–4)—jointly run by British and U.S. archaeologists. Privately financed and organized by wealthy donors (including John D. Rockefeller Jr.) and institutions (including the Oriental Institute and the Field Museum in Chicago and the University of Pennsylvania, as well as the British

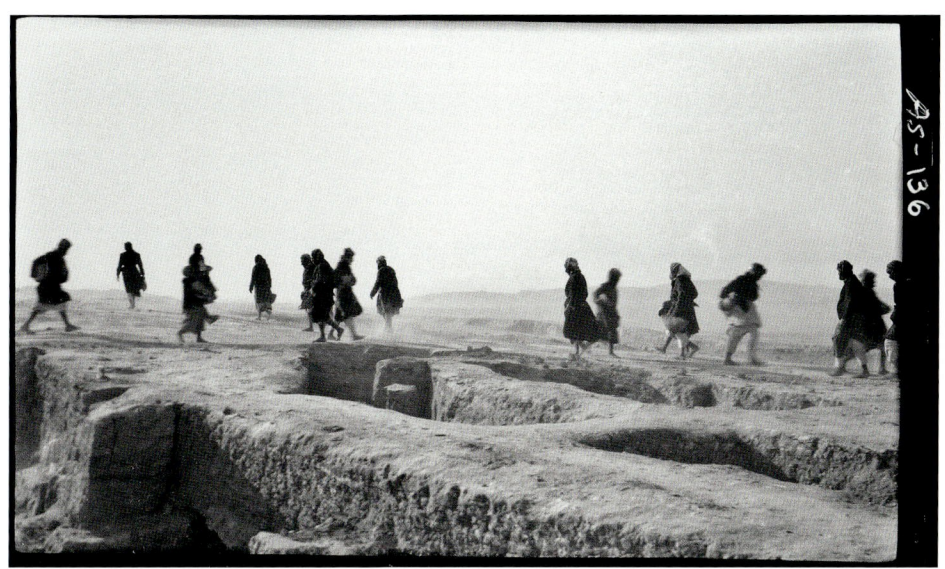

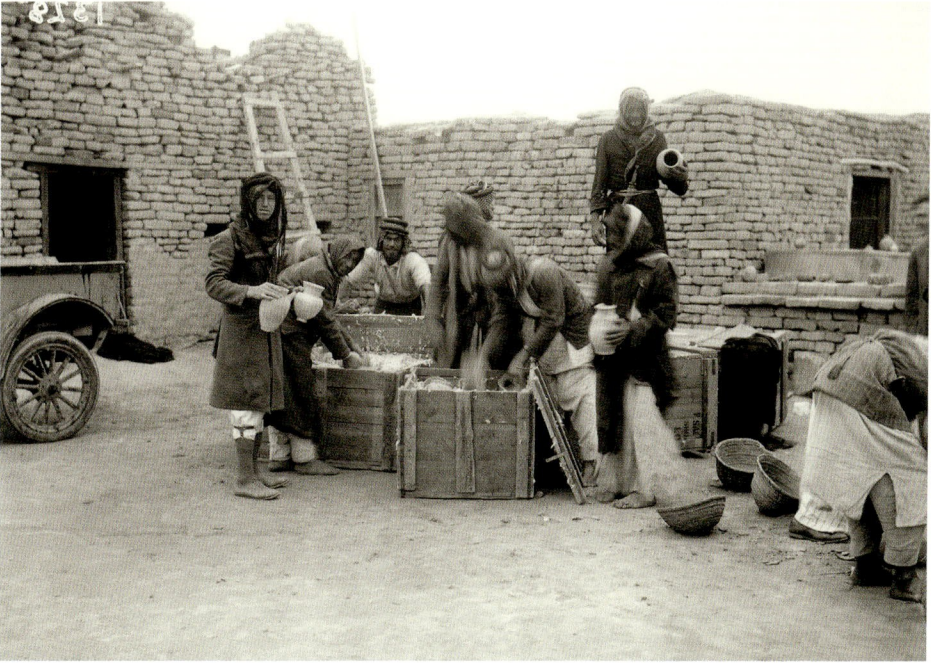

2–3. Workmen walking among open excavation trenches at Tell Asmar. Photograph, ca. 1930. OIM: as0136. Courtesy of the Oriental Institute of the University of Chicago.

2–4. Excavation team packing pottery into boxes, Ur. Photograph, 1929. Penn Museum: 1328. Courtesy of the University of Pennsylvania Museum of Archaeology and Anthropology. Checklist no. 76.

Queen Shub-ad's 5000-Year-Old Golden Head-Dress: an Ur Treasure.

AFTER A PHOTOGRAPH BY COURTESY OF MR. C. LEONARD WOOLLEY, DIRECTOR OF THE JOINT EXPEDITION OF THE BRITISH MUSEUM AND THE PENNSYLVANIA UNIVERSITY MUSEUM TO MESOPOTAMIA.

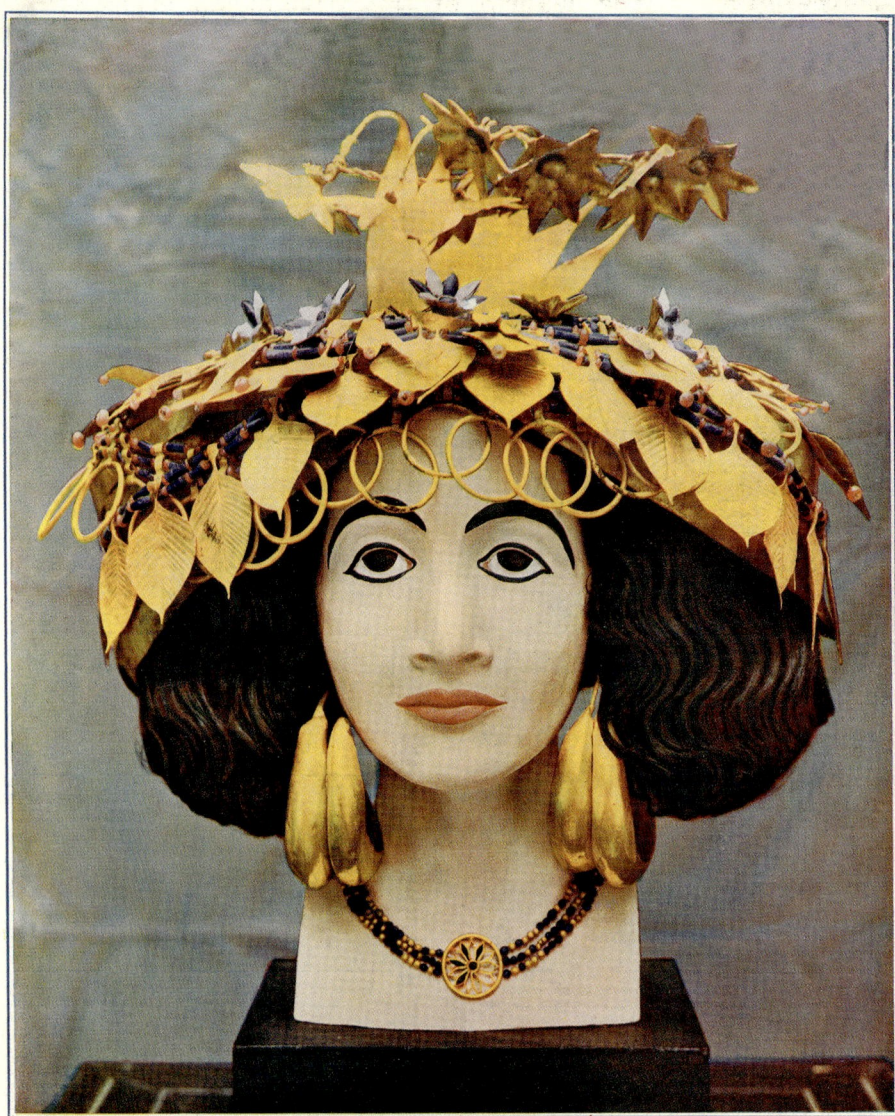

AS WORN BY A QUEEN IN ABRAHAM'S CITY 5000 YEARS AGO: A GOLD HEAD-DRESS FROM UR OF THE CHALDEES, ON A HEAD MODELLED FROM A SUMERIAN WOMAN'S SKULL.

We now reproduce in its actual colours Queen Shub-ad's wonderful head-dress of gold and beads, discovered recently at Ur, already illustrated in black and white in our issue of June 30. Mr. C. Leonard Woolley, the discoverer, writes : " It was found on the queen's skull inside the stone-built tomb chamber. Though crushed by stones and earth, every one of its component parts kept its position in the soil, and their order could be noted with such accuracy that a reconstruction was comparatively simple. The gold ribbon, the basis of the whole, retained its oval form, and, for purposes of removal from the soil, the different strands were fixed by strips of glued paper twisted between them. This gave the outline of the wig. A new wig was made, of these measurements, and dressed in the style illustrated by early Sumerian sculpture, and, when the ribbon was laid over this and the bands which held it were undone, the strands fell naturally into position. The head has been modelled by Mrs. Woolley, over the cast of a nearly contemporary female Sumerian skull, the features being added in wax over the bony structure. Thus was produced a face which, while in no sense a portrait of Queen Shub-ad, must approximate closely to the physical type of the period."

2-5. "Queen Shub-ad's 5000-Year-Old Golden Head-Dress: An Ur Treasure." *Illustrated London News*, August 11, 1928. MMA: ANE.ILN.2. Courtesy of the Department of Ancient Near Eastern Art, The Metropolitan Museum of Art. Checklist no. 91.

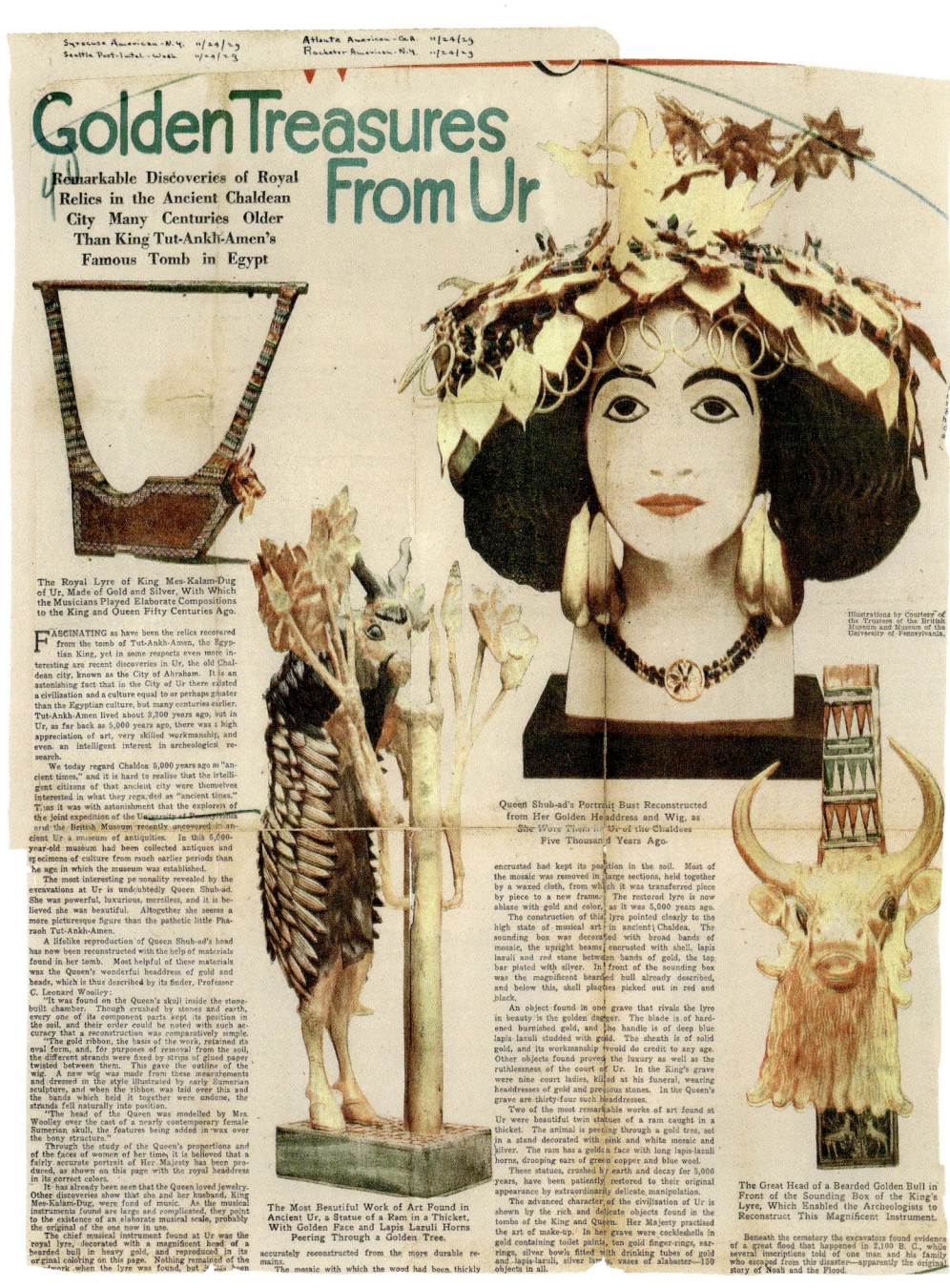

2–6. "Golden Treasures from Ur." *Seattle Post Intelligencer*, November 24, 1929. Courtesy of the University of Pennsylvania Museum of Archaeology and Anthropology. Checklist no. 93.

Museum and the Oxford Museum), these extensive undertakings involved the participation of hundreds of local people and continued until World War II. The finds were divided between Iraq, on the one hand, and the United States and the United Kingdom, on the other. In 1920 Iraq had been established as a League of Nations mandate under British control. A king was appointed the following year, and the country ostensibly gained its independence in 1932.[12] However, negotiations regarding archaeological finds remained under the control of the Colonial Office rather than the Foreign Office. The National Museum of Iraq in Baghdad and the Directorate-General of Antiquities were established by the British Mandate thanks to Gertrude Bell, who became the Honorary Director of Antiquities. She argued for Iraqi interests when the distribution of finds was undertaken, but her power was not sufficient to avoid the problematic division of the Kish tablets: without the knowledge of Iraqi authorities, a thousand tablets were illegally sent from Baghdad to Oxford by Stephen Langdon, director of the Kish mission, before 1933 when the mission ceased.[13]

Precious offerings were unearthed from Ancient Near Eastern tombs in 1923, but the discovery in late 1927 of the so-called Royal Tombs of Ur—the adjective "royal" was critical to ignite the public's interest and imagination[14]—including Queen Puabi's heavy golden accoutrement of diadems, combs, rings, bracelets, and necklaces, was the much needed answer to Carter's find. A decision was made by those responsible for the mission at Ur that news of the discoveries would be managed carefully,[15] with deliberate consideration of what information should be made public, as well as where (Philadelphia, London, or Baghdad?) and when. Woolley devoted himself to writing a press release (see fig. 1-11), and a description of the finds at Queen Puabi's tomb was prepared for the Bureau of Publicity of the University of Pennsylvania, and originally scheduled to be released on January 12, 1928.[16] The importance of the use of the press—print and radio broadcast[17]—which Woolley controlled so expertly, was not confined to the Ur mission. Those responsible for the Kish mission were also aware that publicity was necessary: "...the photographs which you sent to the Museum are splendid and most interesting. A selection has been made from the lot for publicity purposes," wrote Ernest Mackay, director of the mission, to Langdon in Oxford.[18]

The press strategy for Ur worked perfectly: Mesopotamia defeated Egypt (figs. 2–5, 2–6). As Woolley wrote at the end of January 1927, he believed that "the technique of the arts and crafts [of Mesopotamia] is definitively superior" to that of Egypt, and his view on the preeminence of Mesopotamian culture was accepted by the press. For instance, E. L. Rawley wrote in the *New York Times* on January 29 that "[Queen Puabi's] Tomb shows Mesopotamia was more civilized than Egypt."[19] The constant comparison between Mesopotamian culture and that of Egypt suggests that the latter was identified by the public as the paradigm by which to measure any less familiar ancient culture. Based on press coverage, it appears that only an ancient Western culture that compared favorably with the Egyptian held any true interest.

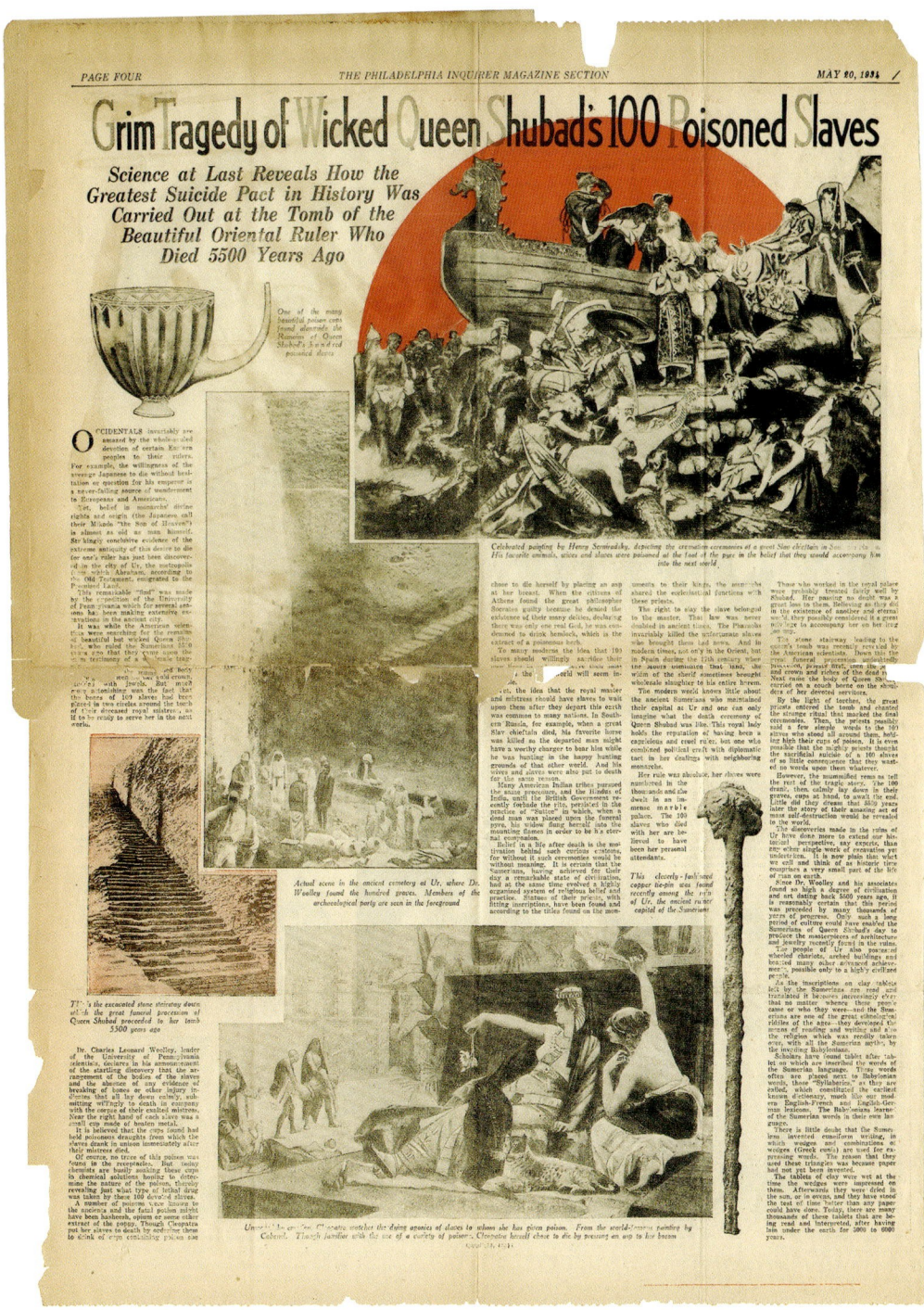

2–7. "Grim Tragedy of Wicked Queen Shubad's 100 Poisoned Slaves." *Philadelphia Inquirer*, May 20, 1934. Courtesy of the University of Pennsylvania Museum of Archaeology and Anthropology. Checklist no. 97.

A gripping headline from one San Francisco newspaper read "When a Mummy Queen 'Lost Her Head.'"[20] We can speculate that though the body found in the tomb was not mummified, the scarce remains of a shattered cranium—the only visible vestiges of Puabi—would not awaken the public's interest and imagination unless, as was often noted, she had been subjected to gruesome acts, thus compensating for the lack of the mummies that had drawn attention to Egyptian finds.[21] Other compelling headlines included: "Evidence that the Queen of Ancient Ur Was Clubbed to Death" (see fig. 1-12), "Ur Tombs Yields—Slain Family," and "Why the Beauties of Ur Were Killed with Their Kings" (see also the article in the *Philadelphia Inquirer*, fig. 2-7).[22] Twenty-first-century sensibilities still react strongly to similar statements, and possibly the only difference between today's perceptions and public opinion from the 1920s is gender awareness: at that time "beauties" could only mean ladies. Kish also offered finds that were just as opportune in terms of public appeal: "Entombed Alive with the Royal Dead: Human victims interred with their monarch to insure his comfort in the Land of the Dead, according to the latest findings of archaeologists in excavations at ancient city of Kish, site of the world's oldest known civilization," wrote Dexley Haynes in the *Washington Post* on October 28, 1928. "No stage setting could suggest more vividly the action of tragedy," added Haynes. "Not even the skeletons of the maidens sacrificed to the 'Rain God' in the Sacred Well of Yucatan could match in graphic qualities the silent testimony of the slaughter of Sumerians." If Mesopotamian finds could not rival those of Egypt, spicy and gory graphic details could attract and appeal to the public.

News from Egyptian missions and the importance of the Tutankhamun tomb often caused intentional or uninformed mistakes in which Mesopotamian culture was confused with Egyptian. One U.S. paper concluded that Queen Puabi was Egyptian,[23] while another presented the golden vases and jewelry from the Puabi tomb as the "work of early Egyptian goldsmiths."[24] The rich tomb of Tut, familiar to U.S. readers, became the standard against which Mesopotamian finds were measured. Meskalamdug, one of the Sumerian kings buried in Ur[25] whose (possible) tomb was discovered in the 1927–28 season, had been discussed in a similar fashion: "Beside this ruler, whose name is believed to have been Meekalamdug [*sic*], the pharaohs of Ancient Egypt are modern. He lived more than 2200 years before Tutankhamen, and consequently the span that separates their lives is greater than that of the entire Christian era."[26]

The comparison between Egypt and Mesopotamia was useful for a public that knew little about the Ancient Near East. But Mesopotamia had attracted travelers and archaeologists since the nineteenth century, due to Biblical references to Mesopotamian cities, kings, and queens. Sumer, however, was not mentioned, except for the city of Ur, and the Royal Tombs of Ur and Queen Puabi had no place in the Old Testament description of the city. It was the patriarch Abraham, described as born in Ur, who brought the city to public awareness. Thus, one way to rouse the interest of a modern viewer was to constantly evoke the relationship between discoveries at Ur—the Biblical city of Chaldees, as it was almost always cited in the press—and Abraham. The result

HOME OF KINGS "DATED" FROM THE FLOOD: A PALACE OF 3500 B.C.

PHOTOGRAPHS AND DESCRIPTION BY COURTESY OF PROFESSOR STEPHEN LANGDON, M.A., B.D., PH.D., PROFESSOR OF ASSYRIOLOGY AT OXFORD, AND DIRECTOR OF THE HERBERT WELD (OXFORD) AND FIELD MUSEUM (CHICAGO) EXPEDITION TO KISH.

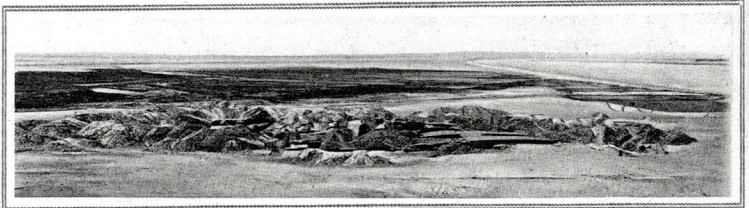

1. "THE ONLY GREAT CONSTRUCTION OF ITS KIND HITHERTO EXCAVATED IN MESOPOTAMIA": THE ANCIENT SUMERIAN PALACE AT KISH AS EXCAVATED—A GENERAL VIEW FROM THE TOP OF A HIGH TEMPLE TOWER EAST OF THE RUINS.

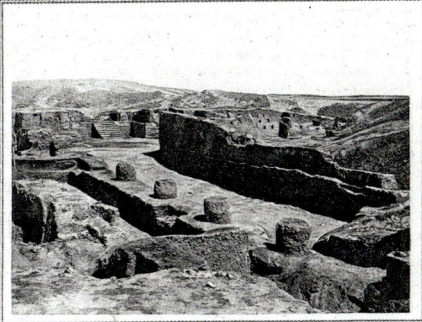

2. THE FIRST "UNDISTURBED AND GREAT MONUMENT OF THE EARLIEST PERIOD OF MESOPOTAMIAN ARCHITECTURE": THE COURT AND PILLARED WALL AT KISH.

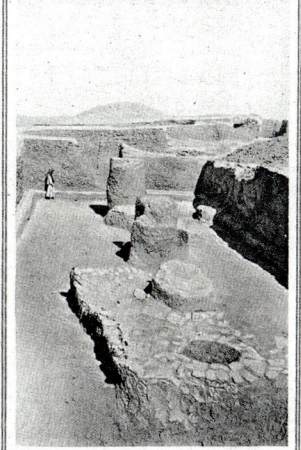

4. "A COMPLETELY NEW ELEMENT IN THE HISTORY OF ARCHITECTURE": THE GREAT HALL OF COLUMNS DISCOVERED THIS YEAR NORTH OF THE COURT SHOWN IN NO. 2.

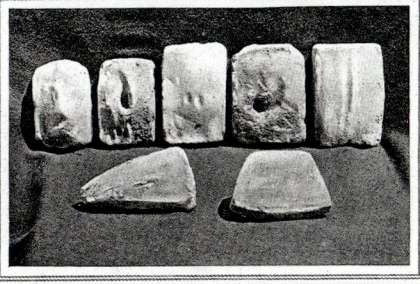

3. MARKED BY THE MASON'S THUMB AND HAND-MOULDED LIKE BISCUITS: TWO OF THE OLDEST TYPE OF BRICKS (ON THE LEFT), WITH OTHERS LATER AND LARGER.

THE wonderful discoveries at Kish, near Babylon, illustrated last year in our issues of March 1 and May 3, have since been greatly developed. The Director of the expedition, Professor Stephen Langdon, refers in his new account to the valuable services of the staff in the field, and expresses gratitude for the generosity of Mr. Herbert Weld and the Field Museum of Chicago. "The work this year," he writes, " has been confined to finishing the extensive palace of the early Sumerian kings of Kish, partially excavated last year, and to continued research on the great mound of eastern Kish, where large numbers of cuneiform tablets had been discovered in 1924. The excavations this season have been conducted by Mr. Ernest [*Continued below.*]

Continued.] Mackay, assisted by Father Eric Burrows, of Campion Hall, Oxford, epigraphist, and by Mr. D. Talbot-Rice. Photograph No. 2 shows the court and pillared wall of the Sumerian palace at the end of last season ; and No. 4 is a view of the great hall of columns discovered this year north of the court. No. 1 is a photograph taken by Mr. Mackay from the top of the lofty temple tower just east of the old palace, and gives a perspective of the building after it had been completely excavated. . . . The original building dates from a period about 3500 B.C., and ceased to be the seat of the kings of Sumer and Accad at the time of the founding of the empire of Agade by Sargon in 2752 B.C. The building is constructed of plano-convex bricks, and is the only great construction of its kind hitherto excavated in Mesopotamia. Its ground plan covers an area of about two acres. Photograph No. 3 illustrates the small biscuit-shaped bricks employed by the earliest architects. The two small bricks at the left are good examples of the oldest type, flat on the lower surface, and very convex on the top, being finished by the moulder's hand like a great biscuit, and marked by the mason's thumb. These measure 8¼ by 5¼ inches, the thickness varying from 1½ to 2½ inches. About 3000 B.C. the Sumerian masons introduced a second type of plano-convex brick, 9½ by 6 inches, and 2¼-2½ inches in thickness, thus approaching, somewhat, the regular flat moulded brick introduced in the twenty-eighth century. Three examples of this type are seen in No. 3, together with two bricks from the outer layers of the columns. This palace furnishes the modern historian for the first time with an undisturbed and great monument of the earliest period of Mesopotamian architecture. The colossal pillar decorations of the southern outer court, and the hall of columns, constitute a completely new element in the history of architecture. The palace of the long line of the kings of Kish, whose kingdom was said to have begun immediately after the Flood, was provided with open fireplaces, great ovens and kitchens, reception halls of vast dimensions, innumerable chambers, and was strongly fortified by a double wall, with moat and drawbridges."

2–8. "Home of the Kings 'Dated' from the Flood: A Palace of 3500 B.C." *Illustrated London News*, May 9, 1925. MMA: ANE.ILN.7. Courtesy of the Department of Ancient Near Eastern Art, The Metropolitan Museum of Art. Checklist no. 24.

RELICS OF SUMER'S FIRST CAPITAL

AFTER THE FLOOD: DISCOVERIES AT KISH.

CHARIOTS AND OXEN OF 3500 B.C.;
AND A WOMAN'S SPLENDID JEWELS.

By Courtesy of Professor S. Langdon, Director of the Oxford-Field Museum Expedition.

NEARLY 6000 YEARS OLD: STONE BOWLS FOUND AT KISH IN A TOMB OF PLANO-CONVEX BRICKS, 25 FT. BELOW PLAIN LEVEL, AND DATING FROM A PERIOD BEFORE 4000 B.C.

ONE OF FOUR CYLINDER SEALS FOUND IN GRAVES OF THE RED EARTH LEVEL AT KISH: A BEAUTIFUL PIECE OF WORK DATING FROM ABOUT 3000 B.C.

SHOWING A DEEP TRENCH WHERE CHARIOTS WERE FOUND: THE SITE AT KISH, WITH A LATE TEMPLE BUILT BY NEBUCHADNEZZAR IN BACKGROUND.

A COPPER REIN-GUIDE FOUND FIXED TO THE END OF A CHARIOT-POLE OF ABOUT 3500 B.C., SURMOUNTED BY A FIGURE OF AN ASS.

JEWELLERY FROM A WOMAN'S GRAVE IN THE RED EARTH STRATUM: A LAPIS AND GOLD BANGLE, BRONZE PINS, SILVER RINGS, ONYX DROPS ON A GOLD HOOP, SMALL GOLD RINGS, AND AN IMPRESSION OF A LAPIS CYLINDER SEAL.

A FOUR-WHEELED CHARIOT 25 FT. BELOW PLAIN LEVEL IN TEMPLE RUINS AT KISH: WHEELS 2 FT. IN DIAMETER WITH COPPER FELLOES NAILED TO THE WOOD.—(ON LEFT) THE SKELETON OF ONE OF ITS DRAUGHT OXEN.

Describing the sixth season's work of the Oxford-Field Museum Expedition at Kish, Professor S. Langdon writes (in the "Times"): "The excavators first exposed the ruins of the temple of the Sargonic period, circa 2700 B.C., to a depth of 25 ft., after which they came upon a sterile stratum 7 ft. thick, reaching a continuous red earth stratum 5 ft. thick, which represents the Sumerian temenos platform on which the great temples were placed about 3000 B.C. In this red layer . . . was found a magnificent mat burial of a woman, with solid gold fillet about her head, gold, silver, and copper ornaments, and a beautiful lapis lazuli seal. Beneath this level the entire area was excavated to a depth of 25 ft. below plain level, and the excavators came upon a long series of brick-vaulted tombs made of small plano-convex bricks . . . just above the virgin soil of the time when this city, said to have been the first capital of Sumer after the Flood, was founded. Stone bowls and spouted painted pots characterise this cemetery. In two of the tombs were found four-wheeled and two-wheeled chariots with the bodies of four oxen which drew them. The oxen were slain to accompany the owner to the lower world, and apparently his servants perished with him. . . . We have reached here a period clearly 1000 years earlier than the oldest Sumerian inscriptions which can be translated. . . . The age to which the vaulted brick tombs belong is to be dated before 4000 B.C. . . . The ruins of this most ancient capital are enormous, and are continuous from 30 ft. below plain level to the age of Nebuchadnezzar and Darius."

2–9. "Relics of Sumer's First Capital After the Flood: Discoveries at Kish. Chariots and oxen of 3500 B.C.; and a woman's splendid jewels." *Illustrated London News*, June 2, 1928. MMA: ANE.ILN.6. Courtesy of the Department of Ancient Near Eastern Art, The Metropolitan Museum of Art. Checklist no. 66.

KHAFAJE STATUARY—WITH A REVELATORY "BEARDED PRIEST."

ILLUSTRATIONS BY THE IRAQ EXPEDITION FROM THE ORIENTAL INSTITUTE OF THE UNIVERSITY OF CHICAGO. BY COURTESY OF DR. HENRY FRANKFORT, FIELD DIRECTOR. (SEE HIS ARTICLE ON PAGE 526.)

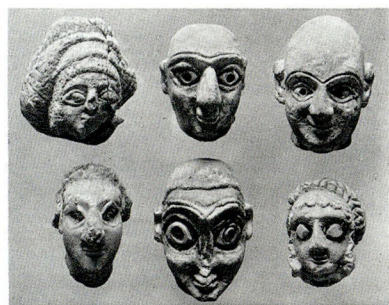 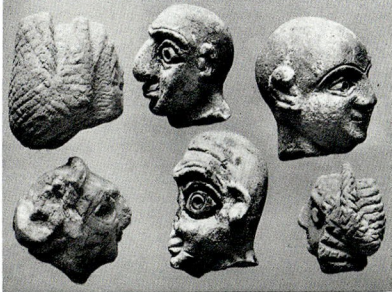

FIG. 5. STATUE HEADS FROM THE KHAFAJE TEMPLE RUINS SHOWN FULL-FACE; WITH EYES INLAID WITH SHELL AND LAPIS LAZULI, FIXED WITH BITUMEN: EVIDENCE OF RACIAL MIXTURE 3000 B.C.

FIG. 6. THE SAME STATUE HEADS IN PROFILE; SHOWING ELEMENTS OF THE MEDITERRANEAN RACE (TOP, RIGHT), AS WELL AS OF THE SHORT-HEADED, BIG-NOSED ARMENOID RACE OF THE MOUNTAINS.

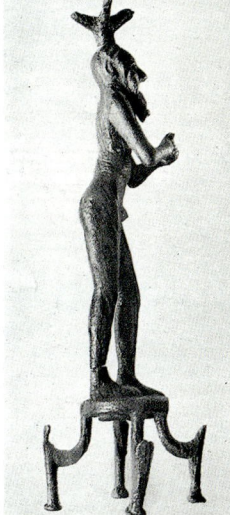 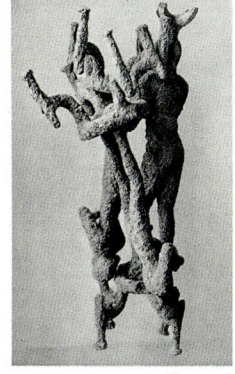 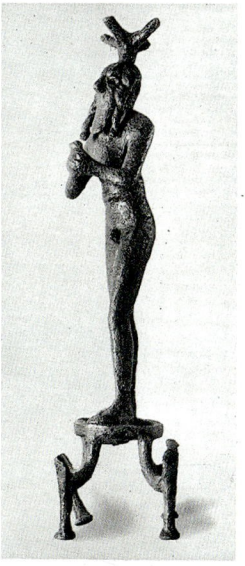

FIG. 8. THE BEARDED PRIEST AND TWO OTHER STATUETTES BEFORE CLEANING; THE PRIEST (RIGHT) OVER 20 INCHES HIGH WITH THE STAND.

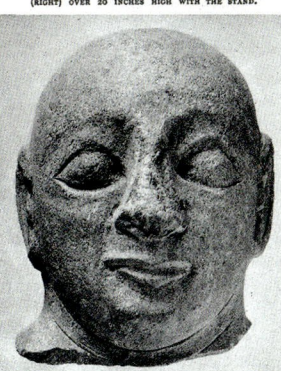

FIG. 7. A UNIQUE DISCOVERY, SINCE SUMERIAN PRIESTS, AS FAR AS IS KNOWN, ALWAYS SHAVED FACE, HEAD, AND BODY: A COPPER STATUE OF A BEARDED PRIEST WITH LONG SIDE LOCKS.

FIG. 9. THE BEARDED PRIEST, NAKED AS PRE-SCRIBED FOR APPROACHING THE GOD: EVIDENTLY A PIECE OF TEMPLE FURNITURE, CARRYING ON THE HEAD A SUPPORT FOR A BOWL OF INCENSE.

FIG. 10. SHOWING QUALITIES OF STYLE TYPICAL OF THE SUC-CEEDING AKKADIAN PERIOD: AN EXCEPTIONALLY FINE HEAD OF DARK STONE FOUND BY MR. DELOUGAZ AT KHAFAJE.

AS Dr. Frankfort explains in his article on page 526, the rooms surrounding the temple court at Khafaje each held a different class of objects—a circumstance which gave rise to the theory that they constituted the communal store-rooms. We can illustrate here only a small selection of the rich remains of statuary found in the rooms; but those illustrated are all of very special interest. From notes on the particular objects shown on this page, or from relevant extracts from Dr. Frankfort's article, we subjoin the following details not embodied in the titles to the illustrations: (Figs. 5 and 6) The nose of one of the figures was anciently broken and repaired by a piece dovetailed into the head, and then broken again—not inexplicable, if one [Continued opposite.]

considers the size of the Sumerian noses.——(Figs. 7 and 9) This unique copper statue represents a priest in the attitude of adoration. It is cast in a closed mould (à cire perdue), while the stand is forged out of plates of copper. The statue as shown was cleaned in the laboratory of the Iraq Museum, Baghdad.——(Fig. 8) These three statues were discovered by Dr. Preusser, evidently hidden in a hurry when the temple was in danger of being captured; they were bundled together and buried underground.——(Fig. 10) This differs from the usual Sumerian statues, above all in its style. The soft and very sensitive modelling deliberately aims at a rendering of the flesh and bone as such (notice the muscles round the eyes and mouth).

2–10. "Khafaje Statuary—With a Revelatory 'Bearded Priest.' *London Illustrated News*, October 8, 1932. MMA: ANE.ILN.10. Courtesy of the Department of Ancient Near Eastern Art, The Metropolitan Museum of Art. Checklist no. 26.

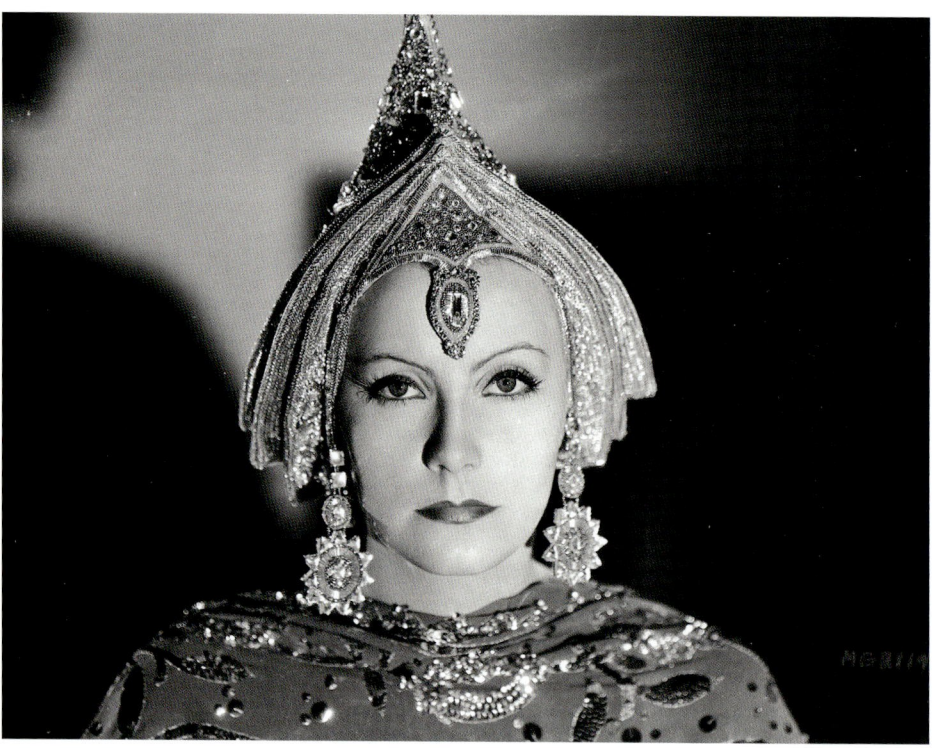

2–11. Greta Garbo in the George Fitzmaurice film *Mata Hari*. Photograph. November 19, 1931. Photographer: Clarence Sinclair Bull. Getty Images: 3170767.

was a close association between Abraham and Queen Puabi in the public perception. Whether Woolley himself believed there was any relationship between a historical figure such as Puabi and Abraham is still debated.[27] But Abraham needed to play a role if Ur and the Royal Tombs were to draw the attention of readers, donors, and even scholars, as some of the latter, including the Ur mission's epigraphist, known as the Reverend Dr. Léon Legrain, and the Rev. E. R. Burrows, were priests or monks (even if they were more "secular" than Woolley, as Richard Zettler has commented).[28] Most of the articles published in the U.S. throughout the 1920s and 1930s situated Ur as "the Home Town of Abraham"[29] rather than as a Sumerian or Mesopotamian city with no true connection to the Bible.

The relationship established by the press between Puabi and Abraham was complicated but providentially conjured a dangerous yet attractive world, one portrayed in cinematic Hollywood terms: "...maybe Abraham and Sarah, his wife, watched her [Queen Puabi's] funeral procession through the streets of Ur; maybe they were even among those invited to her burial, for Abraham was a prominent citizen.... And from her tomb has come a new and rather terrible light upon the customs of the time, and one explanation, perhaps, of why the patriarch was glad enough to put as much distance

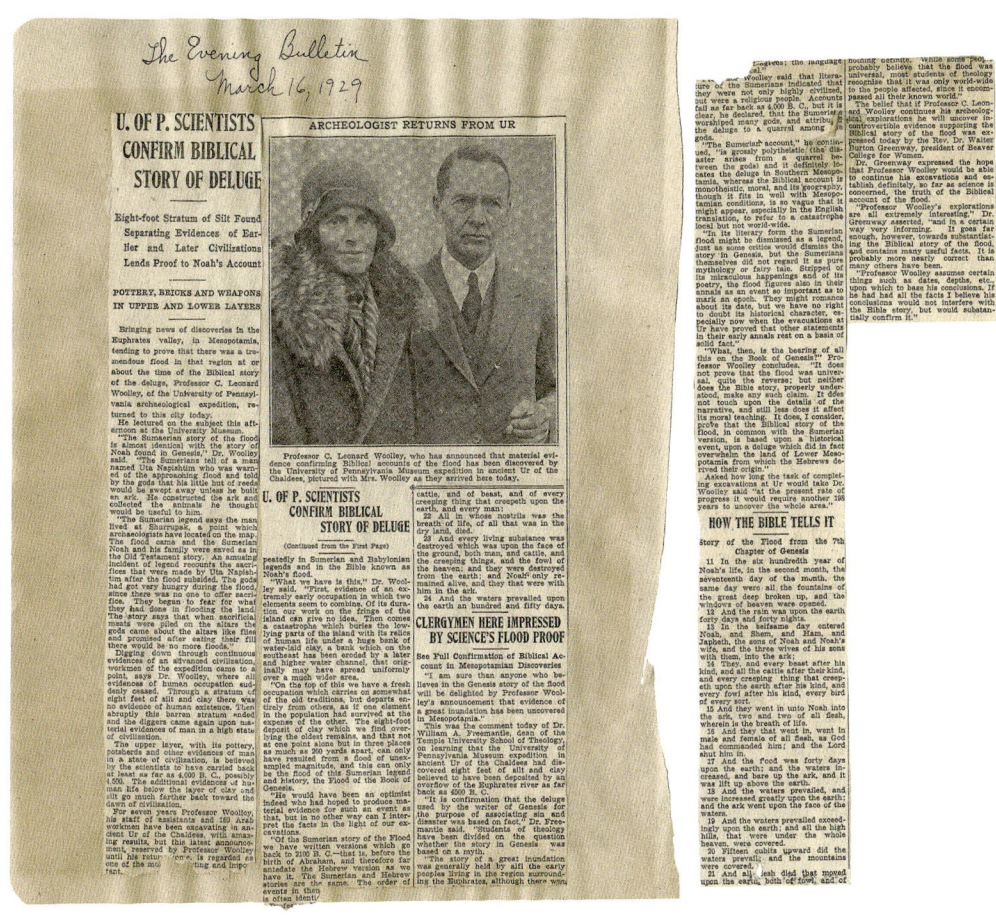

2–12. "U. of P. Scientists Confirm Biblical Story of Deluge." *Philadelphia Evening Bulletin*, March 16, 1929. Courtesy of the University of Pennsylvania Museum of Archaeology and Anthropology.

as possible between himself and his birthplace."[30] Another journalist described Ur in a lively way that was certainly designed to provide a compelling narrative rather than to convey dry scholarly information: "Ur was a laughter-loving city from which Abraham went with Sarah, his wife, and an almost incredibly cruel one. Its combined church, dance hall, theatre hall, theatre, night club and town hall was an immense ziggurat or terraced structure, which was the Temple of the Moon God Nannar and his wife the Moon Goddess. There were balls and fetes and ceremonies there in which everybody, high and low, joined."[31] If we are to believe this description, "Ur of Chaldees" had nothing to envy in Babylon, as perversely envisioned by D. W. Griffith in his 1916 film *Intolerance.* The environment composed by journalists was "a civilization remarkably complete, full of luxury and splendid pageantry and yet incredible cruel. Day after day, night after night, they sang and feasted and drank and offered human sacrifices to their strange gods."[32]

The comparison with ancient Egypt, the association with Biblical figures, and the evocation of a luxurious yet cruel civilization helped to draw an intriguing image of Mesopotamian society and to focus public interest on Sumerian archaeological sites and finds, including Ur, Kish (figs. 2-8, 2-9), and settlements and cities in the Diyala Valley (fig. 2-10). Additional promotion of the most important discoveries from U.S. and British archaeological missions in Iraq was made thanks to the press but also to another powerful weapon: exhibitions at museums on both sides of the Atlantic. Among the small early exhibitions of recent finds in Ur, a largely undocumented show was organized at the British Museum in 1927;[33] and on May 25, 1929, the museum of the University of Pennsylvania opened a display of the "Ur Treasure," including Queen Puabi's funerary items, which had been given to the museum when the finds were divided in Baghdad.[34]

The large London exhibition that took place in 1928[35] included the golden and glittering accoutrement shown on a reconstruction of Queen Puabi,[36] and was a tremendous success,[37] attended by the Prince of Wales and the King of Spain, Alfonso XIII. The polychrome mannequin molded by Charles Woolley's wife, Katharine Woolley, and based on a cast of a slightly later skull from Tell al-Ubaid, provided by Sir Arthur Keith, reflected the features of an Iraqi woman and images of contemporary Hollywood actresses— perhaps Greta Garbo dressed for her role as Mata Hari (fig. 2–11), as Jean Evans has brilliantly pointed out.[38] Since the queen's jewelry and other heavy, shimmering pieces were found in the tomb intact but twisted and flattened on her broken skull, the elements were first assembled on site by Katharine Woolley (fig. 2–12).[39]

A small exhibit of the Ur finds in Philadelphia took place in 1934 at an unexpected venue, one chosen to attract a wide audience—the ninth floor of the now-defunct Strawbridge & Clothier[40] department store—as it was necessary to market an image of Mesopotamia that was as appealing as that of the Egyptian funerary treasures. The show was open only a week, February 21–28, 1934;[41] we do not know if the short duration was due to commercial reasons or because there were still some doubts about the potential of a Mesopotamian exhibition, even one with Queen Puabi's glamorous accessories, to draw crowds. Newspapers reviewed the exhibition positively if briefly,[42] although accompanying images focused not on the jewelry but on the reconstructed wooden harp (from a mold that Woolley cleverly made on the spot) with the original golden bull head.[43]

2–13. Theater program for the Philadelphia production of *The Romance of a People*, 1934. Courtesy of Pedro Azara.

2–14. Interior of the Iraq Expedition House, Tell Asmar: fragments of Sumerian votive statues in the workrooms. Photograph, January 29, 1934. OIM: As. 1098 (P. 24084). Courtesy of the Oriental Institute of the University of Chicago. Checklist no. 5.

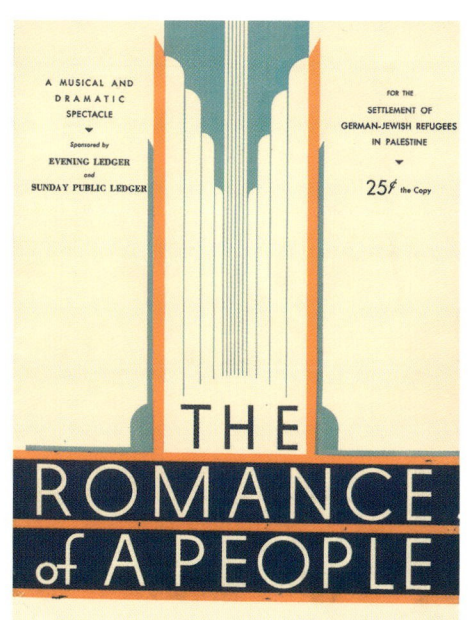

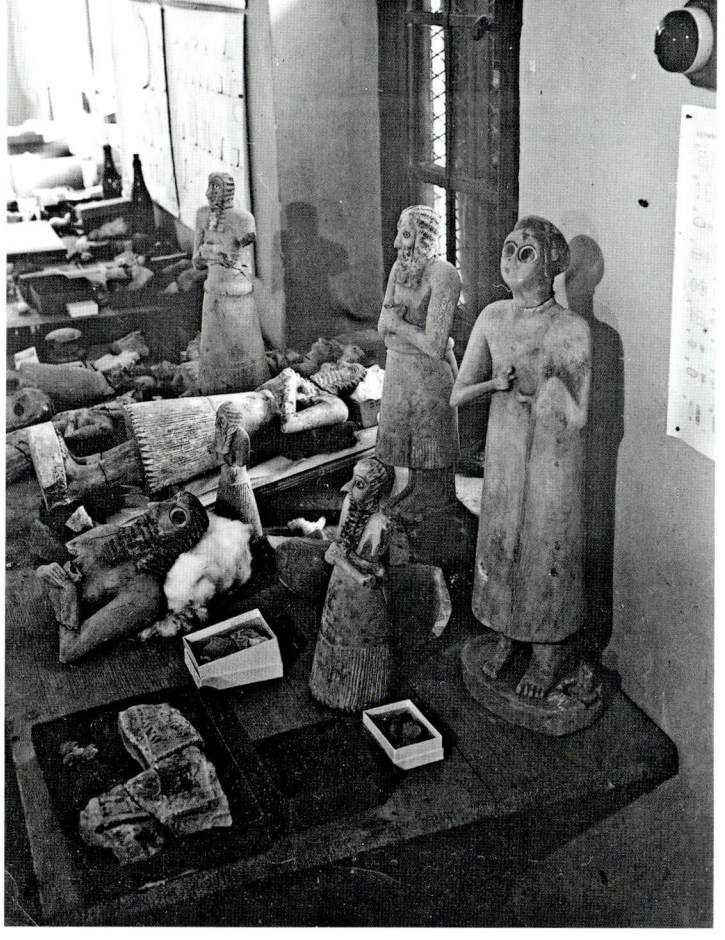

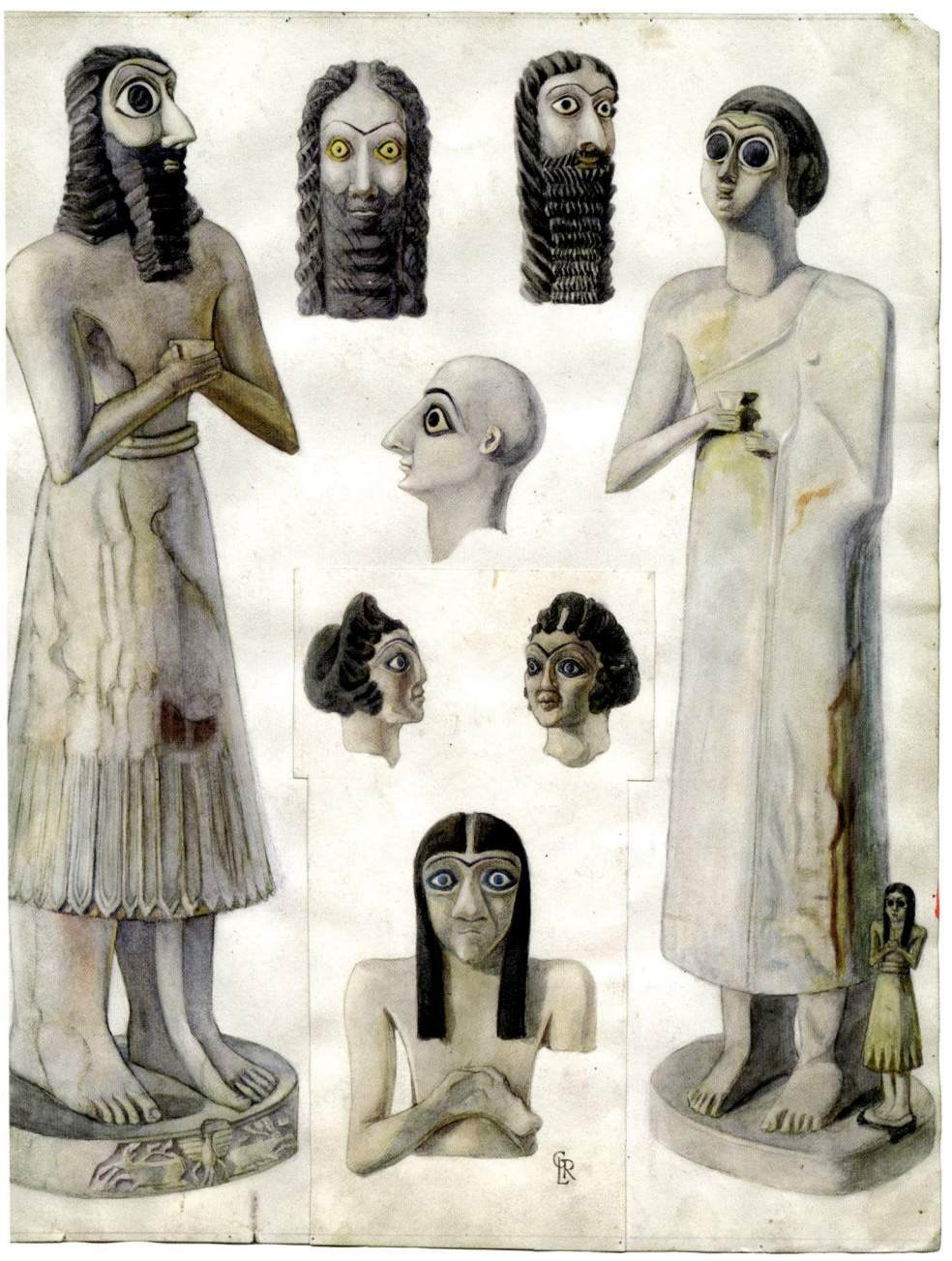

2–15. Reconstruction of votive figurines from Tell Asmar. Watercolor on paper by Rachel Levy. ca. 1934–36. OIM: D. 017485. Courtesy of the Oriental Institute of the University of Chicago. Checklist no. 16.

2–16. "Sumerian Sculpture about 3500 BC: By Dr. Henry [*sic*] Frankfort." *Illustrated London News*, June 9, 1934. Photograph. Courtesy of Mary Evans Picture Library.

2–17. *L'art de la Mésopotamie: De la fin du quatrième millénaire au XVe siècle avant notre ère*, by Christian Zervos. Paris: 1935. Courtesy of Pedro Azara. Checklist no. 188.

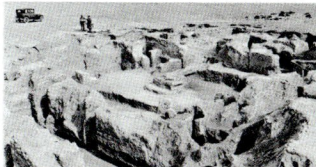

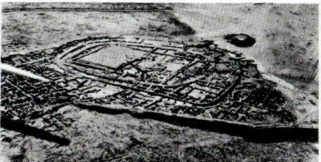

FIG. 1. A TEMPLE DATED BETWEEN 3000 AND 3700 B.C., WHERE THE STATUARY ILLUSTRATED IN THIS NUMBER) WAS FOUND : PART OF THE KHAFAJE SITE EXCAVATED TO THE MAXIMUM DEPTH OF THE FUNNEL-SHAPED HOLES [VISIBLE IN THE ROOMS AROUND THE CENTRAL COURT] PREVIOUSLY DUG BY NATIVE ROBBERS.

FIG. 2. AN AIR PHOTOGRAPH OF THE SITE AT KHAFAJE: A VIEW SHOWING THE TEMPLE CITADEL IN THE MIDDLE, ENCLOSED BY A DOUBLE WALL, WITH THE TEMPLE PLATFORM AT THE LEFT-HAND END.

SUMERIAN SCULPTURE ABOUT 3000 B.C.

ANOTHER GREAT DISCOVERY, AT KHAFAJE, RIVALLING THAT AT TELL ASMAR, WITH POINTS OF DIFFERENCE: A WEALTH OF ANCIENT STATUES, MARKED BY GREATER REALISM AND A PREPONDERANCE OF FEMALE FIGURES, RECOVERED FROM A PLUNDERED SITE.

By DR. HENRY FRANKFORT, Director of the Iraq Expedition of the Oriental Institute of the University of Chicago. (See Illustrations on Pages 911, 912, and 913.)

THIS year's work at Khafaje (the second site which is being excavated by the Iraq Expedition of the Oriental Institute of the University of Chicago, and which lies about twelve miles from Tell Asmar in the direction of Baghdad) is inseparable from that carried out four or five years ago by a host of Arab antiquity robbers ; not that they have approached the site since that time, for now it is closely guarded all the year round by our own armed guards ; but, having completed the excavation of the temple citadel (Fig. 2), we have extended towards part of the town which was honeycombed with holes and had been thoroughly exploited by these native robbers before we obtained the concession to dig. Fig. 2 shows the situation after we had cleared out these holes in order to get an impression of the damage done, and one might well-nigh despair of the possibility of recovering either plans or objects from such a piece of ground.

It is true that the architectural remains are now so fragmentary that they cannot well be reproduced in this journal, but they suffice to allow us to reconstruct with certainty a temple not unlike the earlier stages of the Abu Temple at Tell Asmar. The temple at Khafaje should be dated somewhere between 3000 and 3700 B.C. Mr. P. Delougaz was again in immediate charge of the work.

Fig. 2 shows a general view of the excavations at a moment when work has stopped in order to allow the architects and excavators to consider carefully the complicated evidence obtained by a most meticulous clearing of the mud-brick walls. The central court of the temple, containing a basin with a drain, is sufficiently clear, but the surrounding rooms and chapels show everywhere traces of the funnel-shaped holes where robbers had dug down from the surface in their search for saleable antiquities. In spite of this, the accompanying illustrations show that a wealth of ancient sculpture escaped the plunderers' picks, to reward later our less ruthless methods of approach : but the damage done is well illustrated in the case of Figs. 18 and 20, showing two fragments of the same very fine green steatite vase ; the first was found by us in the process of digging this year, while the second was bought from a London antiquity dealer. This glaring example makes one wonder how many other fragments which would together make

up complete objects have been lost for ever. The vase itself is of unusual importance, since its early character is evident, while different motives which are favourites in later Sumerian and Babylonian art are already making their appearance. Such are the eagle with spread wings—one wing appearing on each fragment—grasping animals in its claws, and the mythical figure with human head and bull's feet struggling with lions on either side. On the other hand, Fig. 19 shows a Protodynastic Egyptian monument of about the same age which bears a very similar style of representation and is made of similar material.

The vase shown at the left-hand bottom corner of the Colour Plate (p. 919) is made of the same material, but the effect is enriched by inlays of red and yellow stone marking the coiled bodies of the snakes depicted thereon. Unfortunately, this vase is too fragmentary to show the whole design. The remaining figures of the coloured plate show various amulets in the shape of animals which are exceptionally finely modelled ; some of them, notably the dark grey ram in the right-hand bottom corner, recalling the most modern sculpture in its simplification of the animal forms. Yet another sculptured vase is shown

in Fig. 23, made of the same green material ; its decoration represents the primaeval architecture of Mesopotamia, whereby houses were built with matting and bundles of reeds ; it is interesting to note that the designs reflecting this architecture were maintained in the rendering of sacred buildings even after bricks had come into common use. The importance of this particular piece is that the triangular *motif* occurs in exactly the same form on a fragment of a green stone vase found by Mr. Ernest Mackay at Mohenjo Daro, in the Indus Valley.

Two more vases are of special importance : the type of ewer of beaten copper (Fig. 8) is known to us from reliefs as having been used when libations were poured out before the gods by priests and worshippers. Figs. 5, 6, and 7 show a unique object of unusual interest. It is a little wagon made of baked clay, which could be drawn in front of the god while incense was burnt or offerings presented in the bowl at the top. It is a complicated affair, constructed, on one side, of two pots of a well-known type ; the projections appearing on the shoulder of each being a conventional relic of what in bygone days had been a spout, carefully modelled to represent the Mother Goddess. This type of pot, the earlier with the real figurine handle and the later showing no more than a debased projection, is commonly found ; but never before as part of a cult object of such an interesting construction. The other side of the lower part of the wagon represents a house with windows, and even the ends of the roofing beams projecting, on each of which a bird is perched, perhaps a symbol of the goddess ; a curious piece of realism is provided by a ladder modelled against the wall. The meaning of the small figures riding bulls is as yet obscure.

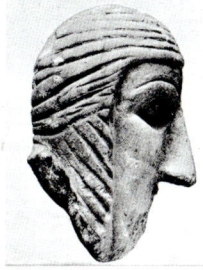

FIG. 4. THE HEAD OF THE STATUE (SHOWN IN FIG. 3) SEEN IN PROFILE : A TYPE "RESEMBLING MORE THAN ANYTHING ELSE EARLY MEDIAEVAL-ROMANESQUE OR EARLY GOTHIC WORK."

Turning to the statuary, we find in the relief of Fig. 2 a representation, perhaps, of the New Year's Festival, which we mentioned in our former article (*Illustrated London News*, May 19, 1934, pp. 761, 776, and 802). The actual feast is shown in progress in the uppermost register of the plaque, while below we see two men moving a large jar of wine suspended from a pole, while one of them carries in his hand a straw ring on which the pointed jar can be safely set down. He is followed by one servant carrying a kid, another with a flat pile of loaves on his head, and finally one with a bowl of onions or some such vegetable. In the lowest register a man is dancing to the tune of a harp. The square hole in the middle was left for a peg to pass through and fasten the plaque to the wall of the temple, no doubt in commemoration of some contribution made to the New Year Festival by a rich inhabitant of the ancient city.

The sculpture in the round is distinguished from that found at Tell Asmar by the great predominance of statues of women. The remarkable flatness of some of these figures (Figs. 9 and 10), and the extraordinary proportions of some stand in contrast with the charm of others (Figs. 16 and 17). The variety in the manner of dressing the hair is also remarkable, the principle being the same in all cases. The hair was first plaited either in one or two plaits, but it was the subsequent arrangement which was dictated either by fashion or individual taste. It is clear that the Sumerian women must have had, on the whole, very long and heavy hair. In some cases (Fig. 15) we see how a long pin was stuck in to secure the coiffure. We have often found the real pins ; they are made of bronze or silver, with a large knob of blue frit or lapis lazuli.

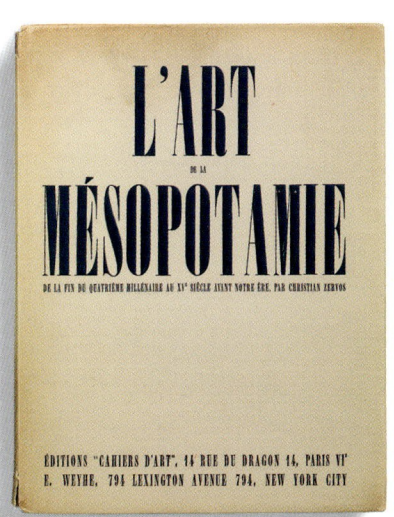

FIG. 3. A LARGE EARLY DYNASTIC STATUE (WITH MISSING PARTS OF THE BEARD AND LOCKS, AND A PORTION OF THE WAIST, RESTORED) : AN EXAMPLE OF STATUARY FOUND IN THE TEMPLE (FIG. 1).

This air view shows part of the extent of the ancient town in contrast with the flat desert and fields around it. The line of separation runs diagonally across the picture from the right-hand bottom corner to the top left-hand corner. Altars and places of libation are seen in the temple courtyard. To the left are the adjoining private houses which have been excavated, bordering on the area which was ransacked by natives before the expedition started work four years ago.

Fig. 13 gives two views of what, but for damage to nose and mouth, would have been one of the finest examples of Sumerian sculpture. The modelling of chin and cheek is most sensitive, and the back view, showing the way in which the heavy plait has been twisted round the head and then tucked in, has been very skilfully contrived by the sculptor. The statues of men include one of the largest Early Dynastic statues so far found (Fig. 3), the head of which (Fig. 4) resembles more than anything else early mediaeval-Romanesque or early Gothic work. The missing part of the beard and locks seen in the front view, and part of the waist, have been restored. The statue stands over 75 cm. high. Fig. 21 shows a most unusual arrangement of the fleece garment which is typical for the Sumerians ; the statue is also remarkable by reason of a mythological scene carved on the back of a piece of stone supporting the legs and connecting the kilt with the base. The break shows how the statues were made in separate parts, and put together by means of wooden or stone pegs fastened with bitumen.

Fig. 12 shows an altogether unusual type, both upper and lower lip completely shaven, leaving a fringe-like beard reminiscent of Farmer Giles. Fig. 14 is a particularly fine example of the realism which seems to predominate in Khafaje in contrast to Tell Asmar ; the collar-bones, neck, and chest muscles are finely indicated ; unfortunately, the upper part of the nose is badly damaged. This same realism is also strongly pronounced in the statue shown in Fig. 11. This is of exceptional importance, as it is one of the few bearing an inscription. In this case the ancient linear script is visible on the right shoulder.

It avers that the statue was dedicated by the High Priest of the Moon-God in Opis to the Moon-God. By this inscription the site of Khafaje is identified as the ancient royal city of Opis, which we know for a time dominated the valley of the Two Rivers. The unusual extent of the Early Dynastic remains at Khafaje is thereby explained, and there is no doubt that important material bearing on the history and culture of the early Sumerians will be found by this expedition in future campaigns.

L'ART
de la
MÉSOPOTAMIE

DE LA FIN DU QUATRIÈME MILLÉNAIRE AU XVe SIÈCLE AVANT NOTRE ÈRE, PAR CHRISTIAN ZERVOS

ÉDITIONS "CAHIERS D'ART," 14 RUE DU DRAGON 14, PARIS VIe
E. WEYHE, 794 LEXINGTON AVENUE 794, NEW YORK CITY

Simultaneous with the Philadelphia exhibition was an event that took place at the Philadelphia Convention Hall. Originally produced for the 1933 Chicago World's Fair, the musical pageant entitled *The Romance of a People* (fig. 2–13) was performed for the first time at Chicago's Soldier Field and dramatically recreated the history of the Jews. The opening on July 3, 1933—symbolically important as the fair's "Jewish Day"—was attended by 125,000 spectators. The program's front page declared that the event was staged "For the Settlement of German-Jewish Refugees in Palestine," and further text noted that *The Romance of a People* was intended to protest Hitler's politics in Germany. When the show was transferred to Philadelphia, the *Philadelphia Inquirer* claimed an explicit relationship between the exhibition of the Ur Treasure and the spectacle of *The Romance of a People*: "The Exhibit is particularly timely just now because 'Ur of the Chaldees' was a city from which Abraham went forth to go into the land of Canaan. Abraham is one of the leading characters in the great pageant 'The Romance of a People,' now being presented in Convention Hall."[45] The newspaper made particular note of "the historical link between the exotic ornaments and the present Jewish pageant now under way."[45] The objects in the Ur exhibition, at least as presented in Philadelphia, were thus transformed into a political "statement."[46]

It was not only material from Ur that was shown in exhibitions dedicated to Mesopotamia. Archaeological missions to different sites located in the Diyala Valley had been undertaken by the Oriental Institute of Chicago. The major finds were stone statues of various sizes, depicting standing male and female figures (fig. 2–14). In Chicago the five finest and best-preserved Diyala statues in the collections of the Oriental Institute Museum were shown at the 1933 World's Fair in a large showcase on the first floor of the Social Science Hall, located on Northerly Island. The works were accompanied by graphic documentation, including small framed photographs on one panel and a large framed watercolor of the statues' reconstruction (fig. 2–15). Whatever the original purpose of these worshiper statues, it is impossible for a contemporary viewer to comprehend the works as they were understood in the third millennium BCE.[47] The hall also held an exhibition on the history of America, giving importance to Maya culture, and—on the first floor—were displayed Egyptian and Mesopotamian items from the Oriental Institute Museum.[48] Yet again, Mesopotamia was competing with Egypt, even if the Diyala statues of worshipers were described as "primitive subjects."[49]

While these recently excavated Mesopotamian artifacts were not promoted as art, the presentation was not exclusively ethnographic. Objects were displayed in glass cases of the type that generally house museum collections of precious three-dimensional objects (in some instances an individual piece was highlighted alone within a case). These exhibitions took place in unexpected locations, including a retail emporium and fair pavilions, mostly to attract as many visitors as possible, particularly those who were not regular museum visitors.

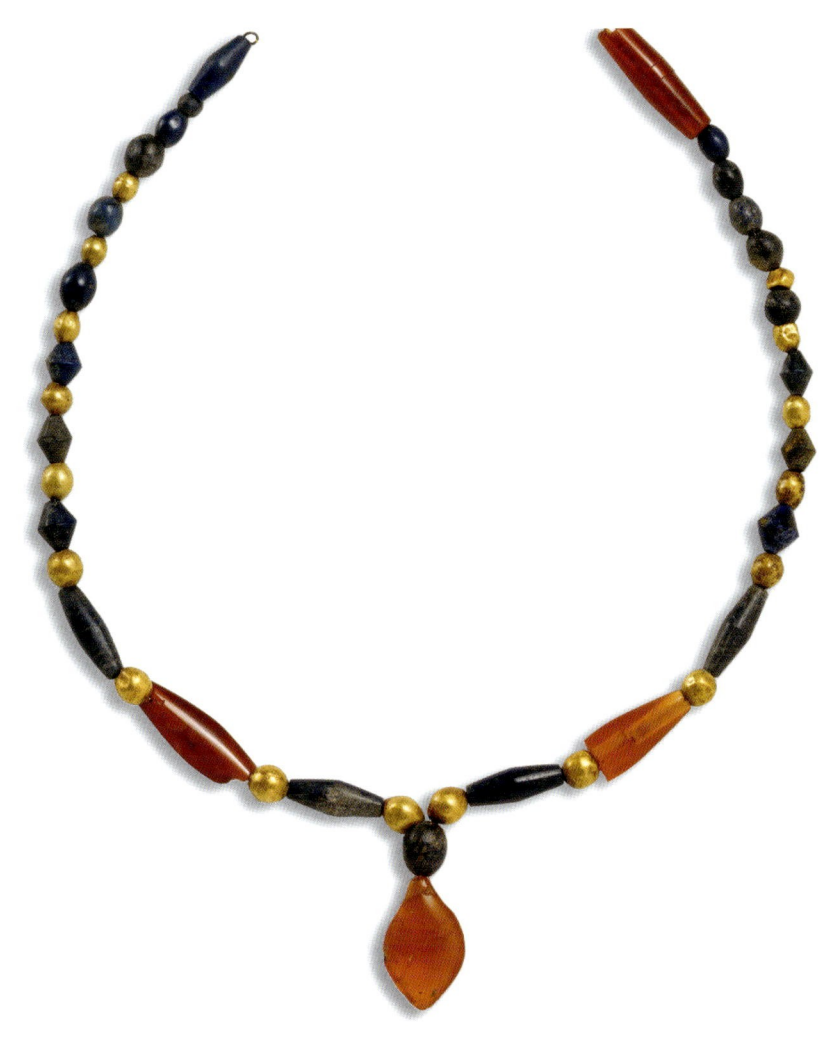

2–18. String of Beads or Necklace, modern interpretation. Gold, lapis lazuli, carnelian. Ur, Tomb PG 807, ca. 2500–2300 BCE. Penn Museum: B17642. Joint Expedition of the British Museum and of the Museum of the University of Pennsylvania to Mesopotamia, 6th season, 1927–28. Checklist no. 127.

Evans has shown how the perception of Mesopotamian sculpture—the term "sculpture" itself originates in the world of art, a place where Mesopotamian idols did not belong—gradually shifted from the ethnographic to the aesthetic in the 1930s, when major discoveries took place at archaeological missions under British colonial control in Kish, Ur, and the Diyala Valley. The art historian Henri Frankfort studied the Diyala statues of worshipers as aesthetic works (fig. 2–16), and placed them at the origin of Western art history in his 1939 publication. Christian Zervos, a well-known defender of modern art, had four years earlier published a monograph based on the Mesopotamian collections

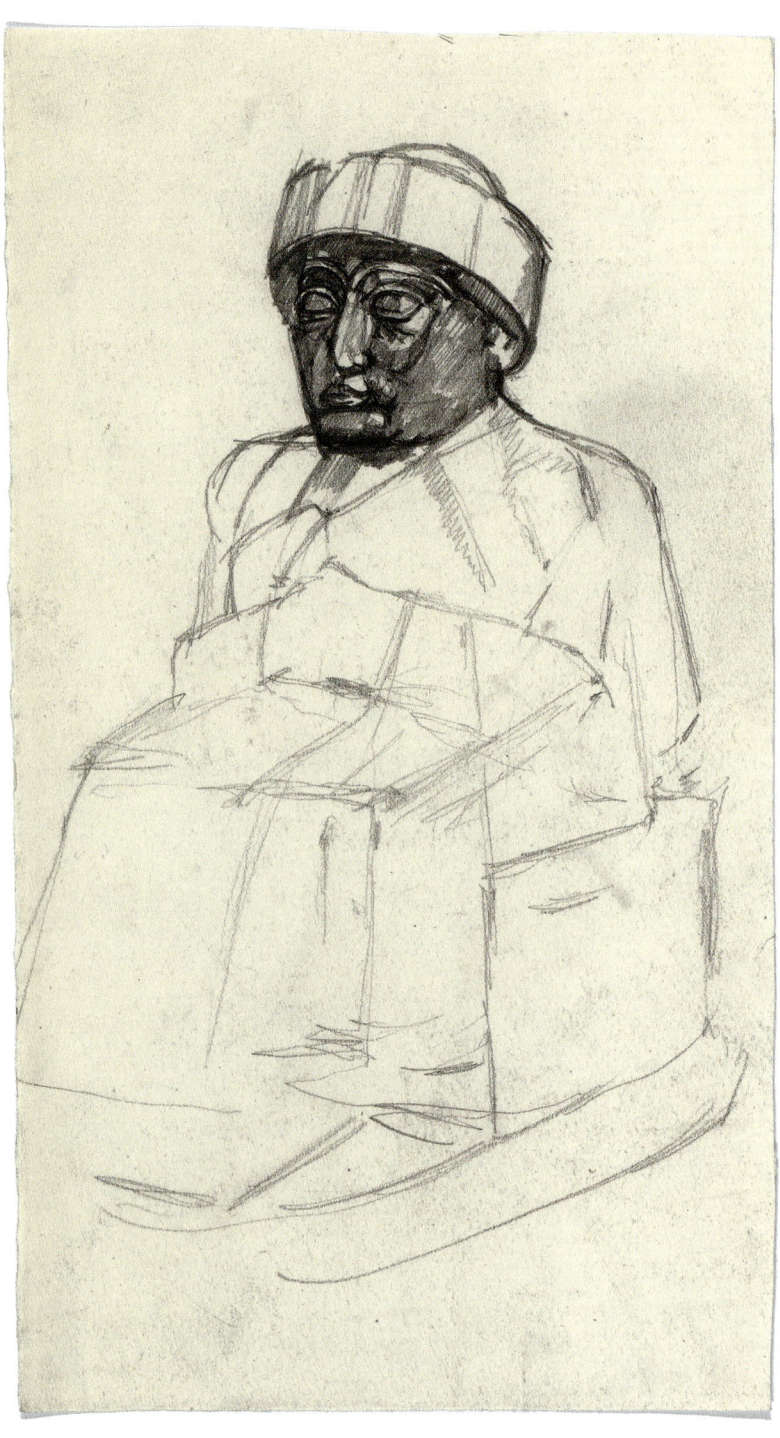

2–19. Alberto Giacometti. *Seated Gudea: After a Sumerian Sculpture*. Pencil on paper. GF: 1994-1808. Courtesy of the Alberto Giacometti Estate. Checklist no. 144.

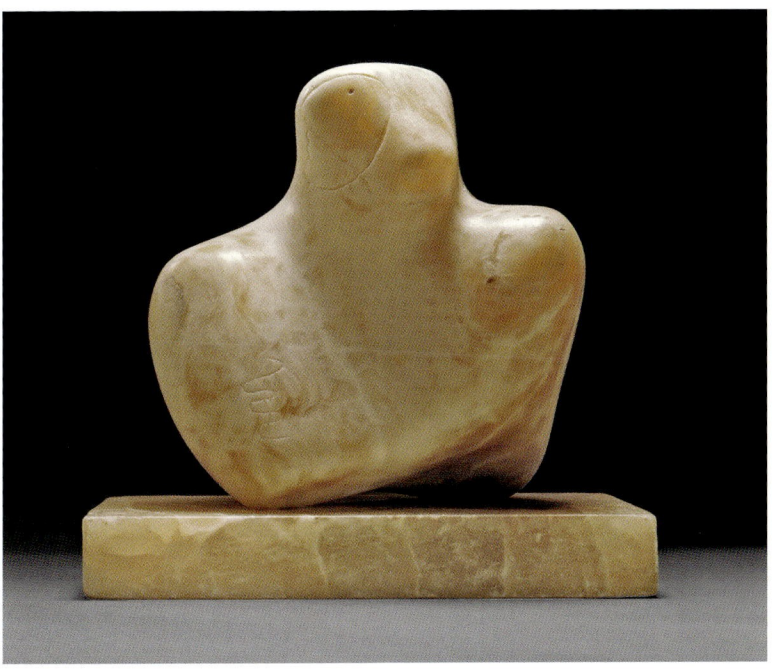

2–20. Barbara Hepworth. *Sculpture with Profiles*. Alabaster, H. 23 cm; W. 23.9 cm; D. 15 cm. 1932. Tate: T06520. Bequeathed by Mrs. Helen Margaret Murray in memory of her husband Frederick Lewis Staite Murray, 1992.

of the Louvre and the British Museum (fig. 2–17).[50] Woolley's own written commentaries on finds excavated at Ur employ vocabulary that belongs to the history and theory of art: the objects were considered "applied arts" in some cases and "sculptures" in others.[51] The transformation of Sumerian finds into works of art thus began just after their discovery. This displacement from the category of magical or sacred handicrafts to the aesthetic realm implied that Sumerian items should be evaluated—and in its finest examples not to their disadvantage—vis-à-vis Greek art. Woolley judged Sumerian statues following mimetic criteria; while he considered that some were not in "the first class," he appreciated others for "the tender modelling of the flesh thrown into relief by the dignified convention of the hair."[52]

Initially viewed as nothing more than artifacts whose aesthetic values, if any, were not the main reason for their existence,[53] these images were slowly seen as embodying ideas in material, sensuous forms, similar to modern sculpture. This shift was inevitable. More than a hundred years earlier, Hegel had defined art as the process by which an idea is made sensible, thus opening the path to the world of art for Mesopotamian artifacts. On the one hand, these were the embodiment of ideas, but on the other, this embodiment was only symbolic: massive, closed, geometric shapes were not sufficient to translate the power of an idea into the material world. Consequently, in Hegel's view Mesopotamian and Egyptian works were on the threshold of art but suffered when compared with Classical examples. Significantly, however, the earliest art had appeared as the result of this "primitive" translation of an idea, as a way to connect with the invisible, even if in an approximate and dubious way. No longer related to the history of the Near East, Mesopotamian handicrafts were thus judged as forerunners to Greek creations, the acme of Western art. Consequently, the colonial and mandated control of the Near East by Western countries (especially Great Britain and France) had deep symbolic justification. The roots of Western civilization, expressed by the creativity of "artists," were located in this part of the world.

The ontological transformation of Mesopotamian handicrafts and fetishes (the words we use here are inevitably conditioned by the vocabulary of the theory of art) into works of art is also evident in the way that the "Ur Treasure" was judged. The jewelry was described as similar to modern examples, and thus pleasing to modern taste: "The necklaces...are so lovely and *artistic* that Milady of 1934 would be glad to wear them" (fig. 2–18).[54] The status of Queen Puabi's outfit was in the 1930s, and continues to be, dependent on contemporary taste and on the way the viewer reacts in front of it, on how it appeals to him or her. Our feelings, connected or not to reason, are the ways by which this outfit is transported to the realm of art; judged as art, it becomes art. The understanding of Queen Puabi's outfit as a work of art is therefore a modern creation. By looking at it from a certain distance, the distance required to appreciate the outfit with a disinterested interest, Queen Puabi's outfit ceases to belong to the sacred world—and enters another world, one that has no "real" power on us but allows us, in a way, to relate to it. In fact, we could say that if works of art still have the power to impress us it is because we adopt an attitude that allows them to be powerful, to exert a power that has been conceded or allowed by us, thus making a work of art a projection of ourselves.

The transubstantiation[55] of spiritual, magical, or practical objects was initiated when modern Western artists began to look at them as works of art. It has often been argued that a work of art exists only when it is interpreted by its artist, in the broader sense of the term, as well as by an active spectator. As Evans and others have pointed out, several modern artists sculpted or drew variations on "primitive" subjects, including Henry Moore (see fig. 1–4), after visiting an exhibition of Sumerian sculptures at the British Museum in the early 1930s. Alberto Giacometti (fig. 2–19) discovered the neo-Sumerian statues of King Gudea when on a visit to the Louvre, and Barbara Hepworth was also fascinated by Mesopotamian statues and busts of worshipers with clasped hands when she saw them in London before World War II (fig. 2–20).[56]

Over a period of just a few decades, their discovery, restoration, promotion, reception, and exhibition produced in the modern viewer a nearly imperceptible change: what had been merely artifacts were now perceived as sculptures, entering the world of art and provoking a sensory and an aesthetic experience in the viewer. The transformation occurred because the viewer's approach to them was altered by the context of their presentation: the banal discussion by the press, as well as thoughtful academic articles on ancient artifacts, presented the Sumerian objects as a prelude to modern art, contributing to shape the modern understanding of their functions. Archaeological finds thus entered the exhibition realm because they became works of art in the eyes of the modern audience. Displayed among other works of art, archaeological material gained a new role, that of inspiring artists. A recent example, included in the exhibition, is represented by Michael Rakowitz's papier-mâché sculptures, which reproduce, in cheap, gaudy, discarded material, Sumerian sculptures from Baghdad's National Museum of Iraq (see fig. 1–23). The ancient sculptures were destroyed or robbed during the 2003 coalition invasion and the dismantlement of Iraqi administrative structures, providing poignant testimony to the power of ancient images and the loss we suffer from their destruction. Our vision shrank, and so did our world.

Early twentieth-century archaeological missions to the Near East began in conjunction with the control of colonial territories and quickly produced material for museum collections that displayed the roots of Western culture and civilization. The notion of art itself is modern; ancient objects, such as those from Mesopotamia, were and could not be art for those who originally lived with them. They were not created to be perceived from a certain distance, to help people in antiquity think about their world, or to provoke the sensory yet distant relationship required for an aesthetic experience. Nevertheless, today we view these items as works of art, and today they belong to the world of art. A double transformation has taken place, first in how we relate to archaeological material, and second in the frequent display of archaeological material as art. This transformation occurred—and continues to hold—because archaeological objects are so often exhibited as art, prompting museum visitors to look at and respond to them as such. This transformation has changed our way of looking at the world, and has perhaps made us better citizens—able to spend time just enjoying the objects, thinking about their meaning, and listening to the voices from the past that are embodied in these forms. But this transformation has a history. This is the history, or the story, we tell in our exhibition.

Endnotes

With many thanks to Richard Zettler for his revision of the essay and valuable comments, and to Jennifer Y. Chi and Roberta Casagrande-Kim for the content editing.

1   Doreen Gildroy, "From the Ancient World," *The American Poetry Review* 43, no. 3 (May/June 2014): 25.

2   See Bahrani 2011b: 125–55; Bahrani 2011a: 104–7. See also Córdoba, Escribano, and Mané 2006/7.

3   Hall and Woolley 1927: 3. (The original orthography of all non-English terms has been retained, with the exception of the deletion of diacritical marks.)

4   For instance, the topographer for the North American and British archaeological mission at Kish was a military man, Colonel W. H. Lane. Mackay 1929: 75.

5   Hall 1923: 180.

6   Hall and Woolley 1927: preface. The Crimean War had allowed the British Museum to obtain the first antiquities from Shahrein (Eridu) in 1855. Hall 1922: 244.

7   Hall 1924: 104.

8   F. G. Kenyon to G. B. Gordon, Mar. 4, 1921, repr. in Dyson 1977: 7.

9   "I doubt whether they [the Iraqis] have yet anyone capable of administering a Museum or caring for antiquities." Kenyon to G. B. Gordon, Apr. 21, 1926, Ur Archives, British Museum Archives (hereafter, BMA), London, CE32/27/72. Unless otherwise noted all material cited from the collection of the BMA is in the Ur Archives.

10   Langdon to Leeds, Jan. 1929, Kish Archives, Ashmolean Museum Archives, Oxford.

11   Ur, Iraq Expedition Records, Correspondence, Exp. V, Jan.–July, 1927, UPennMuseum Archives (hereafter UPMA), Philadelphia.

12   The civil administration of Mesopotamia was under the control of the British secretary of state for India. Thanks to Lawrence's efforts, it was transferred from the India Office to the Colonial Office in 1921. Kenyon to G. B. Gordon, Apr. 21, 1920, Ur, Iraq Expedition Records, Correspondence, Exp. V, Jan.–July 1927, UPMA.

13   The "Kish tablets case" began in 1923 when Professor Saty Mohammed Hilal Al Hosari, General Director of Antiquities in Iraq, sent a first letter to Langdon concerning a large collection of tablets that had not been divided between Baghdad and Oxford. Langdon replied that a division had been established only between items under consideration at that time, which did not include the Kish tablets. The case was only closed in 1984 when a small collection of complete tablets was returned to Baghdad, after the Iran-Iraq war, and after the Ashmolean Museum avoided inclusion in a blacklist of institutions holding what were considered Iraqi proprieties in 1980. All letters related to this case are at the Ashmolean Museum Archives (see Pedro Azara, "La arqueóloga y la moral de la tropa," in Azara 2012: 315–16).

14   It is significant that Woolley used the adjective "royal" to qualify tombs that were yet to be discovered! "We are going soon to get a royal tomb which ought to be the pride of the dig; I have suspected its presence since last season...and though of course it is impossible to say that the contents will be anything remarkable, there can be no doubt that we are getting something of real interest." Woolley to Kenyon, Nov. 1, 1927, BMA, CE32/27/129.

15   On Jan. 5, 1928, Kenyon sent a letter regarding publicity for the finds; and on Jan. 17, 1928, a letter to a Mrs. McHugh, regarding publication of the information in various newspapers. Ur, Iraq Expedition Records, Correspondence, Exp. V, Jan.–June 1928, UPMA.

16   Ibid. The press release was not distributed until Feb. 14, 1928.

17   "The discovery of the Royal Tombs has been broadcast: it does certainly merit publicity." Wooley to R. H. Hill, Jan. 1, 1931, BMA, WY1/13/14/1.

18   Mackay to Langdon, undated letter attached to a clipping from the *Christian Science Monitor*, Aug. 22, 1924. F.M.-Ox. University Expedition to Kish, First and Second Season, 1912–24, box 1, folder 3, Field Museum Archives, Chicago.

19   All the press reports discussed in this text are in the collection of the UPMA. We thank the generous assistance of Alex Pezzati, senior archivist, and Eric Schnittke, assistant archivist, at the UPMA.

20   *Cal Call* [*San Francisco Call*], Aug. 18, 1928.

21   The crushing of Puabi's skull was nevertheless believed to have had some beneficial aspects: "[her] skull was shattered when her husband died so her soul could go with his." *Washington Herald*, Sept. 8, 1929.

22   *Washington Herald*, Nov. 25, 1928; *New York Evening Sun*, Jan. 12, 1928; *Christian* (Pueblo, CO), Aug. 19, 1928.

23   "Treasures Found in Egyptian Queen's Tomb," *Arkansas Gazette* (Little Rock), Oct. 14, 1928.

24   William Ward, in an article clipped from an uncredited publication.

25   The rich deposit of this tomb (especially an intact gold helmet) belongs to the National Museum of Iraq in Baghdad, and it is kept nowadays in the Bank of Iraq due to the instability in the city. Basmachi 1976: 136–37.

26   *New York Evening Post*, Dec. 17, 1927. An almost identical commentary was applied to Puabi in the *California Record* (Stockton), Feb. 14, 1928: "Her tomb antedates that of Egypt's Tut-Ankh-Amen by almost as long a span of time that separates us from the birth of Christ."

27   Woolley (1935: 9) wrote that "at Ur no concrete memorial of Abraham was brought to light," but he also promoted a fund-raising campaign for his archaeological missions that solicited donors "interested in the...beginnings of European civilization, and the antecedents and the illustration of the Old Testament narrative." Ur, Iraq Expedition Records, Correspondence, Exp. V, July–Dec. 1928, UPMA. Did Woolley use the widespread beliefs in biblical sources for financial reasons? In a letter from Woolley to Kenyon dated Dec. 5, 1928, it was noted that the discovery of a tablet with the name of Abraham was to be kept secret: "in the normal course of events we shall get all the tablets [*sic*], but if there were a fuss in the papers, Baghdad would of course keep this one, and we need not invite that risk." BMA, WY I/13/71/1.

28   Personal communication to the authors.

29   *Jewish Tribune,* Dec. 2, 1927.

30   "The Cruel Royal Funeral of Abraham's City of Ur," *Light* (San Antonio, TX), Mar. 4, 1928.

31 "Treasures of Ancient Ur: Remarkable precious objects from the royal graves of the Biblical 'City of Chaldees,' oldest on earth, and the birthplace of the patriarch Abraham," *Chicago Herald Examiner*, July 8, 1928.

32 "Strange New Discoveries in the Tombs of Ancient Ur: Revelation of life 5500 years ago in the Biblical city of Chaldees where beards were put upon the sacred bulls to show their divinity, all the nobles shaved their heads and wholesale human sacrifices were made at the funerals of their kings and queens." Uncredited newspaper article.

33 In June 1927 there was an "exhibition of antiquities excavated at Ur during the season 1927–8...[that] continued open till the end of October, in the Assyrian Basement. This was by far the finest exhibition from the remarkably successful excavations at Ur that has hitherto been shown. Mr. Woolley's discoveries during the past season have been even more sensational than those of 1926–7, and the comparison made last year with finds in the Tutankhamen tomb and the shaft-graves at Mycenae is even more apposite this year." Hall 1928: 65. Another exhibition at the British Museum opened on July 5, 1928, "by which date most of the work of restoration and repair had been done." Woolley 1929: 306. We would like to thank Sarah Collins at the BMA for this information.

34 The earliest exhibition, prepared by the archaeologist Max Mallowan in spite of Woolley's doubts about his capacities, was shown first in Baghdad for "political reasons." Woolley to Kenyon, Mar. 6, 1929, BMA, CE32/28/22/1. Objects from London that were to be shown at the Philadelphia exhibition, organized by Legrain and with items belonging to Philadelphia as well, arrived in March 1929.

35 A letter from Kenyon to Mrs. McHugh, dated Apr. 12, 1928, announced that the larger exhibition of the Ur finds would open in June. In a letter dated May 30, Kenyon fixed the opening for June 20. Ur, Iraq Expedition Records, Correspondence, Exp. V, Jan.–June 1928, UPMA.

36 Bowring 2012: 10.

37 Wooley to Mrs McHugh, July 11, 1928. Ur, Iraq Expedition Records, Correspondence, Exp. V, July–Dec. 1928, UPMA.

38 Evans 2012a: 2. In a letter to Mrs. McHugh, dated June 1, 1928, Woolley wrote that his wife had modeled "a Sumerian woman's head, based on an actual skull." Ur, Iraq Expedition Records, Correspondence, Exp. V, Jan.–June 1928, UPMA.

39 The Woolleys apparently did not work alone in the restoration of the Ur jewelry: "[They] were able to string...[the beads that] had been undisturbed through centuries [with] only the thread rotting away,...temporarily, on the spot. But the real labour fell to the Museum [the university's Museum of Archaeology and Anthropology] women here who have been doing work of this type for several years.... University Museum Aides Restring Beads of Shu-Bad of Ur After Woolley Near East Expedition Finds Treasures: Mrs. Loring Dam, docent, and her assistant [Miss Elizabeth Creaghead] piece together 300 strings of carnelian, lapis lazuli, agate and gold gems." *Philadelphia Bulletin*, June 1, 1929, Pubs. Exhibit Cata./Coll. Guides, Royal Tombs of Ur of the Chaldees, Exhibits from the (~1934) [hereafter Pubs. Exhibit Cata.], UPMA.

40 Richard Zettler has kindly informed us that one and possibly both of the founders of the department store had prominently supported the Penn Museum.

41 A booklet was published to accompany the exhibition. Pubs. Exhibit Cata., UPMA.

42   Newspapers, however, made careful note of the queen's items, as in the *Philadelphia Inquirer*, Feb. 22, 1934: "3400 BC Jewellery Put on Exhibition: Chaldean ornaments dedicated to public at store ceremony." "Chaldean" was a much more popular word than "Sumerian," even if it incorrectly designated late-Babylonian material. The *Philadelphia Record*, on Feb. 22, 1934, also announced: "Royal Jewellery 5000 Years Old on Exhibition."

43   The harp remains on view at the Penn Museum.

44   *Philadelphia Bulletin*, Feb. 22, 1934, Pubs. Exhibit Cata., UPMA.

45   Ibid.

46   Cooper 1993.

47   Evans 2012a: 131–36.

48   Other Ancient Near Eastern antiquities were shown in the Hall of Religion.

49   *Century of Progress World's Fair, 1933–1934 (University of Illinois at Chicago)*, http://collections.carli.illinois.edu/cdm4/item_viewer.php?CISOROOT=%2Fuic_cop&CISOPTR=590&DMSCALE=25&DMWIDTH=600&DMHEIGHT=600&DMMODE=viewer&DMFULL=0&DMX=75&DMY=0&DMTEXT=%2520%2527Science%2527&DMTHUMB=1&REC=5&DMROTATE=0&x=361&y=357 (accessed June 26, 2014).

50   See Frankfort 1939; Zervos 1935.

51   Woolley, "New Examples of Early Sumerian Art," typescript for article published in *London Illustrated News*, 1926, BMA, WY1/3/4.

52   Ibid.

53   Some scholars have argued for the ancient Sumerian reception of these works as aesthetic objects: see, e.g., Bahrani 2014 and Laude 1981, vol. 1: 74–78. While it must have been the case that artists or artisans working for the royal Mesopotamian courts were the most skilled, it is also the case that these ancient objects were not created for the sole pleasure of the senses nor for the embodiment of sensible qualities, as in modern European art.

54   *Philadelphia Bulletin*, Feb. 22, 1934 (emphasis added).

55   This term from the vocabulary of Christian theology denotes an object that changes substantially without altering physically or visibly, and is used to describe what happens when the Eucharistic bread and wine are changed into the flesh and blood of Christ. The word was used in Arthur Coleman Danto's 1981 book *The Transfiguration of the Common Place*, dedicated to the problem of how to define art when, under certain circumstances, everything can be seen as art, from an industrial, functional item to a magical or sacred object.

56   On Moore and Hepworth, see Wood 2003. Several recent exhibitions of Moore's work have included Sumerian sculptures to emphasize the formal relationship between ancient and modern objects. A Gudea head drawn on paper by Giacometti illustrates the title page of Suter 2000.

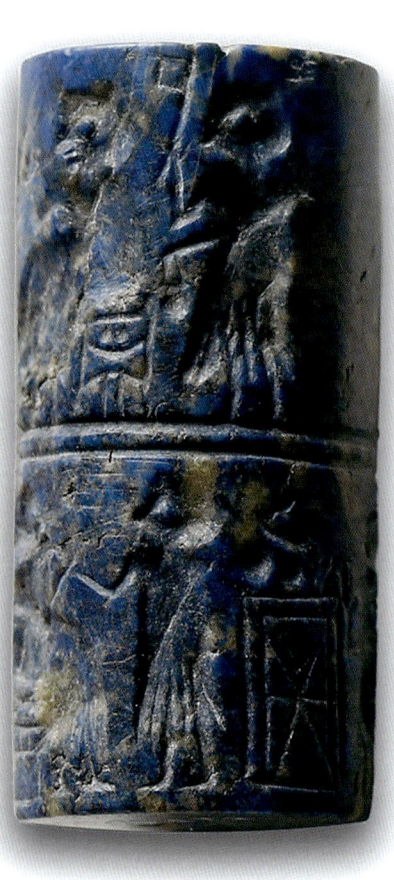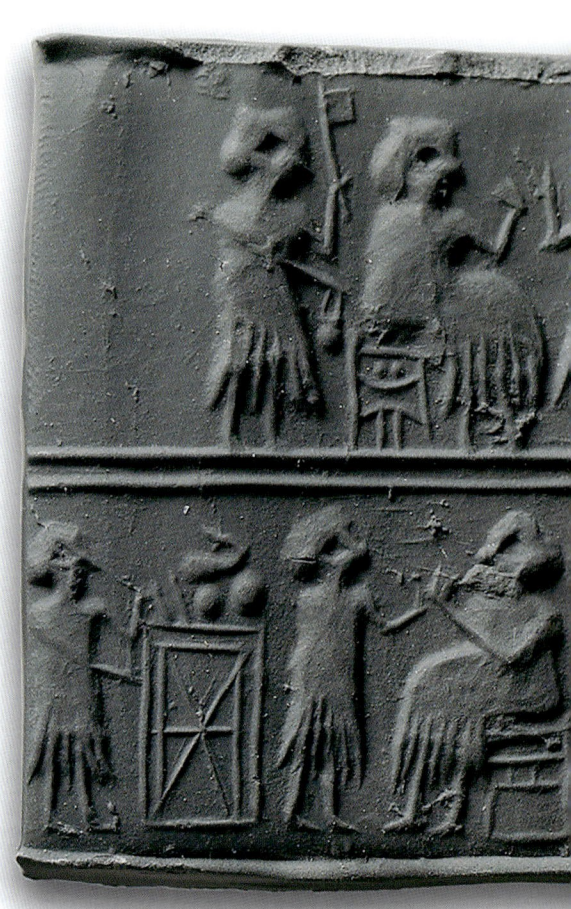

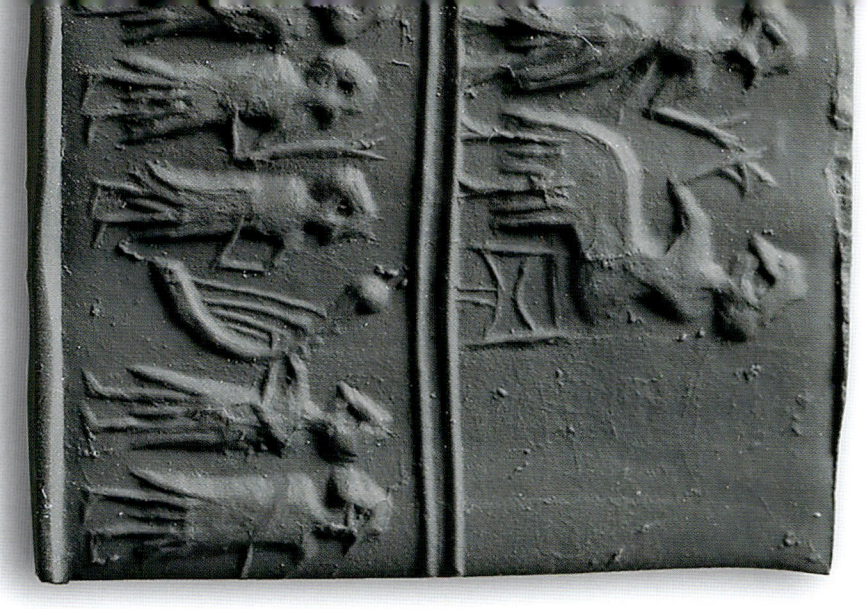

Magnificent with Jewels:
Puabi, Queen of Ur

William B. Hafford and Richard L. Zettler

3–1. Telegram by Leonard Woolley from Basra, January 4, 1928. Courtesy of the University of Pennsylvania Museum of Archaeology and Anthropology. Checklist no. 81. In Woolley's telegram, the queen's name was read as "Shubad" and the text was sent in Latin to encode the message.

The remains of Puabi, the queen, were uncovered in the excavations of Tell al-Muqayyar, ancient Ur (Biblical Ur of the Chaldees), in December 1927. She was identified by her name and title on one of three cylinder seals found with her body, but the field epigrapher Father Eric Burrows originally read her name in Sumerian as Shubad.[1] Her remains were found in a stone tomb chamber more than 8 meters below the surface of the mound, surrounded with burial goods and covered in jewelry that was apparently the height of royal fashion 4,500 years ago.[2]

The field director of the excavations, Charles Leonard (later Sir Leonard) Woolley, announced Puabi's discovery to the directors of the British Museum and the University of Pennsylvania Museum, the two institutions sponsoring and supporting his work, in a telegram dated January 4, 1928.[3] He sent the message in Latin, a code that would be understood by the museum recipients but likely not by the local transmitters (fig. 3–1). The translation read: "I found the intact tomb, stone built and vaulted over with bricks, of Queen Shubad adorned with a dress in which gems, flower crowns, and animal figures are woven. The tomb is magnificent with jewels and golden cups." By sending the

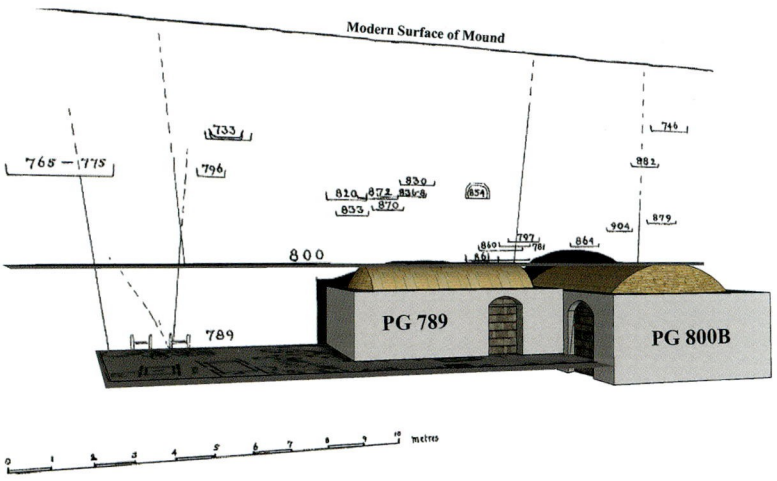

3-2. Three-dimensional reconstruction of Puabi's tomb chamber (PG 800) abutting another funerary chamber (PG 789). The relationship of PG 789, PG 800, and PG 800B is based on textual, photographic, and mapped information. Reconstruction by William B. Hafford, 2014.

telegram in Latin, Woolley hoped to prevent word of the rich finds reaching anyone in the local community who might be tempted to loot the site or the dig house. In fact, as he was beginning the excavations in November 1922, six armed men had attacked his encampment and made off with supplies and personal effects.

Puabi's tomb chamber was found abutting another, nearly identical chamber (fig. 3–2). That tomb, assigned the number PG (Private Grave) 789, had been looted in antiquity and contained only a few scattered remains. The vaulted roof of Puabi's tomb had collapsed, but the chamber had not been looted, and Woolley assigned it the designator PG 800B. His analysis linked this chamber with an arrangement of bodies possibly sacrificed at the time of the queen's death and found at least 1.7 meters above it. He consequently called this the "death pit," and he found another such pit clearly linked to PG 789. The sequence of discovery is clear, but the interrelation of the graves is in doubt. Of the more than 1,800 graves in the "Royal Cemetery" at Ur, Woolley defined a mere 16 as royal (fig. 3–3). His criteria were based on construction, ritual, and wealth—to be royal in his terms a grave had to have an interior main chamber, an exterior death pit, and many prestige goods throughout. PG 789 and 800 were model examples of this typology. Their death pits held dozens of adorned bodies, evidence of ritual sacrifice for the king or queen; their chambers were vaulted and well built, evidence of the importance of the primary burial; and their chambers as well as their death pits contained imported artifacts of particularly high value, evidence of status and wealth.

The first in the sequence that Woolley excavated was naturally that nearest the modern surface, about 7 meters down (fig. 3–4). Here he encountered the death pit he

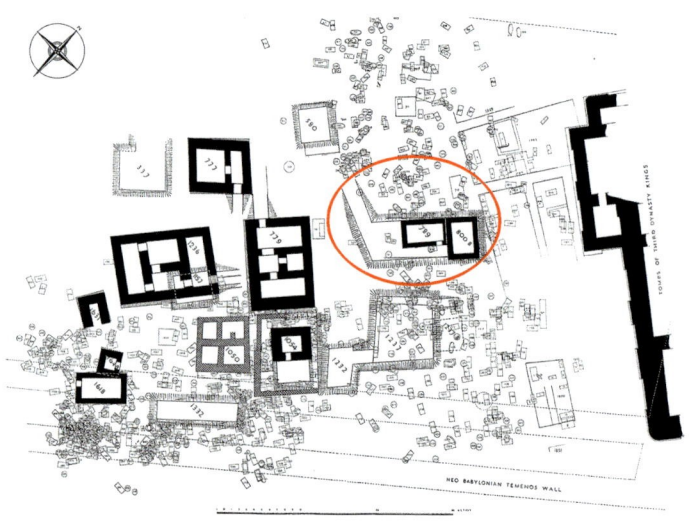

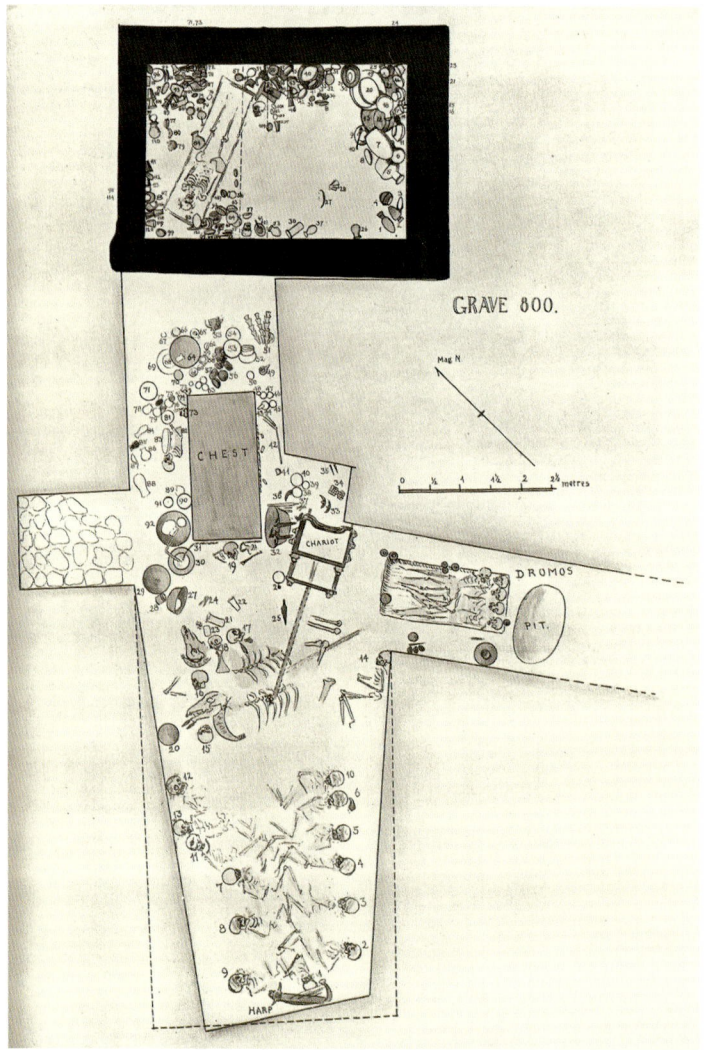

GRAVE 800.

CHEST

CHARIOT

DROMOS

PIT.

HARP

3-3. Plan of the Ur Royal Cemetery. Tombs PG 789 and PG 800 are circled in red (after Woolley 1934: pls. 273, 274).

3-4. Plan of tomb PG 800 as published by Leonard Woolley (1934: pl. 36). The original caption read: "Ground-Plan of Queen Shub-ad's death-pit and tomb-chamber PG/800."

3-5. Plan of tomb PG 789 as published by Leonard Woolley (1934: pl. 29). The original caption read: "Ground-Plan of PG/789, showing the position of objects and bodies."

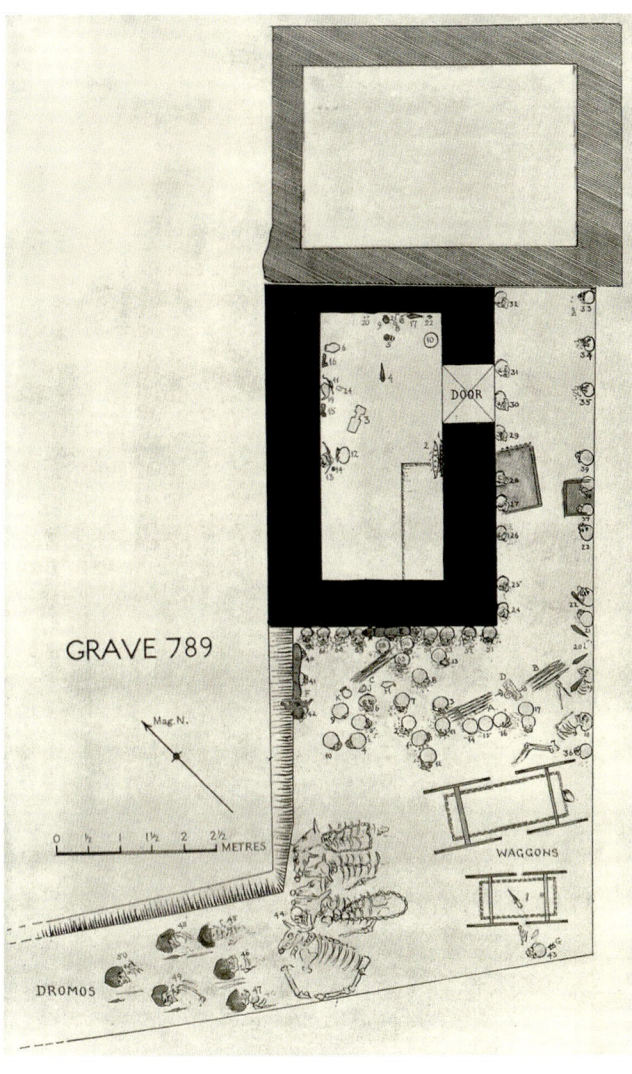

eventually associated with Puabi. Its outlines were difficult to discern, but it was roughly rectangular, approximately 12 by 4 meters, containing twenty-five bodies, a chariot or sled driven by two oxen, and many prestige objects including silver and gold vessels, a gaming board, and musical instruments. Most of the bodies were those of women, though men were present, particularly at the sloped entryway to the pit. One of the men, apparently a groom for the oxen, had a cylinder seal giving his Sumerian name as Lugal-shapada (lugal-ša$_3$-pa$_3$-da).

No built chamber was found at this level. Instead, after removing the remains of a deteriorated wardrobe chest, Woolley found a hole leading to a plundered tomb (PG 789; fig. 3–5) beneath. He initially believed that this was the chamber associated with the death pit.[4] Clearing it from above, he found it to have been looted. A shallow depression along the southeastern wall may have marked the emplacement for the primary burial, but it held no bones. Nonetheless, Woolley assumed it to have been the burial of a king. Elsewhere in the chamber were scattered and highly fragmentary remains of at least three other individuals, one probably male, represented by fragments of a skull with a *brim*, a typical male headdress consisting of two lengths of gold chain with three beads, and two probable females, represented by fragments of skulls and spiral hair rings of gold wire. These individuals Woolley took to be the personal attendants of the deceased king. The looters had left a few artifacts behind as well, including the silver model of a boat and a gaming board.

After excavating the chamber of PG 789, Woolley proceeded to dig below the upper death pit. At the level of the floor of the chamber, he found another death pit. This one measured approximately 10 by 5 meters and contained sixty-three bodies, two wagons, six oxen, and silver and gold objects, though not as many of the latter as in the upper pit. There were also many weapons here, which Woolley took to indicate the male nature of the overall burial. Once again, most of the bodies in the pit were women, though a number of men were present, including six soldiers with spears and helmets at the entrance as if on guard.[5] In fact, Woolley believed that the people in the pit represented the king's retinue, having willingly sacrificed their lives to follow him into the afterlife as guards, grooms, and harem, but recent research has shown that some were brutally killed.[6]

The tomb chamber lay in the eastern corner of the death pit. A doorway at the northern end of its northeastern wall linked it to the pit. The door had been blocked up after the principle burial and before the sacrificial scene in the death pit outside. On digging the passageway leading to the door, Woolley encountered the wall of a second chamber immediately to the north.[7] He assigned this one the designator PG 800B and decided that, in spite of the fact that it was much deeper, it belonged with the upper death pit. He had initially been willing to assign PG 789's chamber to the upper pit, so it was not unthinkable in his view that the principle tomb might be lower. Thus, in his analysis, both PG 800's death pit and its deep chamber (PG 800B) postdated PG 789.

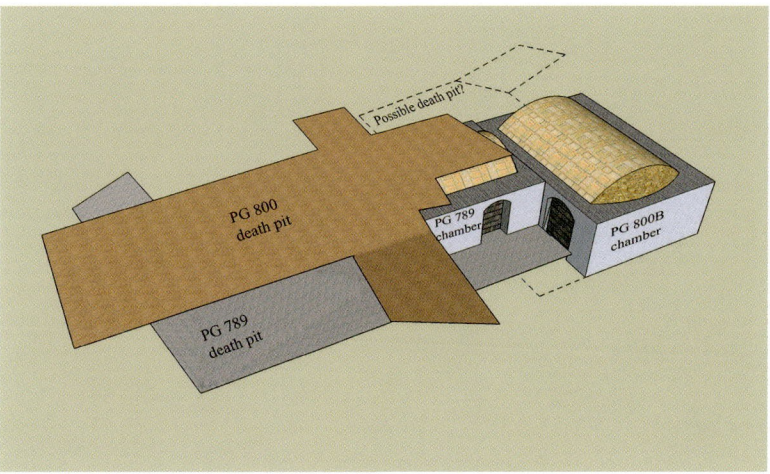

3-6. Three-dimensional reconstruction of tombs PG 789 and PG 800 with possible location of the third death pit shown in dashed lines beneath PG 789. Reconstruction by William B. Hafford, 2014.

Woolley excavated PG 800B from above, claiming there was no door. He believed that the tomb had only been accessed from the upper pit, even though there was no clear evidence linking the two—he had already removed the upper death pit by the time he excavated PG 800B, and it was no longer possible to establish accurate interrelations between upper and lower pits.[8] Nonetheless, he reported the top of Puabi's vaulted chamber as matching the level of the upper death pit.

The unlooted chamber contained the remains of a richly adorned woman, Puabi, the queen. Puabi is not known from other documentary sources, but the fact that the inscription on her seal does not mention her husband may suggest that she ruled in her own right. Inscriptions on the cylinder seals of other queens commonly link them to their ruling husbands, as does, for example, the seal of Ninbanda, whose inscription gives her title and names her as the wife of Mesannepada.[9]

Nonetheless, Woolley believed that PG 789 had once contained Puabi's husband, the king, who had died before her. On her death, so Woolley explained, she wanted to be buried close to this unnamed king, and thus she had her own tomb cut down next to his, with her death pit located above in an elaborate stratigraphic interweaving.[10]

The vaulted roof of PG 800B had largely collapsed, but Woolley found a vast array of objects within the tomb. Some were relatively high up in the fill, which he took to indicate an initial deposition on shelves. Curiously, however, the floor of Puabi's chamber was 40 centimeters lower than the floor of the so-called king's chamber. This is a substantial depth and prima facie evidence that PG 800B actually predated PG 789 rather than vice versa. But there is also compelling evidence of a blocked doorway at the southern end of PG 800B's southwestern wall, very similar to the blocked doorway

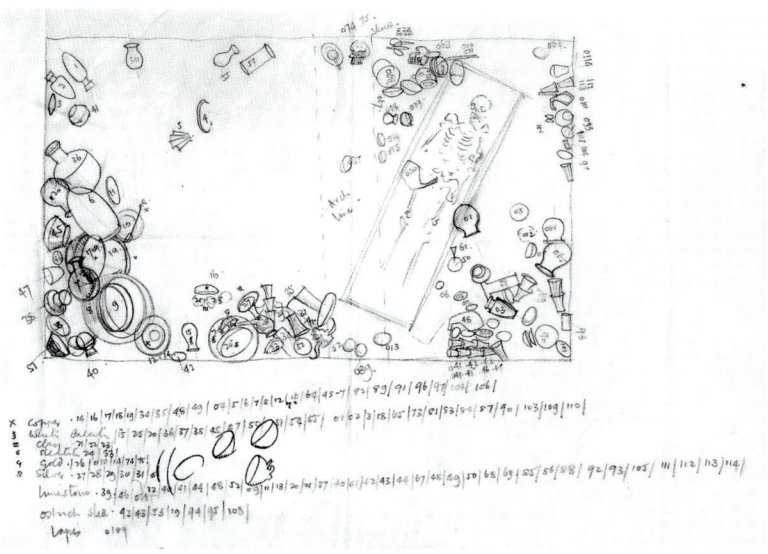

3–7. Excavation drawing of tomb PG 800B with distribution of the finds within the chamber and original numbering from the field notes. Photograph courtesy of the British Museum.

of PG 789's tomb chamber.[11] Woolley himself had observed the possible remains of a blocked doorway on the exterior face of the chamber's southwestern wall, but not on its interior face, and he ruled out the existence of a doorway because it did not fit his understanding of the stratigraphic relationship between PG 789 and PG 800.[12] The doorway would most likely have linked PG 800B to an as yet undiscovered death pit that lay at least partially beneath PG 789, an area Woolley did not excavate (fig. 3–6). If there was no doorway in PG 800B, the body would have been placed in it from above, with the workers climbing out and then completing the vaulted roof from above. The task would have been most difficult, and it is more likely that the normal procedure of placing the body in the chamber through a doorway, leaving, and then blocking the door from the same level would have been conducted.

Woolley found more than 100 objects piled about chamber PG 800B, the majority being vessels of copper, silver, gold, calcite, and clay (fig. 3–7). At least five decorated ostrich-eggshell vessels were also found, as well as a silver pot with a gold drinking tube projecting from it, presumably for drinking beer, and a silver bull's head and shell plaques, both probably from the sound box of a lyre.[13] Two unusually large cockle shells, as well as imitations in gold and silver, containing cosmetic pigments were also found.[14] Puabi would presumably have used these cosmetics in her daily beauty routines.

Three attendants were in the tomb chamber with the deceased queen. Two were stationed near her head, one of whom was likely male due to the daggers and whetstone found with him. The third attendant was located near Puabi's feet and was probably female, as indicated by her gold hair rings, beads, and garment pins.[15]

The queen's remains were laid out on a bier that sat diagonally across the northwestern end of the chamber. She lay on her back with her hands over her abdomen. Just under five feet tall, she was roughly forty years of age at the time of her death.[16] The whole of her upper body was covered with beads of gold, lapis lazuli, carnelian, and agate. These Woolley took to be the remains of a beaded cloak (see fig. 5–1). The arrangement of the beads did not cross the body as would necklaces, but generally ran in vertical lines ending at about the same point near the waist. Puabi also wore a broad belt of tubular gold, carnelian and lapis beads, and a series of large gold rings that Woolley thought had been suspended from the belt.[17] The rings, however, do not have bales for suspension, and it seems more likely that they formed a girdle hanging separately about her hips, lower than the beaded one at her waist. Such an interpretation is supported by Woolley's field cards, which show the rings separated from the upper belt in the ground (fig. 3–8).

Against Puabi's upper right arm were three pins, their points upward, that originally secured a garment. With the pins were amulets of bearded bulls and fish in gold and lapis lazuli along with three cylinder seals, one of which bore her name and title. She wore gold rings on her fingers, some delicately formed in interwoven rope patterns and some inlaid with lapis lazuli:[18] around her right knee was a beaded garter. Near her right hip were four *brim* headdresses, perhaps gifts intended for male deities in the underworld. Near the bier on what Woolley suggested might have been a shelf or small table, was a group of thousands of minute lapis lazuli beads intermingled with small pendants—made of gold foil over bitumen and depicting plants and animals— surrounded by white, powdery material that may have been decayed leather. Woolley reconstructed a wide diadem from these elements, believing it to have been Puabi's spare bejeweled wig.[19] Recent re-analysis suggests that this "diadem" was not a single piece, but thematically linked strings of jewelry probably intended to be worn on the head as individual pieces.[20]

Most spectacular of all was the headdress that Puabi wore in death.[21] At its base were twelve meters of gold ribbon still coiled in ovals as if resting on or wrapping a large wig that had long since decayed. Various strings of lapis, gold, and carnelian beads sat atop, along with four wreaths of gold leaves.[22] Triple willow leaves with inlaid flowers and pear-shaped pendants intermingled with broader leaves originally thought to be mulberry or beech but later identified as poplar.[23] The leaves were tooled and hammered in imitation of natural examples, and some had carnelian beads at their tips. At the back of the head, originally embedded in the hair, was a golden comb, the top of which flared into seven flowers—the crowning glory of the ensemble—while elsewhere in the hair glittered small coils of golden wire. A beaded frontlet with gold rings hung down over Puabi's forehead, and she wore large gold earrings resembling crescent moons, perhaps a tribute to the chief deity of Ur, Nanna the Moon God. Amulets depicting recumbent bearded bulls suspended from a short chain of beads were also found near both ears.

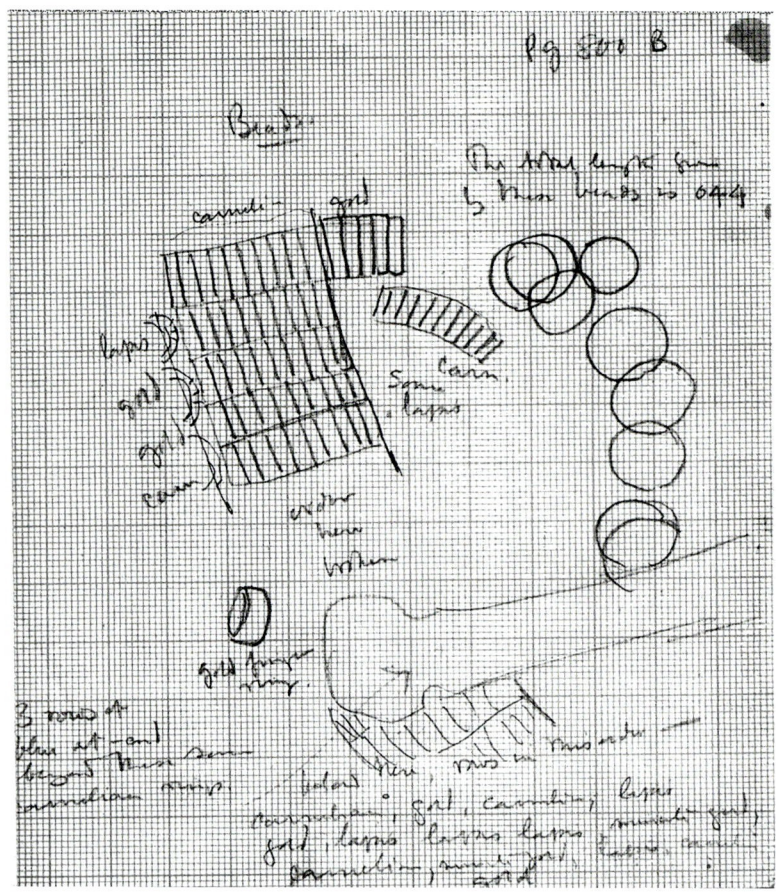

3-8. Field card showing Woolley's original drawing of Puabi's belt as found. British Museum: RC 778-803, 173.

Woolley carefully removed the headdress from the ground, preserving the coils of gold ribbon in what he believed were the actual measurements when worn on the head (fig. 3–9, and see fig. 1–9). Even though the skull had been badly damaged by the collapse of the roof and the weight of the soil above,[24] the ribbon retained its oval form, preserving the dimensions of the original hairstyle or wig. At 38 centimeters in diameter, it would have been a very large wig in order to support the wreaths, ribbon, beads, and hair comb. Combined, the gold and semiprecious stones on Puabi's head weighed 2,215 grams—almost 5 pounds.[25]

In the division of finds between the expedition sponsors and Iraq, most of the artifacts from Puabi's tomb fell to the expedition's lot. When they reached London, Woolley set about finding a method of displaying and publishing them in a manner that would highlight their spectacular impact. He wanted to show the jewelry as it would have been worn, but not on a faceless dummy.[26] His wife Katharine, an accomplished artist,[27] volunteered to make a model head complete with features (fig. 3–10). As a basis,

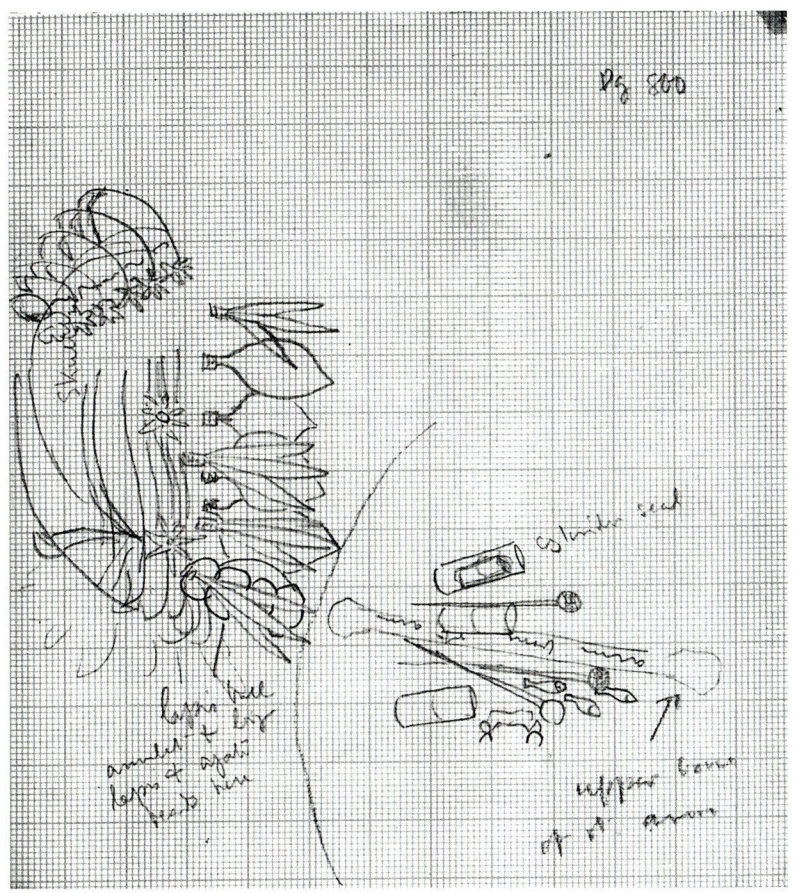

3–9. Field card showing Woolley's original drawing of Puabi's headdress as found. British Museum: Rc 778-803, 167.

she used a plaster cast of a skull from the site of Tell al-'Ubaid, supplied by Sir Arthur Keith of the Royal College of Surgeons.[28] Leonard Woolley believed that the use of a roughly contemporary female skull would allow for the reconstruction of facial features that might approximate those of a woman of that time. Katharine Woolley used wax to build up the face—under Keith's anthropological instruction and approval, as Woolley frequently stated.[29]

A wig was made for the head using the dimensions of the oval gold ribbons, and the jewelry was placed upon it (see fig. 2–5). Woolley later wrote that "the strands [of gold ribbon] fell of their own accord into precisely the lines which they had on the queen's head; the symmetry of the festoons on either side left no doubt as to the correctness of the arrangement."[30] The ultimate creation, however, garnered some criticism, particularly from the curator of the Penn Museum's Babylonian Section, Father Léon Legrain.[31] He believed that only Sumerian sculpture could convey the image of a Sumerian in the eyes of a Sumerian, and that basing the features of a model on such characteristics

97

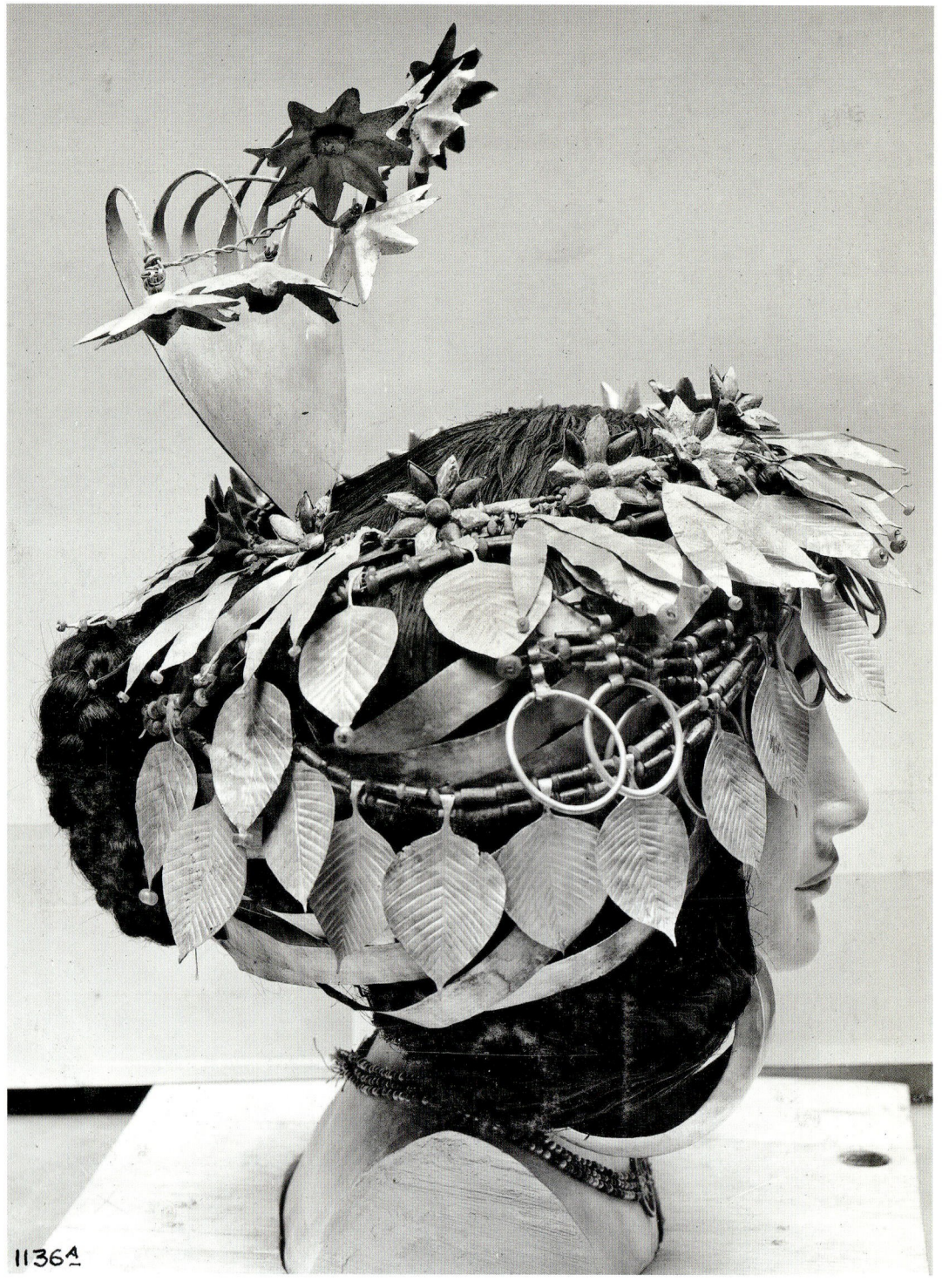

11364

3–10. Early reconstruction of Puabi's headdress by Katharine Woolley. Photograph, 1930. Penn Museum: 1136A. Checklist no. 99.

would result in a more accurate depiction.[32] His argument is almost entirely an aesthetic one, based mostly on an appreciation of Classical art and what he described as "good taste."[33] He stated, "Even if we had the skull of Cleopatra, we should have little suspicion of her beauty and of the curve of the nose which turned the destinies of the Roman Empire."[34]

The artifacts from the 1927–28 season at Ur were first divided with Iraq, then the remaining half was prepared for a summer exhibition in London before a further division with Philadelphia. Katharine Woolley's model head was used in this exhibit to display Puabi's headdress. In the *Times* of London for June 22, 1928, under the headline "Treasures of Ur: Exhibition at British Museum," Woolley stated: "An attempt has been made to reassemble [the headdress] on a modelled head. The result is certainly barbaric; the queen's hair almost disappears beneath a mass of gold, and the whole coiffure is exaggerated in size; but in no other way could one obtain a true picture of the fashions of the period." Despite the "barbaric" impression, the headdress was said to be one of the star attractions of the exhibit, and the *Illustrated London News* ran a full-page black-and-white image of Katharine Woolley's model wearing its golden jewelry on June 30, 1928. So impressive was it that the magazine ran a colorized version on August 11, once again full page (see fig. 2–5).

After the artifacts had been displayed in London in 1928, most of them were then sent to Philadelphia for a second grand exhibit in 1929. There was much discussion of sending Katharine Woolley's model head to Philadelphia at this time. The artifacts were originally scheduled to arrive in January, and the Woolleys themselves were to tour America in March and April. Leonard Woolley wrote of the possibility of shipping the head along with the other artifacts, commenting specifically on the delicacy of the model: "…one difficulty is that the colouring of the head is not fixed & so nothing must be allowed to touch the face etc. I do hope that it will arrive undamaged, but would ask that in any case it be not 'touched up' or doctored in any way pending our arrival. In the exhibition here it has proved the greatest 'draw' of the collection & will I think make an equal sensation in your galleries."[35]

Meanwhile, Legrain was busy refuting the Woolleys' model head and creating his own. Using imagery from seals and statuary, he attempted to reconstruct the hairstyle he believed Puabi would have worn. Some of the seals came directly from Puabi's tomb, but they had little specific detail owing to the difficulty of engraving at such a small scale. More detail was to be found in sculpture, but most of the examples were substantially later in time than Puabi herself.

Legrain decided that the hairstyle in Katharine Woolley's reconstruction was too severely "bobbed," as was the current fashion in the 1920s, and believed that Puabi's long hair would instead have been rolled at the back in a "figure-eight" or elaborate chignon (see fig. 1–7). In his analysis this looped bun would have been bound with the twelve meters of gold ribbon found with her, accounting for its extended oval diameter by assuming that it ran from front to back on the head rather than from side to side. Some ancient Near Eastern female figurines do sport this hairstyle, with a thick band holding the hair in place. In particular Legrain was fascinated by an example of such sculpture, known as *la femme* à *l'écharpe*, that dated around 400 years later than Puabi.[36] He based his model head on the features of this statuette from Tello (ancient Girsu) that now resides in the Louvre; a cast of the statuette is in the Penn Museum.[37] He said of the figure, "She has the high cheek bones, large nose, and large eyes under powerful eyebrows of a true oriental beauty, and in spite of the sculptural effect of her staring eyes, she possesses a charming queenly dignity."[38]

Whether the gold ribbons could have held the mass of hair and allowed for the hair comb at the back is questionable. Furthermore, Legrain's hairstyle could not support all of the wreaths found on Puabi's body; his display included only one as part of the headdress. Indeed, he called into question whether she could have worn all four.[39] In reply, Woolley pointed only to the fact that she had been buried with them on her head, whether she wore them in life or not.

The Woolleys arrived in the U.S. on March 14, but the Penn Museum's exhibit was not yet ready. The artifacts that were expected in January did not arrive until February and March, in two shipments. There is, however, no evidence that Katharine Woolley's model head was included in either shipment, indeed, no evidence of it ever having reached the Penn Museum at all—no acknowledgment of receipt and no further mentions in letters. Moreover, the museum's exhibit of the Royal Cemetery artifacts opened with Legrain's model head on display.

On the day of the opening, May 25, 1929, under the headline "Ur Relics on View: Exhibition open to public at U. of P. Museum today," the *Philadelphia Inquirer* reported that "[t]he image of the queen…has been reconstructed through the patient researches of Dr. Léon Legrain, curator of the Museum's Babylonian section." An image of Legrain with the head he constructed also appeared in the *Waterbury (CT) American* dated March 28, 1929. It may be that the earlier model head was shipped but that Legrain refused to display it, and the Woolleys took it back with them to London; it may have been damaged in the shipment or in the attempt to ship; or it may never have been sent at all owing to Legrain's dislike of it and his determination to make his own. Regardless, the Woolleys' model was not on view in Philadelphia.

When the publication of the Royal Cemetery was nearing completion, Leonard Woolley wanted to illustrate the jewelry in color as worn. Thus, he asked Mary Louise Baker, Penn Museum's archaeological illustrator, to make a watercolor of the model head wearing the jewelry (see fig. 5–5). On May 25, 1933, Woolley wrote that Baker had left Ur with the incomplete Shubad illustration. By July 11, it had been completed in Philadelphia and sent to Woolley, but he rejected it in a letter of September 4, calling it a "parody" and saying that "instead of representing the true physical type it gives something quite different—e.g., the nose is made straight and thin, whereas the peculiar quality of the nose on the skull was its width."[40] He decided instead to use the colorized photo that had appeared in the *Illustrated London News* (see fig. 2–5).

Woolley's monumental definitive report on his excavations of the Ur Royal Cemetery was published in 1934, and included his extensive description of Puabi's tomb PG 800 and its relationship to PG 789, along with details of the discovery of the jewelry and the creation of the model head, which was depicted in color in plate 128. It also had something of the final say on the Woolley-Legrain dispute, justifying the use of Katharine's model head in the publication. Nevertheless, by this point neither head was in use for exhibiting the jewelry. As Penn Museum director Horace Jayne reported in a postscript to his letter to Woolley dated December 23, 1932, "Legrain's head of Queen Shubad is abandoned. We have the coronets and comb separately shown. It is a considerable improvement."[41]

In the creation of his model, Legrain had argued almost exclusively from abstract artistic taste; Woolley had attempted to argue from relatively more concrete science. But the debate concerned difficult, perhaps impossible, questions to answer: How did Puabi wear her hair? What did her eyebrows look like? How exactly did she wear her makeup? Ultimately, decisions on the features of the model distracted from the jewelry itself, and as a result modern displays have not depicted any facial features when a model head has been used.

Endnotes

1   The inscription on the seal reads "KA x Shu.AD, eresh" (Sollberger 1960: 79; Michalowski 2006: 106). The excavators originally read the two cuneiform signs that composed the name in Sumerian as *shub-ad*. Gelb (1957) first proposed reading the two signs in Akkadian as pu_3-AD, citing the parallel writings pu_3-a-bi and pu_3-^{d}a-bi, literally, the word of my father or the word of the (divine) father. Sollberger (1960) followed Gelb, dubbing the name Shubad "meaningless." More recently, Marchesi (2004) questioned the link between pu_3-AD and pu_3-$^{(d)}$a-bi. He argued that the name was likely a shortened form of a longer original, and suggested that AD represented a theophoric element, with the name probably to be read Pu-abum. Puabi's title (*eresh*) means queen, or, more generically, lady, the equivalent of Akkadian *beltu* or *sharratu*

2   Baadsgaard 2008.

3   Woolley's field report dated January 3, 1928, explains that he cabled on the 2nd, but the telegram was not received in Philadelphia until 6:43 a.m. on the 4th. Ur, Iraq Expedition Records, box 2, folder 2, UPennMuseum Archives, Philadelphia (hereafter UPMA).

4   Woolley's field report dated December 6, 1927 Ur, Iraq Expedition Records, box 1, folder 12, UPMA.

5   Bones were most often poorly preserved in the deep soil at Ur, and Woolley primarily based his gender interpretations not on the bones but on the items found with the bodies. Typically if the body had weapons and/or a *brim* headdress, Woolley designated it male, and if it had jewelry and/or a more elaborate headdress, he designated it female.

6   Baadsgaard et al. 2011; Baadsgaard, Monge, and Zettler 2012.

7   Woolley interpreted the placement of the second chamber (PG 800B) as being plastered against the first one he had found (PG 789), yet from his descriptions it seems more likely that the plaster had been placed on the outer face of the standing chamber PG 800B, and PG 789 had been built up against it.

8   Woolley's measurements are inconsistent. He indicates only 1.3 meters between the upper and lower death pits, but also records a 1.5-meter height of the PG 789 chamber walls. Since the PG 789 chamber was at the same level as the lower death pit, its walls by these measures would intrude upon the upper death pit even before the vault began. Zimmerman (1998a) investigated these discrepancies, finding as much as a meter in error. Furthermore, Woolley (1934: 73) acknowledges that the PG 800 death-pit floor sloped down as much as 50 centimeters but does not say in which direction or where his measurements along it were taken.

9   Woolley 1934: pl. 207, no. 216.

10   It is, however, possible that the upper death pit belonged to a completely different tomb, later than both PG 789 and PG 800 (Zimmerman 1998b). If this were the case, there was no built chamber associated, or it was never found. Such is not unknown; see, for example, PG 1237 in Woolley 1934.

11   Zimmerman 1998a; Zimmerman 1998b; Zimmerman and Zettler forthcoming.

12   Woolley 1934: 83–84.

13   Ibid.: 89–91.

14   Bimson 1980.

15   Woolley 1934: 90.

16   Keith 1934: 400.

17   Woolley 1934: pl. 130; but cf. ibid.: 87, fig. 12.

18   Woolley (1934: 88) reports that Puabi had ten gold rings, but his notes and catalog cards show only nine, five apparently from her right hand (U.10877A–D and U.10878) and four from her left hand (U.10949A–B and U.10950A–B). The Penn Museum has five rings, the four catalogued as U.10877A–D (B16717–20), and one of two listed as U.10950 (B16721). The latter is mistakenly identified as U.10878 in Zettler and Horne 1998: 95, no. 31. The British Museum holds U.10878 (BM 121379) and one of the two rings recorded as U.10950 (BM 121378). The Iraq Museum in Baghdad probably has the two rings with the field numbers U.10949A/B (the number assigned in the field) as IM8314/15 (the museum accession number), as in pictures published in the Directorate General catalogue (cf. Directorate General of Antiquities 1942: pl. 20).

19   Woolley 1934: 89.

20   Pittman and Miller, this volume; for the interpretation of the symbolism of the pendants, see Miller 1999, 2000, and 2013.

21   Woolley 1934: 128–29. See Benzel in this volume.

22   There are four wreaths in the final reconstruction of Puabi's headdress, although Woolley only reported three in his field notes. When arranging the jewelry overall, he seems to have decided that the wreath with poplar leaves was too long to have been a single piece and thus made it into two separate ones. One of the two wreaths had leaves with a long, straight tip, the other had leaves tipped with a carnelian bead. Both were reconstructed on two strings of small carnelian and lapis beads. The leaves with carnelian at the ends, however, were made with bales for four strings; hence, its reconstruction on two strings may be inaccurate (Baadsgaard 2008: 225–26). A four-string wreath is also seen on Body 61 of PG 1237 (Woolley 1934: pl. 135).

23   Miller 2000: 149–151. Tengberg, Potts, and Francfort 2008 claim the leaves resemble the Pakistani rosewood (*Dalbergia sissoo*), particularly in the rendering of the venation. Miller (personal communication, 2010) considers shape a more critical aspect. Sissoo leaves are widest in the center, while poplar leaves are widest in the lower third, closer in form to the gold leaf forms of Puabi's wreaths.

24   In fact, the skull was almost completely destroyed. What is preserved of Puabi's physical remains is now in the Museum of Natural History in London. Keith (1934: 400) managed to acquire measurements of the skull, but Molleson and Hodgson (2003: 95) could not confirm them from the fragments. Keith stated: "Even if we do allow for error, there can be no doubt that Queen Shub-ad had an uncommonly capacious skull."

25   Baadsgaard 2008: 362, table 10.1.

26 In a letter to Penn Museum director Horace Jayne dated August 8, 1933, Woolley said, "the head-dress, with which had to go the ear-rings and necklace, if placed on a featureless dummy lost balance terribly, and also the effect in a coloured plate was extremely ugly." Ur, Iraq Expedition Records, box 2, folder 13, UPMA.

27 Katharine Keeling, already a widow at this point, was originally a volunteer artist at Ur. After a few seasons, she married Leonard Woolley and continued as a field artist, producing most of the initial drawings of artifacts. In her autobiography, Agatha Christie tells of Katharine's artwork, saying that in addition to the Puabi bust, "She did a good head of Hamoudi, of Leonard Woolley himself, and a beautiful head of a young boy." Agatha Christie, *An Autobiography* (New York: Dodd, Mead, 1977), 388. The bust of Hamoudi, foreman at the dig, can be found in Woolley 1953: 96f. Katharine was ill after the 1927–28 season and as told in a letter from Woolley to McHugh dated June 1, 1928, "has had to lie up and rest most of the time, but she is also busy making a model of a Sumerian woman's head, based on an actual skull, which will be dressed up with all the regalia of Queen Shubad and will make a splendid show." Ur, Iraq Expedition Records, box 2, folder 2, UPMA.

28 The skull is almost certainly that from Ubaid Cemetery Grave 18, excavated by Woolley in the second Ur season and analyzed by Keith as skull number VIII—reported in Hall and Woolley 1927: 191, 218, and pls. LXV, LXVI. This was the best-preserved female skull at Ubaid and the only preserved skull to date from the "late" period of the Ubaid cemetery, which Woolley believed close enough in time to justify its use to reconstruct Puabi. It is, however, somewhat later than the Royal Cemetery. Furthermore, Keith (in ibid. 218) describes this skull as anomalous: "Forehead full and lofty; skull square in shape; differs from other skulls, but may be merely a family characteristic."

29 Woolley makes this argument in 1934: 85 and in several letters to Horace Jayne and others at the Penn Museum. In a letter dated August 12, 1933, Woolley gives what he says are Keith's direct words on the subject: "…a most skilful [*sic*] restoration of the flesh on the skull we accepted as a type.… Much inference enters into every reconstruction; Mrs. Woolley's inferences, in my opinion, were fully justified." Ur, Iraq Expedition Records, box 2, folder 13, UPMA.

30 Woolley 1934: 86.

31 Father Legrain and Sydney Smith of the British Museum often exchanged letters of a personal nature that show they were none too keen on Katharine Woolley or her work. In a letter to Smith in July 1928, Legrain commented on the model head, calling it "remarkable" in what seems to be a tongue-in-cheek manner. Smith replied in August: "The head of Shub-Ad is as you say remarkable: several ladies of Levantine descent are already claiming it as a portrait but I expect you have guessed the right one." Curatorial, box 7, folder 4, UPMA.

32 Woolley and Legrain argued about this both in person and in scholarly articles. Woolley told Jane McHugh, acting director of the Penn Museum following G. B. Gordon's death, in a letter of September 28, 1928 [Penn Museum Archives Ur Box 2 Folder 3], that "Legrain doesn't approve of the head on the ground that it doesn't resemble Sumerian sculptures, which is true: but then the sculptures are quite inconsistent with the skull types which in my opinion must be decisive." Ur, Iraq Expedition Records, box 2, folder 3, UPMA. Legrain (1931: 6, fig. 9) also did not agree with Woolley's reconstruction of the beaded cloak, preferring to believe that the beads formed a series of long necklaces.

33   Legrain 1929 and 1931.

34   Legrain 1929: 238.

35   Woolley to McHugh September 28, 1928. Ur, Iraq Expedition Records, box 2, folder 3, UPMA. The letter strongly implies that the model head was to be sent, but receipt of it is never acknowledged and it never went on display in Philadelphia.

36   Woolley and Legrain believed Puabi's era to have been earlier than we now know it to have been, and thus Legrain thought this statuette was even farther removed from her in time, around a thousand years. Woolley used this as evidence of the folly of Legrain's reconstruction, but Legrain (1929: 225) used it as evidence of the perseverance of hairstyles.

37   The cast was sent by Francois Thureau-Dangin, received and accessioned at Penn as B15573 on August 27, 1924. The Louvre number of the original piece is AO 295, part of Sarzec's 1881 excavations.

38   Legrain 1929: 238.

39   Ibid.: 241: "It is hard to believe that she wore, when alive, the four at the same time." He believed that the others were extras owned by the queen and placed on her body at death, but not normally worn.

40   Why Baker had begun this painting at Ur and the disposition of the model head in 1933 are unanswered questions. When Woolley rejected the final work in September 1933, he said that "…she had done it without seeing the original, so success would have been difficult to expect." This implies that the head no longer existed and that Baker may have been painting from a photograph. Ur, Iraq Expedition Records, box 2, folder 13, UPMA.

41   Ur, Iraq Expedition Records, box 2, folder 1, UPMA.

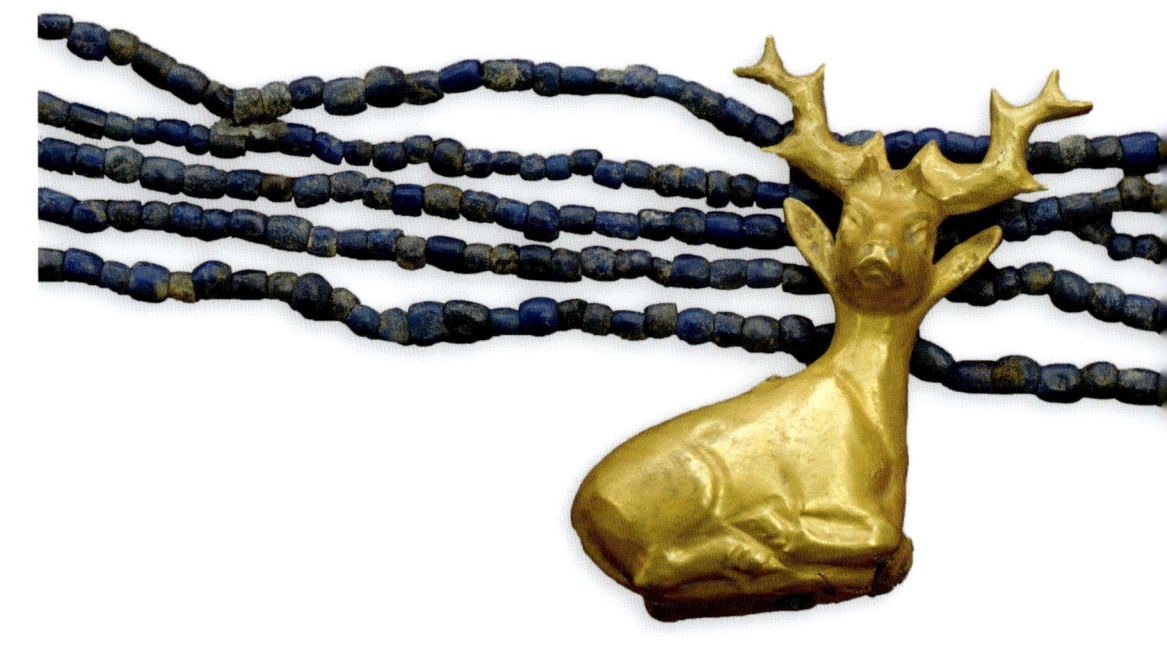

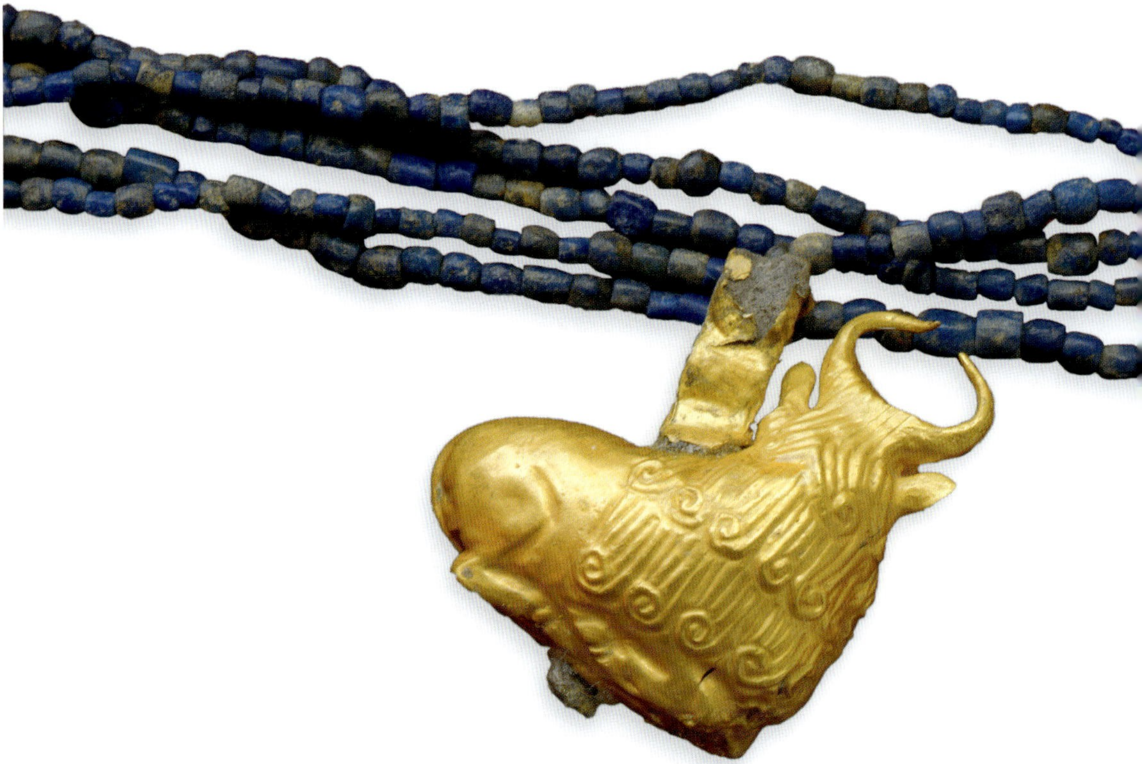

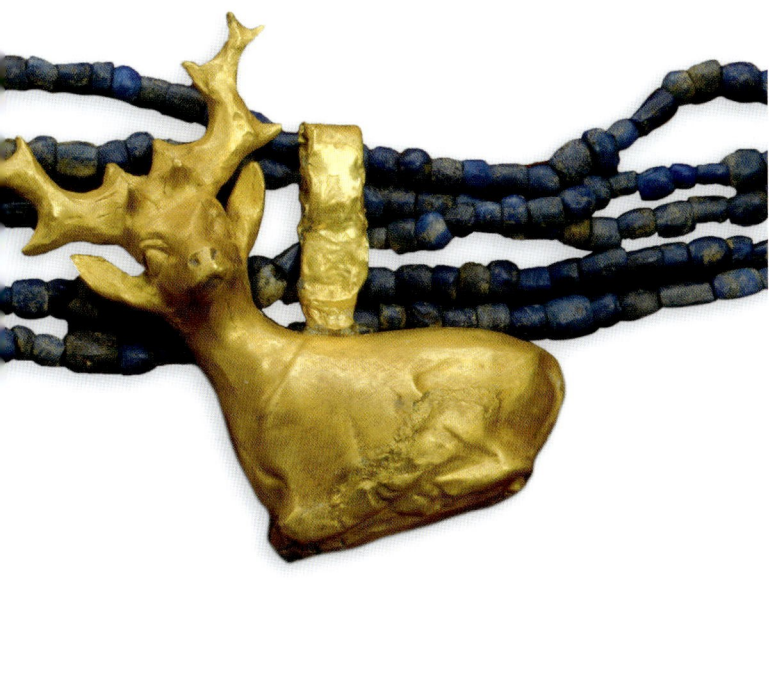

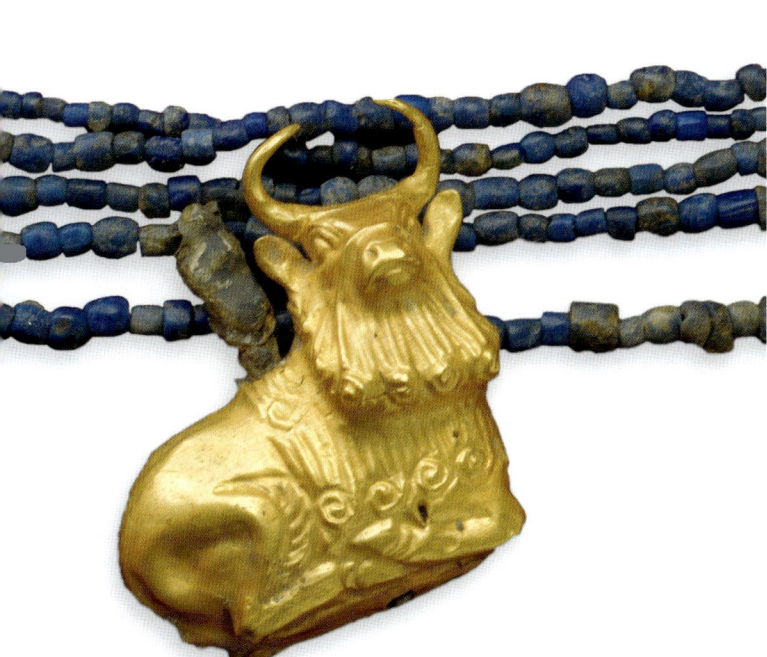

Puabi's Diadem(s): The Deconstruction of a Mesopotamian Icon

Holly Pittman and Naomi F. Miller

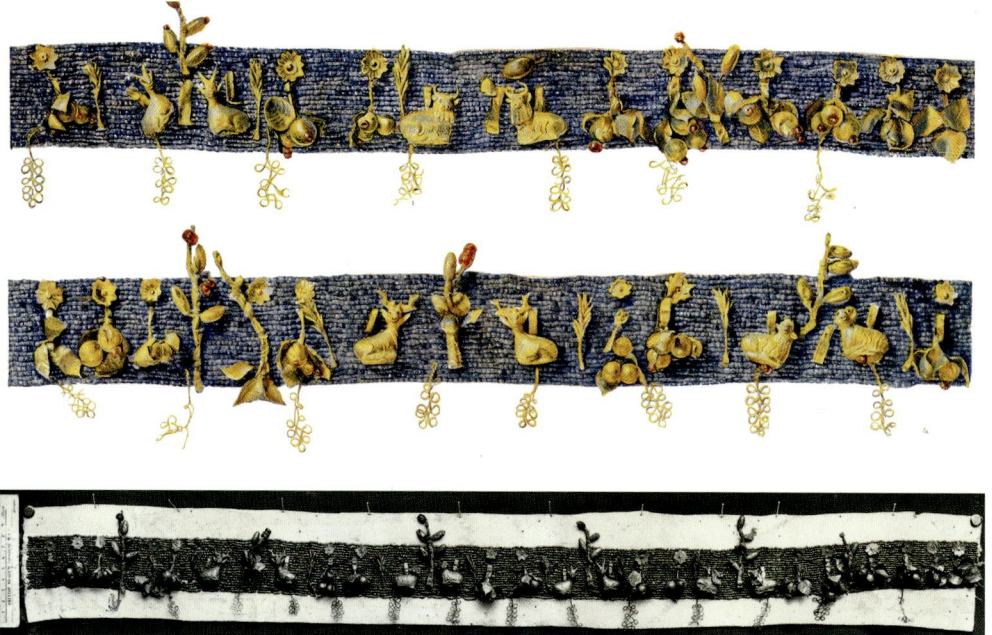

Fig. 4-1a. Watercolor of Puabi's "diadem" (Woolley 1934: pl. 146).

Fig. 4-1b. The original reconstruction of U. 10948, Puabi's "diadem." Photograph, ca. 1928–29. Penn Museum: 1131A. Courtesy of the University of Pennsylvania Museum of Archaeology and Anthropology.

Together with her famous headdress and cape, Puabi's "diadem" was one of the most widely recognized finds from Royal Tomb PG 800 at Ur (figs. 4–1a, b). By the time it was discovered in December 1927, Charles Leonard Woolley and his small team had already uncovered unimaginably rich concentrations of jewelry along with ritual equipment and weapons that had been buried with the deceased and the sacrificed in both royal and private graves. Even so, the overwhelming density of material in Puabi's tomb was stunning, including tens of thousands of beads, pendants and amulets, cylinder seals, and other items of gold, silver, lapis lazuli, carnelian, shell, copper, calcite, and steatite. On her head, Puabi had an elaborate headdress including strands of beads arrayed across her forehead as a diadem. Among the spectacular finds was a dense concentration of beads and pendants that Woolley ultimately constructed as the queen's second "diadem." For decades this "diadem" stood in the literature and in the galleries of the Penn Museum as a comprehensible work of art that was comfortably incorporated into the grave's larger symbolic program. A reconsideration of this canonical object ultimately led to its deconstruction as a monolithic piece, and gradually to its current reconstitution as seven individual diadems (fig. 4–2). No other object from the Royal Cemetery has undergone such radical reassessment during the cumulative processes of retrieval, conservation, curation and exhibition, and research examination. The assemblage can now be appreciated as an entity potent in the Sumerian world of the second half of the third millennium BCE, as well as a work of art that transcends its context and elicits an aesthetic response across space and time.

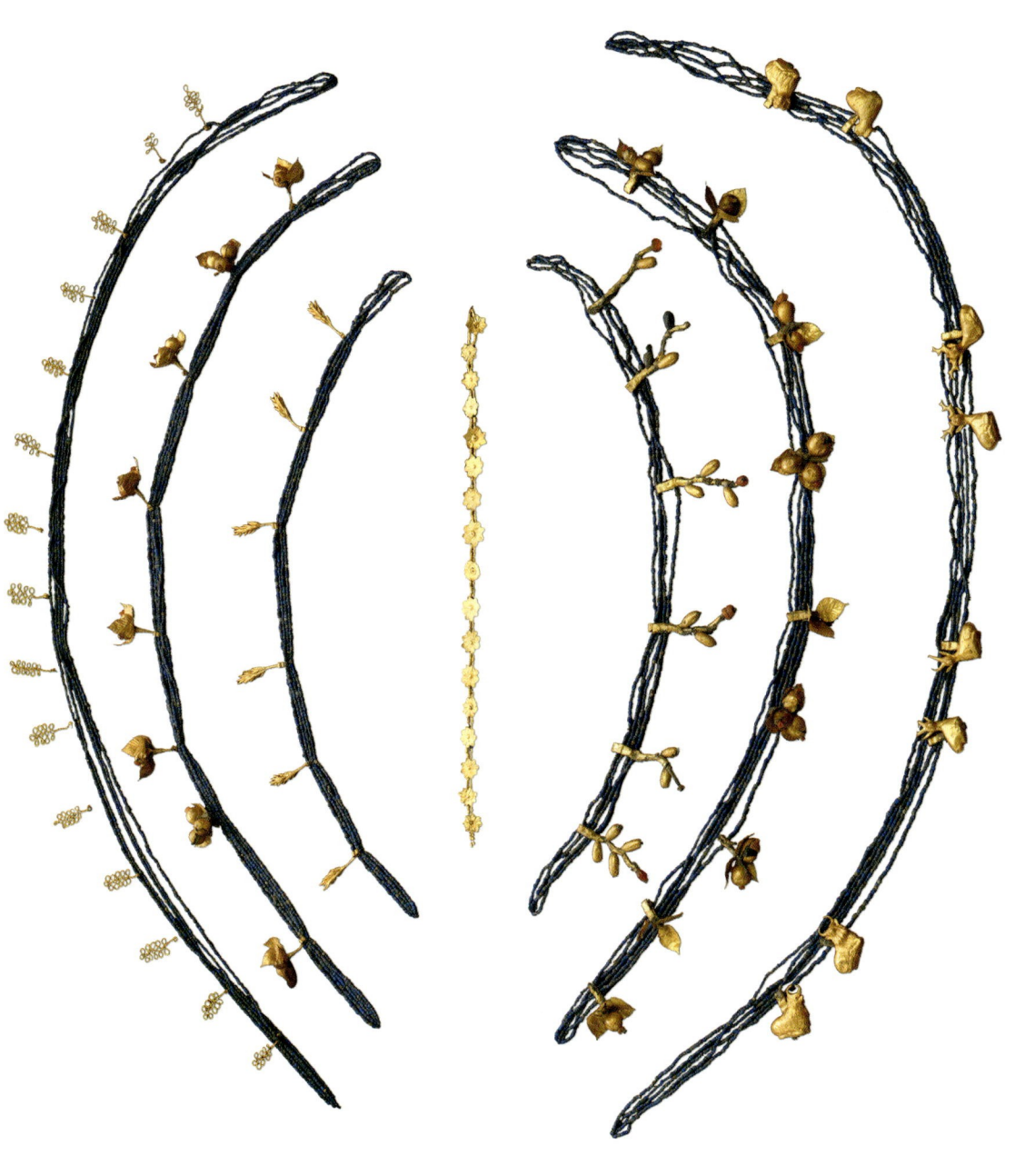

Fig. 4-2. Current reconstruction of Puabi's "diadem." Gold, lapis lazuli, bitumen. Ur, Tomb PG 800, ca. 2500–2300 BCE. Joint Expedition of the British Museum and of the Museum of the University of Pennsylvaniato Mesopotamia, 8th season, 1929–30. Checklist no. 137.

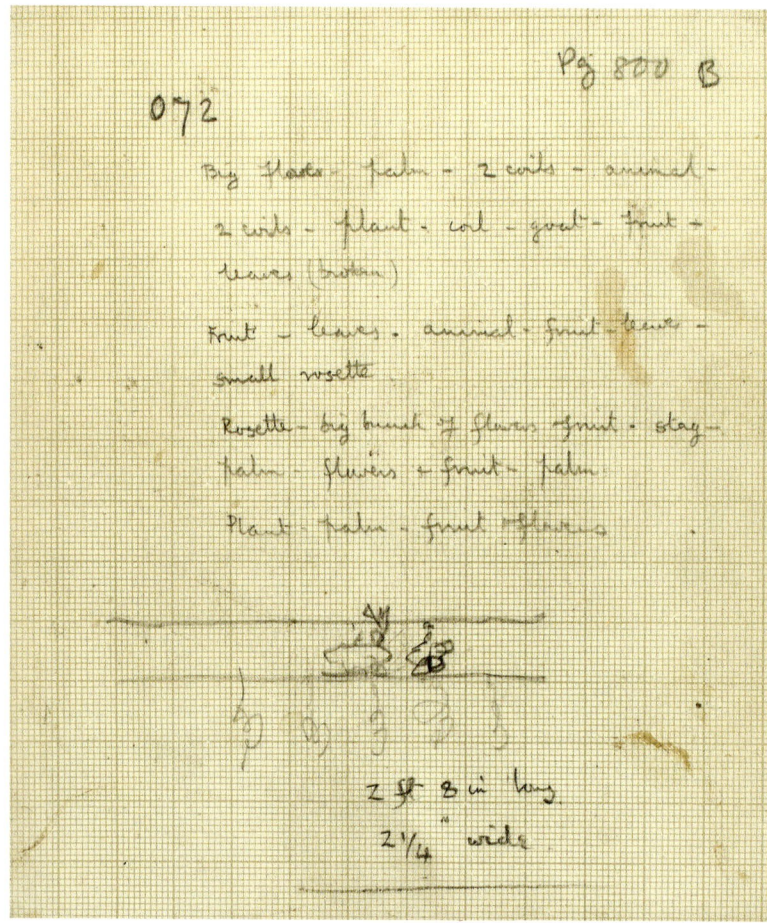

Fig. 4-3. Field card with a sketch of elements of Puabi's "diadem" in situ. BM: RC778-803, 226. Courtesy of the British Museum.

Excavation and Recording

When first uncovered, the "diadem" was a closely grouped concentration of gold, silver, and stone elements floating in the fill above the floor of the tomb. The assemblage was assigned two numbers in Iraq (object card 072 and U. 10948), but when it arrived in Philadelphia it was given the inventory number B. 16684. As of this writing, the assemblage has been renumbered as B. 16684.1 through B. 16684.71.

The jewelry elements assigned to the "diadem" were found beneath an intact white calcite vase (U. 10927; no. 065 on the field plan), one of a cluster of vessels, tumblers, and bowls against the northwestern wall of the tomb chamber (see fig. 3–7). Woolley gave this collection of jewelry three field numbers: Field card 070, which became U. 10980, was described in the final catalogue as "Beads: gold and silver double conoids. From the queen's cloak PG/800, Pl. 130 (*v.* 10975)." Field card 071 became U. 10981 and was similarly described in the final report as "Beads: large carnelian cylinders and date-shaped beads. From the queen's cloak. PG/800. Pl. 130. (*v.* U. 10975)" (Woolley 1934, 2: 566). Although found some distance from Puabi's body, these two groups of beads were probably assigned to her cloak because they were much larger than the other elements comprising the final group of beads and pendants.[1] Finally, field card 072 briefly described "a series of animal figures, flowers and plants set on minute beads of gold and lapis (U. 10948)." This group became U. 10948, and it is these elements that Woolley defined as a "diadem."

The first step in Woolley's thinking about this mass of jewels can be traced through the object cards, which identified 072 as a:

> Gold Crown formed of beads and figurines, etc. sewn onto a fillet of leather. The background was composed of minute beads of lapis and gold—the latter short tubular lengths. Against them stood out

A. 4 pairs of animals viz. 2 antlered stags ht .0035; 2 bearded bulls ht .003; 2 gazelles ht 0035; 2 rams ht 0025

B. small 8-petalled rosettes dia 0015

C. plant ornaments, viz. Ears of corn l. 0035; Pomegranates, bunches composed of 3 fruits and 3 leaves l. 004; plants with simple stems (gold leaf over silver) and gold and carnelian pods l. 006;

D. 8 Twisted wire palmettes l. 0035. For the order of them see Field Notes

The field notes report more detail and probably reflect the order in which Woolley observed the objects in the ground:

> 072
>
> Big flowers—palm—2 coils—animal—2 coils—plant—coil—goat—fruit and leaves (bottom)
>
> Fruit—leaves—animal—fruit and leaves—small rosette
>
> Rosette—big bunch of flowers fruit—stag—palm—flowers and fruit—palm
>
> Plant—palm—fruit and flowers

The sketch beneath this list depicts a long narrow strip with squiggles representing various elements; hanging from the strip are six further squiggles certainly denoting the palmettes. Below this drawing appear the measurements: "2 feet 8 inches long and 2 1/4 inches wide" (fig. 4–3).

This list and sketch—which records the figural pendants on a background of small lapis beads—offer the most detailed account of what Woolley saw in the ground and thus are the single most important records for the elements' subsequent reconstruction. In direct contradiction to his drawing, however, Woolley reported in the catalogue section of the excavation's final publication that the diadem "coiled in a circle and collapsed on itself (PG 800. Pls. 140-1. [P. CBS 16684])" (Woolley 1934, 2: 565). Thus, sometime between the initial sketch and the final publication, Puabi's gold crown had been transformed into a "diadem."

Gold Crown to Diadem—The Final Report

Woolley continued to consider the collection to be a headdress or "Gold Crown" in his report from the field of January 3, 1928.[2] Following his presentation of the queen's headdress, he introduced the crown, which was found "by the side of the bier," suggesting that it was closer to Puabi's body than he had previously recorded in the field report. He described the headdress as consisting of a fillet of thin leather on which small beads of gold and lapis were stitched. The beads created a backdrop for small gold rosettes, thin twisted wire, carnelian and gold representations of fruit and foliage, and four pairs of gold animal figurines.

It appears that the evolution from a gold crown to a diadem had occurred in London in preparation for the exhibition of the finds at the British Museum in June 1928, as reported in the *Illustrated London News* on June 22. Although we have no image of the object, the registration entry dated March 1, 1929, records that the Penn Museum received the diadem assemblage restored on a white ground in a long strip, but we do not know whether in London the strip was displayed flat, or in a circle to suggest its use as an ornament for the head.

When Woolley returned to work at the southwest end of the cemetery in 1929, he discovered an analogous find, in what would become PG 1618, that led him to understand the function of U. 10948 in Puabi's tomb as an extra diadem that had been arranged on a wig. In a letter from the field dated December 31, 1929, he described finding the remains of a wig to which were attached a gold earring and a gold frontlet, and then connected it to U. 10948.[3] This appears to have been the moment when Woolley concluded that if U. 10948 was indeed a diadem, then it must have been attached to a wig, and there must have been some kind of support (a shelf or small table), although nothing of the kind was observed in the initial excavation. By the time he composed the final report, Woolley was unqualified in his description of the wooden support near Puabi's bier on which he found the jewels making up a "magnificent diadem," such as the numerous small lapis lazuli beads that lay against a strip of white powdery material, which was presumed to be leather at one point, and which Woolley interpreted as the background to which the beads were sewn. He also described a number of gold ornaments that had retained their sequence and spacing in situ on top of the background of lapis lazuli beads. Based on what was found in PG 1618, but without specific archaeological parallels in Puabi's tomb, Woolley concluded that this was her spare diadem and was originally fixed to a wig placed alongside the queen in the grave.

Woolley's catalogue entry, as cited above, confirms that he embellished the field records, situating the diadem close to the body and adding the remains of a table and leather, neither of which were noted in his initial descriptions. The entry also reports that the diadem was coiled in a circle, although in the physical reconstruction Woolley had chosen to restore the elements in the configuration of the strip that he found and recorded (fig. 4–1b).

Other Diadems in the Royal Cemetery

The diadem found in PG 1618, which served as the functional archetype for U. 10948, was for a male and consisted of simpler elements than those of Puabi's assemblage. In the final report Woolley elaborated on the description provided in the earlier field report, providing the exact find spot of the man's diadem in the southeast corner of the coffin, behind the skull and on top of a fibrous dust, which he believed to have been human hair. Additionally, Woolley listed the diadem's components, including a fillet of gold ribbon (U. 13790) and two hair rings of spirally coiled gold wire (U. 13791; Woolley 1934, 2: 129–30).

Woolley also reported that fragments from a diadem similar to Puabi's were found in PG 777, but "there the workmanship was distinctly poorer" (Woolley 1934, 2: 89). Although Woolley did not include a photograph or illustration in the final report, he recorded the individual elements of the headdress of the deceased: a silver broad-palmed comb ending in balls of lapis lazuli, silver hair ribbons, a wreath of carnelian and lapis lazuli beads with gold ring pendants, and the remains of a diadem that closely resembled Puabi's made up of small cylindrical lapis lazuli beads, gold and silver flower rosettes attached to pairs of gold leaves, and small silver-wire palmette pendants, all of which were crushed and decayed but which were undoubtedly, in his view, used in a diadem (U. 9786-7; Woolley 1934, 2: 57; see fig. 4–4 as displayed at the Penn Museum in the 1930s). PG 777 was badly disturbed and looted in antiquity so it was not possible to determine whether the diadem was worn by the primary deceased or by a female attendant. Woolley felt it was likely to have been worn by the primary deceased because the diadem is comparable to Puabi's and because no attendant was found wearing

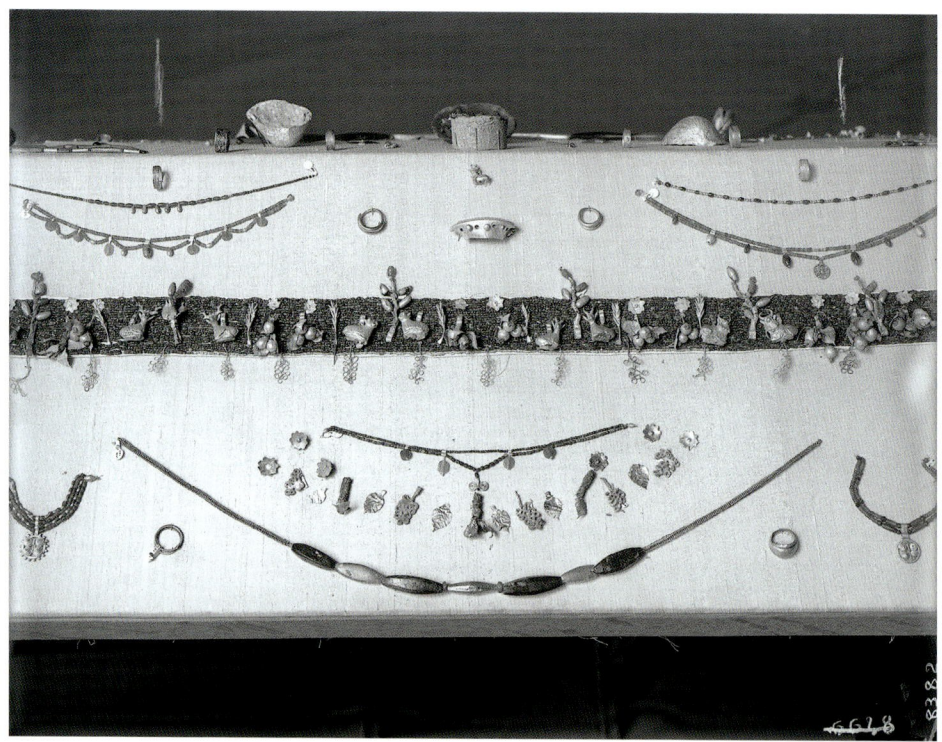

Fig. 4-4. Showcase for Puabi's "diadem" and the diadem from PG 777, at the Ur Gallery, Penn Museum, 1930s. Courtesy of the University of Pennsylvania Museum of Archaeology and Anthropology, Penn Museum: 8382.

anything similar (Woolley 1934, 2: 57). Although there were no animal pendants, the vegetal elements on the object seem comparable to those of U. 10948, and the small palmette pendants in silver wire are identical in form to those found in Puabi's tomb.

In his letter of December 31, 1929, Woolley also observed a close similarity between Puabi's diadem and the cluster of jewelry found near the body of Meskalamdug in PG 755. In the final report this cluster comprised a gold pin (U. 10005), a number of coiled-wire hair rings (U. 10019), a gold finger ring (U. 10029), silver finger rings (U. 10030), a coil of silver ribbon, gold and lapis triangles (U. 10017), a wreath of gold leaves hung from a double chain of lapis and carnelian beads (U. 10027), a wreath of silver ring pendants (U. 10026), gold and lapis beads (U. 10028), two lapis lazuli amulets (a frog [U. 10008] and a ram [U. 1009]), a copper pin with a head in the form of a squatting monkey (U. 10010), and a lump of silver (U. 10012; Woolley 1934, 2: 158; see fig. 4–5). Woolley described the jewelry as of the kind carried only by women, and further suggested that the individual pieces were offerings made by a woman, since the tomb had no skeletal remains and gave no evidence of secondary interment or human sacrifice. It seems that what linked this collection of jewelry elements to Puabi's diadem was the presence of the two lapis lazuli amulets.

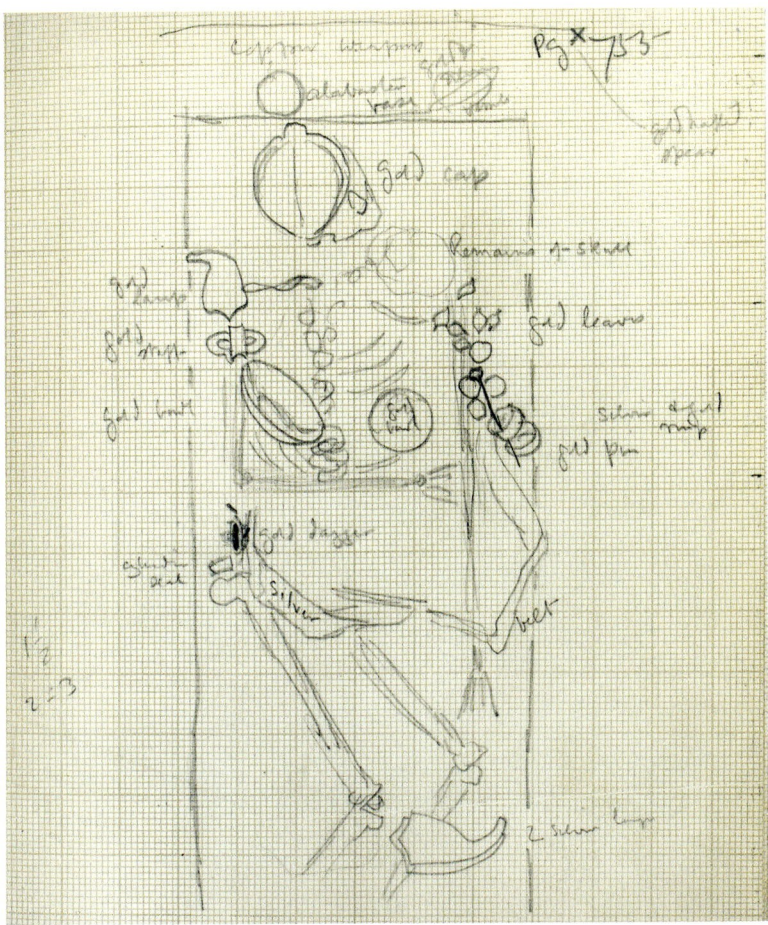

Fig. 4-5. Field card with a sketch of the cluster of jewelry found near the body of Meskalamdug in PG 755. BM: RC686-777, 148. Courtesy of the British Museum.

Several other "private" graves of the Early Dynastic cemetery also had jewelry comparable to the collection found in Puabi's grave. Woolley did not consider these graves "royal" because they lacked structures and sacrificed attendants. However, as with PG 755, some of these graves were certainly the last resting place for members of the so-called elite. One such grave, PG 1068, was that of the "Little Princess," who was interred with elaborate ornamentation surrounding her head (Woolley 1934, 2: 162–63).

PG 1130—which to judge from its location was ancillary to PG 1054 (fig. 4–6)—provides the best evidence to support Woolley's interpretation of the collection of ornaments in Puabi's tomb as parts of a headdress. He described a number of elements that serve as analogs for Puabi's "diadem," most strikingly, the gilded figures of recumbent bulls and pendants in the shape of fruit (Woolley 1934, 2: 165; see fig. 4–7). Interestingly, Woolley described the find in PG 1130 as a "bandeau" in the final report (2: 163) but

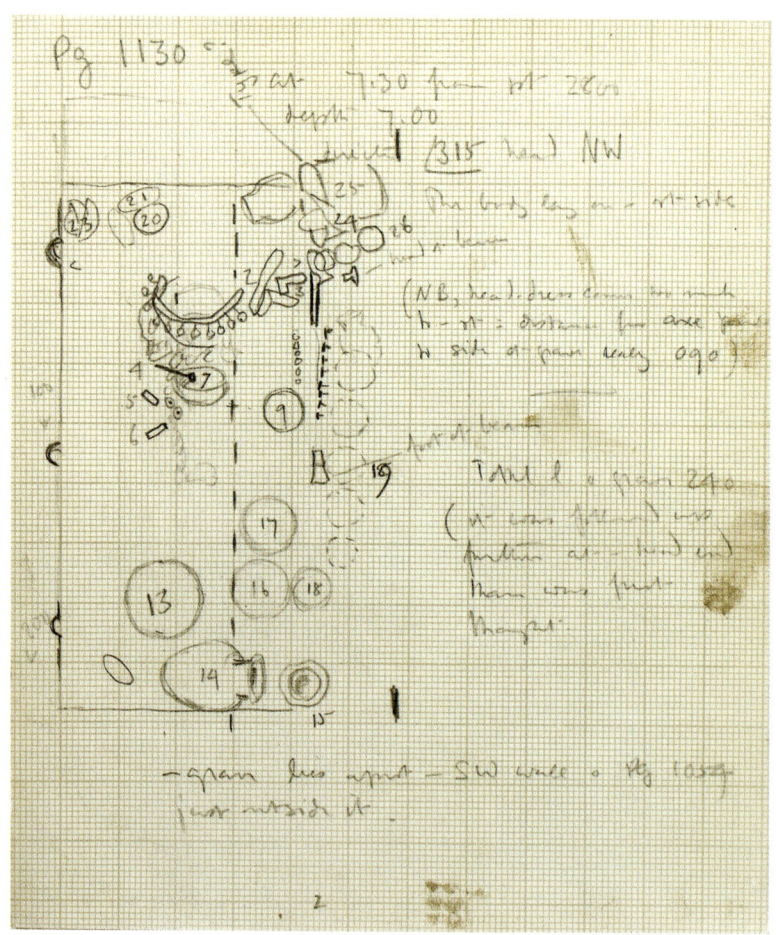

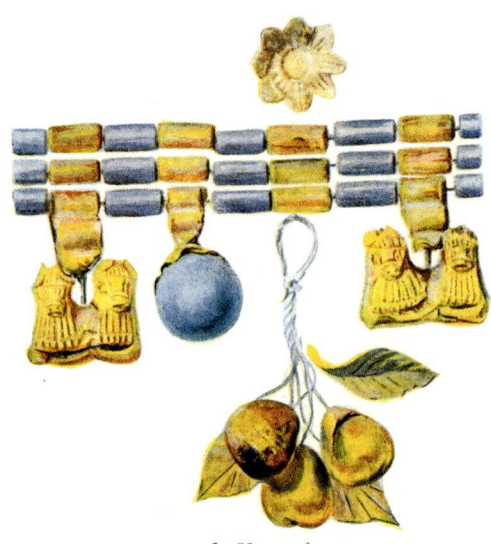

⅓. U. 11776

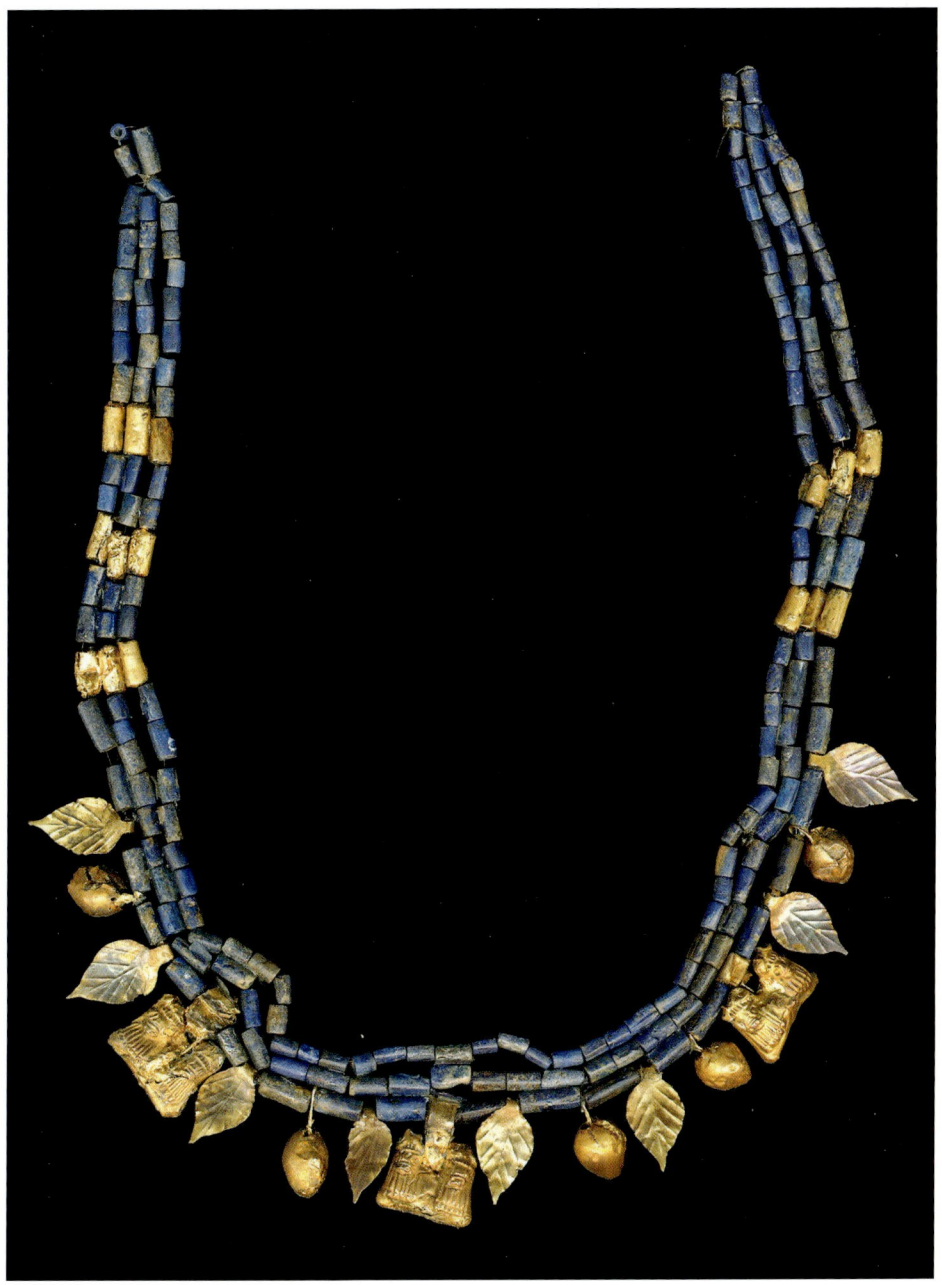

Fig. 4-6. Field card with a sketch of the location of jewelry, a diadem, and other tomb items in PG 1130. BM: RC1130-1237, 1. Courtesy of the British Museum.

Fig. 4-7. Watercolor of a detail of a diadem (U. 11776) from PG 1130 (Woolley 1934: pl. 142).

Fig. 4-8. Diadem (U. 11776) from PG 1130. Courtesy of the British Museum.

as a "diadem" in the catalogue: "Gold diadem consisting of a ground of gold and silver tubular beads on which hang figures of two seated gold bulls and bunches of gold and silver, etc, leaves and fruit" (2: 573, pl. 142; see fig. 4–8).

From "Diadem" to Diadems

At some point, probably in London, Woolley constructed the "diadem" with more than 9,500 lapis and about 50 gold beads sewn to a white cloth strip some 2 feet 8 inches long (fig. 4–1a). The pendants were apparently glued or sewn onto this beaded ground. While the arrangement does not exactly match what he described in the field, it does suggest a patterned distribution of pairs of facing animals separated by an upright "branch" with fruit. The "ears of corn" were also oriented upright, while the "pomegranates" were deployed in pairs between the animal sets. Fifteen palmettes dangled beneath the lapis lazuli strip. This was a dazzling display of gold and carnelian on a lapis ground that would have encircled a wig just over 10 inches in diameter. While the iconography was incoherent, it was the abundance of wealth and striking colors that fascinated all who saw it.

Puabi's so-called diadem maintained its integrity as restored by Woolley for more than eighty years. It was first displayed in Philadelphia at the Penn Museum in the late 1920s (see the essay by Azara and Marín in this volume). When the Near East galleries were refurbished in 1983 under the supervision of Maude de Schauensee, that arrangement was retained (fig. 4–9), but for the first time the "diadem" was presented on a circular mount. For more than seven decades, Woolley's reconstruction was never closely examined, but rather was accepted as the most elaborate example of the "diadem" type.[4] That changed in the late 1990s when research for the traveling exhibition of the Royal Cemetery materials in the Penn Museum's collection called for a major reconceptualization (fig. 4–10).[5]

In preparation for the traveling exhibition, the curators Richard Zettler, Donald Hansen, and Holly Pittman led a graduate seminar that focused on the archaeology of the cemetery and various categories of objects to be included in the exhibition. Participants examined pieces to prepare them for conservation and display. Looking closely at the "diadem," it became obvious that Woolley's reconstruction made no sense. The most obvious clue to the disjunction between the elements and his reconstruction was the relationship between some of the pendants and the lapis lazuli ground on which they had been placed. While the animal pendants were logically arranged so that the bales (loops for suspension) attached to the back of each animal were at the top, it was apparent that the vegetal elements—in particular the "branches of shrubs in gold with gold and carnelian pods or fruit" and "ears of corn in gold"—had been attached to the ground of lapis beads upside down. Their bales were at the bottom, an untenable orientation for objects meant to be suspended from strings that passed through each opening of the multiple-bale system. Thus, it was decided that the pendants would be

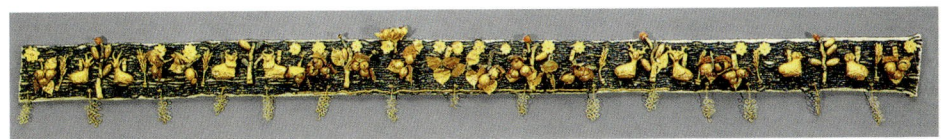

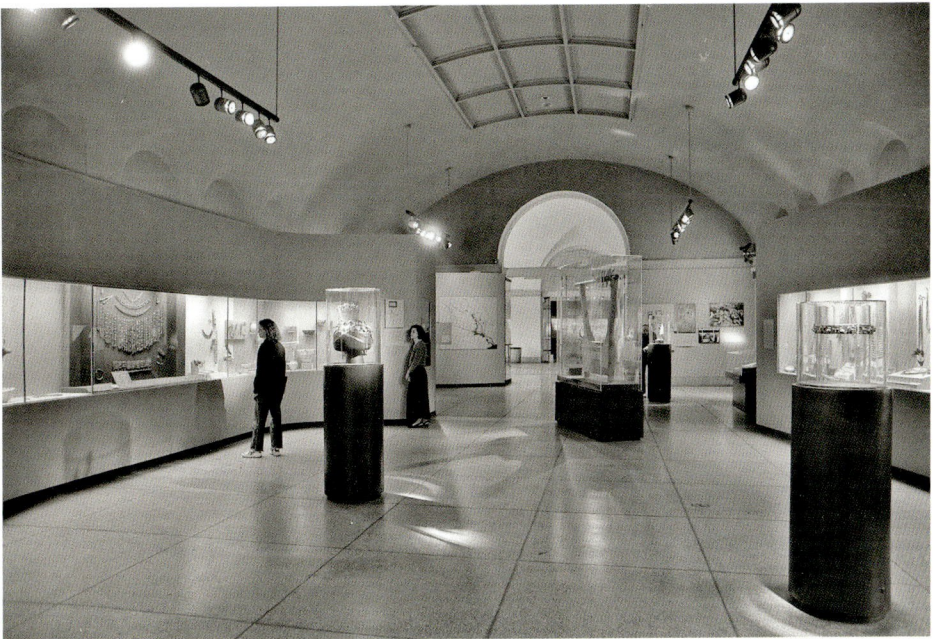

Fig. 4-9. Puabi's "diadem" as restored and on view in 1983 (Zettler and Horne 1993: 93, fig. 30).

Fig. 4-10. View of the Ur galleries at the Penn Museum, 1983. Courtesy of the University of Pennsylvania Museum of Archaeology and Anthropology, Penn Museum: 148678. Puabi's diadem is on display in the case in the right foreground.

taken off the lapis lazuli beaded ground, and rearranged grouped by type with respect to gravity. This is the presentation that was shown during the traveling exhibit.

It seems that what had informed Woolley's initial reconstruction most closely was indeed the arrangement he had originally seen in the ground, as recorded in his sketch of the jewelry and other artifacts. Indeed this is the most impressive aspect of Woolley's field recording. For the most part he understood that the arrangement in the ground did not represent the original configuration of objects when they were deposited, but rather their arrangement after any of the organic supports had deteriorated and caused the objects to come to rest in what finally became the fill of the tomb. When considered as a single object, Woolley's reconstructed "diadem" conformed to the outline of the crushed skulls that he had saturated with wax and then removed in one solid mass from the ground. Indeed the "diadem" as it had been reconstructed reproduced the drawing that Woolley made in the field.

What Woolley understood to be one object, essentially intact, has proven upon closer examination to more likely be a group of objects that, while related, almost certainly were never meant to be understood as a single "diadem." They have now become the "diadems," each with a different theme defined by their respective pendants (fig. 4–2).

The Pendants

It is the presence of figural pendants that separates U. 10948 from most other examples of jewelry assemblages found in the tombs. As Woolley reported, remarkably few amulets and amuletic pendants were discovered in the Royal Cemetery, and by far the largest concentration was found associated with Puabi. They are in all cases small, usually not more than 4 centimeters in length. Their subjects are animals, plants, and a third type comprising the geometric pattern of a circle of loops—Woolley's palmettes. The first task for the reconstruction that began in 1997 was to accurately identify the real-world referents of these pendants by evaluating the characteristics of present-day and ancient flora and fauna.

Naomi F. Miller, then a research scientist at the Museum Applied Science Center for Archaeology at the Penn Museum, was asked to identify the species depicted on the vegetal pendants. Although her results were not available for the catalogue that accompanied the traveling exhibition,[6] in a subsequent study she corrected and elaborated on Woolley's identifications.[7] The plant forms are somewhat stylized but clearly represent specific plants.[8] Woolley's "ears of corn" represent rather the inflorescence of the male date-palm (*Phoenix dactylifera*), a spadix with multiple branches. Woolley's "branches of shrubs in gold with gold and carnelian pods or fruit," when correctly oriented, are obviously bunches of dates on the stem. Finally, Miller confirmed Andrew Cohen's suggestion[9] that the three-leaved and three-fruited pendant Woolley described as a cluster of pomegranates with leaves most likely represented apples.[10]

The assemblage also includes seventeen gold rosettes (fig. 4–11), a common design element in Mesopotamian imagery from very early times that typically has eight segments, as here. Sometimes rosettes seem to represent a flower and/or a star, as in Puabi's headdress (see fig. 5–11). As early as the fourth millennium BCE, this motif may refer to the goddess Inanna in some instances.[11] Cohen argues that the rosettes should be identified as apple blossoms, associating them with the fully formed apples of the larger pendants,[12] noting that ancient Mesopotamians were familiar with apple cultivation. However, they would have known that apple flowers are pentamerous (with reproductive parts occurring in multiples of five). More generally, there are no eight-petaled flowers in nature.

Miller also tackled Woolley's twisted-wire "palmette" (fig. 4–12),[13] arguing that the form depicts the configuration of rope used to gather sheep for milking.[14] This unusual

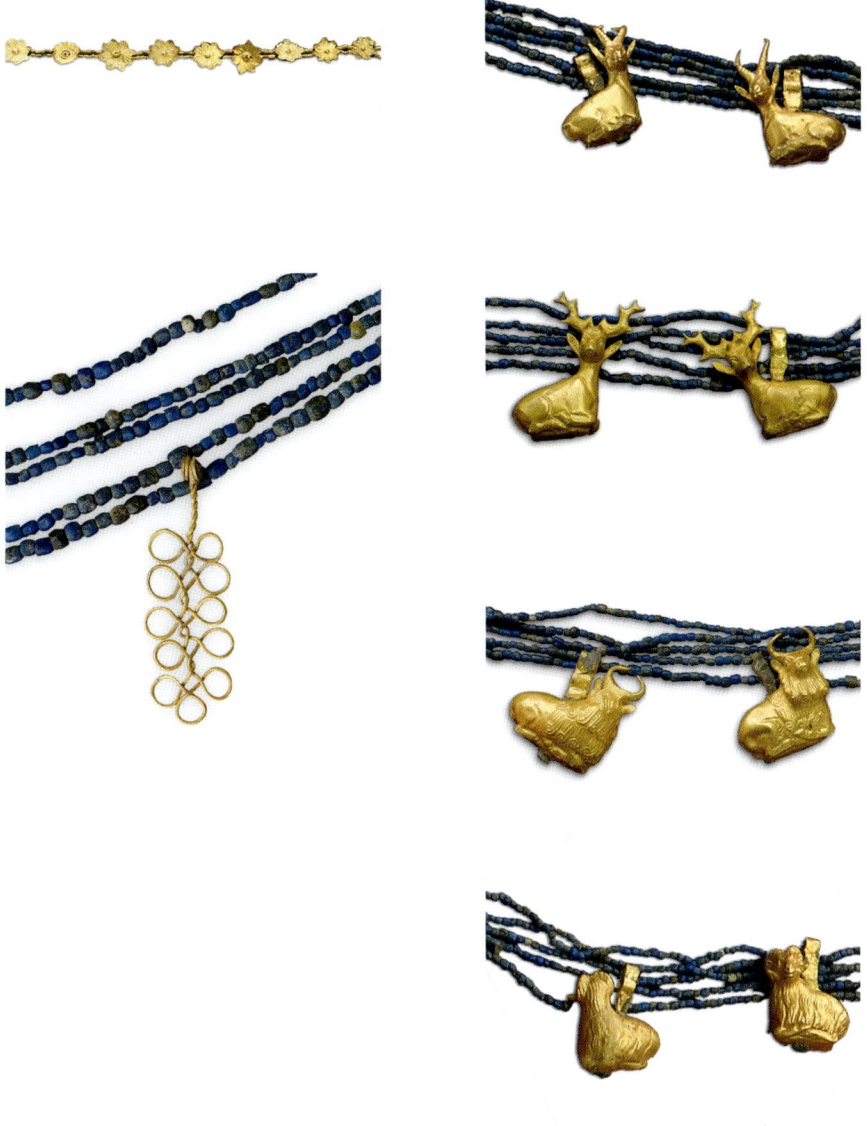

Fig. 4-11. Detail of rosettes on Puabi's headdress. Ur, Tomb PG 800, ca. 2500–2300 BCE. Joint Expedition of the British Museum and of the Museum of the University of Pennsylvaniato Mesopotamia, 8th season, 1929–30. Checklist no. 137.

Fig. 4-12. Detail of the "diadem" from tomb PG 800 (see fig. 4-2): wire "palmette."

Fig. 4-13. Gazelle amulets.

Fig. 4-14. Bearded stag amulets.

Fig. 4-15. Bearded bull amulets.

Fig. 4-16. Bearded ram amulets.

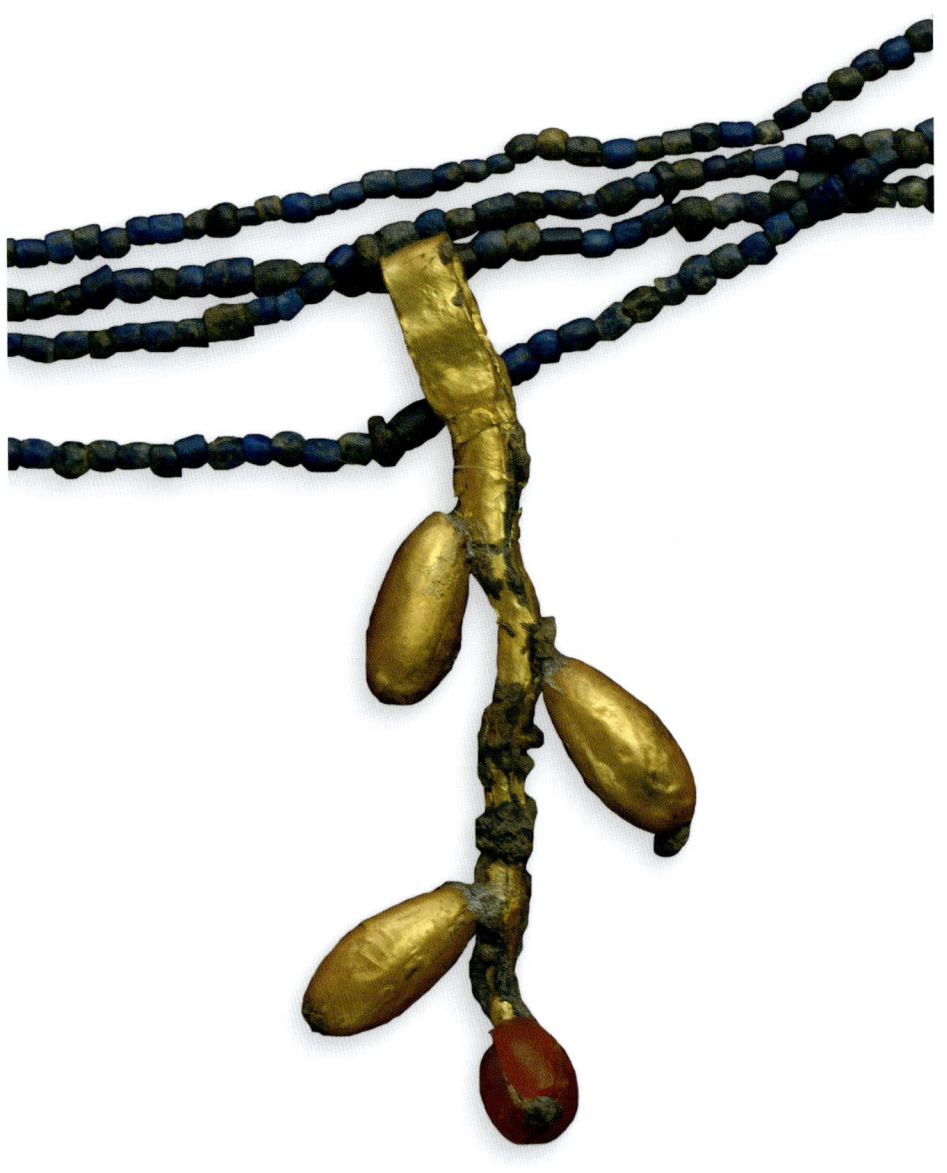

Fig. 4-17. Detail of fig. 4–2: fruiting female date inflorescences.

pendant type, in silver, was reportedly found associated with only one other burial/ grave (PG 777).

Superficially, the animal pendants appear to be nonproblematic representations. They are specific enough so that we can confidently propose identifications of gazelle, stag, bull, and ram (figs. 4–13 to 4–16). The gazelle is rendered in extraordinarily realistic terms, down to the sweet expression on its face. All of the animals are represented with

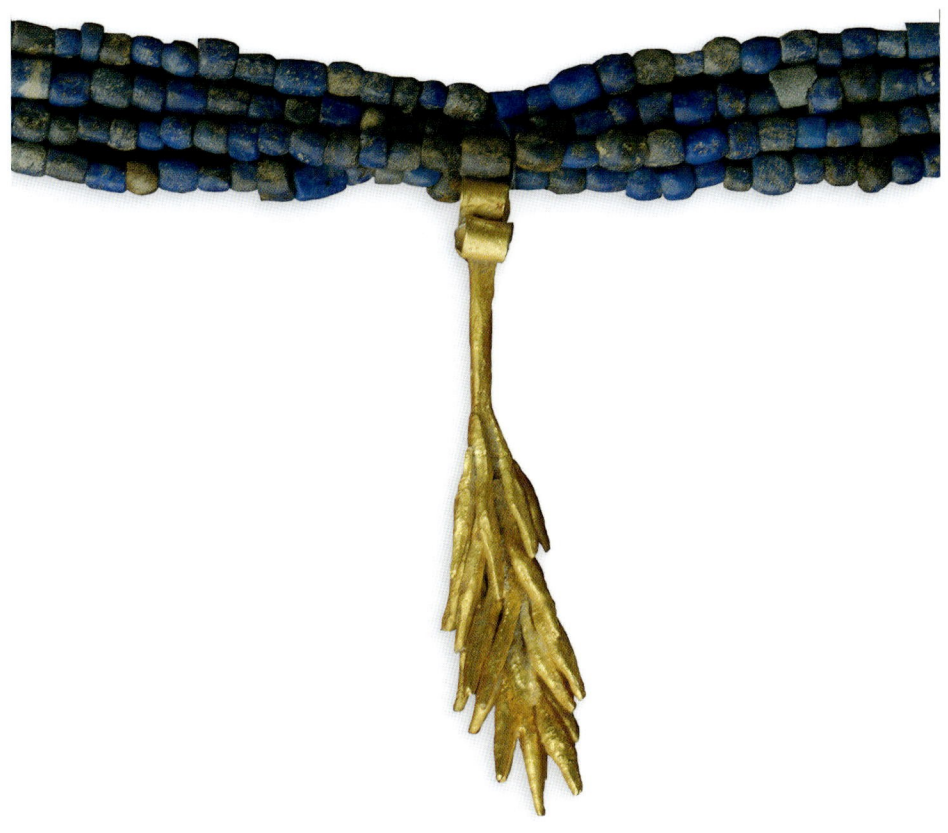

Fig. 4-18. Detail of fig. 4–2: male date spadix inflorescences.

horns, which signify maleness. Although adult female gazelles do have horns, in most species they are shorter than those of their male counterparts.[15] The bull is intriguing as it is represented with a hairy chest and back but with a beard that is clearly false.[16] Since neither wild nor domestic bulls have beards, the bull pendants are most likely to represent a mythological character. In contrast to the gazelle, stag, and possibly the bull, the ram is recognizably a domesticated animal because of its large horns curved tightly against the skull.[17] It is clear from the artisans' depictions of the other animals that they had the skill to include projecting horns had they wanted to. Note that contemporary depictions of domestic rams on glyptic generally retain the representational tradition of broadly spread horns that had prevailed since the Uruk period.[18]

The seven groups that emerged from Woolley's composite make up the current reconstruction, based on the similarity of the bales and the subjects of representation. All of the animal pendants have the same system of suspension, with a long, wide double loop attached to the center of each animal's back, and each hangs from two strands of lapis beads. Although expertly rendered in the round, the pendants were arranged

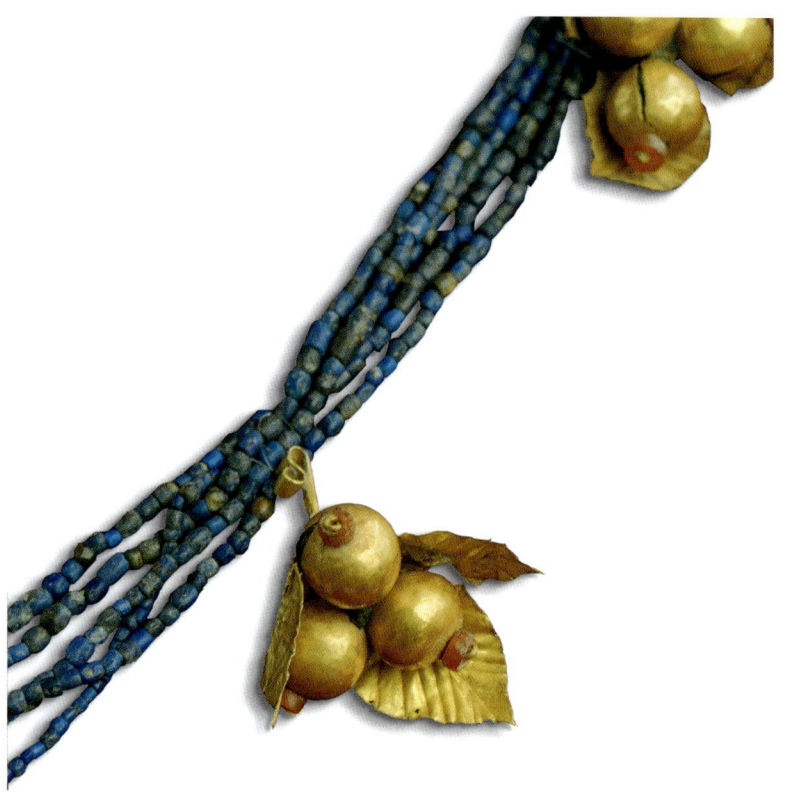

Fig. 4-19. Detail of fig. 4–2: apple clusters with large bales.

in facing pairs, but the original relationship of each set cannot be determined from Woolley's records. The vegetal pendants are more diverse. The fruiting female date inflorescences (fig. 4–17) are larger than the other pendants, have two loops for suspension, and hang from two strands. The male date spadices (fig. 4–18) have two small suspension loops and hang from two strands. Judging from the size of their bales, the apples belong to two groups. Eight of the clusters have the larger bales (fig. 4–19) that match those of the male date inflorescences. The other eight have smaller bale systems identical to the bales of the female date inflorescences. The rope twists have single suspension loops constructed of wrapped wire. Finally, the rosettes (see fig. 4–11) have a completely different system for attachment, consisting of a single hole in the middle of the blossom, suggesting that, uniquely among the elements, they might have been sewn onto a backing of some sort.

It seems that the collection Woolley unified through his reconstructed "diadem" was instead an aggregation of separate, probably thematically and functionally related strings of lapis beads supporting distinct groupings of pendants. If when excavated they were distributed over a length of 2 feet 8 inches with a width of some 2 1/4 inches, it is likely that what he observed in the ground was an ensemble of jewelry that had once been wrapped in leather or cloth. Included in that ensemble must also have been the gold and silver conoid beads (070) and the large carnelian cylinders and date-shaped (i.e., ovoid) beads (071) that Woolley assigned to the queen's cloak. Because they were of an entirely different type, he apparently did not associate them with 072, which had no large beads of any kind. However, once we deconstructed the "diadem" into a number of individual pieces, it was possible to consider them as belonging to the assemblage of jewelry that was not on the body of the dead queen, but was rather deposited under the vessels along the wall of the chamber. Indeed, it is in this new configuration that analogs found within the cemetery can be evaluated, shedding light on the possible function of the ensemble. The closest analog is clearly the "bandeau" found across the head of a deceased in PG 1130. Accurately reconstructed by Woolley, with the bull and apple pendants suspended among lapis and silver beads, this object was indeed worn as a head ornament. PG 777 had a related construction with only vegetal pendants, including the only other examples of the "palmettes," this time in silver. Finally the mass of jewelry found next to the body of Meskalamdug in PG 755 compares to the final deposition of the "diadem" ensemble in PG 800. In both cases, pendants were found associated with masses of small beads in lapis and gold. It seems that as the strings of the various ensembles disintegrated, the small beads fell beneath the larger figural pendants and the pendants all fell in on each other, creating the impression—preserved in Woolley's drawing—of a single item with all of the pendants attached to it.

The Diadem Group as a Work of Art

As a themed group of diadems, the ensemble is a work of art that both provokes an aesthetic response and carries meaning. This was true in the time of Queen Puabi, for whom those strands of beads and pendants were carefully wrapped and placed by her side, and it continues to be the case for modern viewers. There are two ways in which the so-called diadem assemblage can be understood in aesthetic terms. The first concerns its materials and the superb quality of its workmanship. The second delves more deeply into the symbolic meaning that the pendants carried for the Sumerians.

Through textual evidence and selected examples, Irene Winter has introduced the issue of "aesthetics" into our consideration of ancient Mesopotamian artifacts. In a diachronic consideration of the aesthetic value of lapis lazuli, she demonstrates that its deep-blue, lustrous quality was associated with divinity and royalty.[19] Other scholars have noted that lapis was believed to have special magical powers.[20] Carnelian and gold also had high aesthetic value for the ancient Sumerians. The goddess Inanna is associated with these materials through the valence of abundance and fertility; her significance in terms of the iconography will be discussed below. The preponderance of lapis in the Royal

Cemetery tell us both that it was highly prized as a material, and that at the particular moment of the Royal Tombs there was an abundance of these prized materials that required they be taken out of circulation in bulk to make way for additional quantities. Charles Redman and Andrew Cohen[21] have understood the extraction of wealth from circulation among the living as a conscious strategy among the ruling elite during this period, intended to define its status and contribute to the process of the emergent institution of kingship. Certainly what is preserved in the Royal Cemetery is the residue of elaborate ritual processes undertaken at the highly dangerous and liminal moment of the death of a key player in the political and religious hierarchies.

Winter has also considered the positive aesthetic value for the Mesopotamians of craftsmanship of "surpassing" quality.[22] While the texts in which these values are expressed do not date to the period of the Royal Cemetery, Cohen observes that "objects such as the spangling diadem (or set of apparel) from PG/800…with its gold and carnelian plant forms and animals sewn to a background of lapis lazuli beads, is captivating to us and must have been equally so when seen on a corpse as part of a larger ensemble of jewelry."[23]

Archaeologists commonly assume that the placement of grave goods in a burial carried cultural meaning. This could include notions of an afterlife in which the items would have been used. Alternatively, burial goods could have reflected the status and position of the deceased in life, perhaps associated with an assumption that they would maintain that status in the afterlife. For Mesopotamia in general, and Puabi in particular, we may ask: were the items meant to signal her elite status in life, or were they included for her personal use after death? Although recorded several hundred years after the Royal Cemetery,[24] several Mesopotamian literary texts concern death and the Netherworld, and it is possible that the iconography of grave goods referred to beliefs about the afterlife.

Scholars have occasionally compared the rich jewelry found in the graves of the Royal Cemetery to a Mesopotamian myth that records Inanna's descent to the Netherworld, in which she prepares for her visit by dressing in her finery—that is, the *mes*, or the fundamental powers of the cosmos. We are told that the gatekeeper to the Netherworld demanded that Inanna relinquish her regalia, one piece at a time. Thus, when she arrived in the presence of Ereshkigal, queen of the Netherworld, Inanna was completely naked, and thereby stripped of all her powers. Dina Katz has convincingly argued that while Inanna arrived in the Netherworld naked, not all deceased are required to be unclothed when they reached the afterlife.[25] Thus, there is no reason to think that the diadems of a mortal queen would have been demanded for her entry into the Netherworld.

Another text describes the death of Ur Namma, the founder of the third dynasty of Ur, who brings gifts to the primary gods of the Netherworld so that he can join them in their pantheon. This myth makes no reference to a requirement of naked entry into the

Netherworld, but it does suggest that gifts were presented to the gods by high-ranking deceased. Nevertheless, there are no grounds on which we can argue that any of the materials found in the Royal Cemetery should be considered as gifts for Netherworld denizens. In ritual texts contemporary with the Royal Cemetery, offerings and gifts are presented to the gods by all categories of mortals. However, the arena for this gift giving is always within the context of the temple or the house of the god, and usually such gifts are inscribed with the name of the donor and a dedication to the deity. Nothing from any of the Mesopotamian burials from any period has been identified as a gift that the deceased would bring to the gods of the Netherworld. Gifts to the gods are instead the obligation of the living, and take the form of food and libations accompanied by elaborate and highly prescribed ritual performances.

In her original discussion of the date pendants, Miller commented that "it is perhaps not surprising that so much jewelry symbolic of fertility and renewal was put in a tomb that is practically an advertisement for the good life in the afterlife."[26] Cohen's compelling 2007 study, *Death Rituals and Royal Ideology,* considers a symbolism for the Puabi pendants that assumes, but does not require, them to be part of a single object. Specifically, he interprets the ensemble as a celebration of abundance and fertility, with reference to Inanna and her consort, Dumuzi. Cohen observes that both dates and apples are associated with Inanna and applied metaphorically to sexuality, abundance, and fertility. Apples are mentioned in the incantations associated with male potency. The apple tree sometimes serves as a metaphor for the god Dumuzi, the lover of Inanna in many Sumerian literary works, who is sometimes referred to as a date farmer as well as a shepherd. Miller suggested that the wire pendants, too, might refer to Dumuzi's flock.[27] Since the Mesopotamians imagined the Netherworld as a dreary place with no food, water, or other joys of the living, it may be that the *absence* of sheep in the underworld is represented, given the funerary context of the objects.[28] Although the plant imagery is consistent with tropes of fertility and abundance, the specter of death should not be dismissed in this funerary context. Indeed, the animal pendants bring that idea to the fore.

Of the four male animals, the bull least resembles an actual creature. In temperate climates domestic bulls do not have hairy chests, but it is not clear whether the gold pendants are meant to depict aurochs (wild ox), which became extinct in the seventeenth century.[29] The beard is clearly false, attached by a cord across its nose.[30] The sun god, Utu, is commonly depicted as a bull with a false beard. According to Polonsky, "Sumerian verbs used in connection with the lapis lazuli beard express that the beard was 'worn,' that it 'adorns,' and that it may be 'affixed' to the visage" of Utu.[31] Therefore, the bull pendants represent Utu, whom Enki "placed in charge of the whole of heaven and earth, the father of the Great City [the Netherworld]," as recorded in the myth "Enki and the World Order" (ETCSL c.1.1.3, lines 368–80).[32] He is the son of Enki, brother of Inanna, and therefore brother-in-law of Dumuzi. Moreover, Enki is the lord of the Abzu ("[cosmic] underground water"),[33] and his boat is named the "Stag of the Abzu."[34] In

"Gilgamesh, Enkidu and the Nether World" (c.1.8.1.4), Enki's boat goes to the Nether-world, while in other texts it plies the waters between heaven and earth, representing the quintessence of the liminal state between life and death.

The gazelle also figures in mythology related to the Netherworld. Cohen first recognized that it might represent Dumuzi.[35] The relationship between Utu and Dumuzi underlies the events of Dumuzi's dream (c.1.4.3): Chased by demons, Dumuzi calls out, "Utu, you are my brother-in-law, I am your sister's husband!...Please change my hands into gazelle hands, change my feet into gazelle feet, so I can evade my demons" (lines 165–73). Rams, too, are mentioned in Dumuzi's dream. As he envisions himself dead Dumuzi cries, "[M]y rams were scratching the earth with their thick legs for me" (lines 25–39). The scratching of the earth is a metaphor for mourning: "that your rams were scratching the earth...for you means that I shall lacerate my cheeks with my fingernails" (lines 56–69). These references suggest that the bearded bull, stag, and gazelle represent characters in the Dumuzi story: Utu, Enki's boat, and Dumuzi himself. In this context the ram may symbolize Inanna's mourning for her lover-consort-husband.[36]

Cohen also equates the diadem assemblage with a garment called the *suh*, which in the Early Dynastic period is said to be Inanna's head or neck band.[37] Texts describe this type as sometimes decorated with lapis lazui. Since we believe that the individual pieces of jewelry, in their newly reconstructed form, can now be understood to comprise U 10948, and could easily have served as headbands analogous to that found in PG 1130, it is possible that Cohen's interpretation of the *suh* is correct. It is also possible to extend this interpretation to the various sets of pendants. There were at least five annual rituals associated with the agricultural cycle, and there were others associated with the divine and with dead ancestors. From the Lagash texts, we know that elite females frequently sponsored banquets and feasts commemorating and celebrating various occasions. It is possible that the distinct strands of Puabi's diadem were related to distinct rituals in which she participated, some associated with Dumuzi and Inanna, others with the agricultural cycle, and others with dead ancestors. There is nothing to suggest that this jewelry was only for the burial chamber, and it could easily have been worn by the queen in life. In ancient Mesopotamia the themes of abundance and procreation—the primary responsibilities of the newly emerging political and economic elites—were reinforced and reiterated in every aspect of the world of both the living and the dead. Puabi's diadems can now be fully appreciated as a paradigmatic example of how multiple themes were signaled through works of art for the ancient inhabitants of Ur, and how they convey their meanings for the wider public today.

Endnotes

1   They continue to be associated with the beads on the cloak, and one (U. 10981) can be identified as the only strands having silver beads.

2   Ur, Iraq Expedition Records, Correspondence, Exp. V, Jan.–July 1927, box 2, folder 2, Penn Museum Archives.

3   Ibid., box 2, folder 5.

4   Maxwell-Hyslop 1971: 5.

5   Zettler and Horne 1998.

6   Pittman 1998.

7   Miller 1999, 2000.

8   Miller 2000.

9   Cohen 2005: 128–29.

10   Miller 2000: 154.

11   See the references in Barrett 2007: 25.

12   Cohen 2005: 128.

13   Among the denizens of the Penn Museum, this object type is fondly referred to as a "rug beater."

14   Miller 2013.

15   Wronski et al. 2010: fig. 2.

16   We are indebted to zooarchaeologist Katherine M. Moore for this observation. Cohen (2005) proposes an identification of the wisent (European bison); that identification is unlikely on morphological grounds as the shoulders of the wisent, like those of the American bison, appear humped.

17   According to Katherine Moore (communication with the authors, Oct. 30. 2014), "the combination of the long coat, the tight coiling of the horns, and the placement of the ears within the coil" make it virtually certain that the caprid is a domestic ram. Note that Cohen (2005) asserts that the caprid is a wild ram based on the curvature of the horns.

18   See, for example, Amiet 1980: figs. 1143, 1157.

19   Winter 1999.

20   See, for example, Benzel 2013.

21   Redman 1978; Cohen 2005.

22   Winter 2009. Woolley often remarked on the high quality of workmanship of the various objects found in the Royal Tombs. While he extolled the superb execution of the pendants in Puabi's "diadem," he observed that although "the craftsmanship of comparable amuletic pendants found in PG 777 was distinctly poor...the little animals from Shub-ad's headdress are exquisitely modelled, the plants and ears of corn are very charming, and the general effect is one of great richness and delicacy." Woolley 1934, 2: 89.

23   Cohen 2005: 151.

24   We follow Cohen's (2005: 29–36) particularly good discussion of how to apply the later stories to the interpretation of mid-third millennium symbolism.

25   Katz 1995.

26   Miller 1999: 30.

27   Miller 2013.

28   Ibid: 132.

29   Vuure 2005.

30   See also Zettler and Horne 1998: cat. 10 (harp ornament from Ur, St. Louis Art Museum, acc. no. 260: 1951).

31   Utu emerges from the Netherworld every morning at sunrise and decrees the fates and renders judgments. Polonsky 2002: 211.

32   Kramer 1960.

33   "The Pennsylvania Sumerian Dictionary," http://psd.museum.upenn.edu/epsd/index. html.

34   The sign form for the animal avatar for Enki's boat is dara$_3$, usually translated as "wild goat" with no further explanation. In the Warka sign list, one variant of DARA$_3$ ≈ ALIM$_x$ from Uruk IV is clearly a stag (Green and Nissen 1987: 184–sign 71). The boat-shaped lyre from the Royal Cemetery features a stag (Schauensee 2002); it, too, might represent Enki's boat, given a translation of DARA$_3$ as "stag."

35   Cohen 2005: 130.

36   Cohen (ibid.), too, points out the maleness of the animals. He identifies the ram as wild, but somewhat contradictorily implies that it is part of Dumuzi's (domesticated) flock.

37   Ibid.: 130–31. Cohen's argument holds whether it is based on Woolley's reconstruction or the current view that there are several diadems.

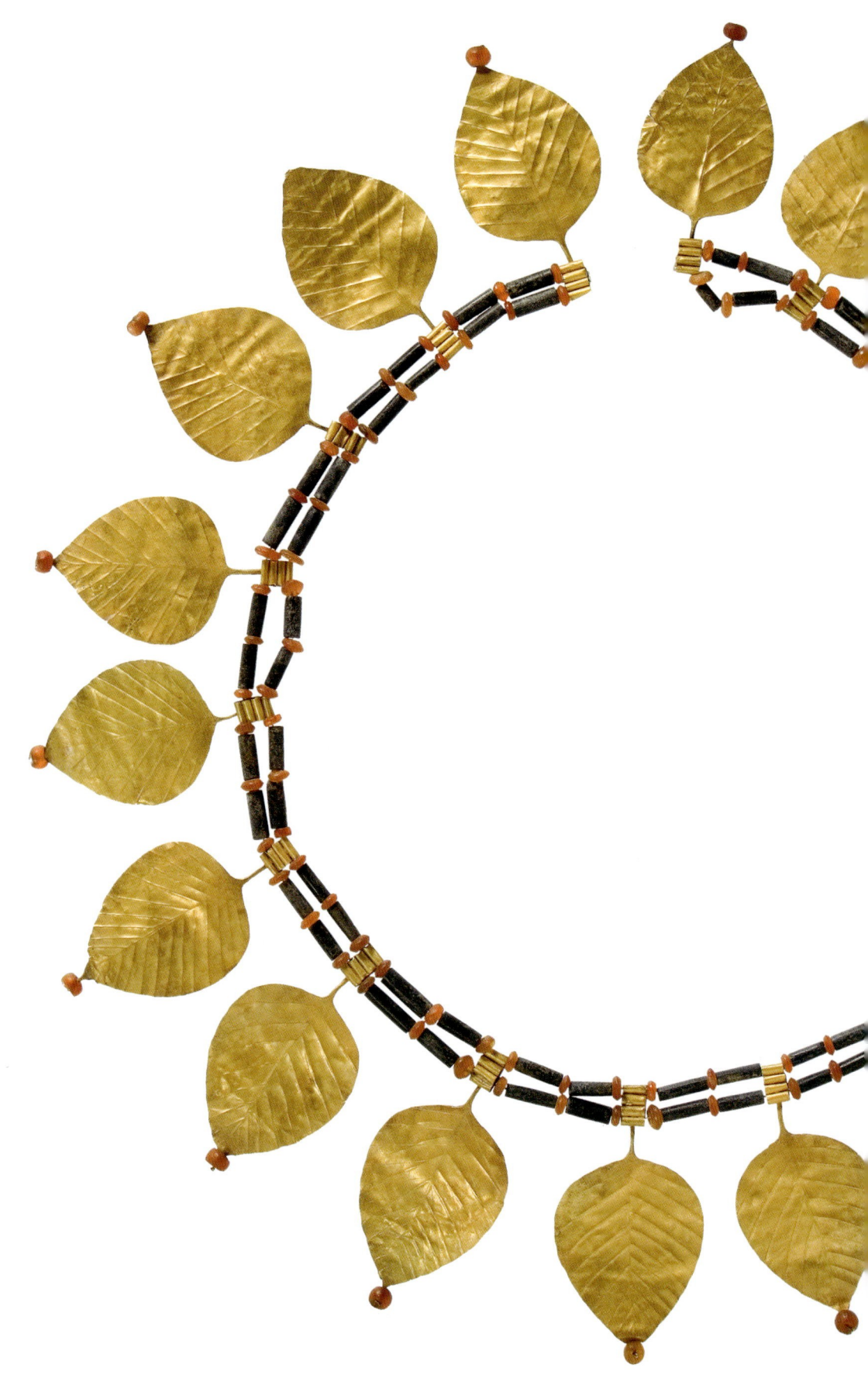

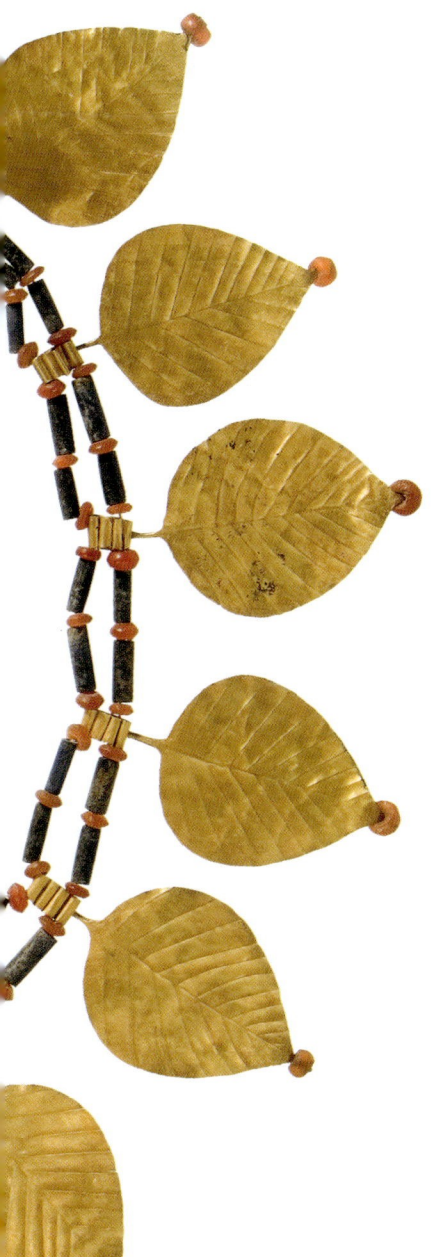

What Does Puabi Want (Today)? The Status of Puabi as Image

Kim Benzel

Introduction

The title of this essay quite deliberately and from the outset returns the question of who Puabi was and what she might have looked like to Puabi herself (fig. 5–1). I am consciously invoking the work of two scholars who have delved deeply into the nature of images: Zainab Bahrani and W. J. T. Mitchell.[1] In her work Bahrani defines what an image was in antiquity, while Mitchell does the same for a more general history of art and argues, along with Alfred Gell for example,[2] that images need to be considered as if they were animated beings, "driven by desire and appetites,"[3] rather than as inert or inanimate objects. Mitchell asks:

> Why is it that people have such strange attitudes toward images, objects, and media? Why do they behave as if pictures were alive, as if works of art had minds of their own, as if images had a power to influence human beings, demanding things from us, persuading, seducing, and leading us astray? Even more puzzling, why is it that the very people who express these attitudes and engage in this behavior will, when questioned, assure us that they know very well that pictures are not alive, that works of art do not have minds of their own, and that images are really quite powerless to do anything without the cooperation of their beholders?[4]

But in the case of Puabi, there are already problems with respect to her image, real or imagined, as it has been discussed for the nearly hundred years since her discovery. First, we must define what constituted an image and the aesthetic conception of it in Puabi's time versus ours.[5] Second, if images are dependent on interactions with their beholders, be they believers or nonbelievers, then how can we discuss any image of Puabi if she conceivably had *no* beholders, given that she was found dead and buried far underground and out of sight?[6] Is not every discussion about the image of Puabi, in whatever form one wishes to accept that image, ignoring that we, the discussants, are removing her from her original context? That is, are we not exposing an image that was in all likelihood never meant to be seen, or whose power lay not in the literal seeing of it? It is possible that neither her well-documented archaeological context nor her problematic reception into modern, Western aesthetics is doing Puabi or her image justice, since the simple fact of her archaeological discovery, even properly executed, may in this sense have manipulated or even missed the original intent of her image.[7] It is this line of questioning that gets to the heart of the exhibition *From Ancient to Modern: Archaeology and Aesthetics.*

5–1. Queen Puabi's headdress, beaded cap, and jewelry in their current reinterpretation and display at the University of Pennsylvania Museum of Archaeology and Anthropology. Gold and various stones. Ur, Tomb PG 800, ca. 2500–2300 BCE. Joint Expedition of the British Museum and the University Museum of the University of Pennsylvania, 6th season, 1927–28. Checklist nos. 109–12.

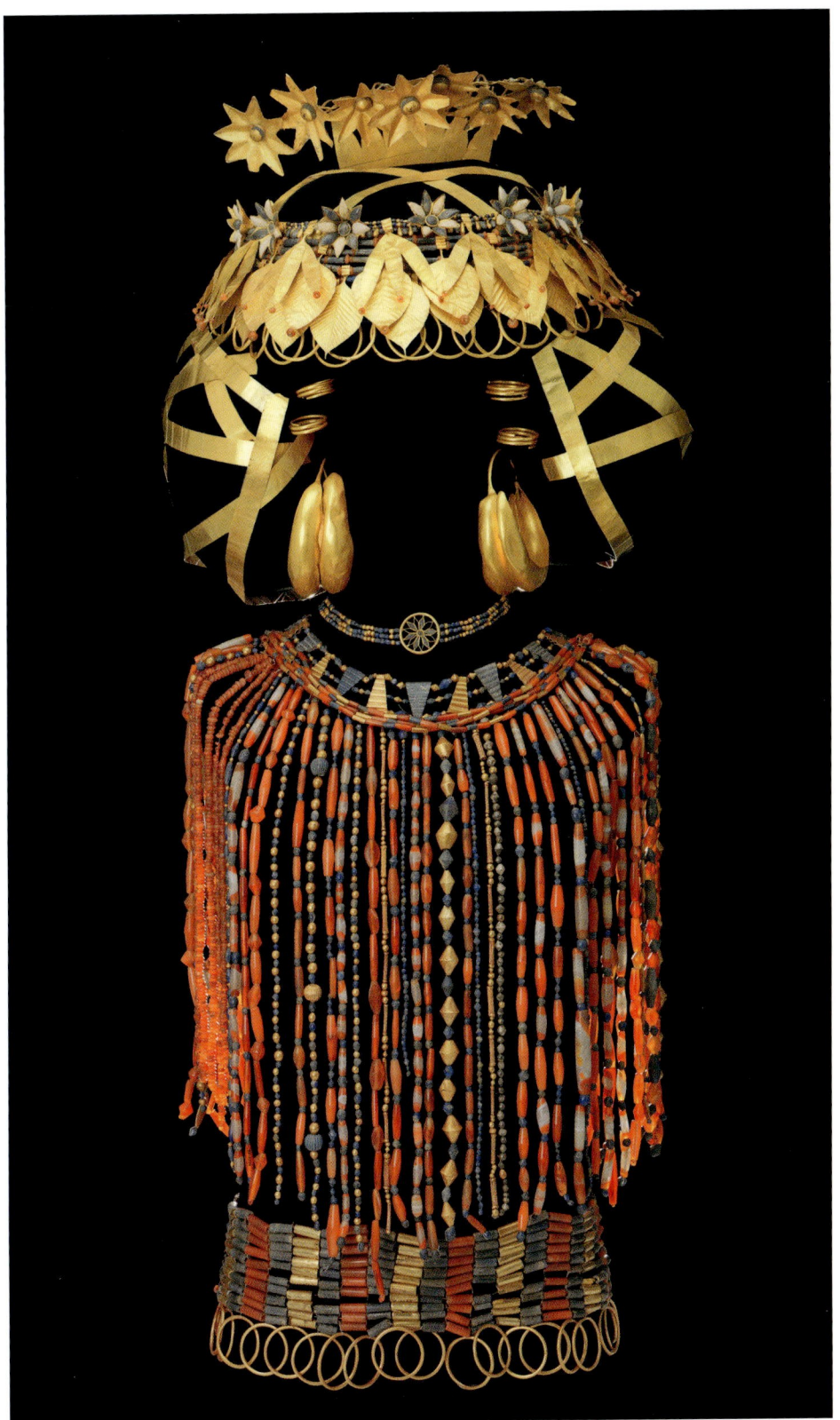

The exhibition aims to illustrate the multiple layers of meaning that a single object can convey over the course of its existence—from its creation to its final ancient context, its discovery, and finally its interpretation and cultural use by modern scholarship. In doing so, the exhibition investigates several iconic works of material culture from ancient Mesopotamia in ways that significantly contribute to the understanding of these works and their reception (and misplaced reception) in modern times. Indeed a good deal of the exhibition explores how the images on display and the archaeology and aesthetics associated with those images have at various times and in various ways led us astray. However, the exhibition adopts a particular and restricted definition of aesthetics, one that takes its cues from a primarily modern and Western definition that often sees itself as universal: "The notion of art itself is modern; ancient objects, such as those from Mesopotamia, were and could not be art for those who originally lived with them. They were not created to be perceived from a certain distance, to help people in antiquity think about their world, or to provoke the sensory yet distant relationship required for an aesthetic experience."[8]

It is true that looking at the Diyala sculptures or at Puabi—now that they have been excavated and are visible to us—through this lens of modern, Western aesthetics has been and remains a skewed enterprise, and that returning the works to their original state as archaeological (and functional) material is crucial to any proper understanding. Jean Evans and Jack Green have made a powerful case for this in their essay in this volume.[9] However, I would argue that both archaeology and aesthetics are capable of driving slanted interpretations, as can be seen all too well in the press coverage of the archaeological excavations at Ur.[10]

Mesopotamian Aesthetics

What is often missing in scholarly discourses on reception and aesthetics related to non-Western and premodern cultures are discussions of if, and how, each of those cultures might have defined or expressed *in their own terms* a particular sense of reception and/or aesthetics. Pointedly, one might ask if is there a distinctly Mesopotamian sense of aesthetics that differs in significant ways from a modern, Western sense, and if so, would that Mesopotamian aesthetic offer us a way of looking at Puabi in more culturally appropriate terms. What if a Mesopotamian aesthetic revealed that the archaeology associated with the discovery and the continued research on Puabi are just as stuck in a modern, Western interpretation as any reception of her was, and may still be, stuck in a modern, Western aesthetic?

Irene Winter has provided a foundational framework for the study of Mesopotamian aesthetics, in which she relies on the culturally specific vocabulary and syntax used in the ancient Mesopotamian textual record to express artistic value and experience.[11] Of particular interest with regard to the image of Puabi (which inherently and overwhelmingly

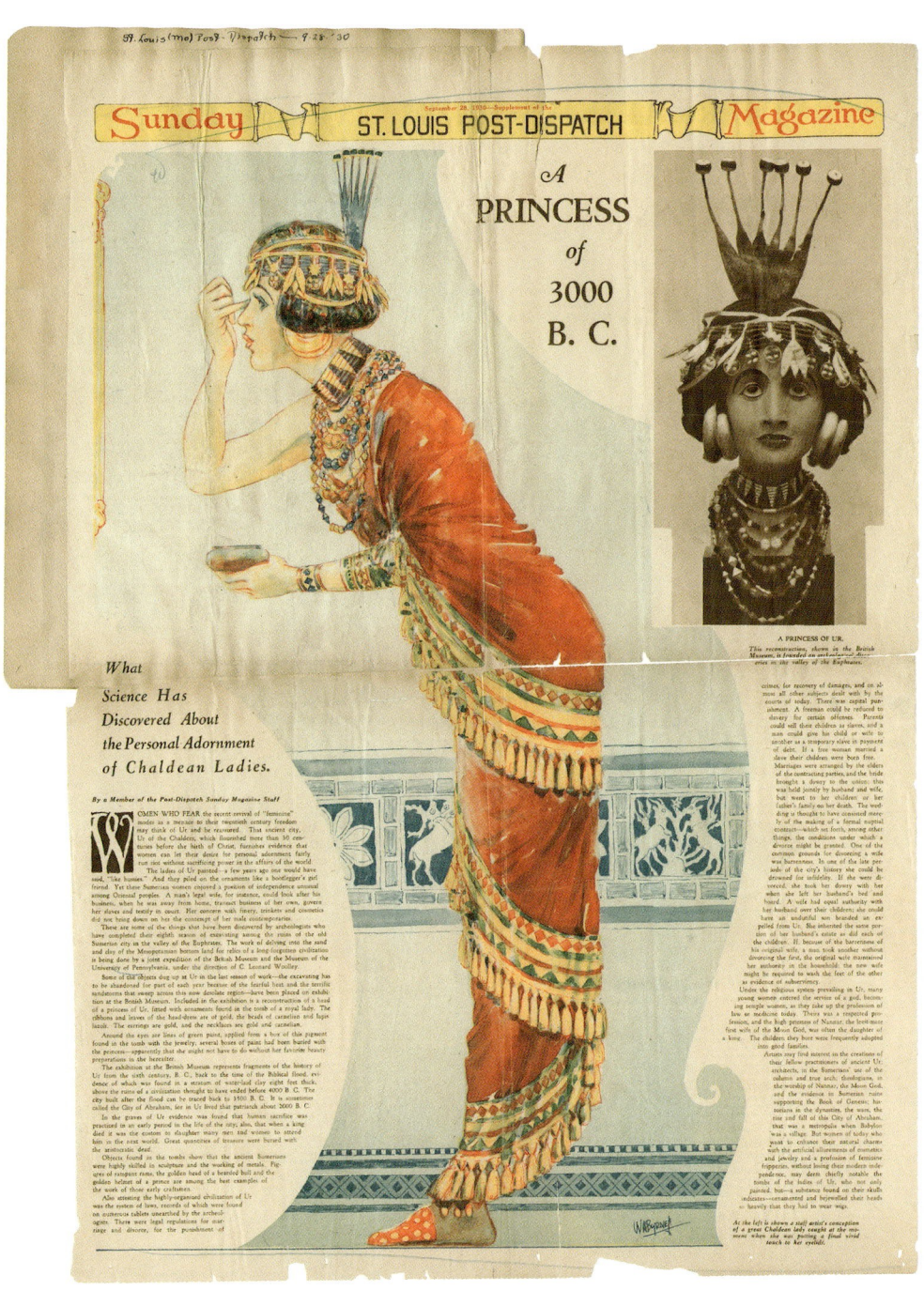

5–2. "A Princess of 3000 B.C.: What science has discovered about the personal adornment of Chaldean ladies." *St. Louis Post-Dispatch Sunday Magazine*, September 28, 1930. Courtesy of the University of Pennsylvania Museum of Archaeology and Anthropology. Checklist no. 95.

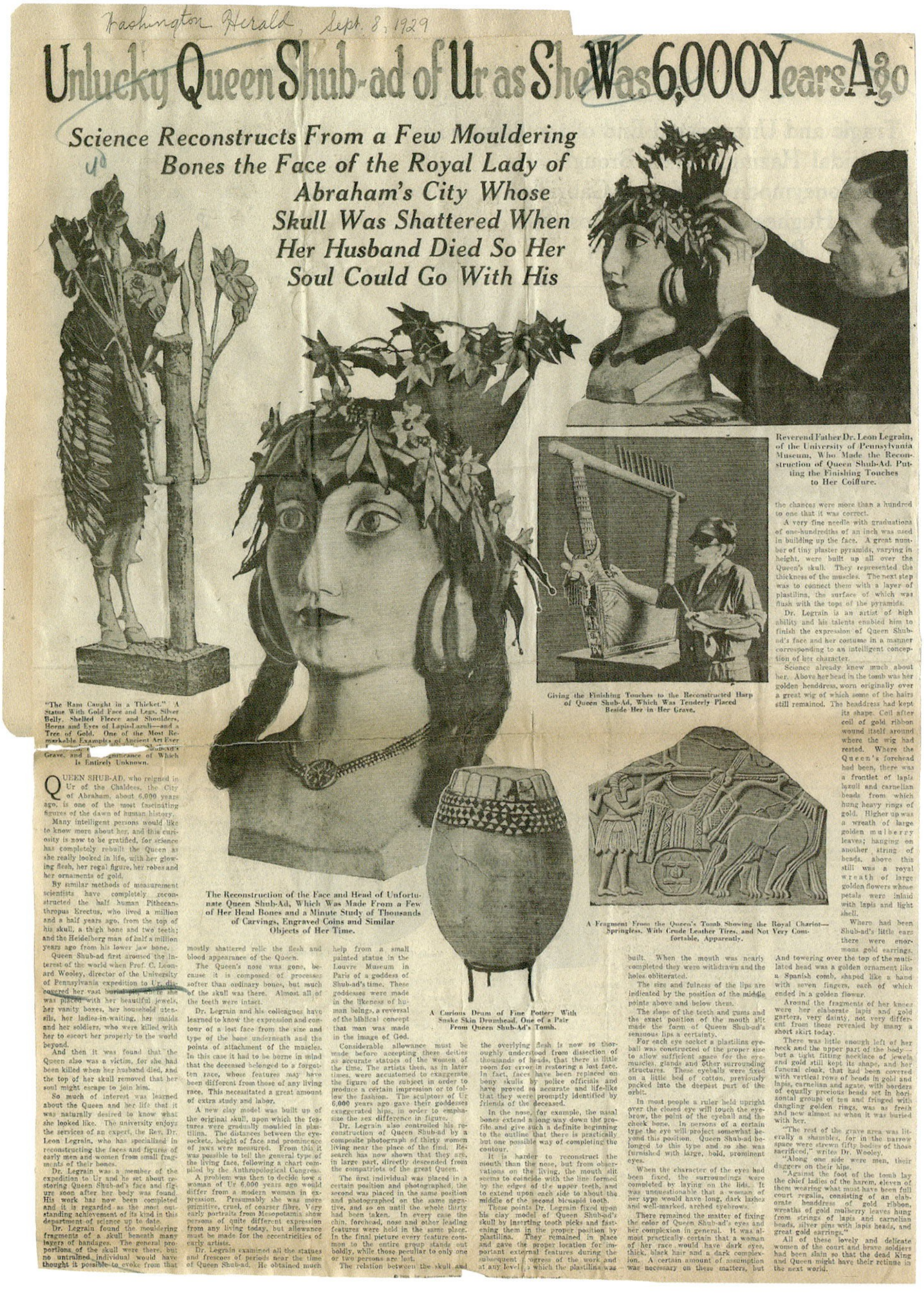

Washington Herald, Sept. 8, 1929

Unlucky Queen Shub-ad of Ur as She Was 6,000 Years Ago

Science Reconstructs From a Few Mouldering Bones the Face of the Royal Lady of Abraham's City Whose Skull Was Shattered When Her Husband Died So Her Soul Could Go With His

"The Ram Caught in a Thicket." A Statue With Gold Face and Legs, Silver Belly, Shelled Fleece and Shoulders, Horns and Eyes of Lapis-Lazuli—and a Tree of Gold. One of the Most Remarkable Examples of Ancient Art Ever [illegible] Shub-ad's Grave, and [illegible]gnificance of Which Is Entirely Unknown.

The Reconstruction of the Face and Head of Unfortunate Queen Shub-Ad, Which Was Made From a Few of Her Head Bones and a Minute Study of Thousands of Carvings, Engraved Coins and Similar Objects of Her Time.

Reverend Father Dr. Leon Legrain, of the University of Pennsylvania Museum, Who Made the Reconstruction of Queen Shub-Ad, Putting the Finishing Touches to Her Coiffure.

Giving the Finishing Touches to the Reconstructed Harp of Queen Shub-Ad, Which Was Tenderly Placed Beside Her in Her Grave.

A Curious Drum of Fine Pottery With Snake Skin Drumhead, One of a Pair From Queen Shub-Ad's Tomb.

A Fragment From the Queen's Tomb Showing the Royal Chariot—Springless, With Crude Leather Tires, and Not Very Comfortable, Apparently.

QUEEN SHUB-AD, who reigned in Ur of the Chaldees, the City of Abraham, about 6,000 years ago, is one of the most fascinating figures of the dawn of human history.

Many intelligent persons would like to know more about her, and this curiosity is now to be gratified, for science has completely rebuilt the Queen as she really looked in life, with her glowing flesh, her regal figure, her robes and her ornaments of gold.

By similar methods of measurement scientists have completely reconstructed the half human Pithecanthropus Erectus, who lived a million and a half years ago, from the top of his skull, a thigh bone and two teeth; and the Heidelberg man of half a million years ago from his lower jaw bone.

Queen Shub-ad first aroused the interest of the world when Prof. C. Leonard Wooley, director of the University of Pennsylvania expedition to Ur, discovered her vast burial pit where she was placed with her beautiful jewels, her vanity boxes, her household utensils, her ladies-in-waiting, her maids and her soldiers, who were killed with her to escort her properly to the world beyond.

And then it was found that the Queen also was a victim, for she had been killed when her husband died, and the top of her skull removed that her soul might escape to join him.

So much of interest was learned about the Queen and her life that it was naturally desired to know what she looked like. The university enjoys the services of an expert, the Rev. Dr. Leon Legrain, who has specialized in reconstructing the faces and figures of early men and women from small fragments of their bones.

Dr. Legrain was a member of the expedition to Ur and he set about restoring Queen Shub-ad's face and figure soon after her body was found. His work has now been completed and it is regarded as the most outstanding achievement of its kind in this department of science up to date.

Dr. Legrain found the mouldering fragments of a skull beneath many layers of bandages. The general proportions of the skull were there, but no untrained individual would have thought it possible to evoke from that mostly shattered relic the flesh and blood appearance of the Queen.

The Queen's nose was gone, because it is composed of processes softer than ordinary bones, but much of the skull was there. Almost all of the teeth were intact.

Dr. Legrain and his colleagues have learned to know the expression and contour of a lost face from the size and type of the bone underneath and the points of attachment of the muscles. In this case it had to be borne in mind that the deceased belonged to a forgotten race, whose features may have been different from those of any living race. This necessitated a great amount of extra study and labor.

A new clay model was built up of the original skull, upon which the features were gradually moulded in plastilina. The distances between the eye-sockets, height of face and prominence of jaws were measured. From this it was possible to tell the general type of the living face, following a chart compiled by the Anthropological Congress.

A problem was then to decide how a woman of Ur 6,000 years ago would differ from a modern woman in expression. Presumably she was more primitive, cruel, of coarser fibre. Very early portraits from Mesopotamia show persons of quite different expression from any living today, but allowance must be made for the eccentricities of early artists.

Dr. Legrain examined all the statues and frescoes of periods near the time of Queen Shub-ad. He obtained much help from a small painted statue in the Louvre Museum in Paris of a goddess of Shub-ad's time. These goddesses were made in the likeness of human beings, a reversal of the biblical concept that man was made in the image of God.

Considerable allowance must be made before accepting these deities as accurate statues of the women of the time. The artists then, as in later times, were accustomed to exaggerate the figure of the subject in order to produce a certain impression or to follow the fashion. The sculptors of Ur 6,000 years ago gave their goddesses exaggerated hips, in order to emphasize the sex difference in figure.

Dr. Legrain also controlled his reconstruction of Queen Shub-ad by a composite photograph of thirty women living near the place of the find. Research has now shown that they are, in large part, directly descended from the compatriots of the great Queen.

The first individual was placed in a certain position and photographed, the second was placed in the same position and photographed on the same negative, and so on until the whole thirty had been taken. In every case the chin, forehead, nose and other leading features were held in the same place. In the final picture every feature common to the entire group stands out boldly, while those peculiar to only one or two persons are lost.

The relation between the skull and the overlying flesh is now so thoroughly understood from dissection of thousands of heads, that there is little room for error in restoring a lost face. In fact, faces have been replaced on bony skulls by police officials and have proved so accurate and life-like that they were promptly identified by friends of the deceased.

In the nose, for example, the nasal bones extend a long way down the profile and give such a definite beginning to the outline that there is practically but one possible way of completing the contour.

It is harder to reconstruct the mouth than the nose, but from observations on the living, the mouth slit seems to coincide with the line formed by the edges of the upper teeth, and to extend upon each side to about the middle of the second bicuspid tooth.

These points Dr. Legrain fixed upon his clay model of Queen Shub-ad's skull by inserting tooth picks and fastening them in the proper position by plastilina. They remained in place and gave the proper location for important external features during the subsequent progress of the work and at any level to which the plastilina was built. When the mouth was nearly completed they were withdrawn and the holes obliterated.

The size and fulness of the lips are indicated by the position of the middle points above and below them.

The slope of the teeth and gums and the exact position of the mouth slit made the form of Queen Shub-ad's sensuous lips a certainty.

For each eye socket a plastilina eyeball was constructed of the proper size to allow sufficient space for the eye-muscles, glands and other surrounding structures. These eyeballs were fixed on a little bed of cotton, previously packed into the deepest part of the orbit.

In most people a ruler held upright over the closed eye will touch the eyebrow, the point of the eyeball and the cheek bone. In persons of a certain type the eye will project somewhat beyond this position. Queen Shub-ad belonged to this type and so she was furnished with large, bold, prominent eyes.

When the character of the eyes had been fixed, the surroundings were completed by laying on the lids. It was unquestionable that a woman of her type would have long, dark lashes and well-marked, arched eyebrows.

There remained the matter of fixing the color of Queen Shub-ad's eyes and her complexion in general. It was almost practically certain that a woman of her race would have dark eyes, thick, black hair and a dark complexion. A certain amount of assumption was necessary on these matters, but the chances were more than a hundred to one that it was correct.

A very fine needle with graduations of one-hundredths of an inch was used in building up the face. A great number of tiny plaster pyramids, varying in height, were built up all over the Queen's skull. They represented the thickness of the muscles. The next step was to connect them with a layer of plastilina, the surface of which was flush with the tops of the pyramids.

Dr. Legrain is an artist of high ability and his talents enabled him to finish the expression of Queen Shub-ad's face and her costume in a manner corresponding to an intelligent conception of her character.

Science already knew much about her. Above her head in the tomb was her golden headdress, worn originally over a great wig of which some of the hairs still remained. The headdress had kept its shape. Coil after coil of gold ribbon wound itself around where the wig had rested. Where the Queen's forehead had been, there was a frontlet of lapis lazuli and carnelian beads from which hung heavy rings of gold. Higher up was a wreath of large golden mulberry leaves; hanging on another string of beads, above this still was a royal wreath of large golden flowers whose petals were inlaid with lapis and light shell.

Where had been Shub-ad's little ears there were enormous gold earrings. And towering over the top of the mutilated head was a golden ornament like a Spanish comb, shaped like a hand with seven fingers, each of which ended in a golden flower.

Around the fragments of her knees were her elaborate lapis and gold garters, very dainty, not very different from those revealed by many a short skirt today.

There was little enough left of her neck and the upper part of the body—but a tight fitting necklace of jewels and gold still kept its shape, and her funeral cloak, that had been covered with vertical rows of beads in gold and lapis, carnelian and agate, with borders of equally precious beads set in horizontal groups of ten and fringed with dangling golden rings, was as fresh and new almost as when it was buried with her.

"The rest of the grave area was literally a shambles, for in the narrow space were strewn fifty bodies of those sacrificed," writes Dr. Wooley.

"Along one side were men, their daggers on their hips.

"Against the foot of the tomb lay the chief ladies of the harem, eleven of them wearing what must have been full court regalia, consisting of an elaborate headdress of gold ribbon, wreaths of gold mulberry leaves hung from strings of lapis and carnelian beads, silver pins with lapis heads, and great gold earrings."

All of these lovely and delicate women of the court and brave soldiers had been slain so that the dead King and Queen might have their retinue in the next world.

5-3. "Unlucky Queen Sub-ad of Ur As She Was 6000 Years Ago." *Washington (D.C.) Herald*, September 8, 1929. Penn Museum. Courtesy of the University of Pennsylvania Museum of Archaeology and Anthropology.

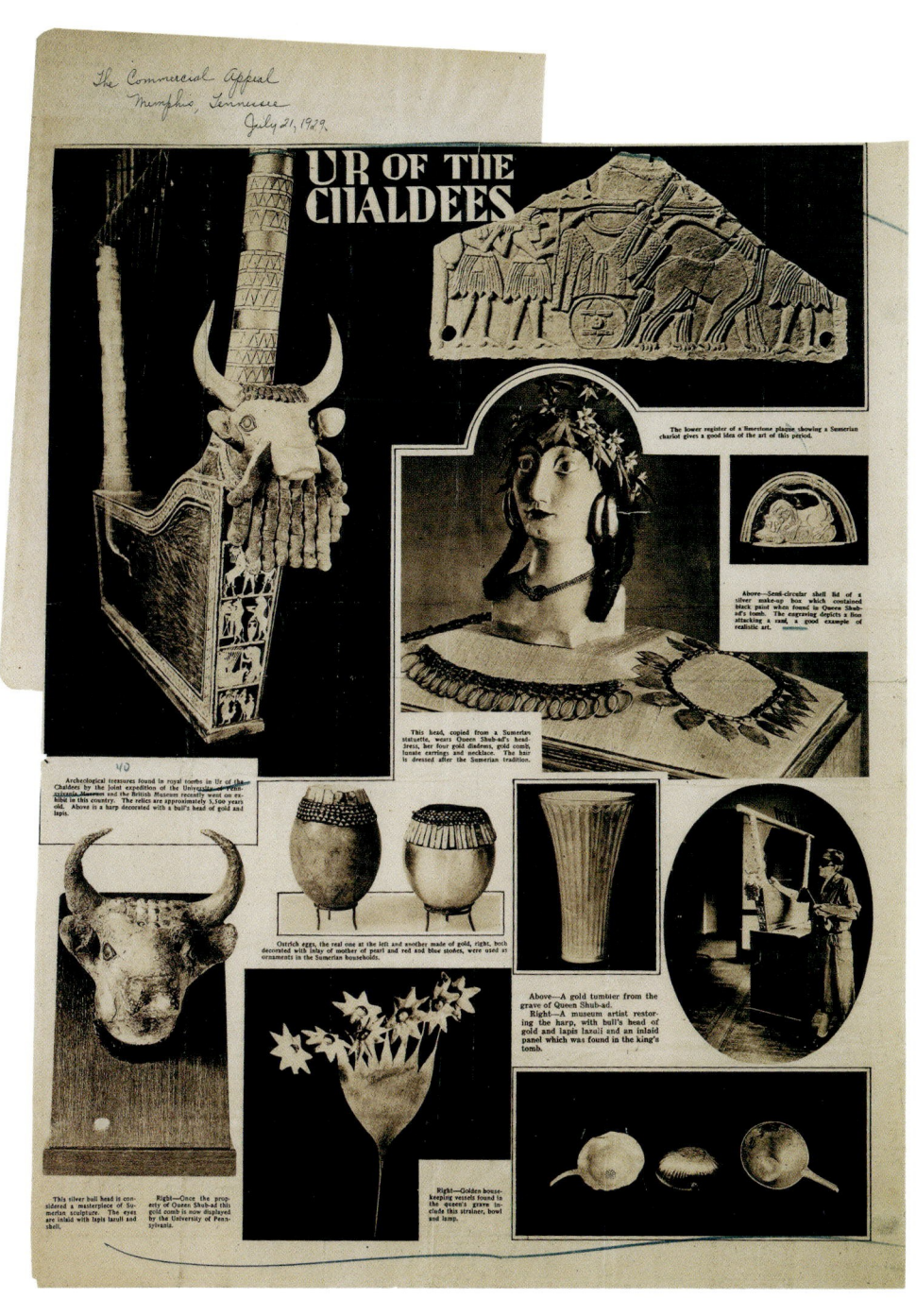

5–4. "Ur of the Chaldees." *Memphis (TN) Commercial Appeal* (Memphis, Tennessee), July 21, 1929. Courtesy of the University of Pennsylvania Museum of Archaeology and Anthropology. Checklist no. 94.

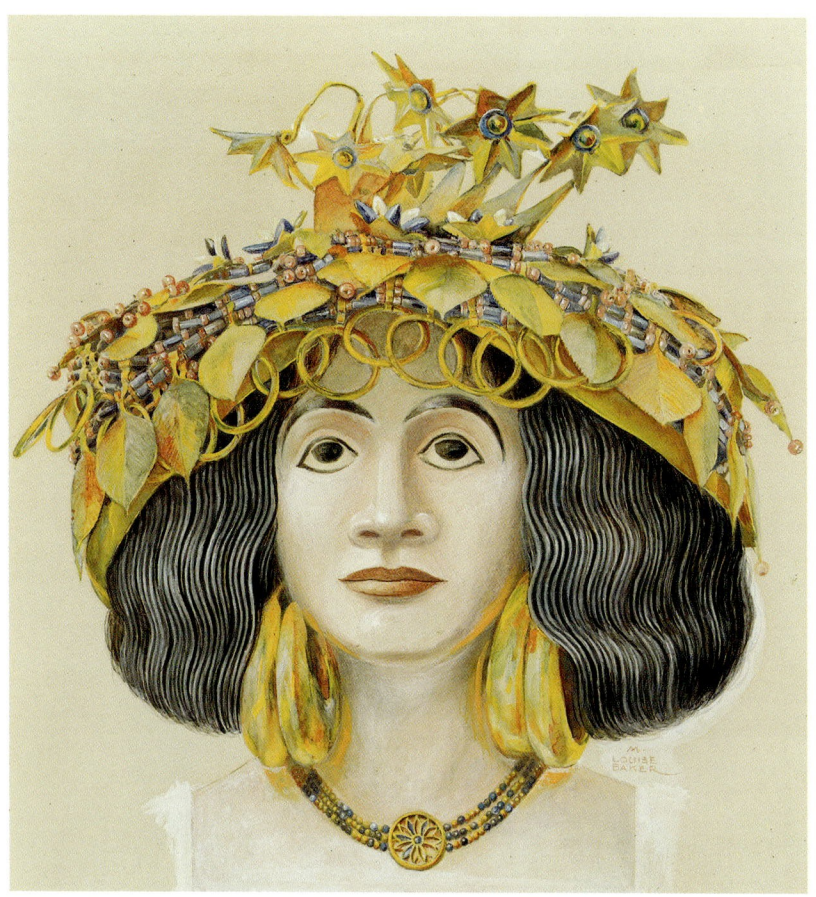

5–5. Puabi and headdress. Watercolor by Mary Louise Baker, ca. 1936. BMAG: 1964 A2626. Birmingham Museum Trust. Checklist no. 102.

foregrounds her jewelry) is Winter's focus on making and technique as key components in Mesopotamian aesthetic judgment, or, as she calls it, the "value of skilled production."[12] Winter reveals that Sumerian literary sources place clear and notable value on the skill with which an object was made, favoring descriptions such as "expertly fashioned," "skillfully made," "executed in a refined manner," or "brought to a perfect end" over those that refer to an object as simply "beautiful."[13] Furthermore, she observes that it is "the emphasis on skill and expertise in the process of making that is recorded as part of the value of the end product"[14] that rendered an object "fitting," "admirable," "awesome," or "great."[15] In other words, "the properties related to production" must be seen "as inseparable from, and part of, the overall stimulus leading to aesthetic response itself."[16] There is thus a direct link between making and perceived aesthetic and cultural value.[17] Winter reminds us that this, of course, is very different from the modern, Western notion of aesthetics based on Kant's writings, which "quite explicitly precluded such a relationship between a 'pure' judgement of beauty and an assessment of technique, or perfection."[18]

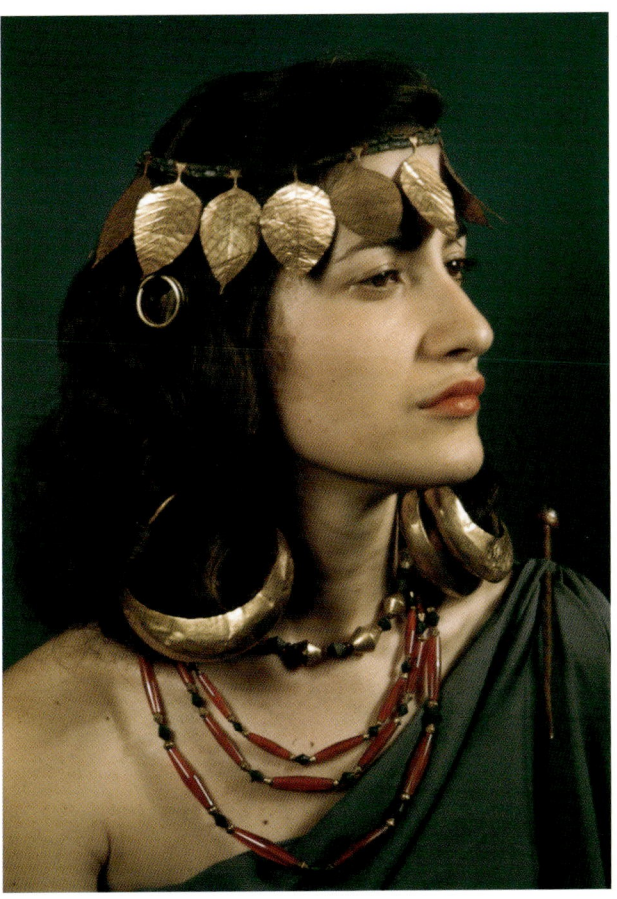

5-6. Gloria Shihadeh Albany (later Swift) wearing Puabi's jewelry. Photograph, ca. 1944. Penn Museum: 160118. Courtesy of the University of Pennsylvania Museum of Archaeology and Anthropology.

Elsewhere, Winter has elaborated on additional features of a distinctly Mesopotamian aesthetic, such as certain visual attributes: the broad category comprising light, luster, shine, luminosity, and radiance is one such physical attribute that in Mesopotamia carried "high aesthetic valence," as well as "aspects of power and awe" that physically manifest divine presence.[19] Luminosity, as it relates to the sacred, is also connected to purity and holiness, since "that which is pure and holy will shine, and conversely, that which shines manifests the sacred."[20] In fact, according to Winter, what is distinctive about the Mesopotamian artistic tradition is not just the close relationship between making and aesthetic value but "the degree to which aesthetic and emotional responses are closely intertwined and the degree to which the sacred seems to be manifest through visually affective, hence aesthetic, qualities."[21] Implied in these equations is also some measure of agency on the part of the object or image imbued with these qualities, indicative of the interconnectedness of aesthetics and agency that exists within the Mesopotamian representational system.[22]

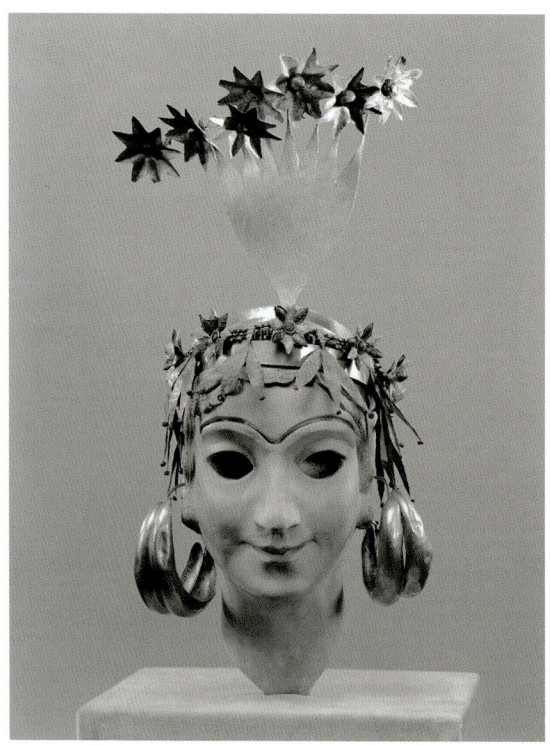

5–7. Model of Puabi and headdress in the reconstruction by Mrs. Levey. Photograph, December 1955. Penn Museum: 61895. Courtesy of the University of Pennsylvania Museum of Archaeology and Anthropology.

If we now return to the exhibition *From Ancient to Modern: Archaeology and Aesthetics* and the image of Puabi with a better-defined sense of what might have constituted aesthetic criteria in ancient Mesopotamia, it may be possible to distinguish between actual creation and the context of creation. What if the creation—the making—of Puabi's jewelry (and thus her image) carried both key Mesopotamian aesthetic values and possible interpretations for Puabi (her identity and function) before any archaeological context came into play, perhaps even independent of that context (which is not to say that the image had no function in its context),[23] because the context was one in which the image was perhaps never seen by a human audience? What if the final product, the image of Puabi, was important not in the physical, literal manner of a picture but in some metaphysical way, unrelated to our understanding of an image today?

Scholars typically investigate the identity and function of an individual in antiquity by relying on inscribed evidence, if it exists, as well as on the archaeological context in which he or she functioned. In most cases, such inquiries focus on what the material culture associated with the person reveals or projects about his or her identity; only occasionally are these objects considered capable of actively creating that identity. In

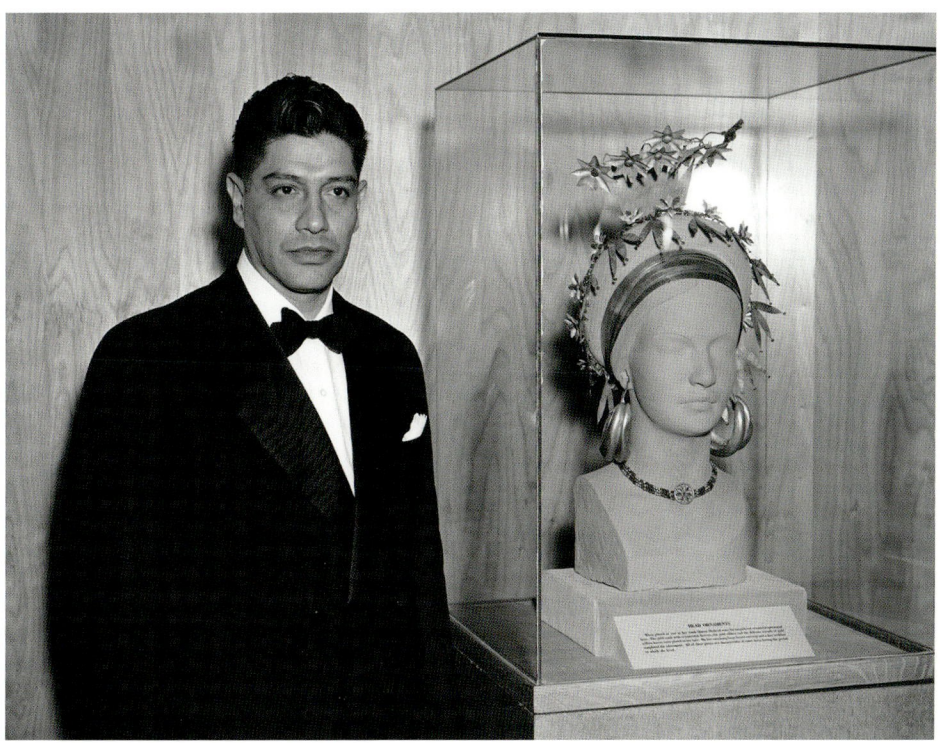

5–8. The Mexican designer Antonio Lebrija next to the reconstructed head of Puabi and her headdress. Photograph, 1955. Penn Museum: 249489. Courtesy of the University of Pennsylvania Museum of Archaeology and Anthropology.

Mesopotamia, however, identity could inhere both in the individual's body and in the objects that were in contact with it. In fact, objects otherwise considered inanimate were not limited to passive decorative or symbolic functions; they could do things, they could make things happen, they could elicit responses.[24] They could quite literally become Mitchell's animated beings "driven by desire and appetites." And in this Mesopotamian notion of agency, the image itself could be one of these inanimate yet potentially animated beings.

It is with this concept in mind that I approach the question of Puabi's image, treating the jewelry not as mere ornament, insignia, or representation of personhood but as an active participant in its very formation. Moreover, I extend this logic to include how the jewelry, and thus Puabi's identity and image, were actually manufactured, both physically and conceptually, and how they fit nicely into the selected criteria for Mesopotamian aesthetics established above.

Puabi: The Aesthetics of Technique

With few exceptions, most scholars have interpreted the archaeological discovery of Puabi's jewels primarily as a reflection in burial of a significant level of power, wealth, and prestige among the ruling kings and queens of Ur[25]—hence, the name "Royal Cemetery." In addition, the majority of research on Puabi continues to assign to her the role of queen to a king,[26] even though it has been demonstrated that Puabi's tomb is stratigraphically unrelated to the tomb of this imagined husband and king.[27] While Puabi may well have been royalty, there is no evidence confirming that she was queen to any king.

In a departure from the generally accepted narrative, I propose that her jewelry was not simply a rich but passive collection of prestige goods, but rather that it can be read in terms of active ritual, even cultic, production—thereby creating an identity and image for its wearer that was either different from that of royalty, or at the very least, beyond that of royalty alone. In this scenario the ensemble of jewelry, regardless of its original and exact arrangement,[28] produced an image of Puabi that had aesthetically little to do with the glamorous and exotic, yet modern and Western, Greta-Garbo-as-Mata-Hari-like figure[29] that was first introduced to the world in the late 1920s (see fig. 2–5; see also figs. 1–7, 2–11, 5–2 to 5–4), or with various other iterations over the years (figs. 5–5 to fig. 5–9). Each of these reconstructions is so much imbued with the aesthetic of its time that it is possible to identify the decade of almost every one by visual analysis alone. Ironically, it may be that the several "faceless" versions of Puabi over time best fit the original intent of both the image and context (fig. 5–10).

In order to establish the role of making, and some of its visual results, within Mesopotamian aesthetics, I will present a small selection of Puabi's jewels, particularly those in gold adorning her head (figs. 5–1, 5–11).[30] The ornaments of gold appear to be rather simple in technique, made primarily of undecorated, hammered gold sheet; however, with closer examination, it becomes apparent that the methods used to hammer and assemble each piece were deceptively complicated and time-consuming.

Gold in its native state—that is, gold between 70 and 90 percent pure—is thought of as extremely malleable and ductile. Indeed, in smaller amounts that is true. However, many of the gold ornaments found with Puabi—all of which likely fall within the purity range of native gold[31]—were made from substantial, single pieces of metal. Each piece entailed enough hammering to shape it that the metal would have become quite hardened in the course of manufacture and therefore would have required considerable and repeated annealing (i.e., evenly reheating metals so that they regain their malleability for further hammering or other kinds of manipulation without melting or blistering). Even smaller ornaments included extensions, such as the suspension loops, that no longer qualified them as small enough to be easily worked without constant annealing. Furthermore, there seems to have been a premium placed on fashioning individual elements from a single piece of gold whenever possible, even at the cost of additional, intensive labor. The making of this jewelry is thus noteworthy for its almost prescriptive consistency and

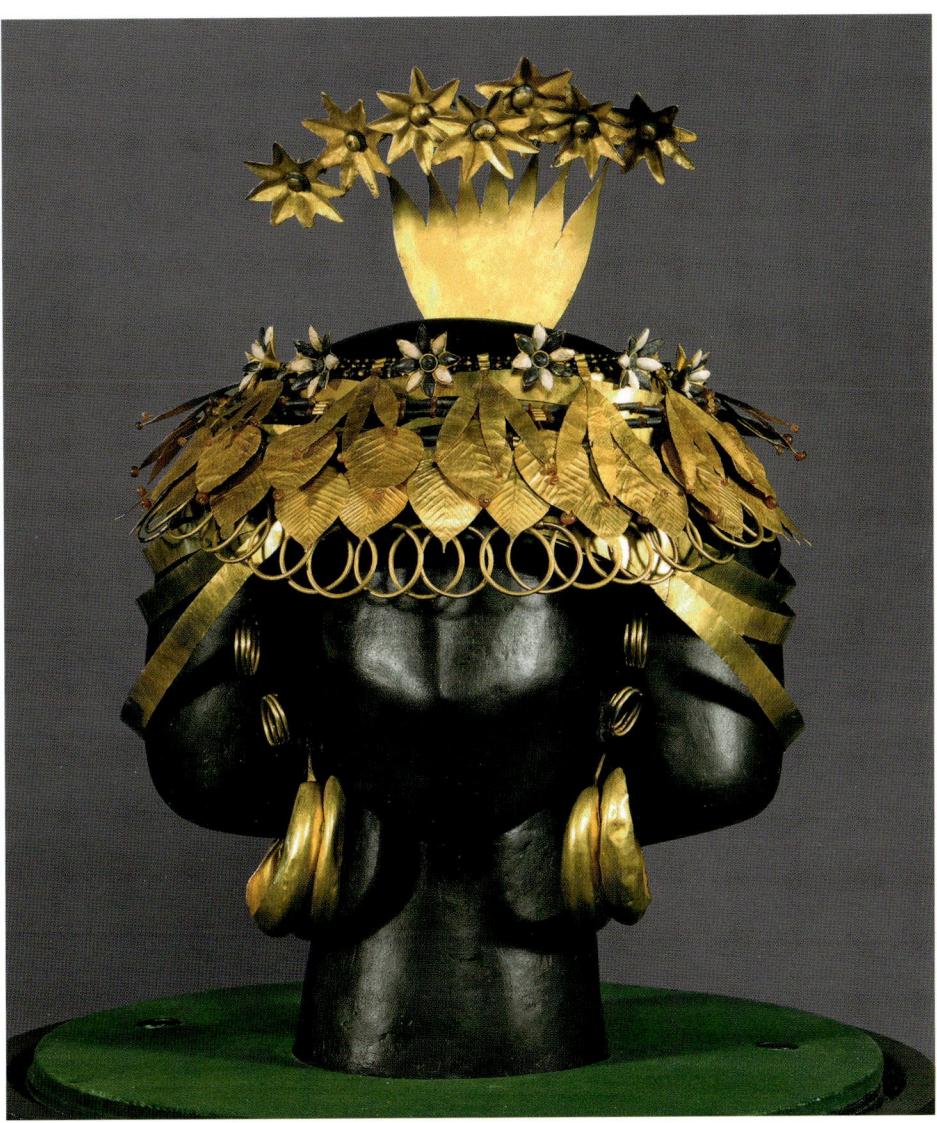

5–9. Model of Puabi and headdress in the late 1990s reconstruction by the University of Pennsylvania Museum of Archaeology and Anthropology. Photograph, ca. 1997. Penn Museum: 15. Courtesy of the University of Pennsylvania Museum of Archaeology and Anthropology.

repetition of a restricted technical repertoire, based primarily on hammering, that, unlike intricate decorative techniques such as granulation, did not advertise the labor and expertise involved. Finally, considerable advance planning would have been necessary to form Puabi's assemblage because individual pieces made in such a highly prescriptive way were likely conceived together. These were not jewels collected over a lifetime or retained as heirlooms and then buried with Puabi simply because they belonged to her. They were made for a particular purpose—her burial.[32]

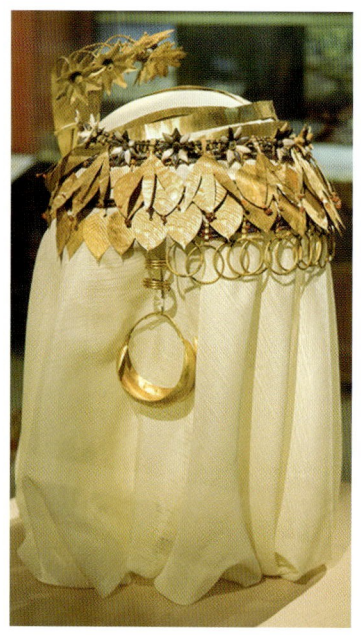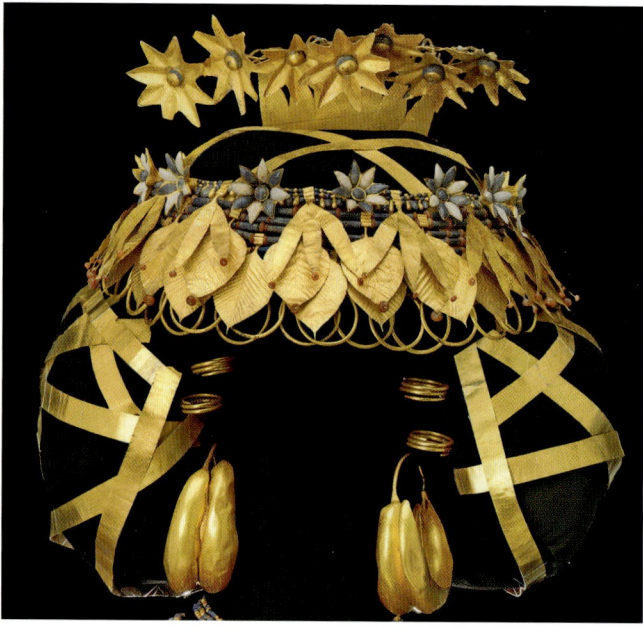

5–10. Puabi's headdress in a reconstruction by the University of Pennsylvania Museum of Archaeology and Anthropology. Undated photograph (ca. 2000–2010). Courtesy of the University of Pennsylvania Museum of Archaeology and Anthropology.

5–11. Queen Puabi's headdress in its current reinterpretation and display at the University of Pennsylvania Museum of Archaeology and Anthropology. Gold and various stones. Ur, Tomb PG 800, ca. 2500–2300 BCE. Joint Expedition of the British Museum and the Museum of the University of Pennsylvania, 6th season, 1927–28. Checklist no. 109.

Beginning at the top of Puabi's body with the large hair comb (fig. 5–12), it becomes apparent that a tremendous effort was made to create this sizeable and heavy ornament out of as few pieces of gold as possible: its body was made out of a very large and thick sheet of gold. In order to obtain from a single piece of gold the wire pin at one end of the comb, and the wide splay into seven prongs at the other, the goldsmith must have possessed an intimate knowledge of the mechanics and movements of gold as it was hammered repeatedly. At five of the comb's six points where the body divides into the seven prongs, visible stress marks are visible, due to insufficient annealing of the gold, proving once again the complexity of this technique (fig. 5–13).

In the case of this comb, I imagine that the goldsmith would have begun hammering at one of the short ends of the elongated solid gold mass and then continued hammering to produce the large flat surface that makes up the body. This implies that the goldsmith had to plan the comb's final size and shape from the beginning: in fact, if at the end of the hammering process the mass of gold was not sufficient for the desired design, he would have been forced to begin from scratch or resort to soldering or brazing (i.e., fusing) additional sections to the main body. Thus, while one's first impression of the comb is that, although quite large and lovely, it is rather simply made from an undecorated sheet of gold, it becomes clear that its manufacture was anything but straightforward and easy to execute.

Turning to the botanical wreaths that adorned Puabi's head (figs. 5–14 to 5–16), we find that the predominant technique employed to make the gold leaf elements was also hammering. The goldsmith fashioned each of the many leaves from a single unit of gold, hammering in one direction to make the leaf shape and in the other direction to form the suspension loop for stringing—similar to the way that the comb was produced. In the case of the wreath pendants, the shaping of each leaf was a fairly simple procedure; nonetheless, frequent annealing was required both for the hammering of the shape and for the chasing that was done to delineate the veins.

As with the allotment of gold for the comb, the hammering of the leaves entailed planning not just for the leaf design but also for the narrow strip of gold that continued beyond the fine stems and, once it had been folded into the desired shape, served as the suspension loop for each leaf (figs. 5–17, 5–18). While the three separate wreaths have three separate design variations of this loop, they share a fundamental aspect of technique: the use of a single, continuous—and seamless—piece of metal whenever possible.

In the case of the two poplar-leaf wreaths (figs. 5–14, 5–15), the strip of gold extending from the leaf stem was folded and rolled, almost ribbon like, into tubes intended for strands of beads (see figs. 5–17, 5–18). The amount of annealing, and therefore time, needed to hammer and fold each of the many loops was again considerable. Once more, a significant amount of skill was required to calculate and accomplish the transformation of a single unit of gold into both the leaf shape and the suspension loop. An easier and more practical way, considering that gold leaves were found in many other tombs at the cemetery (figs. 5–19, 5–20), would have been to produce multiple tubes that could be laid side by side, soldered together, and subsequently attached to the leaf to form the loop. In this system if something went wrong in the making of the ornament, the goldsmith could replace one part rather than starting from scratch to create an entirely new leaf and loop out of a single piece of gold. Yet the goldsmith chose the more difficult and time-consuming method. Was this to avoid breaking the gold into various bits, which would require joining the parts, thereby compromising the seamlessness of the pieces, both physically and conceptually? Was the goldsmith circumventing the use of solder, which would have added impurities to the gold and compromised the physical and conceptual purity? Was there a particular method prescribed for ritual reasons?

Puabi's hair ribbon, perhaps the least outwardly impressive of all her jewelry, constitutes a hammering tour de force (fig. 5–21). The ribbon of gold is remarkably plain and devoid of any decoration; yet it represents the epitome of technical expertise due to the enormous skill and time—and constant annealing—required for its making. The extreme

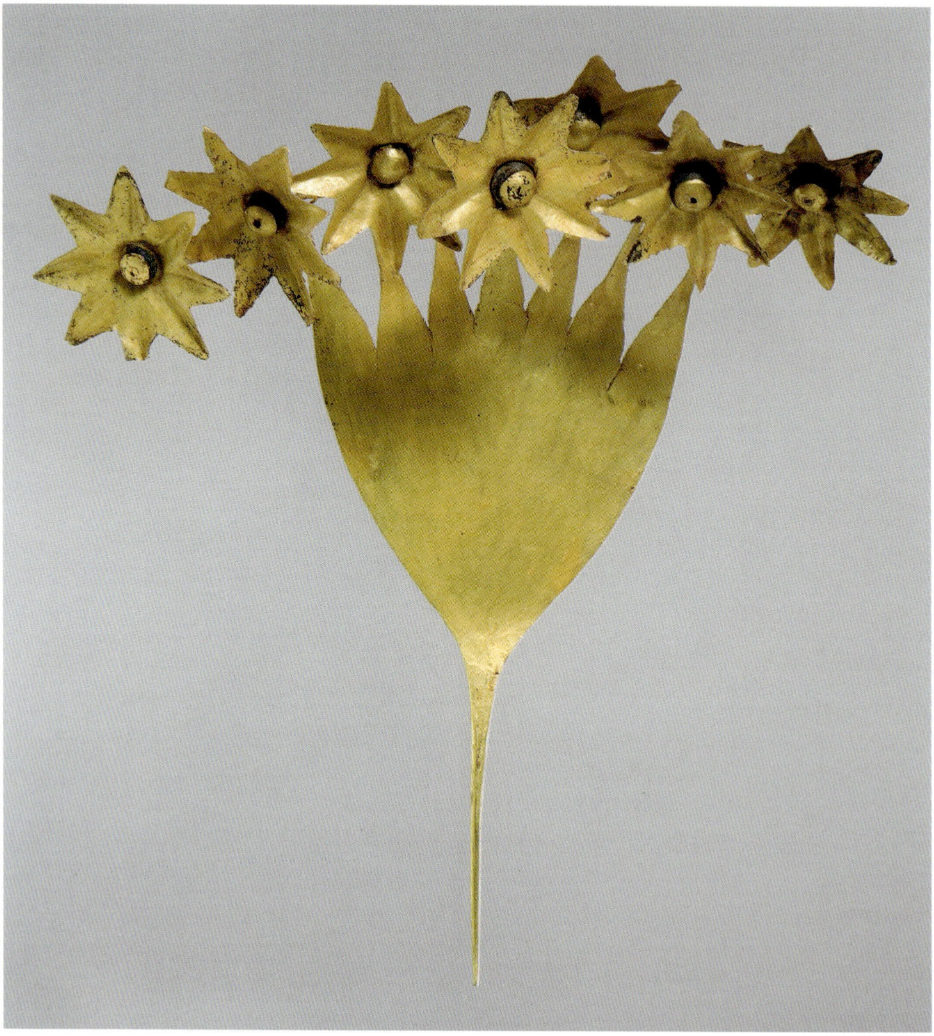

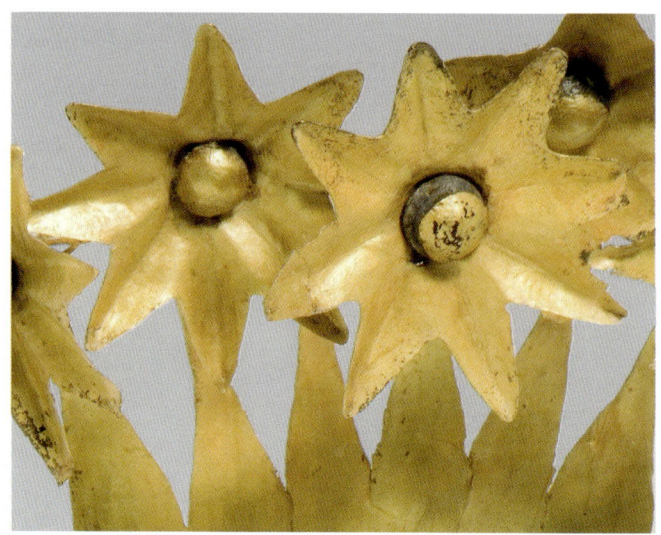

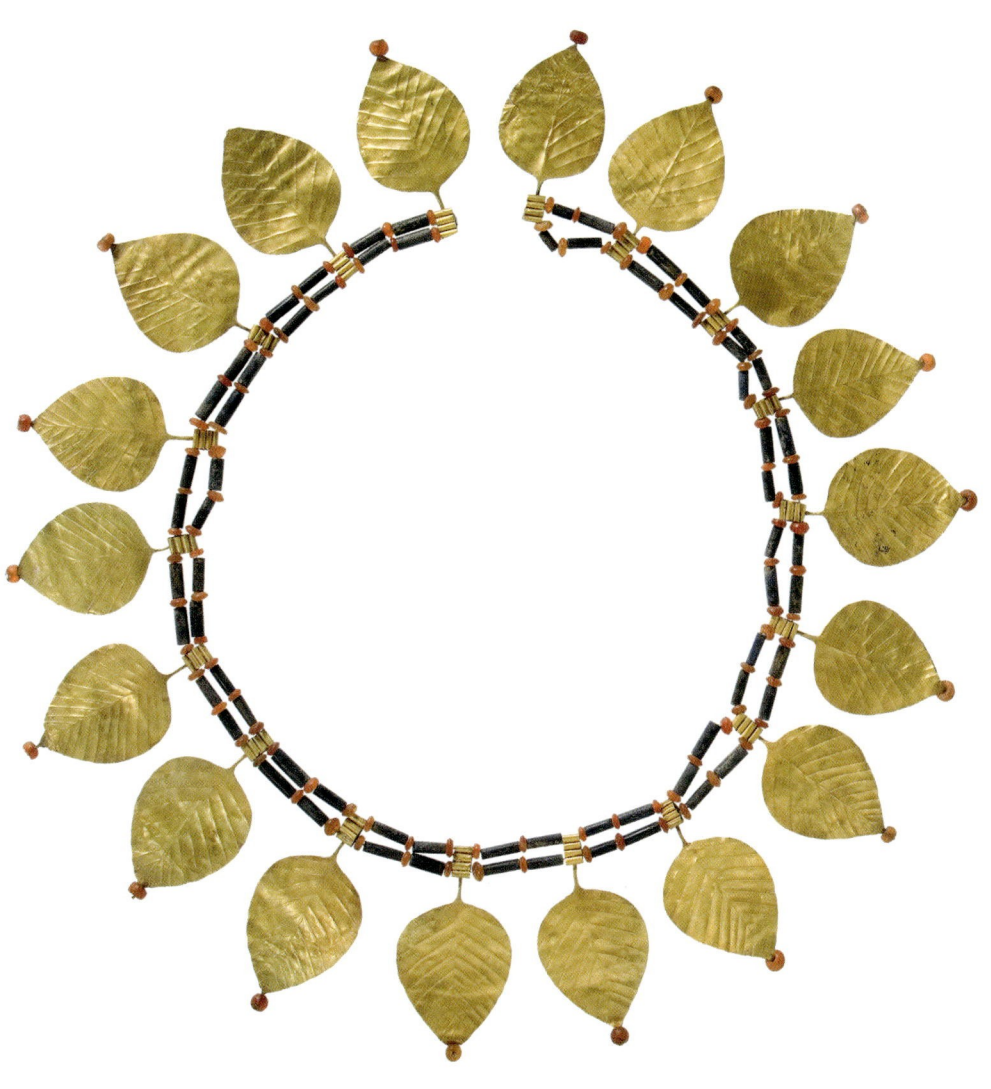

5–12. Puabi's hair comb. Gold, lapis lazuli. Ur, Tomb PG 800, ca. 2500–2300 BCE. Penn Museum: B16693. Joint Expedition of the British Museum and the Museum of the University of Pennsylvania, 6th season, 1927–28. Checklist no. 109.

5–13. Detail of the hair comb's points.

5–14. Wreath. Gold, lapis, and carnelian. Ur, Tomb PG 800, ca. 2500–2300 BCE. Penn Museum: B17709. Joint Expedition of the British Museum and the Museum of the University of Pennsylvania, 6th season, 1927–28. Checklist no. 109.

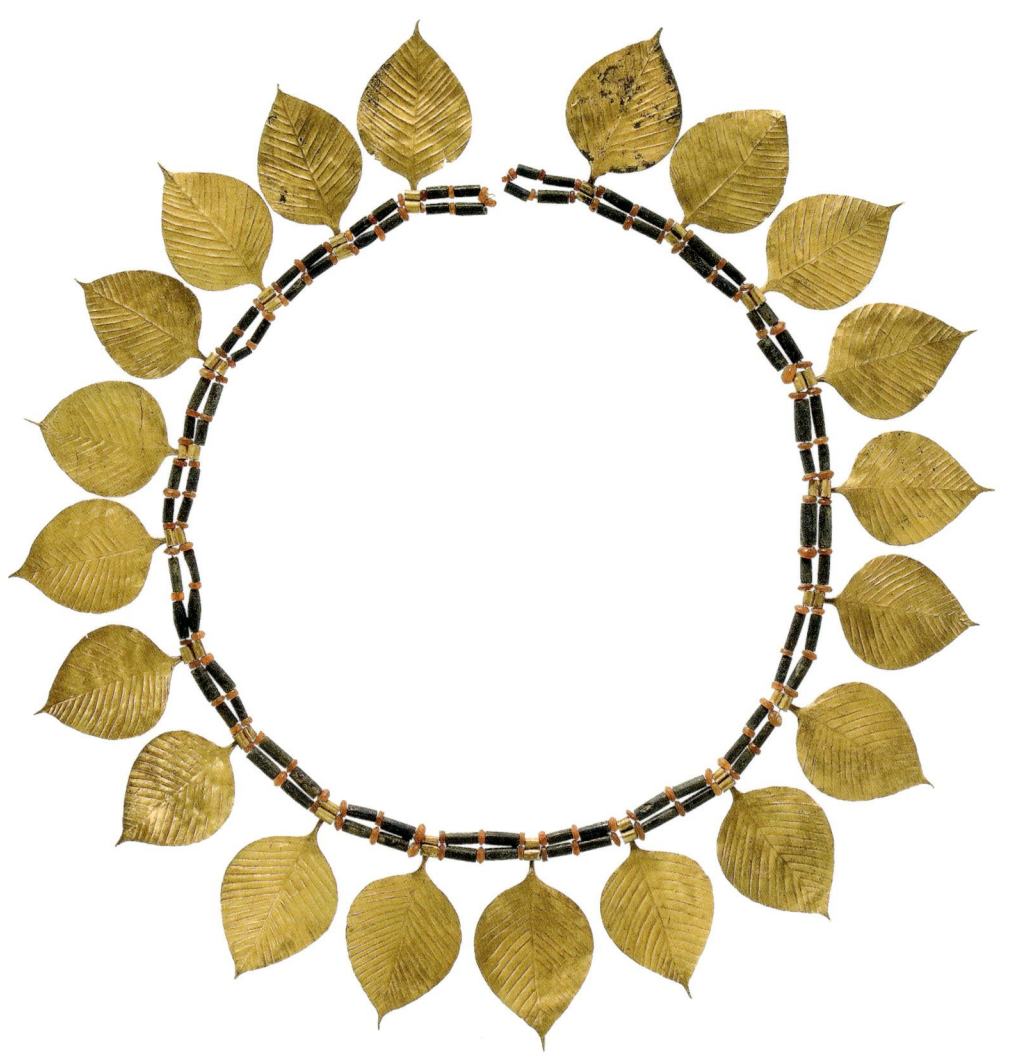

5–15. Wreath. Gold, shell, lapis, and carnelian. Ur, Tomb PG 800, ca. 2500–2300 BCE. Penn Museum: B17710. Joint Expedition of the British Museum and the Museum of the University of Pennsylvania, 6th season, 1927–28. Checklist no. 109.

length and straightness of the gold strip made this ribbon the most difficult piece of Puabi's jewelry to produce accurately and without breakage. As with the previous examples, the goldsmith would have had to begin from scratch if the metal had split, cracked, or broken. Even in their completely undecorated state such ribbons, and there are scores of them in the Ur burials, best exemplify the virtuosity involved in the craft of hammering at Ur.

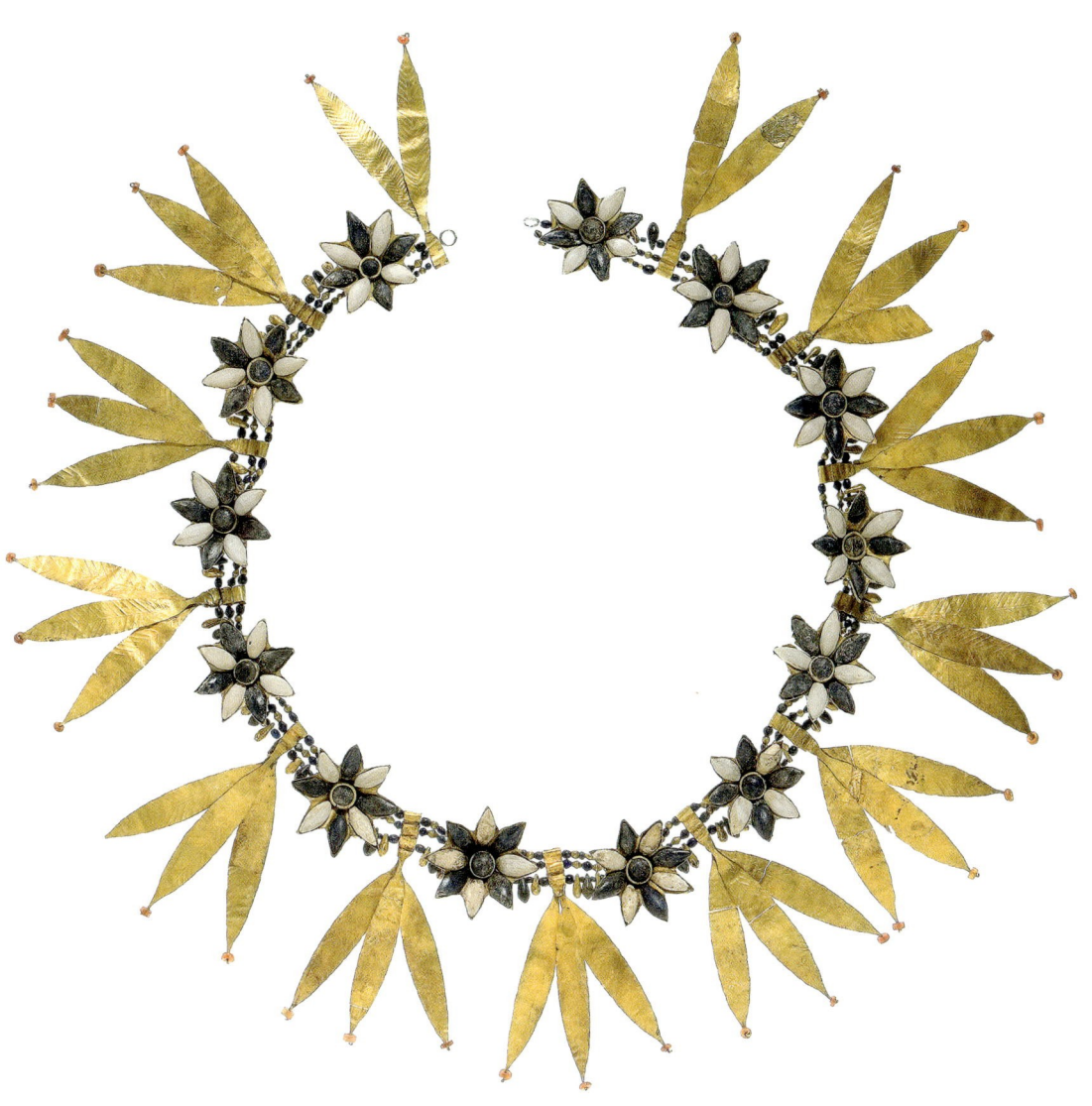

5–16. Wreath. Gold, lapis, and carnelian. Ur, Tomb PG 800, ca. 2500–2300 BCE. Penn Museum: B17711. Joint Expedition of the British Museum and the Museum of the University of Pennsylvania, 6th season, 1927–28. Checklist no. 109.

Conclusions

From this brief examination of only a selection of Puabi's jewelry, several technical aspects must be reiterated and stressed because they have as much conceptual as technological significance. First, the goldsmith was undoubtedly an expert at his or her craft. As we have seen, the amount of hammering required to shape the comb or hair ribbon, although not a complicated technique, called for considerable knowledge of the mechanics of the metal as well as a feel for where to begin and how to hammer the gold, so that the overall design of large or long ornaments could be achieved in a seamless manner. The primary

151

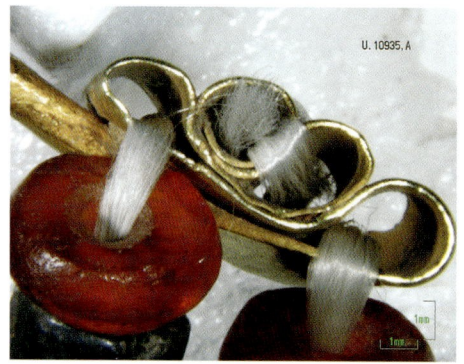
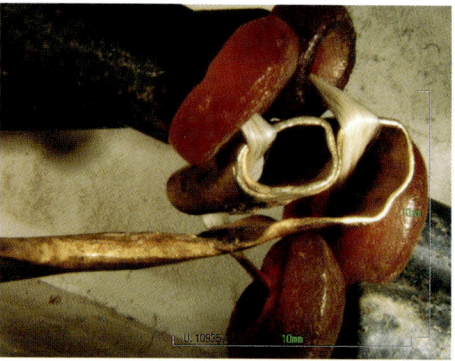

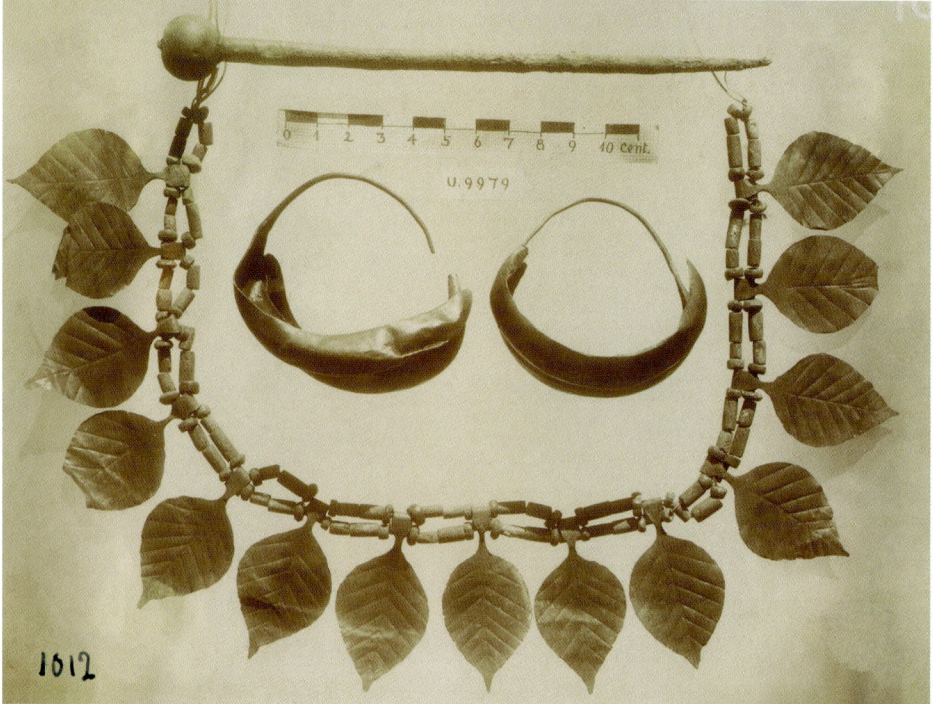

5–17. Microscopic detail of the suspension loop of wreath B17709 (see fig. 5–14). Courtesy of Kim Benzel.

5–18. Microscopic detail of the suspension loop of wreath B17710 (see fig. 5–15). Courtesy of Kim Benzel.

5–19. Earrings, wreath, and pin from tomb PG 789. Photograph. Philadelphia, 1930. Penn Museum: 1012. Courtesy of the University of Pennsylvania Museum of Archaeology and Anthropology.

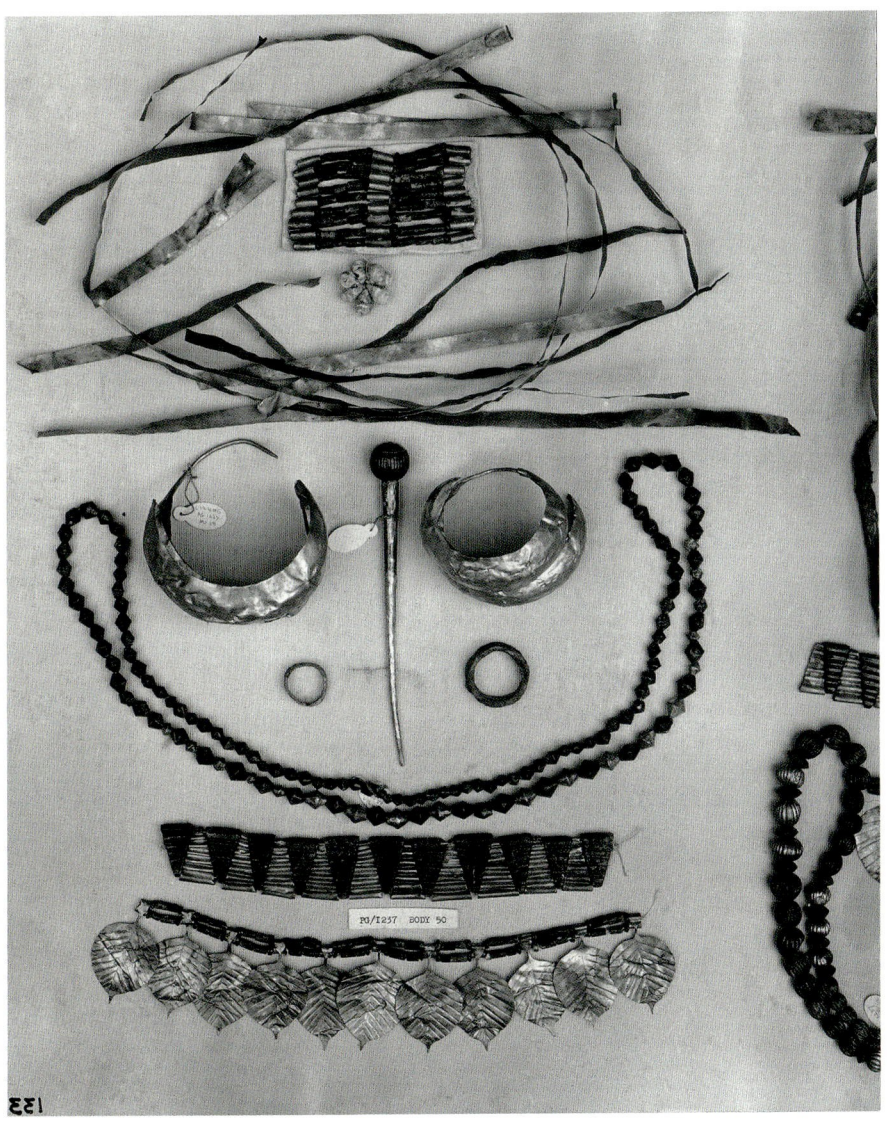

5–20. Headdress, wreath, earrings, pin, and necklaces from tomb PG 1237. Photograph. Philadelphia, 1930. Penn Museum: 1012. Courtesy of the University of Pennsylvania Museum of Archaeology and Anthropology.

components of hammering are thus skill and time—technical elements that remain largely hidden in the final product but that are far from insignificant.

Furthermore, it is crucial to note that the hammering of flat sheet is the primary metal-working technique used to produce Puabi's ornaments, resulting in surfaces that actively enhanced the sheen of the gold and exploited the resulting reflection of light, or shine. This approach created in technique the semantic equivalent to the Sumerian word for "shine" that was associated with the Sumerian term for "gold." Indeed, shine is an

153

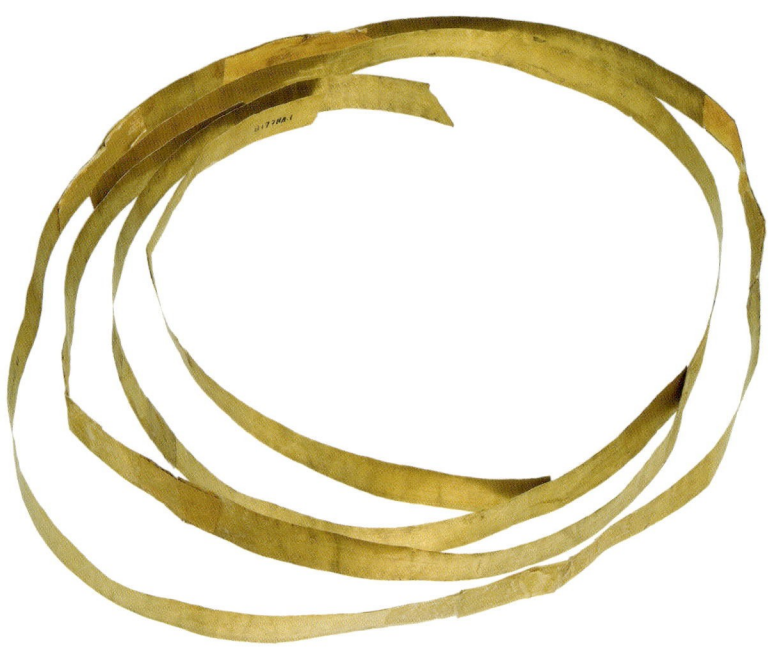

5-21. Puabi's hair ribbon. Gold. Ur, Tomb PG 800, ca. 2500–2300 BCE. Penn Museum: B1771A. Joint Expedition of the British Museum and the Museum of the University of Pennsylvania, 6th season, 1927–28. Checklist no. 109.

inherent quality of the metal, not one achieved by human manipulation. Furthermore, the Sumerian sign indicating "shine" could also signify "holy" or "sacred," and thus the two concepts were often equated and/or conflated.[33] Therefore, I would argue that in the case of Puabi's jewelry, the technology itself exhibits agency, and that shine—and conceivably some aspect of the sacred—were deliberately produced in its very making. I believe strongly that the technique of hammering such a large quantity of flat metal sheet was very consciously chosen or prescribed. This combination of material and semantic properties in the associated technical processes represents a subtle yet sophisticated use of repetition or doubling, a conceptual operation that is well-known in the visual and literary imagery of Mesopotamia,[34] and seen here in technological form. In other words, the preference for hammering evident in the making of Puabi's jewelry unambiguously produced the shine and radiance that constituted a key category of aesthetic value in Mesopotamia, one that is closely associated with awe, power, and divine presence.

Repetition is essentially a by-product of hammering and constitutes a second aspect of manufacture at Ur that is also obscure but fundamental, once again both in its technical importance and in conceptual significance. The very act of annealing, the foremost component of continuous hammering, accounts for the tremendous amount of time

154

expended to make Puabi's jewels; yet it is not overtly appreciable in the final products. It is interesting to note that on a conceptual level, the act of repetition is also a primary factor in ritual procedure, so that the technological process of repetitive hammering could conceivably have related the making of this jewelry to a ritual undertaking.

Seamlessness was mentioned above and comprises a third and crucial aspect of the jewelry technology at Ur for several reasons, again both physical and conceptual. For one, the use of a single piece of gold whenever possible preserved the integrity and relative purity of the metal as well as the visual unity of the piece. The use of separate elements would have interrupted both the material and the form, and the use of solder quite literally would have added impurities to the metal by way of the baser elements it contained. Easier means were available during this period, so one must assume the choice was not by default but deliberate.[35]

This approach has implications not only for the compositional or economic value of the gold but also for the potential ritual value or symbolism of the finished object. The procedure chosen achieved in technical terms the semantic equivalent to the Sumerian word for "pure," which is also associated with the Sumerian term for "gold" presumably because, like "shine," that quality too was deemed inherent to the metal.[36] In fact, and perhaps not surprisingly, the Sumerian sign indicating "pure" is the same as that used for "shine," which, as stated above, is also that used to signify "holy" or "sacred," suggesting that all three concepts could be conflated in certain contexts. Thus, one might again argue that the technique itself had agency, that "purity"—as well as "shine" and "sacredness"—were consciously being produced in the making. This consideration, in conjunction with those already discussed, points to the possibility that Puabi's jewelry carried a cultic charge, which in turn could be transferred to her identity and image. The entire progression of this charge was seemingly activated first and foremost by the materials and methods of manufacture.

Finally, seamlessness quite literally hides the hand of the mortal maker, thereby leaving open the question of who made the object, and how, and giving the impression that the object simply "exists" rather than being made in any sense. A similar operation is well known from ancient Near Eastern texts that describe the making of cult statues, where the process entailed rituals that purposefully obscured the role of the sculptor, allowing a statue to miraculously emerge in its fully finished and animated state, as if made by the gods.[37] I believe that a related conceptual maneuver was likely being carried out in the technical processes chosen for the making of Puabi's jewelry.

These hidden aspects of technology are rarely explored because they are for the most part poorly understood, or even completely unnoticed. The finished product generally provides the starting point for all art historical investigations, leaving technique and process to the fields of studio art and conservation. Based on my analysis of Puabi's jewelry, the technical aspects of the creative endeavor provide additional ways in which to read the jewelry. Thus, the making of Puabi's golden ornaments, especially those adorning her head, entailed procedures typical of ritual and cultic production—repetition, prescription, and seamlessness—all of which were consistently applied at great additional expense of labor. In the process, aspects of shine, purity, and possibly the sacred were constructed on and in both the dead body and the live image of Puabi and thereby in her person and identity, in ways that go beyond those associated with gender, wealth, prestige, and royalty.

Considered in this light, the jewelry produced for Puabi easily fits the descriptions given in Sumerian texts of "expertly fashioned," "skillfully made," or "brought to a perfect end"—and does so quite literally and physically based on the technical procedures actually used. As pointed out by Winter and Bahrani, the Sumerian terminology for crafting reflects a sense of great value attached to the objects it describes—a value that stems as much from the skilled craftsmanship exhibited in the finished objects as from the operative values of the raw materials out of which they are made, or the distinguished function they may have served. Especially in phrases such as "brought to a perfect end" the wording implied a mandate for a prescribed procedure attached to the making of valued objects that resulted in a seamlessness—a hidden perfection—that could not but be perceived to stem from a magical or sacred source, or even in some measure to activate the magical or the sacred because it effectively erased the hand of the mortal maker.[38] I would emphasize that there seems to have existed a "correct" and "perfect" way of making Puabi's jewelry, and other jewelry at Ur—one that satisfied several categories of specifically Mesopotamian aesthetic criteria while offering the possibility of an alternative interpretation even before consideration of the archaeological context.

For the type of investigations just undertaken of Puabi's jewelry, Alfred Gell's work on the "magical efficacy," or "enchantment," of technology and the agency of the creative process is particularly relevant.[39] He considered "art as a component of technology"—"as the outcome of technical process, the sort of technical process in which artists are skilled."[40] As a result, Gell stressed a distinction between "beautiful" objects, which can include natural entities such as animals and sunsets, and objects that are "beautifully made" or "made beautiful"[41]—a distinction that was likewise embedded in Sumerian artistic practices and the terminology associated with them. For Gell, this "madeness"[42] of things called art—this "skilled crafting"—was part of a larger, "often unrecognized technical system, essential to the reproduction of human societies, which [he called] the technology of enchantment."[43] As an anthropologist, Gell departs from the modern, Western manner in which works of art are typically judged and valued (by an assessment of their "beauty") to give greater, or at least more nuanced, value to the processes by which they were made (by an assessment of how they are "made beautiful"), thereby concluding that "the way an art object is construed as having come into the world…is the source of the power such objects have over us—their becoming rather than their being."[44]

With this statement, Gell not only addresses the complex issue of the agency of objects and its connectedness to their aesthetic dimension, but also redirects the accepted modern and Western sense of aesthetic judgment to better align with that of any number of premodern and non-Western cultures, including that of Mesopotamia. I have no doubt that Gell would have responded to Puabi's jewelry aesthetically, as a work of art whose hold over him stemmed in large part from "the power that the technical processes have of casting a spell over us so that we see the real world in an enchanted form."[45] Bahrani, in her discussion of Gell's contributions, agrees: "Technological processes, linked to processes of ritual enchantment, produce a unique category of aesthetic things."[46]

Having made the case for a distinctly Mesopotamian aesthetic that allows for the image of Puabi to participate in the realm of art as much as that of archaeology, I will conclude by returning to the last of the problematic questions posed at the start: What of the fact that Puabi was buried; that she (her image) may not have been seen, or meant to be seen; that she (her image) ostensibly did not have an audience? Do images and the aesthetic consideration of them require a viewer? In ancient Mesopotamia, the production of objects meant for supernatural or metaphysical purposes and thus not dependent on mortal or physical audiences constituted a large and vital component of its material culture. Bahrani categorizes certain of these objects—such as foundation figurines—not by shape or medium but by representational status, as works "made, not for display, nor for an audience or viewership, but for *concealment*."[47] Although Bahrani specifically excludes burials from this category, I would argue that Puabi's jewelry (and thus her image and identity) nonetheless effects a related phenomenon, in that the power and/or meaning lay not in the literal seeing of it but in the making and wearing of it, whether in life or in death, seen or unseen.

The schema may be comparable to one at work in the myth of the goddess Inanna/ Ishtar's descent to the Netherworld, where she is made to discard her jewelry and garments, one piece at a time, and in the process loses a measure of her divine power with each item taken.[48] In this metaphysical conception of Inanna/Ishtar, her image equals the sum of her jewelry, and her jewelry *is* her identity and her power—in part, I would argue, by virtue of the way it was made and the aesthetic values that the making embodied and manifested. Objects and images in Mesopotamia lived comfortably in such metaphysical and often unseen realities, where aesthetics, agency, and identity were all part of a system of image making that served to disrupt or interrupt reality rather than refer to or copy it.[49] And because the image in Mesopotamia existed easily in less physical and literal realities than we are accustomed to today, efforts to match Puabi to other extant images of Sumerian women have never amounted to much.[50] That is why a faceless and incorporeal Puabi may ultimately best suit her ontological status as an image—purely the sum of her animated and aestheticized jewelry (see fig. 5–1). In her own time, Puabi may have wanted only to be seen by the divine and as divine; because of her archaeological discovery, she exists today in a highly physical and visible realm and can actually want different things from us, her new audience. It is the ongoing job of art historians and archaeologists, among others, to figure out exactly what those things are.

Endnotes

1 The groundbreaking work by Bahrani (1995, 2003, 2008) on the ontological status of images in antiquity is ongoing, articulated most recently in Bahrani 2014; the influential work by Mitchell (1986, 1994) on image theory is well-known, but here I give special homage to *What Do Pictures Want?* (2005).

2 Gell 1998.

3 Mitchell 2005: 6.

4 Ibid.: 7.

5 For the importance of defining the terms "image" and "aesthetics" in their appropriate cultural (here, ancient Near Eastern) contexts, see, among other of their writings, Winter 1995 and Bahrani 2014.

6 It is possible, though not confirmed archaeologically or otherwise, that the burial of Puabi and others at Ur entailed a procession of the ornamented corpses to their graves in a spectacle that was very much visible to the public (see Cohen 2005; Gansell 2007); see also also note 32 below.

7 Here, I would like to stress that I am in no way attempting to undermine or challenge the critical importance of proper archaeological excavation and research. I am simply observing, along with scores of others before and with me, that even the best-performed archaeological investigation can in one way or another influence the reception and interpretation of objects, as is so clearly demonstrated in the present exhibition and its accompanying catalogue.

8 See Azara and Marín, in this volume.

9 Evans (2012a) has also made this the underlying premise of her groundbreaking book on the lives of Sumerian sculpture. Yet, in both her book and her coauthored essay in this volume, she makes it clear that an ancient object can also "be an agent of spiritual or emotional experience for the observer, whether past or present." Evans and Green, in this volume.

10 See Zettler, in this volume.

11 Winter 1995, 2003, 2008; see also Bahrani 2014, esp. 43, 213.

12 Winter 2003: 403ff.

13 Ibid.: 406–10; even when the word "beautiful" is used, it is applied to the workmanship, as in an inscription on a statue from a later period: "the workmanship of which was beautiful to look at" (Bahrani 2014: 43). For a thorough treatment of what happens when modern scholars look for ancient objects to be beautiful, see Evans 2012a, esp. 46ff.

14 Winter 2003: 408.

15 Winter 1995: 2571; Winter 2003: 406.

16 Winter 2003: 418.

17 See also Bahrani 2014, esp. 43, 213.

18 Winter 2003: 416; and see Bahrani (2014, esp. 25), who argues that ancient objects can also be received and appreciated within the terms of modern and Western notions of aesthetics.

19 Winter 1995: 2572–75. See also Cassin 1968; Bruschweiler 1987; Winter 1999, 2012. Bahrani has recently extended this idea to include something akin to the millennia-later aesthetic concept of the Sublime, in which the aesthetic response is associated with the awe-inspiring magnificence of nature. See Bahrani 2014: 45–47.

20 Winter 1995: 2573; for more on this topic, see also Benzel 2013: 26ff.

21 Winter 1995: 2575.

22 As outlined in great detail by Bahrani 2003 and 2014.

23 See Bahrani (2014: 29ff.) on the inseparability of the aesthetic dimension of an ancient object from its sociohistorical context.

24 Bahrani 2008: 78; see also Bahrani 2014: 84–85.

25 For a critical analysis of Woolley's excavations of the cemetery, see the essays by Hafford and Zettler, and Pittman and Miller, both this volume.

26 As per Woolley's original interpretation (1934: 73ff.)

27 Zimmerman 1998b; see also Evans 2012a: 198.

28 See Pittman and Miller, in this volume.

29 Evans 2012a: 2.

30 For a complete treatment of Puabi's jewelry from this perspective, see Benzel 2013.

31 See ibid.: 32 n102.

32 The reasoning for this is manifold: the jewelry shows little sign of wear; certain pieces would not be supportable if the wearer were standing upright; and some ornaments have not been finished on their backsides; see also ibid.: 117ff. The last two of these observations could conceivably contradict the idea that the corpses of Puabi and others would have been seen upright in public, as remarked in note 6 above.

33 For more on the philological aspects of "shine," "holy, and "sacred," see ibid.: 26ff. See also Benzel forthcoming.

34 Bahrani 2002.

35 For more on the techniques available during this period, see Benzel 2013: 172ff.

36 For more on the philological aspects of "pure," see ibid.: 26ff.

37 For example, see Walker and Dick 1999, and Dick 2005; see also Bahrani 2003, 2014.

38 Bahrani 2014: 242 n31.

39   Gell 1992.

40   Ibid.

41   Ibid.: 43.

42   See also Koerner 1999 on the "madeness" of art objects.

43   Gell 1992: 44.

44   Ibid.: 46; see also Gell 1998 for the agentive qualities of artworks.

45   Gell 1992: 44.

46   Bahrani 2014: 38–39.

47   Ibid.: 89.

48   Sladek 1974.

49   Bahrani 2014: 67.

50   See, for example, Gansell 2007: 44.

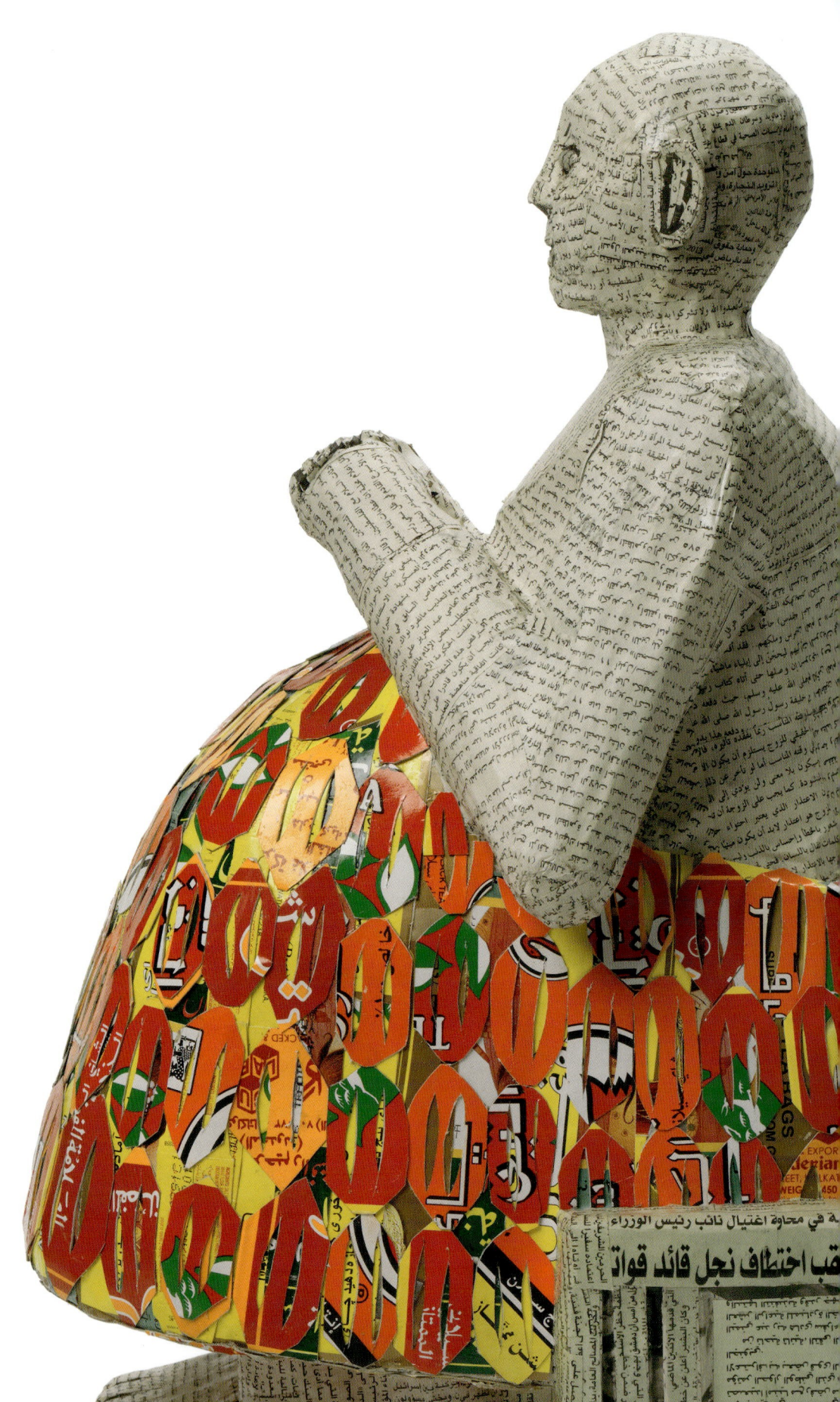

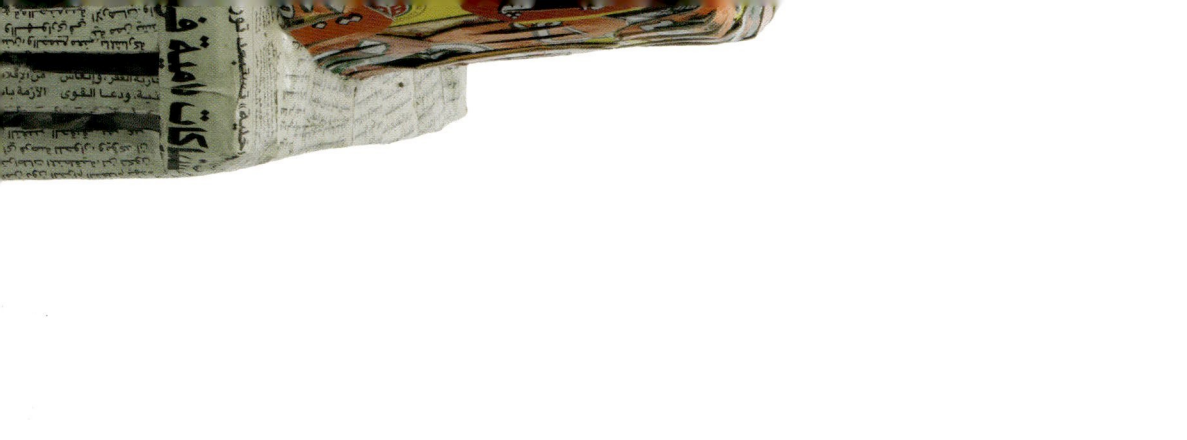

Ground to Gallery: The Discovery, Interpretation, and Display of Early Dynastic Sculpture from the Iraq Expedition of the Oriental Institute

Jack D. M. Green and Jean M. Evans

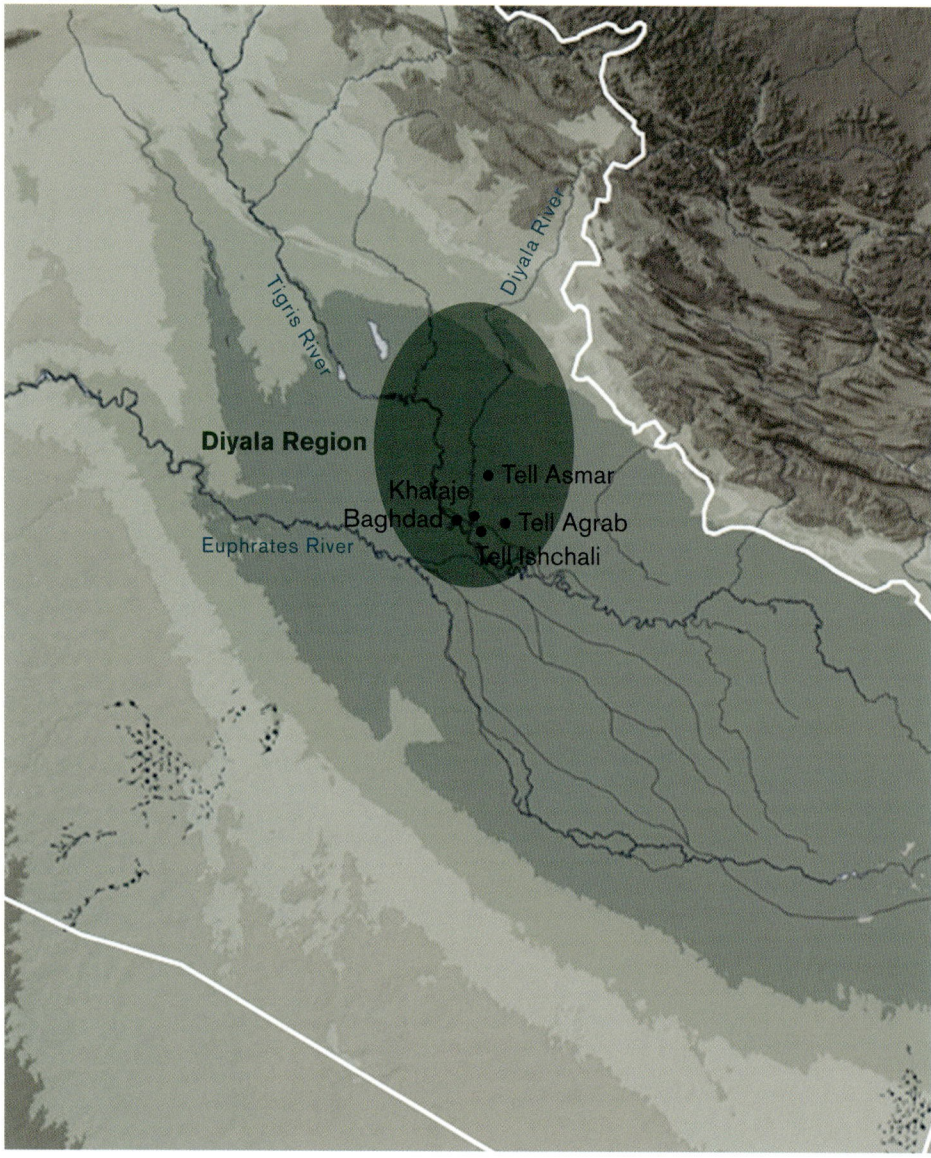

6-1. Map showing the Diyala region of Iraq and sites investigated by the Iraq Expedition of the Oriental Institute of the University of Chicago (1930–37).

The discovery of ancient Sumer was unique in ancient Near Eastern archaeology because there was no recognizable trace of the civilization in biblical, classical, or postclassical traditions. The mid-nineteenth-century rediscovery of the ancient Near East had taken place at the Assyrian capitals in northern Iraq. Subsequent archaeological excavation, however, increasingly shifted to southern Iraq, in search of Sumer. During the late nineteenth and early twentieth centuries, numerous sites yielded archaeological remains identified as Sumerian, and knowledge of Sumerian language and culture grew exponentially.[1]

In 1930 an archaeological sequence for the earliest known remains in southern Iraq was formulated at the first annual conference of archaeologists held in Baghdad.[2] Four cultural phases—Ubaid, Uruk, Jamdat Nasr, and Early Dynastic—were defined on the premise that distinct material assemblages are contemporary wherever they are encountered. The Iraq Expedition of the Oriental Institute of the University of Chicago began excavations in the Diyala region of Iraq, east of Baghdad, in the same year (fig. 6–1). One of the major results of the Diyala excavations was the further refinement of the established chronology. Over seven seasons of fieldwork the Iraq Expedition excavated numerous uninterrupted, stratified assemblages that allowed for the observation of subtle changes from level to level. The Early Dynastic period (ca. 2900–2350 BCE), in particular, had been an ill-defined time variously referred to as prediluvian, Lagash, pre-Sargonid, plano-convex, and early Sumerian. In 1935 the Early Dynastic period was subdivided into ED I, II, and III on the basis of the Iraq Expedition excavations.[3]

Hundreds of Early Dynastic statues and fragments of statues were excavated by the Iraq Expedition. In late nineteenth- and early twentieth-century ancient Near Eastern scholarship, what is now known as Early Dynastic sculpture was with few exceptions described as "Sumerian." The Diyala region is located geographically outside of Sumer, but the designation reflects the Sumerian culture and cultic practices in which it was reasonably assumed such sculpture originated. Modern scholarship today refers to Sumerians primarily as the inhabitants of the geographical region of Sumer.

In contrast, the study of Sumerians was dominated well into the twentieth century by racial inquiry. The origins of a Sumerian race were at the core of debates devoted to a complex issue known as the "Sumerian problem."[4] Early scholars believed that the examination of monuments could contribute to a resolution of the racial issues. Although differences were recognized, statues, relief carvings, skeletal remains, and living human beings comprised a single scientific category of ethnographic data that sought an understanding of the Sumerians as a physical, racial type (fig. 6–2). The identification of various races thus was the principal reason for examining sculpture—and an array of other visual imagery on relief carvings, cylinder seals, and inlays—excavated in the ancient Near East. Ancient visual culture therefore informed scientific inquiry ranging from early classifications of the Sumerian language to the identification of so-called Sumerian skeletal remains.[5]

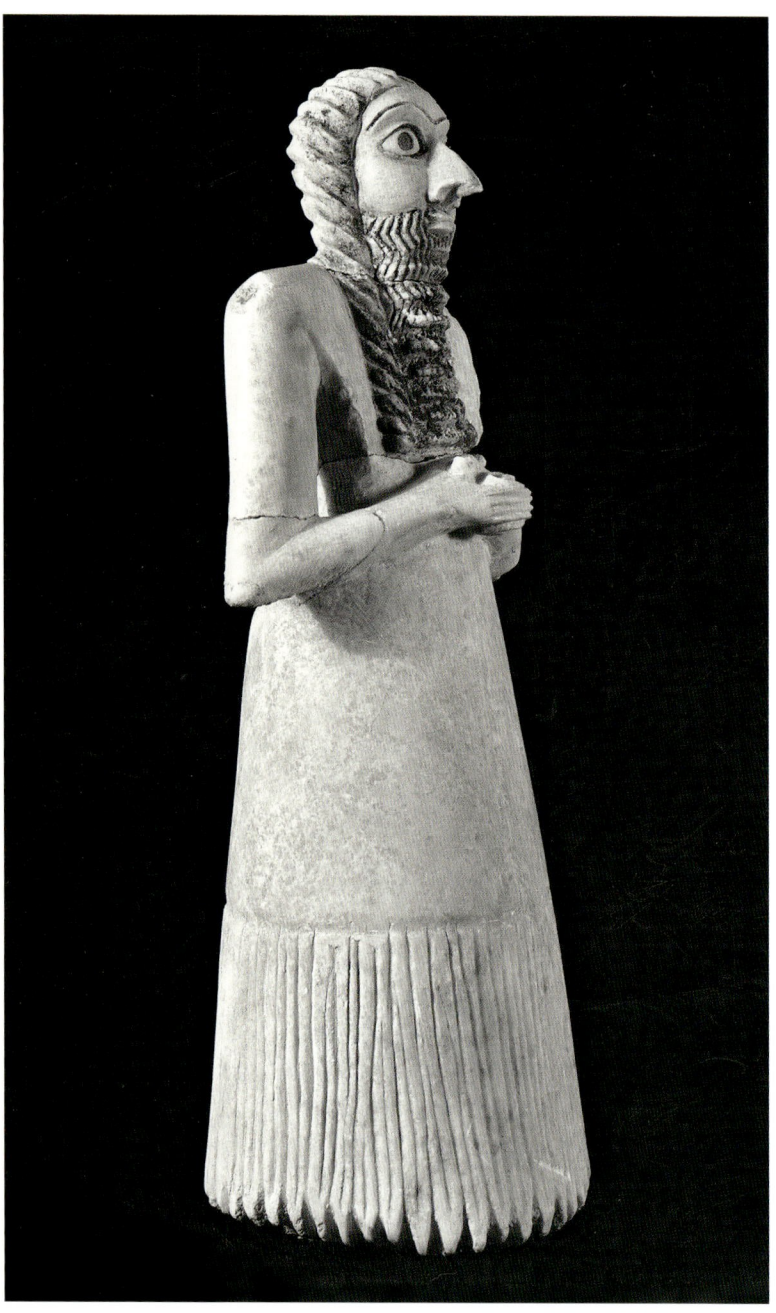

6–2. Standing Male Figure. Gypsum, alabaster, shell, black limestone, bitumen. Eshnunna (Tell Asmar), Early Dynastic period (ca. 2900–2600 BCE). MMA: 40.156. Fletcher Fund, 1940. Photograph: P. 2398, courtesy of the Oriental Institute of the University of Chicago. Checklist no. 140. The caption published in 1934 read: "A statue showing extremely well the physical type of the early Sumerians." See also fig. 1–2.

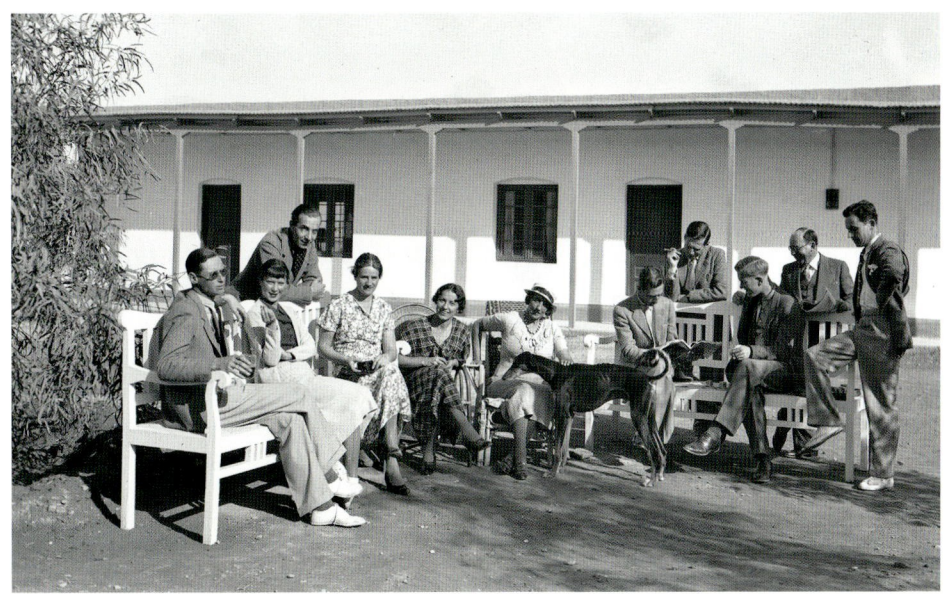

6–3. Excavation team outside the Iraq Expedition House, Tell Asmar. Photograph, December 1934. OIM: P. 24527. Henri Frankfort is standing behind the bench at the right, holding a cigar.

Consequently, the aesthetic reception of Sumerian sculpture was overshadowed in early ancient Near Eastern studies by the so-called Sumerian problem. When the Iraq Expedition conducted the Diyala excavations, however, a major methodological shift was occurring in the study of ancient monuments. In a departure from the racial emphasis of earlier studies of Sumerian sculpture, the Diyala publications utilized art historical methodologies, largely due to the efforts of Henri Frankfort (1897–1954), the field director of the Iraq Expedition and a major scholar in the field of ancient Near Eastern studies (fig. 6–3).

The Tell Asmar sculpture hoard (fig. 6–4), in particular, made a great impression on the excavators. Frankfort wrote to James Henry Breasted (1865–1935), the director of the Oriental Institute, shortly after the hoard was excavated. He apologized for the "rhapsodic disorder of the story" of the "sensational" discovery; he found it "very hard to remain seated at my desk under these circumstances."[6] The archaeologist Seton Lloyd (1902–1996), who physically excavated the Asmar hoard, wrote in a letter to his mother that "it will take me a long time to forget the intense excitement of lying on my tummy for almost two days, extracting one priceless antiquity after another from a hole in the ground, always with the feeling of awful responsibility."[7]

Frankfort proposed a publication of the Diyala sculptures that would focus on "the interest of the sculpture in the history of art," and envisioned a lavishly illustrated volume that would "put our finds into the hands of the increasing number of people who

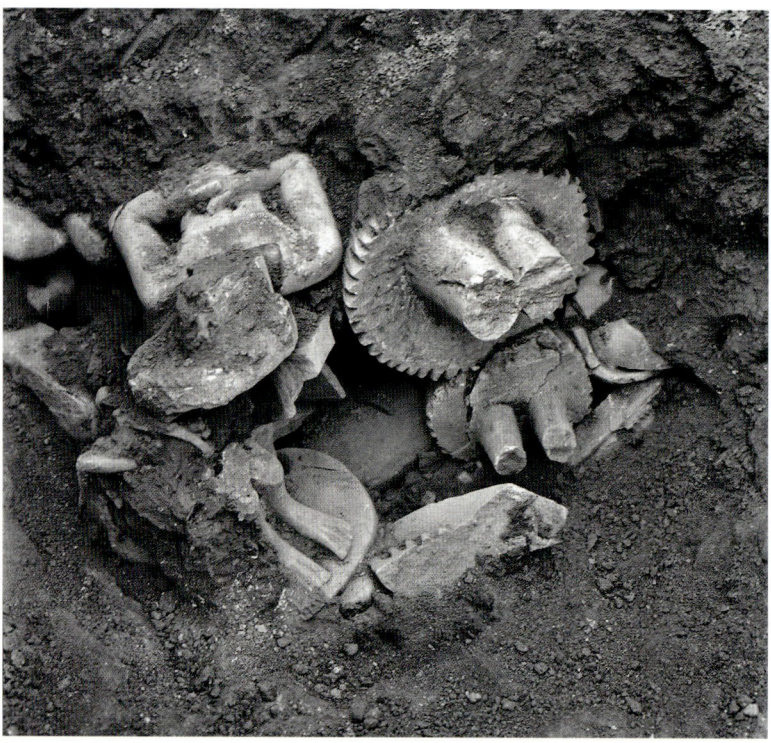

6–4. The hoard of statues at Tell Asmar in situ, Locus D17: 9. Photograph, 1934. OIM: As. 1091. Courtesy of the Oriental Institute of the University of Chicago.

are keen on oriental art."[8] He maintained that the Early Dynastic sculptures excavated in the Diyala region represented the most ancient "monumental stone sculpture," not only in the art history of Mesopotamia but in that of the world. He believed that the Asmar hoard (fig. 6–5), in particular, formed the "foundation of all sculptural achievement." The statues therefore could provide "an understanding of the phenomenon of art itself."[9]

The Sumerians had long been considered "primitive" since they were seen as the earliest civilization in world history. The discovery of the most ancient "monumental stone sculpture" accorded well with preconceived ideas of what Sumerian culture should represent, and thus was well poised to be received as "primitive" art.[10] According to then-current methodologies, ancient peoples resembled modern "primitive" peoples,[11] and the latter were seen as representative of an ancient stage in human development, as ancestral versions of Europeans. By the 1930s the aesthetic sensibility through which the arts of "primitive" cultures were embraced was well established in the Western art world. Moreover, abstraction resonated with an early twentieth-century aesthetic sensibility that viewed it as a fundamental quality of both "primitive" art and modern Western art. The shared vocabulary of abstraction was consequently applied

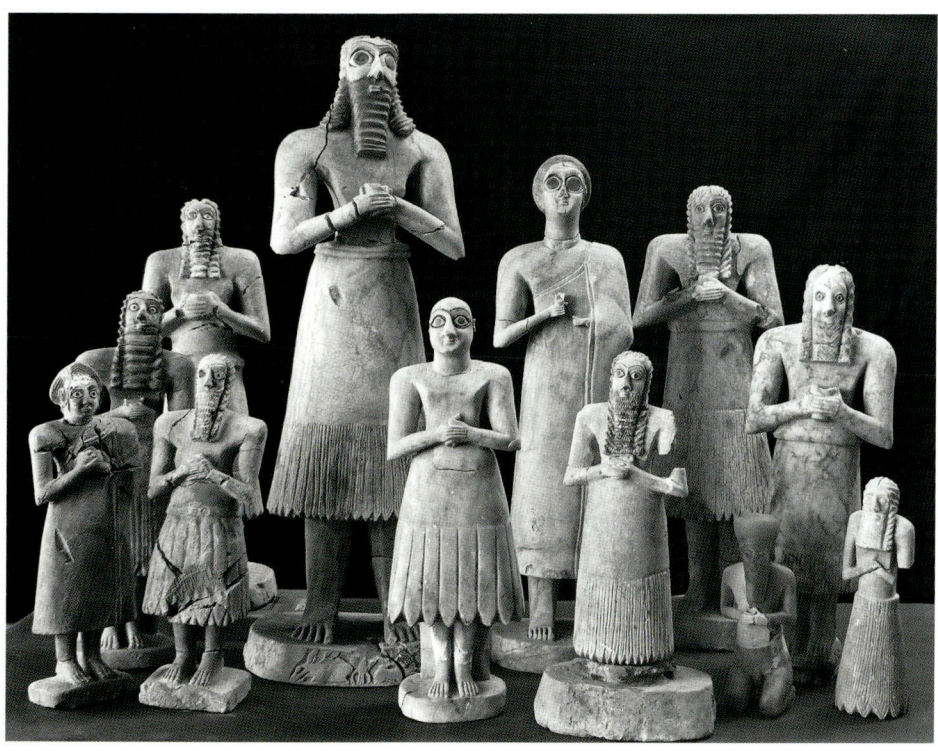

6–5. Group of figures from the Square Temple (Abu Temple), Tell Asmar. Photograph, ca. 1934. OIM: As. 1152. Courtesy of the Oriental Institute of the University of Chicago. Checklist no. 6. The statues are now divided among the Iraq Museum in Baghdad, the Oriental Institute of the University of Chicago, and the Metropolitan Museum of Art.

to the arts of various cultures across time and space. Frankfort published his final two volumes on the Diyala sculptures, *Sculpture of the Third Millennium B.c. from Tell Asmar and Khafajah* and *More Sculpture from the Diyala Region* (hereafter abbreviated as *Sculpture* and *More Sculpture*), in 1939 and 1943, respectively. Using the formal analyses of traditional art history,[12] two broad Early Dynastic sculptural styles were recognized and considered chronologically significant. The hoard of twelve well-preserved statues buried in the Abu Temple at Tell Asmar was designated the prime example of an earlier sculptural style, characterized by the simplification of corporeal forms into geometric, or "abstract," shapes (fig. 6–6), while a later style was described as "realistic" (fig. 6–7).[13] Outside the sphere of ancient Near Eastern studies, Sumerian art had already been accepted within the formal canons of abstraction.

A decade before Frankfort had published *Sculpture*, E. H. Rothschild, author of *The Meaning of Unintelligibility in Modern Art*, had reviewed in 1929 a British Museum catalogue of Babylonian and Assyrian sculpture and declared that "Sumerian art, in some respects, stands alone in the near eastern tradition for spontaneity and vigor and for a direct and significant expression of plastic power."[14] In *Sculpture,* Frankfort similarly described the sculptures in the Tell Asmar hoard as exhibiting a

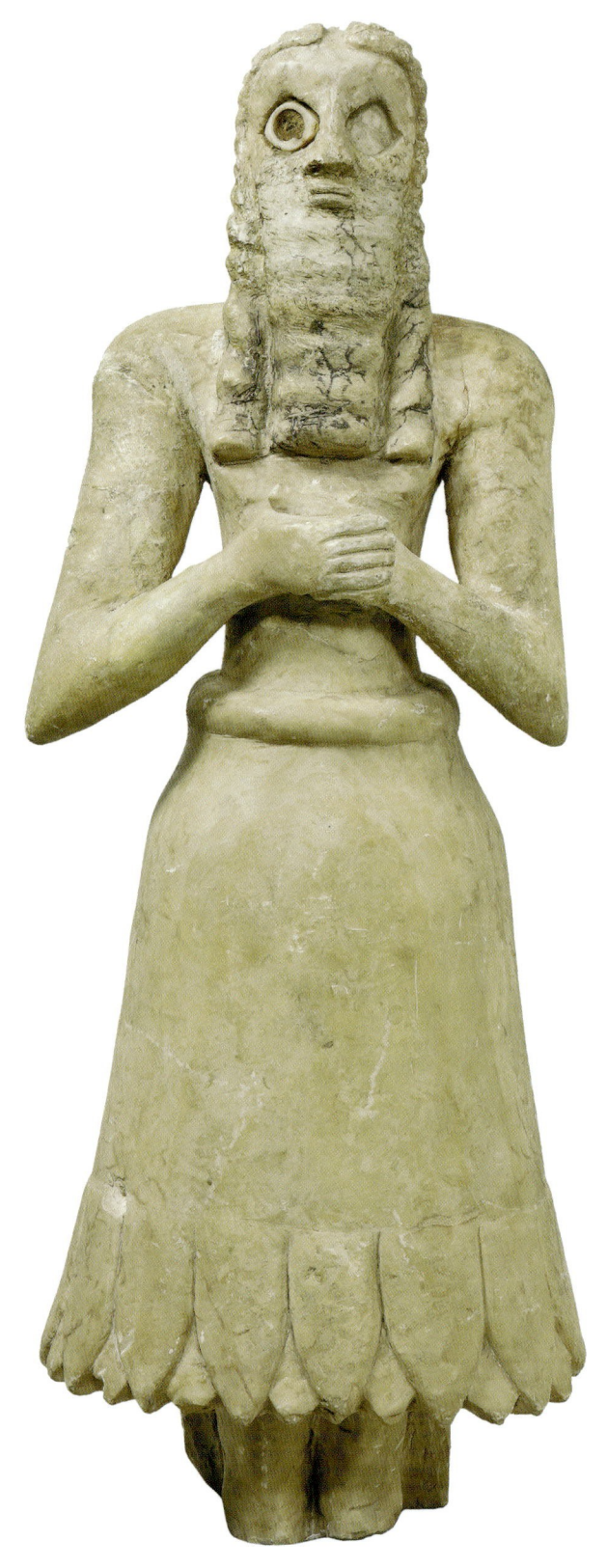

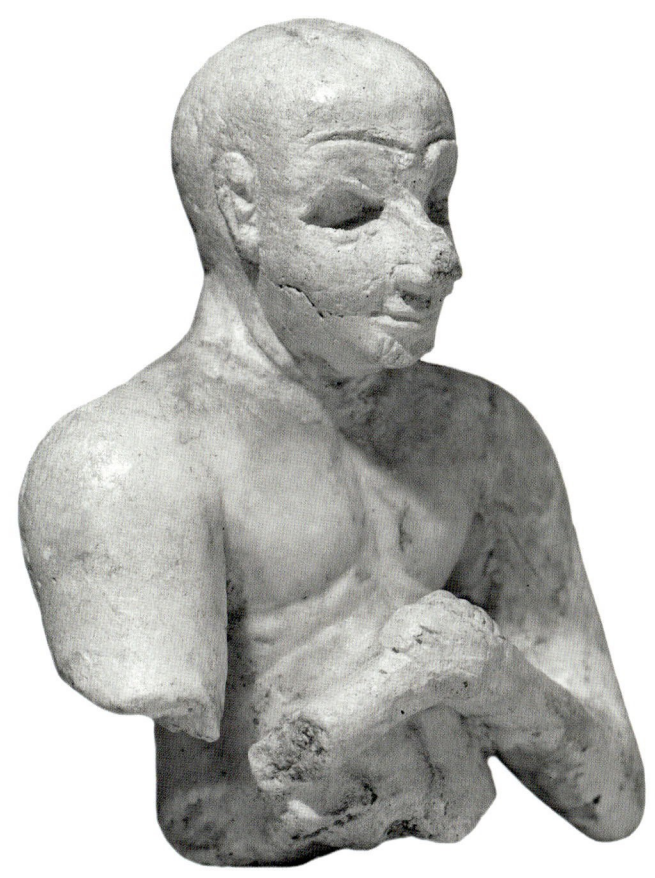

6–6. Standing Male Figure. Gypsum, shell, bitumen, Khafajah (Sin Temple IX), ca. 2700–2500 BCE. OIM: A12434. Iraq Expedition of the Oriental Institute, 1930–37. Checklist no. 54. Example of Frankfort's "abstract" sculptural style.

6–7. Top Half of a Male Figure. Gypsum, Khafajah (Sin Temple IX), ca. 2700–2500 BCE. OIM: A12387. Iraq Expedition of the Oriental Institute, 1930–37. Checklist no. 50. Example of Frankfort's "realistic" sculptural style.

"spontaneous stylization" executed with "great vigor" and "extraordinary power."[15] Descriptions of fundamental shapes, masses, and forms of expressive power, vigor, and spontaneity belonged to the collective vocabulary for describing abstraction in the early twentieth century. The innovation of Frankfort—in *Sculpture, More Sculpture,* and other publications—was that he oriented the art historical reception of Diyala sculpture within this vocabulary. As a result, he was instrumental in effecting a methodological shift in the study of Early Dynastic sculpture away from the racial issues of the "Sumerian problem."

The understanding of so-called primitive art as a collection of universal visual attributes promoted comparisons among radically different artistic traditions.[16] The emphasis on formal analysis in early twentieth-century art history thus allowed Frankfort and other scholars, as well as critics and artists, to link Sumerian sculpture to abstraction both in other "primitive" cultures and in modern Western art. Aesthetic form in this respect was not linked to a particular time or place. Frankfort, for example, wrote articles about contemporary abstractionists such as his friend the sculptor Barbara Hepworth, and took his Oriental Institute class on Egyptian art to a Picasso exhibition at the Art Institute of Chicago.[17] The cylinder, according to Frankfort, was the fundamental form in Mesopotamian art, whereas the cube was the fundamental form of Egyptian art, which therefore shared affinities with modern Cubism.[18] Finally, James Johnson Sweeney, who organized one of the earliest African art exhibitions in America and later became director of the Guggenheim Museum, found in 1943 an austerity reminiscent of Sumerian sculpture in the paintings of Seurat.[19]

For several decades already, scholars have reflexively examined the processes underlying conceptions of universal form in "primitive" art. Rejecting the notion that any actual tradition can be defined as primitive, it is now recognized that the idea of the primitive, like that of the Orient, is located in its relationship with the Western beholder.[20] In the early twentieth-century response, however, "primitive" art stood alone, unencumbered and unmitigated by cultural context. The "primitive" as such was a collection of visual attributes construed by the West as universally characteristic of primal artistic expression. The result was a blank slate onto which Western meanings and perceptions were projected, fantasized, and realized.[21]

It is important to acknowledge that the emphasis on form that linked Sumerian sculpture to abstraction in the sculpture of other "primitive" cultures, as well as to modern Western art, originated in the specific time and place of the early twentieth-century Western art world. Formal analysis is a tenant of traditional art history and a legitimate approach to studying art, but the emphasis on formal art historical analysis in the early study of the Sumerians created a vacuum that divorced Early Dynastic statues from a fuller exploration of their use and meaning in the temple. Some modern scholars continue to perceive affinities among disparate cultures across space and time by utilizing the same early twentieth-century paradigm for the aesthetics of "primitive" abstraction. However, there is no universal meaning for abstraction as such. Only a consideration of Early Dynastic sculpture in its ancient context can determine the significance of these statues for the culture that produced them.

Reconstructing Early Dynastic Sculpture in Temple and Ritual Settings

Early Dynastic statues were temple objects.[22] Inscribed examples indicate that the most common request to accompany the dedication of an Early Dynastic statue was for a long, healthy, and prosperous life for the donor.[23] Through dedication the donor thereby sought the benevolence and protection of the resident deity of a temple. Early Dynastic statues, it is commonly argued, were displayed in the sanctuary so that as representations of the donor they could perform, with clasped hands, an eternal prayer before the divine.

Reconstructions of Early Dynastic statues in the ancient temple are still primarily informed by the early reception of the Diyala sculptures as art because the practice of isolating objects for attentive looking is as particular to Western culture as is the museum space in which such activity occurs.[24] In the late nineteenth and early twentieth centuries, the dominant display model for sculpture in museums was its installation against a wall (fig. 6–8).[25] Early Dynastic statues were reconstructed in static rows against the long walls of the most important part of the temple and set in isolation from other temple objects (fig. 6–9).[26] In this manner, the statues as reconstructed in ancient context resembled their display in the modern museums for which they ultimately were destined.

These archaeological reconstructions have remained a part of modern scholarship, even though Early Dynastic statues were never actually found set up for display as such.[27] Many statues were hoarded and buried in temples. Others were built into the mud-brick architecture and cultic installations of temples, and still others were found in various locations throughout the temple rather than in the sanctuary. If we dismantle the early archaeological reconstructions of Early Dynastic sculpture, a fuller consideration can be given to the ancient evidence for rituals of sculpture.[28]

Why was sculpture dedicated in such abundance during the Early Dynastic period? One theory concerns the desire to overcome restricted access to the temple. The concept of materiality comes into play here.[29] That is, the object world of the statue is distinct from the world of the donor after dedication has occurred: as a material, physical form the statue was separate from the donor. Symptomatic of this quality of separateness, the temple statue assumed functions beyond the eternal prayer encoded by the donor in the dedicatory act.

Textual evidence from the late Early Dynastic e_2-mi_2 archive of the city-state of Lagash demonstrates that temple statues were the recipients of offerings when the queens of Lagash visited temples on the occasions of festivals.[30] Dates and oil were the most frequent offerings to statues. In one instance, the queen Sasa made offerings to statues during the festival in the courtyard of the temple of the goddess Bau.[31] Archaeological evidence demonstrates that, more generally, entrances, courtyards, and small rooms are all legitimate findspots reflecting the life of Early Dynastic temple statues. Both textual and archaeological sources therefore indicate that statues were not always sequestered in the sanctuary, where access was limited to the few who

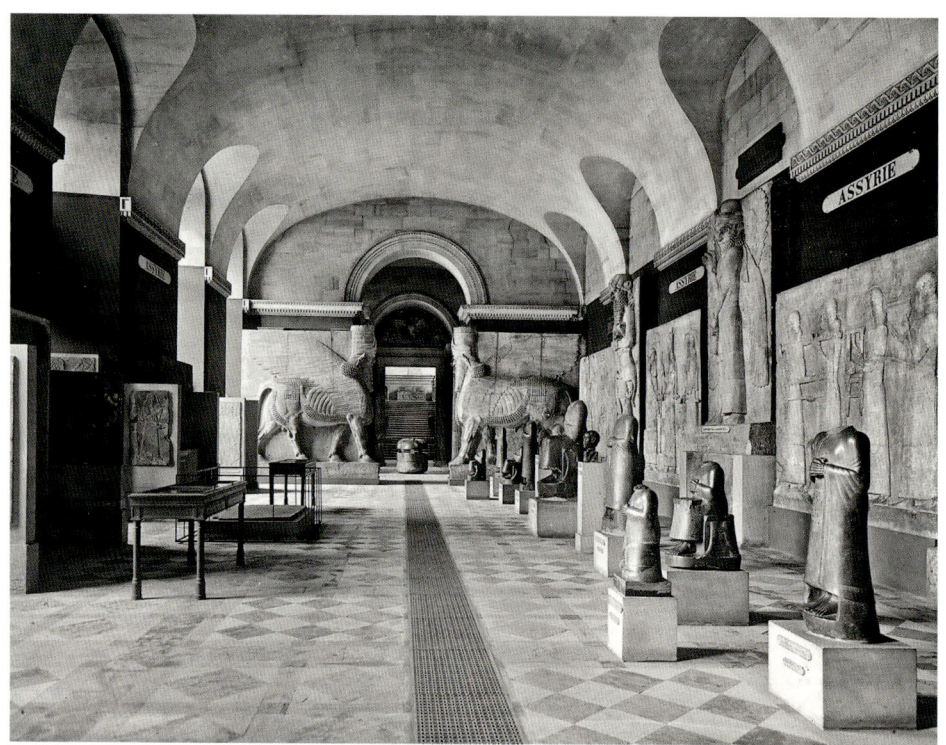

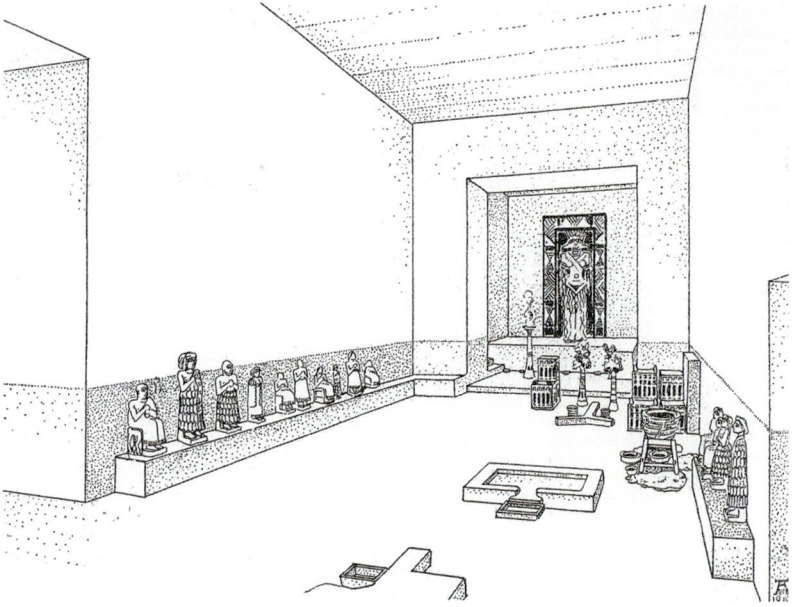

6–8. Louvre Museum, Assyro-Chaldean Gallery, ca. 1900.

6–9. Reconstruction of the Ishtar Temple G sanctuary at Ashur (Andrae 1919: table 11a).

catered to the needs of the god. In their release from the sanctuary, the statues became available to, and encountered, a wider audience. They potentially negotiated the very terrain of access as the recipients of offerings.

The Early Dynastic queens of Lagash made offerings that highlight the extent to which statues were external to the individual who donated. There is only one example in the Lagash texts in which a queen made an offering to her own statue.[32] On all other occasions, the queens made offerings to statues of donors who were still alive and those of donors who were deceased. There are also instances when the queens administered offerings to statues simply described as *alan*, the Sumerian term that we translate as "statue" or, more generally, "image." It is possible, then, that offerings to statues formed a social practice that existed beyond the donor. The textual evidence would suggest that the social practice of tending objects, including *alan*, was one instance in which an individual could be present in the temple.

All these offerings—to statues of known persons, either living or deceased, and to statues of unnamed individuals—can be related conceptually. Temple statues served as intermediaries between the human donor and the divine. In a similar manner, temple statues also acted as intermediaries between the temple visitor and the divine and formed the focal point for offerings that mediated between the living and the deceased. In all these instances, intercession is possible only with the mediation of the temple statue—not the individuals themselves who are represented by the statue.

Given that a temple visitor might tend to a statue even when he or she was not the donor of the statue, and even when the identity of the individual represented was unknown, the *alan* was the focus of cultic activities in its own right. Moreover, its consistent style—a frontal human figure with clasped hands—made the *alan* identifiable within a larger typology of other dedicatory objects, and thus the temple statue would have been the focus of cultic activities because of its visual appearance.[33] The quality of abstraction that is characteristic of the entire corpus potentially aided the effectiveness of this visual image by allowing for a degree of consistency, and consequently could have facilitated through time and space the generation of social bonds that were mediated by the material presence of the *alan*. The appearance of the Early Dynastic temple statue is critical for an understanding of its life inside the temple: one significant factor underlying the abstraction of Early Dynastic sculpture was likely the desire for a consistently recognizable form that signified a temple statue to a greater degree than it signified a specific human donor.

Displaying the Sculptures: Reception and Reinterpretation in Museum Settings

A number of studies have explored the history of museum displays in their historical and social contexts, but there has been limited focus on museum displays devoted to ancient Mesopotamia.[34] More specifically, the exhibition of Early Dynastic sculptures has seldom been explored in detail.[35] As discussed above, traditional (often classically informed) curatorial practice and museum display had an impact on the way in which Early Dynastic sculpture was presented within archaeological reconstructions of the early twentieth century. This art historical emphasis has overshadowed the statues' interpretation, their academic reception, and ultimately their modern display and reception by museum visitors. The following discussion assesses the "second lives" of the Sumerian sculptures after their archaeological discovery, as they have been reframed and reinterpreted in the context of modern museum displays. What messages were being communicated by the curators responsible for exhibiting the objects, and how might those objects have been received by museum visitors? Here we trace the history of their exhibition by the Oriental Institute of the University of Chicago, touching briefly on their presentation elsewhere.

The role of these sculptures as museum objects is significant considering the number of people who have viewed them in modern times. Taking into account an average of 50,000 annual visitors to the Oriental Institute,[36] it is likely that over the past eighty years more than 4,000,000 individuals have physically encountered the Early Dynastic sculptures at that venue alone. Presumably this is far greater than the number encountering them in antiquity, even if the statues were permitted out of the sanctuary.

Through articles in the *Illustrated London News* (fig. 6–10), Henri Frankfort propelled the discovery of the Tell Asmar hoard of sculpture and findings at Khafajah to an international audience,[37] making this extraordinary assemblage of human images accessible to the public for the first time. Shortly after their excavation and initial public exposure in the spring of 1934, the first public display of this Early Dynastic sculpture in the United States took place. Five of the statues that were part of a formal division of objects from the Iraq Expedition were shown in a single case within the Oriental Institute's exhibit at the Chicago World's Fair of 1933–34, also known as *A Century of Progress* (figs. 6–11, 6–12).[38] The most relevant and image-rich pages of Frankfort's article in the *Illustrated London News* provided graphic support, with a full page devoted to Rachel Levy's watercolor of a selection of the best-preserved statues (see fig. 2–15).[39] Her rendering helped to convey the immediacy, excitement, and importance of the discovery, as well as to provide visitors with a reconstruction of the statues as they may have appeared with their original pigment and inlayed materials. The Oriental Institute exhibit also included other artifacts, a series of casts of objects from the Egyptian Museum in Cairo, paintings and photographs from the Oriental Institute's Persian Expedition to Persepolis, architectural models, and an Egyptian mummy from the Oriental Institute's collection.

Studies of the Chicago World's Fair of 1933–34 have tended to focus on its modern approaches to architecture and science, as well as its social legacy.[40] The slogan of the fair, "Science Finds—Industry Applies—Man Conforms," highlighted the primacy of the scientist in modern culture and the ability of humankind to conquer nature in the present and future. Movement was a major theme, with action-packed displays highlighting technological advances. Such futuristic displays contrasted with conventional exhibits of artifacts and static models representing the past. Some exhibits at the World's Fair focused on Chicago's achievements over the previous hundred years (hence, "A Century of Progress"), whereas the Hall of Social Science, the Hall of Religion, the Land of a Million Years Ago, as well as the Art Institute of Chicago and the Field Museum, served as venues that featured the ancient past.[41] In the Hall of Social Science, for instance, ancient artifacts were included in its focus on the positive social consequences of scientific advancements.[42] Yet the overall impact of the past on contemporary life as conveyed at the World's Fair appears to have been minimal and generally at odds with the prevalent message of technological advancement.[43]

James Henry Breasted wrote a short report on the Oriental Institute's exhibit at the time of its opening at the Chicago World's Fair, beginning with a discussion of these remarkable statues, indicating the perceived importance of their display to the public, and their crucial contribution to art history:

> In completing its exhibit at the Century of Progress Exposition the Oriental Institute has just installed a group of five statues, or perhaps better, statuettes, which are the oldest sculptures ever found in Asia. They were excavated by the Iraq Expedition of the Oriental Institute at the ancient cities of Eshnunna and Opis which the Institute is systematically clearing and investigating. Opis was the oldest Semitic capital of Babylonia, the identity of which was first established by discoveries of the Institute expedition during the past winter. The statues arrived from excavations only a few weeks ago and have since been undergoing the usual processes of conservation to prevent their suffering any damage in a climate different from that of their ancient habitat. While the modern art student will not regard these sculptures as beautiful, they disclose the power of *primitive art*[44] and the faces are fascinatingly interesting. They are rendered exceedingly impressive by the use of extraordinarily large eyes.
>
> The source of the statues is likewise very interesting. Winter before last the expedition at Eshnunna cleared a temple of the time of Sargon, of the 26th Century B.C. Further excavation <u>under</u> this building disclosed below it a second temple. On clearing the holy-of-holies of this third and lowest temple they found buried alongside the rectangular base, on

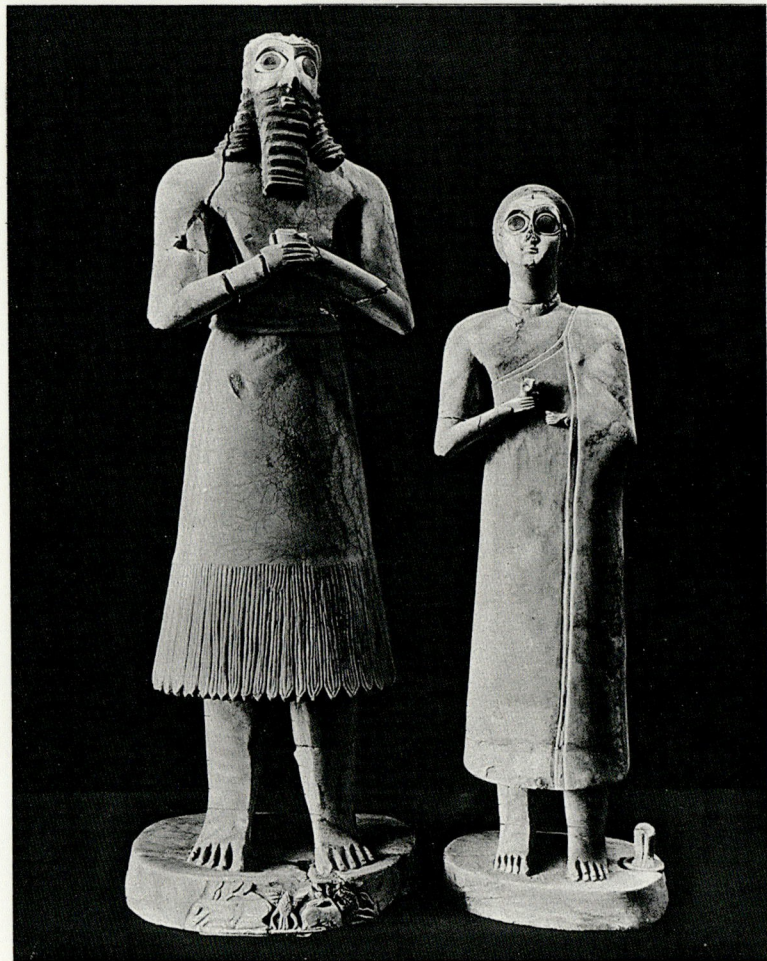

THE ILLUSTRATED LONDON NEWS.

The Copyright of all the Editorial Matter, both Engravings and Letterpress, is Strictly Reserved in Great Britain, the Colonies, Europe, and the United States of America.

SATURDAY, MAY 19, 1934.

A REMARKABLE DISCOVERY OF THE FIRST KNOWN SUMERIAN CULT-STATUES: THE LORD OF FERTILITY AND THE MOTHER GODDESS, OF ABOUT 3000 B.C. (HEIGHT OF THE GOD, INCLUDING BASE, ABOUT 30 IN.)

Here and on five other pages (two in colour) we illustrate new discoveries made at Tell Asmar, fifty miles north-east of Baghdad, by the Iraq Expedition of the Chicago University Oriental Institute, as described by Dr. Henry Frankfort on page 776. Mr. Seton Lloyd was again in immediate charge of the work at the temple, and Dr. Thorkild Jacobsen of that at the private houses. From this temple, which is of the Early Dynastic Sumerian period, datable to about 3000 B.C., came twelve complete statues, including the first cult-statues (shown herewith) ever found in Babylonian excavations. The character of the goddess is indicated by the small statuette of her son, of which only the feet are preserved, let into the base. The base of the god's statue bears his triple symbol—gazelles, plants, and the lion-headed eagle, Imgi. The hair is blackened with bitumen, and the eyes inlaid with black limestone and shell. The cup which each grasps suggests the annual New Year feast following the union of god and goddess to ensure fertility.

6–10. Front page of the *Illustrated London News*, May 19, 1934.

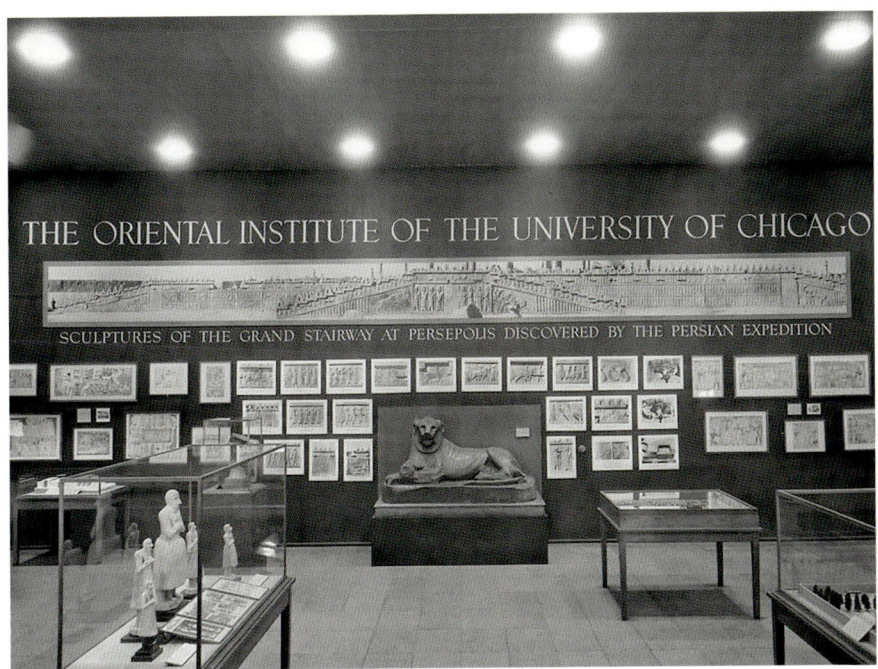

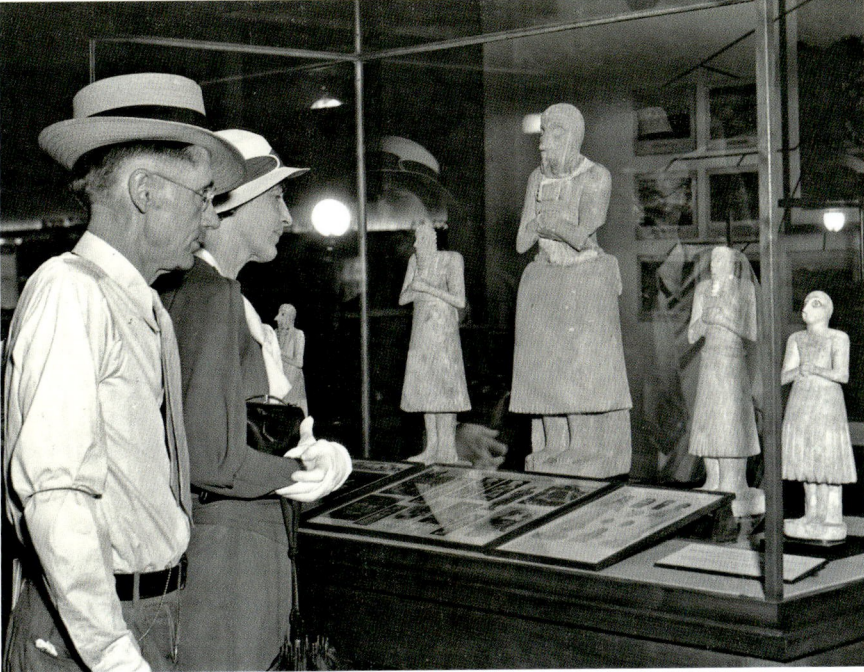

6-11. "Century of Progress" International Exposition, Chicago, 1933–34. Photograph, 1934. OIM: P. 24146. Courtesy of the Oriental Institute of the University of Chicago. Checklist no. 18.

6-12. Visitors to the World's Fair "viewing the primitive subjects." "Century of Progress" International Exposition, Chicago, 1933–34. Photograph, 1935. OIM: COP_17_0003_00087_002. Courtesy of the University of Illinois at Chicago: Century in Progress Archive.

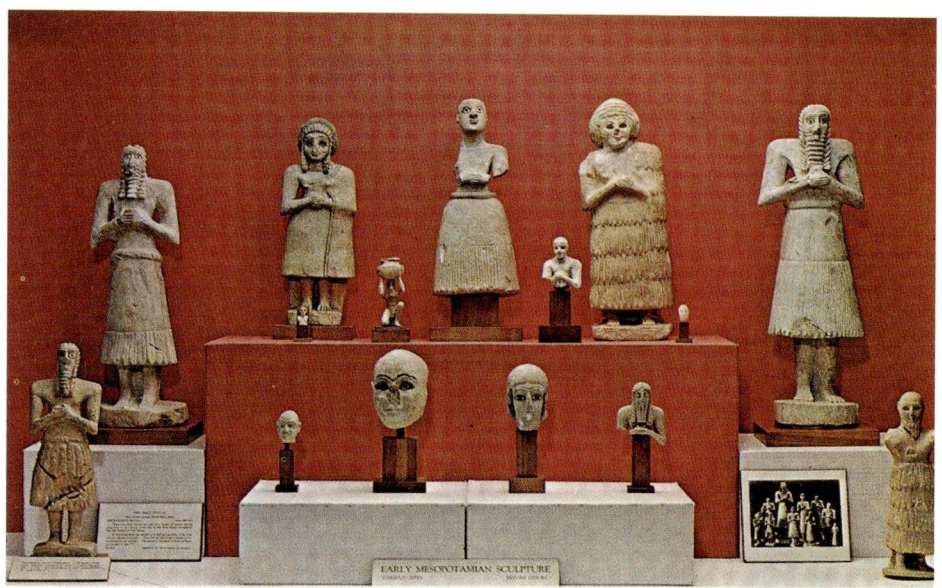

6-13. Postcard of installation of Diyala figurines at the Oriental Institute. Paper, ca. 1960–70. Checklist no. 20. The caption on the reverse reads: "The University of Chicago, Oriental Institute. Statues from Mesopotamia. From Various Sites in Iraq. Before 2200 BC.".

which the divine image had once been set up, a group of no less than twelve statues lying in a pit beneath the floor, piled one upon the other like a heap of cord-wood. They were all for the most part in an extraordinarily good state of preservation and constitute a discovery of unrivalled importance and of unprecedented age, for they date from no less than 3000 B.C. The visitors to the Exposition will enjoy the first public exhibition of these remarkable works of earliest known Asiatic art.[45]

Although the original labels for the display have not been located, the word "primitive" was not only used by Breasted but also appeared in a caption for an image by the fair's photographers that features an artist viewing the statues (fig. 6–12).[46] The use of this term emphasizes how the sculptures were intended to be viewed by visitors: both as sensational new discoveries and as examples of "primitive art."

The implication that the statues were "primitive" relates not only to their perceived abstract form and early date, but also to their status as precursors to the artistic achievements of subsequent centuries, as represented by the surrounding artifacts, casts, and images displayed at the Chicago World's Fair. For example, a replica of the bust of Nefertiti, an icon of New Kingdom Egyptian art, was featured next to the statues.[47] Along one wall within the exhibit space were numerous photographs of Achaemenid reliefs from Persepolis, a major artistic achievement of the first millennium BCE. Unfortunately, no records are available at the present time to indicate how the Early

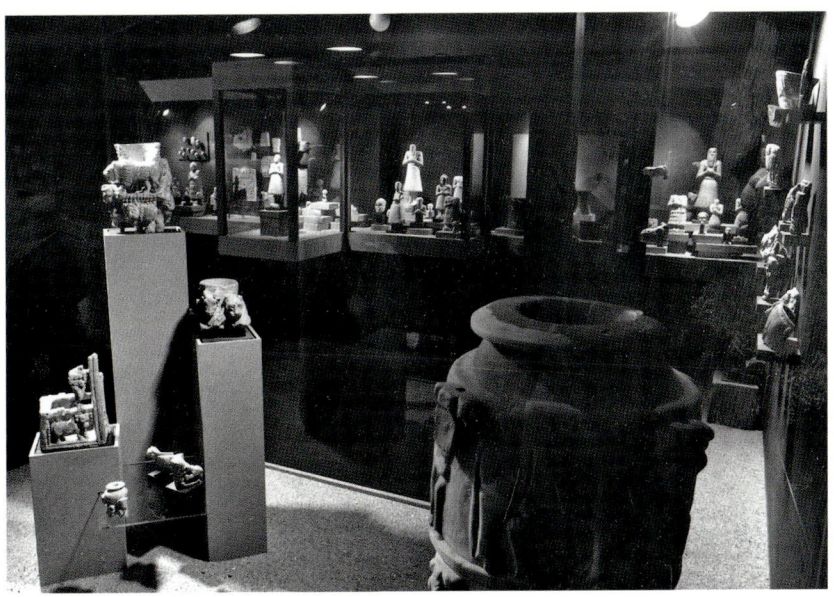

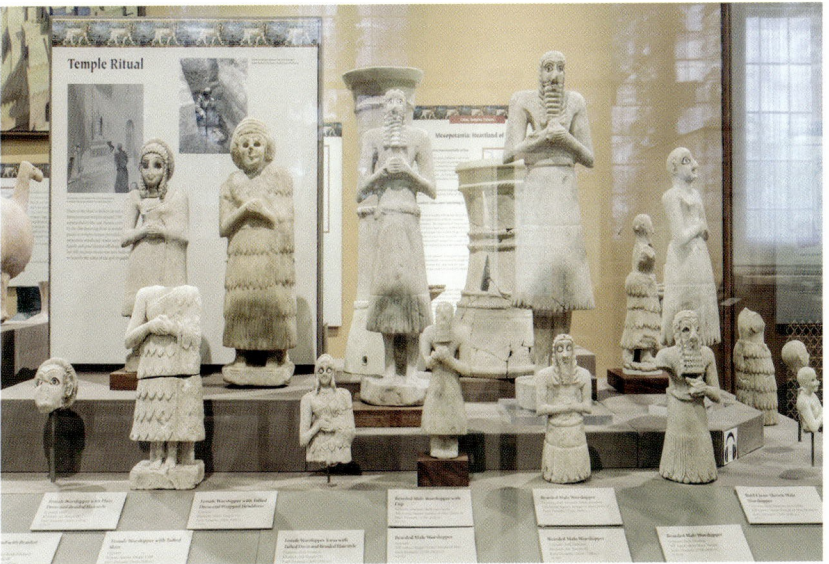

6–14. A view of the Mesopotamia Hall at the Oriental Institute Museum, University of Chicago, completed in 1977. Photograph. OIM: P.64069. Courtesy of the Oriental Institute of the University of Chicago.

6–15. The Diyala sculptures at the Oriental Institute Museum displayed in the Edgar and Deborah Jannotta Mesopotamian Gallery, 2003. Photograph, 2014. OIM: D.027541. Courtesy of the Oriental Institute of the University of Chicago.

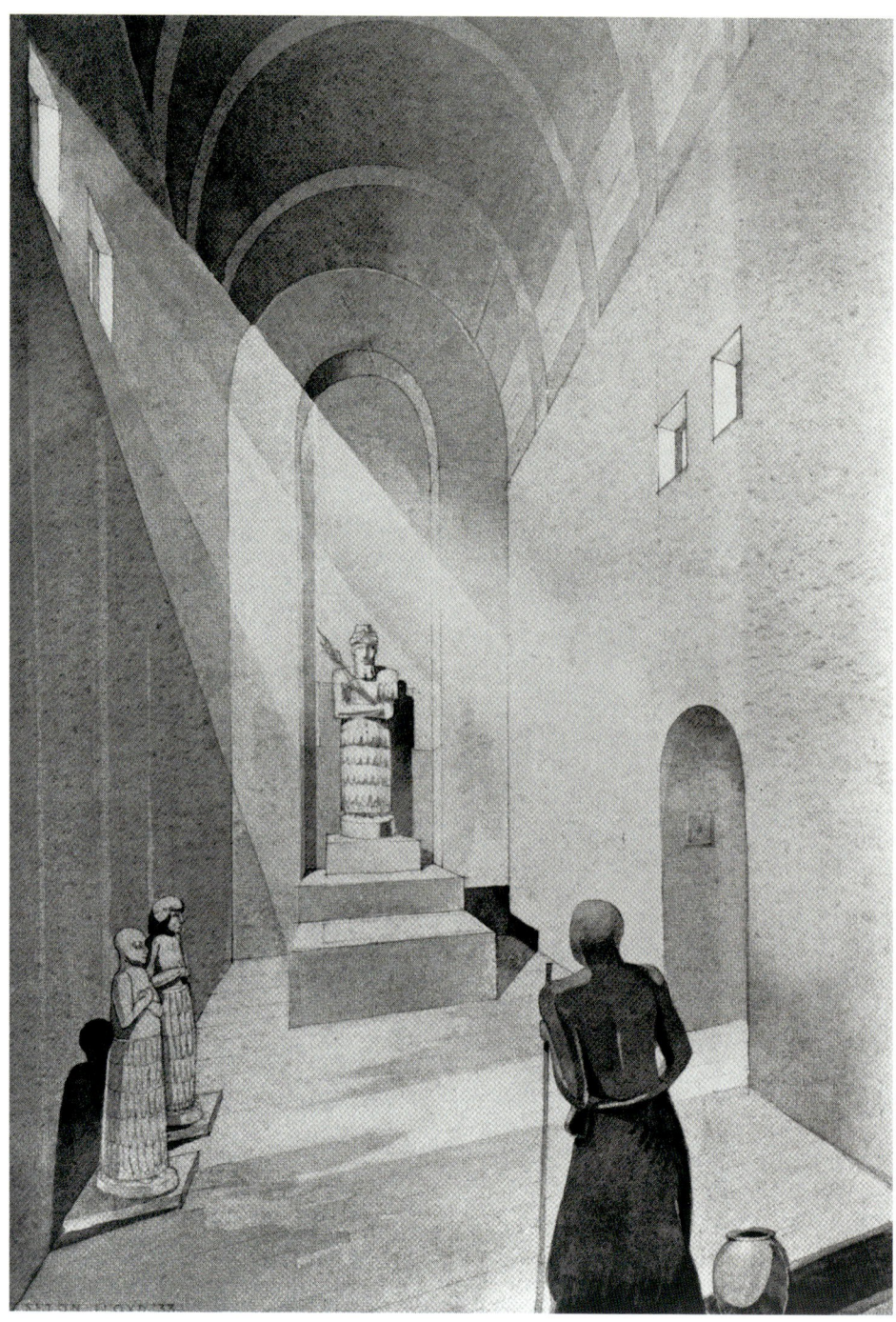

6-16. Seton Lloyd's 1933 reconstruction of Tell Asmar, Abu Temple.

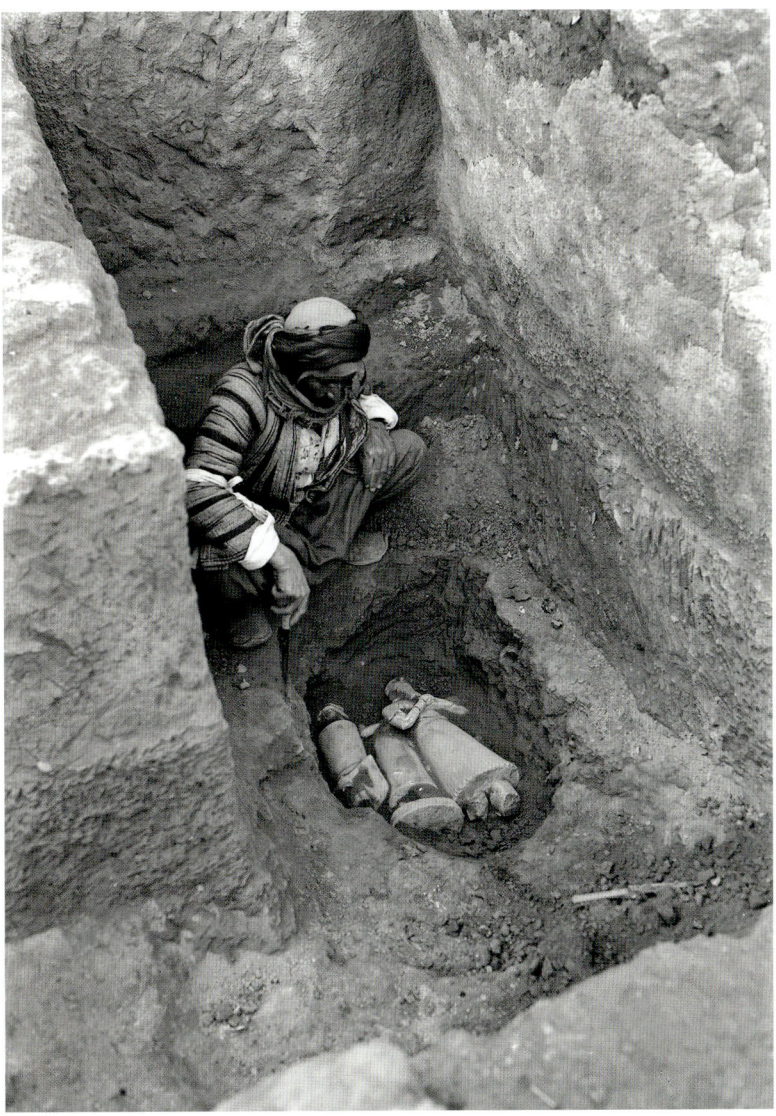

6–17. Statues in situ with one of the excavation workers, Tell Asmar. Photograph, January 1934. OIM: P.26904. Courtesy of the Oriental Institute of the University of Chicago.

Dynastic sculptures were received by visitors to the World's Fair, or whether they had a widespread cultural impact as "primitive art" as a result of this presentation.

The Oriental Institute's first permanent display of Early Dynastic sculpture was installed in the mid-1930s and continued until the mid-1970s. It grouped several of the Diyala statues on a series of plinths against a red background, a visually appealing and symmetrical arrangement that strongly reflected the variety of forms, dimensions, and levels of preservation (fig. 6–13). The inclusion of a black-and-white photograph of the

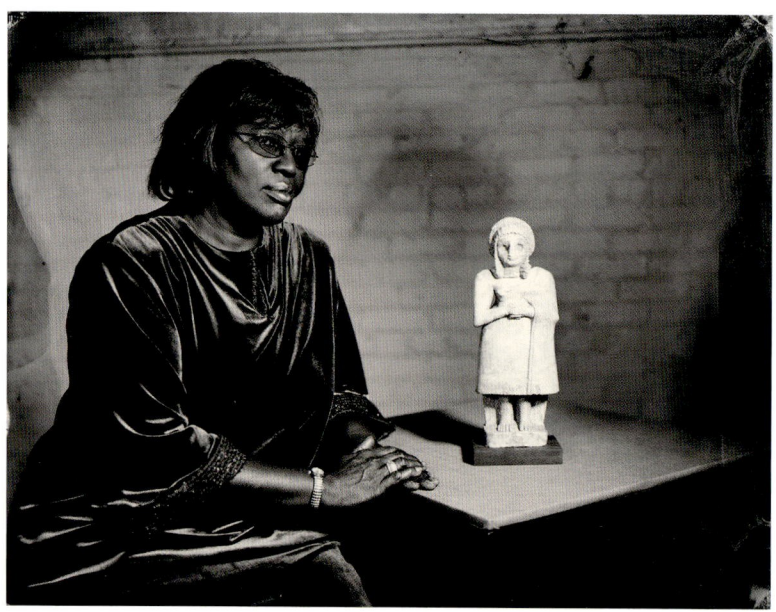

6–18. Diane Mayers Jones with one of the female Diyala statues. OIM: A12412. Photo: Jason Reblando.

best-preserved Tell Asmar statue group prior to its division helped to provide a better sense of the types of statues discovered, and a link to the treatment of this group as an assemblage (see fig. 6–5). Other examples of intact sculptures were displayed individually in single display cases nearby. The relatively small size and fragmentary nature of the sculptures precluded their open display beyond the confines of glass and wood trim.

The redesign and installation of the Oriental Institute's Mesopotamia Hall in 1977, initially overseen by curator Gustavus F. Swift III and subsequently by acting curator Judith A. Franke, afforded a more dynamic, educational, and atmospheric exhibit with in-case lighting, and presented the full range of sculptural fragments and statues across a series of interconnected customized display cases (fig. 6–14).[48] The elevation of some sculptures on raised slabs alluded to their original presentation as cult statues in a Mesopotamian temple or shrine. The layout may have referenced, in part, Walter Andrae's famous and imaginative reconstruction of a temple at Assur, with its statues positioned along the walls (see fig. 6–9).[49] The new installation at the Oriental Institute also presented a large number of sculptures and fragments as an eclectic, diverse assemblage of archaeological objects in varying levels of preservation. A blown-up image of the photograph of the twelve statues of the Tell Asmar hoard prior to its division was also included in the exhibit.[50]

Although it is still unclear how the statues were presented in temple settings during antiquity, the contemporary visitor commonly expects to see objects within a museum setting exhibited as art, to be admired for their aesthetic qualities or examined for art historical study.[51] The notion, however, that an ancient object cannot be an agent of spiritual or emotional experience for the observer, whether past or present, is a false one.[52]

The most recent reinstallation of the Edgar and Deborah Jannotta Mesopotamian Gallery of the Oriental Institute, under the direction of Karen Wilson (completed in 2003), presented the Diyala statues in a more understated way, with fewer statues and fragments exhibited than previously, and those on view spread across a large table case and part of a wall case (fig. 6–15). This arrangement reflects an attempt to return to the simplicity of displaying the statues as individual objects, reflecting the curator's own background and scholarly interests as an art historian. The selection was also made to reflect the diversity of costumes and hairstyles represented on male and female sculptures, and a way to understand these as images of people.[53] The exhibit indicates the importance of the statues within the sphere of temple ritual, reinforced by an imaginative illustration of the Tell Asmar Square Temple shrine as reconstructed by Seton Lloyd (fig. 6–16). The archaeological context and the excitement of discovery is emphasized through the addition of a photograph from the Tell Asmar excavation that shows an in situ cache of statues (fig. 6–17). The photograph currently provides a useful talking point for guided tours, in which the value of archaeological context can be emphasized over art historical significance.

From Aesthetics to Politics: Early Twenty-First-Century Presentations of Early Dynastic Sculpture

At the Oriental Institute, Early Dynastic sculpture has been displayed in several special exhibits, often reflecting greater flexibility and innovation in the way the objects are curated and presented to the public. The 2008 exhibit *Catastrophe! The Looting and Destruction of Iraq's Past*[54] presented one of the Tell Asmar hoard statues alongside a field register from Tell Asmar and an excavation photograph, highlighting the value of archaeological context and recording. The 2012 exhibit *Picturing the Past: Imaging and Imagining the Ancient Middle East*[55] displayed one of the sculptures alongside Levy's watercolor, providing material "reality" in comparison with the artist's colorful and somewhat imaginative reconstruction.[56] The 2013 photographic exhibit *Our Work: Modern Jobs—Ancient Origins*[57] featured a portrait of Chicago-based fashion designer Diane Mayers Jones alongside one of the Early Dynastic sculptures from Khafajah (fig. 6–18). The intention of this exhibit was to connect the lives of people in the past with individuals in the present through an exploration of occupations, professions, inventions, and skills. Each of the twenty-four photographic portraits by Jason Reblando was presented alongside a transcribed and edited interview. Although the female statue was paired with a fashion designer because of its costume, Mayers Jones found that her strongest connection with the object was not the garment, but rather the interpretation of the statue as a religious or pious figure: "It's amazing just reading about how she's a worshipper and how you can see her hands cupped together in reverence to God. I'm a

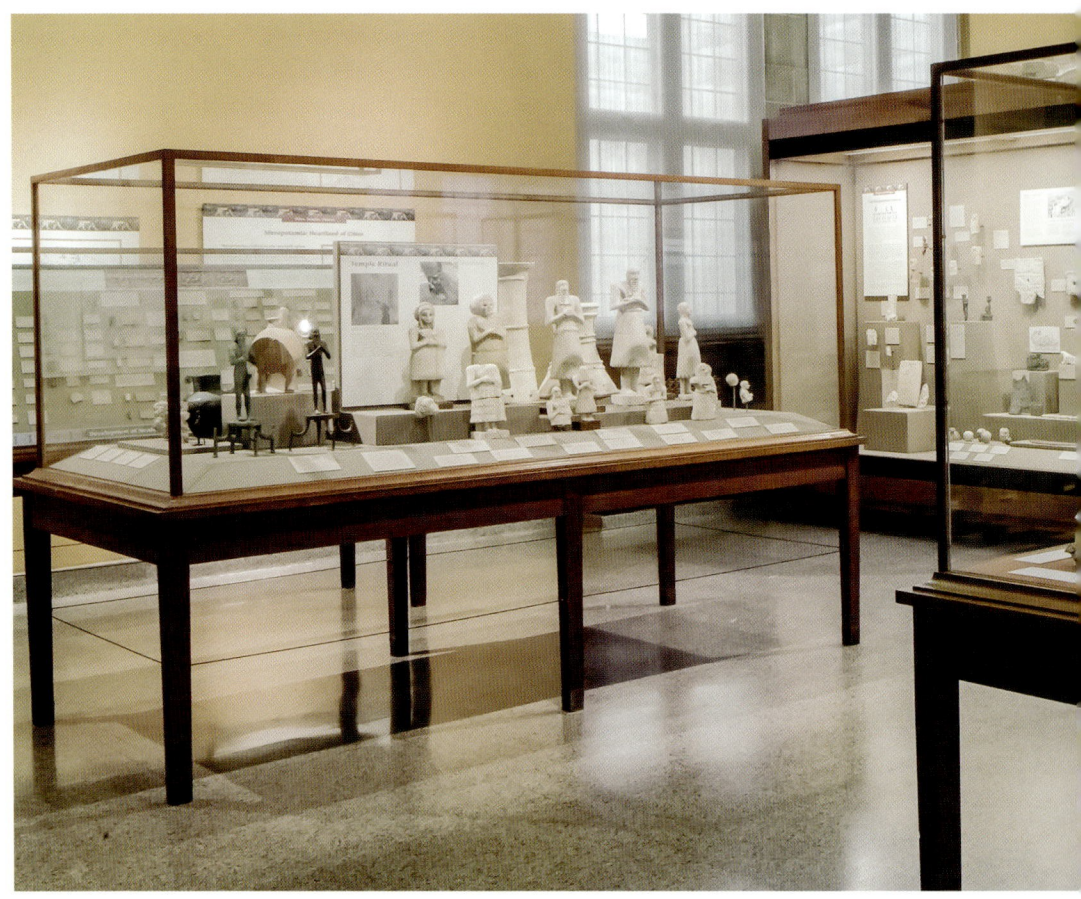

6–19. *The Invisible Enemy Should Not Exist*, on view in the Edgar and Deborah Jannotta Mesopotamian Gallery at the Oriental Institute Museum. Photograph, 2014. OIM: D.027553. Courtesy of the Oriental Institute of the University of Chicago.

very religious person, and it makes me think of myself, because I'm very into the church scene as you call it, so I'm always putting my best foot forward in an effort to be closer to God."[58]

The fashion designer's comment demonstrates that these sculptures can be encountered and perceived in various ways by museum visitors, albeit filtered through the lens of the information provided by the museum curator (when labels are actually read). Such objects need not always be placed in secular, scientific, or art historical frameworks. They may also evoke personal or even spiritual meanings to museum visitors.[59] Mayers Jones's statement also reminds us that the sculptures represent people from the past—people who had families, occupied positions of social status, and expressed their religiosity through rituals and as donors to the temple.

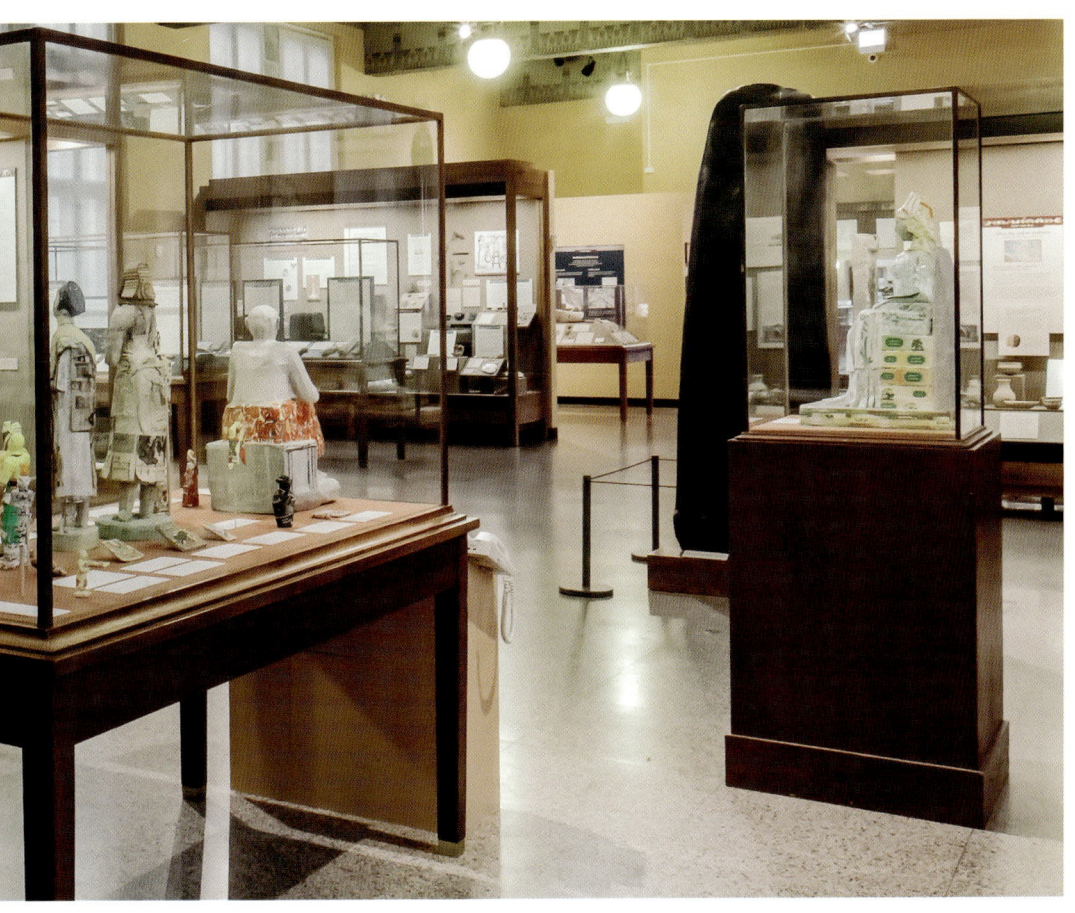

Early Dynastic sculpture has more recently been framed in a modern cultural and political setting that highlights the plight of cultural heritage in Iraq. The Chicago-based artist Michael Rakowitz has utilized the famous Early Dynastic statuary from the Iraq Expedition to the Diyala region, among other iconic ancient Mesopotamian objects from the Iraq Museum in Baghdad, as part of his project entitled *The Invisible Enemy Should Not Exist*, which he began in 2007 and continues to supplement (see checklist nos. 149–77).[60] Rakowitz has formed a narrative about the looting of the Iraq Museum and Iraqi cultural heritage in the aftermath of the U.S.-led invasion of April 2003. Exhibit labels prepared by the artist present the current status of the object's known (or unknown) whereabouts, and the events surrounding the invasion and plundering of the Iraq Museum. His works include a series of modern reconstructions of artifacts from the Iraq Museum that were thought to be damaged, looted, or stolen. The objects were created using images presented on the Oriental Institute's 2003 "Lost Treasures of Iraq" database,[61] as well as information posted on Interpol's website. Made from the packaging of Middle Eastern foodstuffs and local Arabic newspapers, Rakowitz's works express in his view "moments of cultural visibility found in cities across the United States."[62]

It should be noted, however, that a significant number of objects that were unaccounted for or of unknown status at the time of their recreation by Rakowitz have fortunately since been documented, including many Early Dynastic statues from the Oriental Institute's Iraq Expedition currently displayed in the Iraq Museum. Through their presentation in international contemporary art exhibitions in the United States, Europe, and the Middle East, Rakowitz's works have become visible icons of the damage, looting, and continual threats to the cultural heritage of Iraq. His playful use of brightly colored newspaper and lightweight ephemeral packaging in the creation of these papier-mâché works is ironic given the generally light monochrome color as well as the density, durability, and heaviness of the surviving ancient sculptures. The aestheticism and materialism that has surrounded traditional art historical treatment of the original statues is also subverted through the further simplification and abstraction represented by Rakowitz's creations.

The vibrancy of these contemporary works indicates their role as bright beacons drawing attention to tragedies of the recent past, as well as to the ongoing plight of cultural heritage in Iraq. Rakowitz's project is especially relevant as ancient Mesopotamian artifacts continue to be looted from sites in Iraq and Syria for sale on the illicit antiquities market. In addition, his adaptation of the museum-label format to present pertinent facts about the objects (museum inventory number, date range, description), evokes the scientific objectivism of the curator or archaeologist. Such details have also been important in identifying missing or looted objects from the Iraq Museum.

During the Oriental Institute Museum's 2014 exhibit of *The Invisible Enemy*, the reconstructions of objects from the Iraq Museum were displayed directly opposite the Early Dynastic sculptures in the museum's own collection (fig. 6–19). Reunited yet still divided, the contemporary works by Rakowitz and their original companions stood face-to-face in the Mesopotamian gallery of the Oriental Institute.[63]

The tone of *The Invisible Enemy* as presented at the Oriental Institute was not intended to be overtly political. The exhibit, however, could clearly be interpreted as political by visitors, since it highlighted the tragic and preventable looting of the Iraq Museum that stemmed from the U.S.-led invasion. Rakowitz's work amplifies the impact on the material cultural of Iraq, and as these losses become more widely known, his project has the potential to change the iconic status of ancient Early Dynastic sculpture as well as other well-known objects from the Iraq Museum.

The appreciation, study, and display of the Diyala sculptures have shifted within the past decade from a largely art historical focus toward a more contextually driven emphasis based on archaeology and ancient texts as well as an awareness of their threatened state as victims of conflict. The presence and public display of the statues in the Oriental Institute continues to remind us of the ongoing challenges faced in Baghdad, where the other large group of statues from the Iraq Expedition to the Diyala region is exhibited. The Iraq Museum and its contents remain under the threat of looting, damage, and destruction given the country's precarious security.

Conclusions

A clear barrier to understanding the function and context of Early Dynastic sculpture has been its early categorization in art historical terms, and a failure to explore the social and cultural role of the statues within the context of ritual action and deposition, including the parts played by the individuals who donated the statues and those who visited temples and made offerings in their presence. The statues continue to live on within museums and in exhibits, while the meanings attributed to them, including their politicized significance, continue to evolve over time, influenced by archaeologists, museum curators, artists, and members of the public. The aesthetic or art historical approach, with minimal object labeling and a desire to isolate the object for attentive looking, has tended to dominate the display of Early Dynastic statues in museums, including the Oriental Institute.

While the reason for the increased presence of temple sculpture in the Early Dynastic period may have been related to an attempt to overcome restrictive access to the temple, the modern museum has permitted even greater access to these objects and images. This essay has demonstrated that while the statues were initially presented to Western audiences primarily as "primitive art" and great artistic achievements, displays from the early twenty-first century have increasingly attempted to frame them in terms of their archaeological and historiographical context. Following the looting of the Iraq Museum in 2003, the statues have also been used as symbols of a fragile and threatened heritage. The continued role of these sculptures as archaeological artifacts, human images, art objects, and politicized symbols reflects their enduring ability to evoke beauty, mystery, personhood, power, and presence. Visitors to museums, the secular temples of our time, continue to respond to and be inspired by these images, layering multiple meanings onto them. Artists continue to be inspired by their abstract forms and wider role as icons of cultural heritage. The sculptures therefore continue to mediate social interactions, although no longer as intercessors between the realms of the living and the dead, or between the living and the divine, as in the early Mesopotamian temples. They now serve as a way of mediating between past and present, enabling visitors to gain an impression of ancient Mesopotamian people, their physical appearances as well as their religious practices.

Endnotes

1   For a history of archaeology in Iraq, see Pallis 1956; Bernhardsson 2005.

2   Frankfort 1932a: vii, 1–5, 48–51.

3   Frankfort 1935a: 79–87; Frankfort 1936: 35–59, and the "Chronological Table" at the end of the volume with comments preceding it. For an analysis of the Early Dynastic subdivisions, see Evans 2007.

4   For a comprehensive treatment of the Sumerian problem and a translation into English of the major scholarly contributions up to 1960, see Jones 1969. See also Rubio 1999; Bahrani 2006.

5   For the ethnographic reception of Sumerian sculpture, see Evans 2012a: 15–45.

6   Quoted in ibid.: 55.

7   Quoted in ibid.

8   Quoted in ibid.: 56.

9   Frankfort 1939: 1. See also Frankfort 1935b: 121; Frankfort 1936: 41; Frankfort 1939: 18, 39–40; Frankfort 1943: 1.

10   For the reception of Sumerian sculpture as "primitive," see Evans 2012a: 46–75.

11   Fabian 1983: 32, 106–7; Bahrani 2003: 75–84.

12   Frankfort 1939; Frankfort 1943.

13   Frankfort 1935a: 55–78; Frankfort 1935b; Frankfort 1939: 19–36; Frankfort 1943: 1–16; Frankfort 1954: 23–31.

14   Rothschild 1929.

15   Frankfort 1939: 18, 19–20, 22.

16   Connelly 1995: 5.

17   Frankfort 1935c; Jacobsen 1995.

18   Frankfort 1932b.

19   Sweeney 1943: 10.

20   Connelly 1998: 89.

21   For example, see Errington 1994: 215; Steiner 2002: 136–39.

22   See Evans 2012a.

23   Braun-Holzinger 1991.

24   For early archaeological reconstructions of the context of Early Dynastic sculpture, see Evans 2012a: 76–110. Alpers 1991.

25   Moser 2006: 148, 187.

26   Andrae 1922: table 11a.

27   See, for example, Braun-Holzinger 1977: 11; Braun-Holzinger 1991: 237–38; Spycket 1981: 50; Winter 1989: 581–82 and n23.

28   For rituals of Early Dynastic sculpture, see Evans 2012a: 111–45.

29   The literature on materiality is vast, but for further bibliography, see Kopytoff 1986; Gell 1998; Miller 1999; Meskell 2004.

30   For the Early Dynastic e_2-mi_2 archive and offerings to statues recorded therein, see Evans 2012a: 131–37.

31   Förtsch 1914: DP 54.

32   Ibid.

33   Evans 2012a: 136.

34   Moser 2006; Shaw 2003, but see Evans 2012a: 81–88.

35   See also Evans 2014: 647, for a description of the display of one of the Early Dynastic sculptures (Aruz 2003: 59–61, cat. 24a) in the exhibit *Art of the First Cities:The Third Millennium B.C. from the Mediterranean to the Indus* at the Metropolitan Museum of Art in 2003.

36   Emberling 2008: 31.

37   Frankfort 1934a. See also Frankfort 1934b for discussion of the discoveries of Early Dynastic sculpture at Khafajah, another site excavated by the Iraq Expedition. The *Illustrated London News* was a popular weekly magazine in Great Britain with a wide readership that appealed to the aspiring middle classes. It had a strong focus on the history of art and antiques alongside an eclectic range of topics, features, and news. The presentation of major archaeological discoveries in the *Illustrated London News* could be considered equivalent to a feature article in *National Geographic* magazine in more recent times.

38   The Oriental Institute's exhibit was within the Hall of Social Science, one of over fifty halls at the Chicago World's Fair. The exhibit was open to the public in the summer and fall of 1934, the second year of the World's Fair.

39   Frankfort 1934a: 777; Evans 2012b.

40   Ganz 2012; Shrenk 2007.

41   Century of Progress 1934.

42   Shrenk 2007: 25.

43   However, archaeology and prehistory had played an important role in the early international expositions in Europe, as demonstrated by Müller-Scheessel 2001.

44   Emphasis added.

45   James Henry Breasted, "The Oriental Institute Exhibit at A Century of Progress Exposition," typescript, June 25, 1934, Director's Office Correspondence, 1934, Century of Progress, Oriental Institute Archives.

46   The original caption by the fair's official photographer, Kaufman & Fabry Co., is preserved in the Century of Progress Records, 1927–52, University of Illinois at Chicago: COP_17_0003_00087_002 (CARLI digital collections): "These five statuettes, exhibited on the upper floor of the Social Science Hall are the oldest ever found in Asia, dating from about 3,000 B.C. The Oriental Institute is exhibiting them to the public for the first time at the World's Fair; they were evacuated early this year at the site of ancient cities of Eshnunna and Opis. Above photograph shows Miss P. McLaughlin, Cincinnati artist, and L. Stienes, of Fairmont, Nebraska, viewing the primitive subjects."

47   Teeter 2012.

48   Franke 1977.

49   Andrae 1922: table 11a.

50   Evans (2014: 647) remarks on the presentation of a single Tell Asmar statue with a backdrop of Rigmor Jacobson's famous image of the statues at *Art of the First Cities* at the Metropolitan Museum of Art in 2003. This contrast of the collective against the singular statue appears to prioritize the aesthetics of the sculpture as an art object, while also evoking a sense of adoration or cultic focus.

51   Ibid.: 648; Oriental Institute 1982: 14; the Oriental Institute Museum, even though an archaeological institution, presented the statues as "one of the highlights of Mesopotamian artistic achievements."

52   Gell 1998. Although aesthetic values may vary from culture to culture, including in the premodern era, Gell argued that "art" objects can be secondary agents with ritual or expressive power that can entrap and captivate the recipient. In this sense, art and objects reframed within museum displays can have agency.

53   Karen Wilson, communication with the authors, 2014. Some modifications were subsequently made in the labeling of the display under the direction of Geoff Emberling in 2010. This included the addition of greater detail regarding context and site information on labels so as to emphasize more clearly the archaeological provenience of the objects. These relabeling efforts were part of a general concern within the Oriental Institute to present the sculptures as archaeological rather than as art-museum objects.

54   Emberling and Hanson 2008.

55   Green, Teeter, and Larson 2012.

56   Evans 2012b.

57   Green and Teeter 2013.

58   Ibid.: 34–37.

59   Falk 2006. Within the field of museum studies "Spiritual Pilgrim" is one of the visitor categories proposed in Falk's innovative approach to understanding the museum experience from the point of view of visitor identity and motivation. The category has been renamed "Recharger" in recognition of visitors who seek a "contemplative, spiritual, and/or restorative experience," including those who may experience the museum as a place where religious or spiritual beliefs can be confirmed (Falk and Dierking 2013: 48).

60   For more information about the exhibit (Mar. 18–May 25, 2014), see the Oriental Institute website https://oi.uchicago.edu/museum-exhibits/special-exhibits/michael-rakowitz-invisible-enemy-should-not-exist (accessed Sept. 11, 2014).

61   The database was compiled by Clemens Reichel (then research associate) and Charles E. Jones (then head librarian, Research Archives) in collaboration with McGuire Gibson (professor of Mesopotamian archaeology). The 2003 web feature continues to be accessible online, although it has not been recently updated: http://oi-archive.uchicago.edu/OI/IRAQ/iraq.html (accessed Sept. 11, 2014).

62   http://michaelrakowitz.com/projects/the-invisible-enemy-should-not-exist (accessed Sept. 10, 2014).

63   The decision on their presentation came about through a discussion between the artist and Jack Green, chief curator at the Oriental Institute Museum, during the installation of The Invisible Enemy Should Not Exist at the Museum of Contemporary Art, Chicago, 2013.

Appendix: Back to the Beginning; The Aesthetics and Allure of Field Records

Clemens Reichel

The Diyala excavations—first undertaken by the Oriental Institute (1930–37) and later by the University of Pennsylvania (1937–39) at Tell Agrab, Tell Asmar, Khafaje, and Ishchali—represent a benchmark in the archaeological exploration of Iraq (see the contribution by Evans and Green in this volume). The scope and size of these excavations remains unrivalled to the present day, covering more than a millennium of Mesopotamia's early archaeological history (3000–1800 BCE).

The expedition's publication record—five volumes on architecture, and four on select classes of artifacts—played no insignificant part in the wide use of the Diyala archaeological sequence, which has remained a backbone of early Mesopotamian chronology.

The price of paper publications, unfortunately, acted as a filter that severely limited the data set that could be made available. What was recorded in the field on hundreds of catalogue cards, notebook pages, photographs, elaborate sketches, and drawings was condensed into a few pages, often with minimal illustrations. Like many other final excavation publications, the Diyala volumes are summaries—streamlined accounts that highlight the main narrative while leaving out details that may have seemed secondary or insignificant to the excavators but that may be of great interest to scholars today.

By selecting excavators from the United States, England, Germany, Denmark, the Netherlands, and the Ukraine, Henri Frankfort—who in 1930 was still a novice to the excavation of complex mud-brick architecture—had built an international team with very different levels of expertise. Since the final publications were largely redacted by Frankfort (and, following his death in 1954, by Pinhas Delougaz, who was appointed to the Oriental Institute's faculty after the end of the excavations), they reflect relatively little of the individual skills and recording techniques of these excavators. Fortunately for us their field notes and plans, preserved in the archives of the Oriental Institute Museum, provide a detailed account of their insights and their evolving understanding of the complex archaeological contexts with which they were confronted. More than that, they bear testimony to the artistic skills of a generation of excavators trained in the art of architectural and artifact illustration.

The archival materials left by Conrad Preusser, field director of the excavations at Khafaje during the 1930–31 season, provide a good example to illustrate this case. A German-born architect trained by Walter Andrae at the site of Ashur, he was intrinsically familiar with mud-brick excavations, and hence provided some of the technical expertise that Frankfort's team so desperately needed. At Khafaje, Preusser almost immediately discovered the Temple Oval, a monumental temple complex dated to the Early Dynastic period. The published plans of this building reflect the Oriental Institute's architectural conventions of the time, showing walls in solid black and rooms as empty spaces; features such as hearths, drains, and benches were indicated in a highly schematic way. Following the conventions of the Ashur excavators, by contrast, the walls in Preusser's 1930–31 field plan (fig. 7–1) were largely rendered in outline.

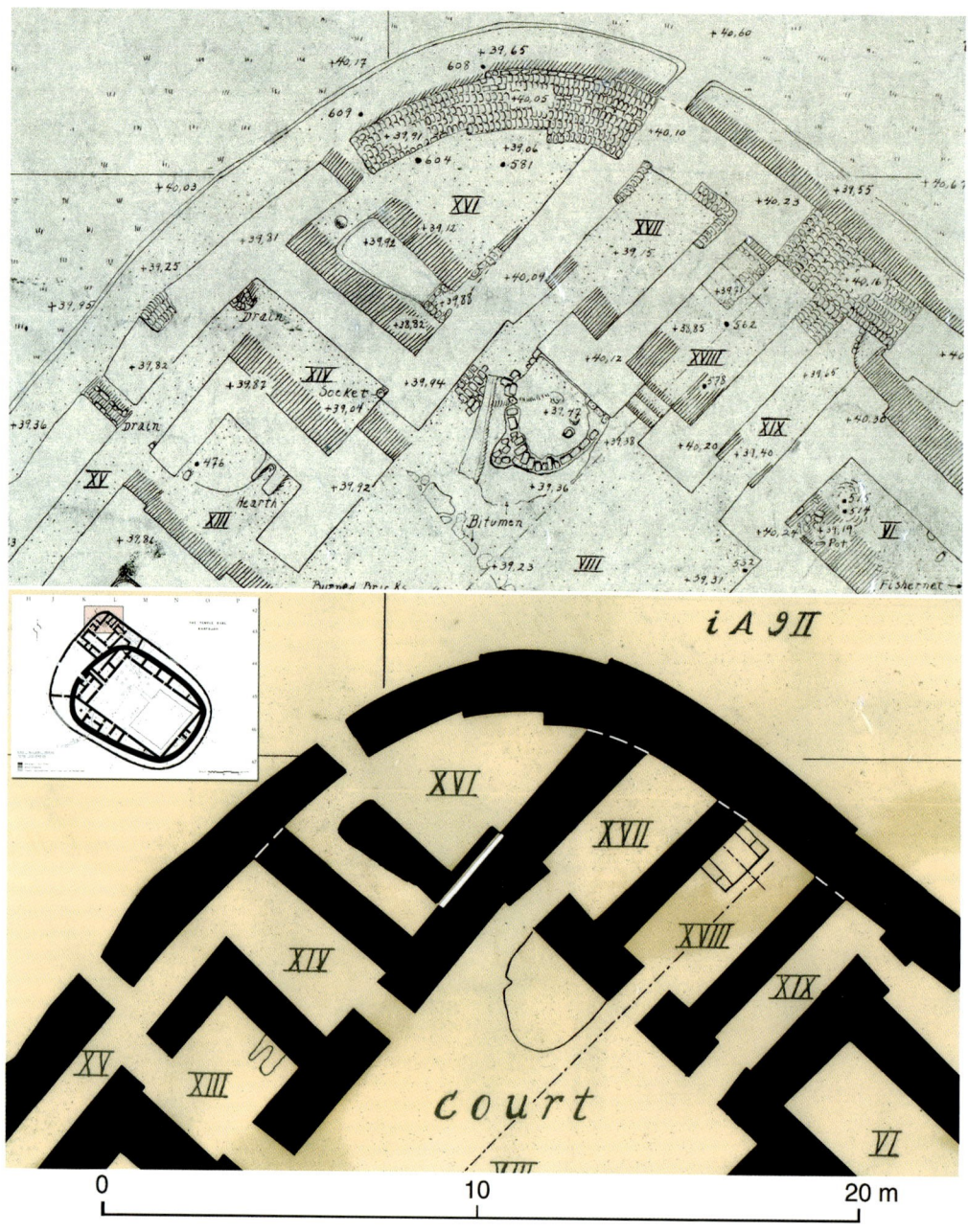

7–1. Temple Oval at Khafaje, northern corner. Top: field plan. Bottom: inked plan. Inset: plan of the Temple Oval showing the location of the northern corner.

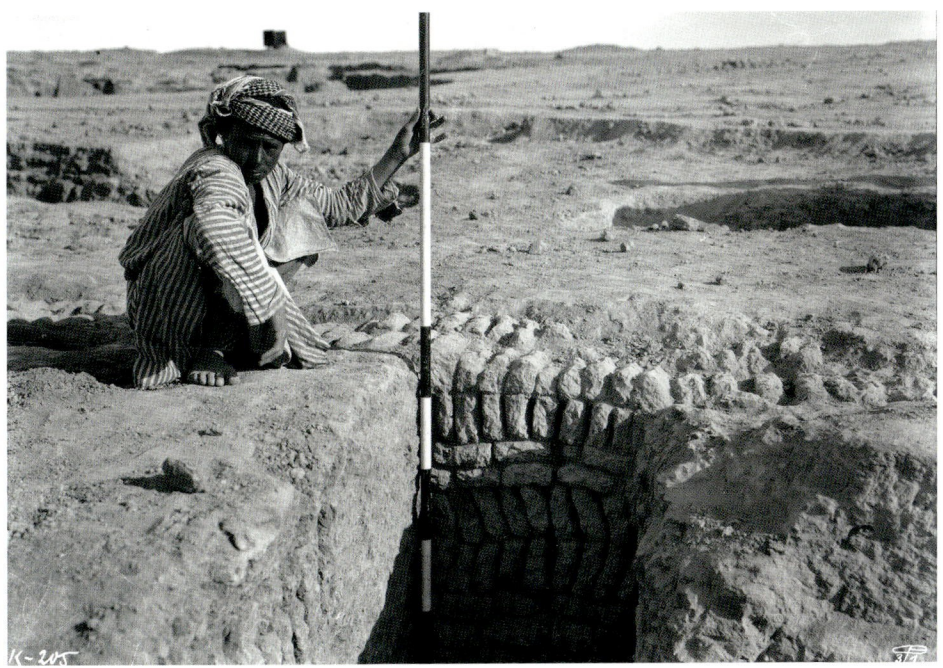

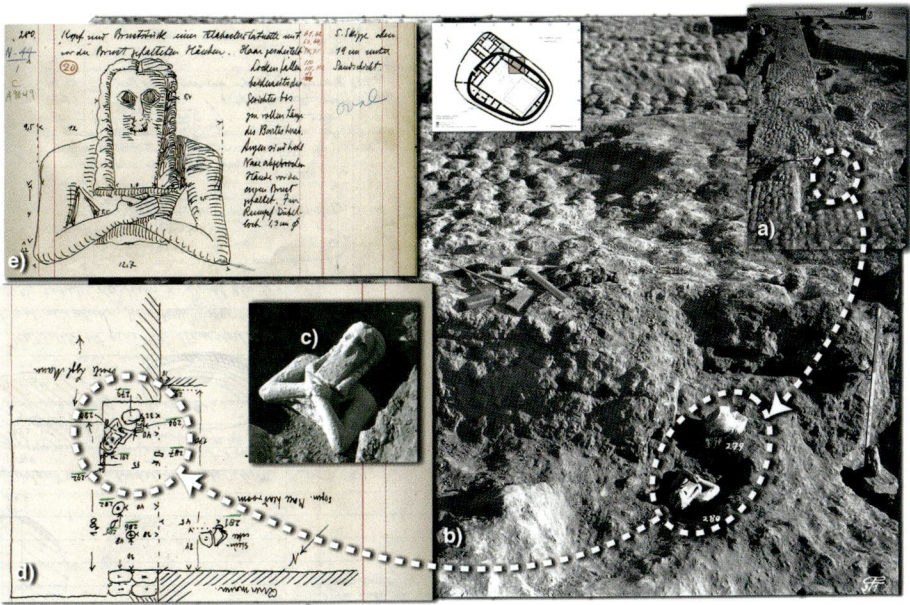

7-2. Temple Oval at Khafaje, wall with a section of bricks laid in characteristic "herringbone" pattern, 2600–2400 BCE, as articulated by excavators. Photograph by Conrad Preusser, 1930–31.

7-3. Temple Oval at Khafaje, excavation of Statue Kh. I 280 (upper body fragment). a) Northern building wall, showing findspot of statue. b) Close-up of find context. c) Close-up of statue in situ. d) Sketch in the field register showing find circumstances and its relation to other artifacts. e) Description and sketch of the statue. Inset: Plan of Temple Oval, showing location of findspot. Photographs, sketches, and descriptions by Conrad Preusser (1930–31); plan by Hamilton Darby.

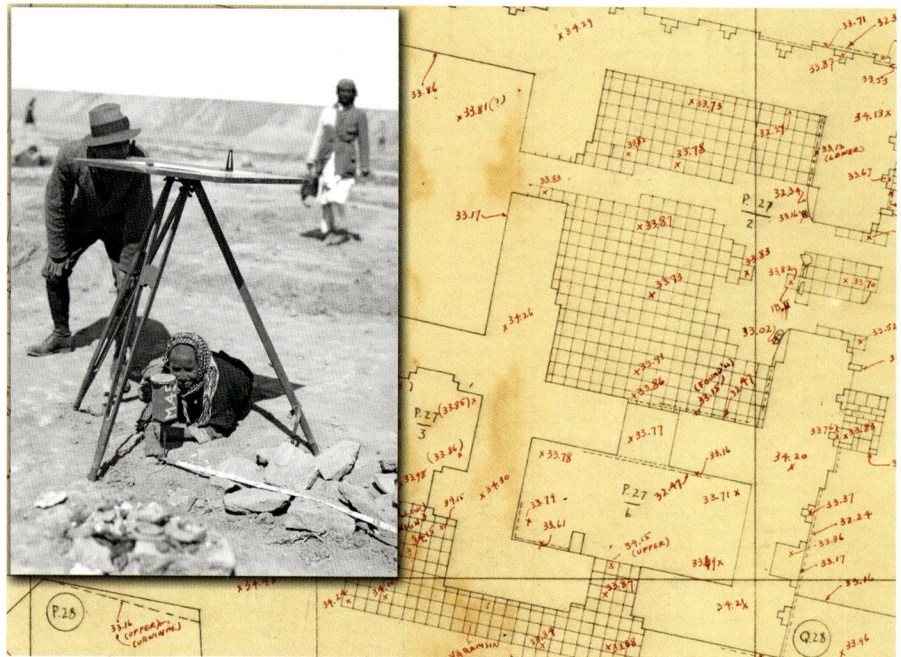

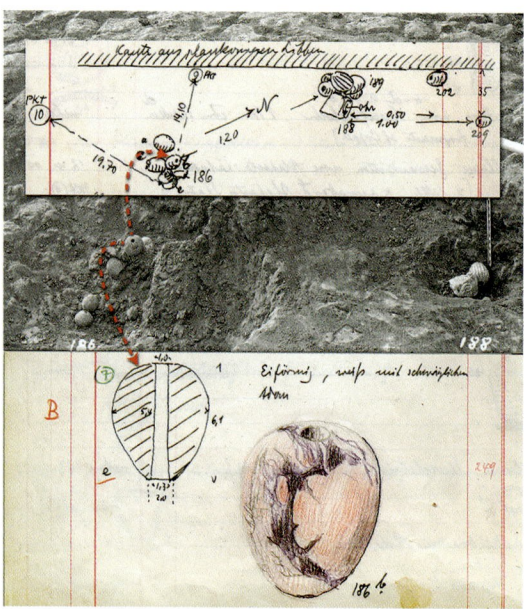

7–4. Plan of Naramsin Audience Hall, Tell Asmar; red numbers indicate top and bottom elevations of walls and floor elevations, 1934–35 season. Inset: Hamilton Darby setting up a plane table for mapping over measuring point, Khafaje, 1931–32.

7–5. Temple Oval at Khafaje, excavation photograph of mace heads in situ; white numbers indicate find numbers. Top: Detailed sketch of find circumstances and relations to other artifacts. Bottom: Find register entry for mace head Kh. I 186b with colored sketch and description (red "B" in left margin indicates that it was allocated to Baghdad, i.e., the Iraq Museum). Photograph, drawings, and descriptions by Conrad Preusser, 1930–31.

In spite of his architectural training, he focused on faithfully recording features, floor, and even destruction assemblages such as piles of bricks, slabs of bitumen, or reed impressions in mud plaster that had fallen from the roof. Some wall sections that he had articulated—by removing the wall plaster and by outlining the "herringbone" brick-laying pattern that are characteristic of Early Dynastic architecture (fig. 7–2)—were faithfully rendered brick-by-brick in the plan. The same level of detailed recording can be found in Preusser's find register (fig. 7–3). In neat German handwriting, he not only record-ed the artifact's provenance, find date, measurements, and description, along with a detailed sketch of each item, but also added sketch plans of find contexts, showing the spatial relationship of items to each other as they were found. These sketches are annotated with measurements, either indicating the relative position of an artifact to identifiable features such as wall lines, or triangulations to known points.

The impact that these field records have on modern viewers probably depends on their level of expertise with archaeology. Architectural recording conventions have changed considerably since the 1930s, when a preference was placed on "neat" floor plans, with wall lines that were drawn with a ruler and rooms that were rendered as empty spaces. Over the past decades, however, the emphasis on architecture has given way to an archaeological focus that values the importance of floor assemblages for the reconstruction of activity areas and functional interpretations. Modern plans of ancient Near Eastern mud-brick architecture generally try to "facsimilize" the unevenness of mud-brick architecture by rendering walls through hand-drawn lines, providing a feel that more accurately reflects the building material's inherent lack of straight lines and right angles. The departure from the aesthetics of older architectural mapping conven-tions gives Preusser's field plans and sketches, themselves largely free of the "dicta-torship" of rulers and calipers, a contemporary, almost modern feel. To scholars, these plans and field registers also promise information that is not present in the published volumes. Find contexts mapped out in the field register can be added to a new Temple Oval master plan even if these recording techniques are not entirely consistent: once the reference points are identified in the plan, artifact assemblages can be mapped in through distance measurements to known points as provided in the field register. Such an enhancement opens new avenues toward modern-day functional analyses of the building. Nowadays archaeologists pay significantly more attention to the relationships of artifacts with each other and with their architectural environment. A floor assem-blage, for example, *must* be kept apart from higher destruction debris since it relates to the actual function of the building during its use-life. Even the latter, however, can provide useful information if properly recorded: artifact assemblages from the roof, for example, might indicate the function of an upper space. Locational analyses undertaken through GIS (geographic information systems) programs can help to revise or refine our understanding of a building's function.

These are only two examples of how the Diyala field records can enhance our under-standing of the excavated architecture. Floor and wall elevations were recorded on field plans but were never published (fig. 7–4). Adding them to the existing plans not only provides a vertical dimension in the reading of the plan but also helps to contextualize provenanced artifacts in relation to their associated floor levels.

At a time of escalating conflict in the Middle East that impacts Iraq's cultural heritage, the field photographs, drawings, and sketches on catalogue cards and in field registers continue to be of lasting value (fig. 7–5). In 2003, during the looting of the National Museum in Baghdad that followed the Iraq War, several hundred cylinder seals from the Diyala excavations were stolen. With the persistence of threats against Iraq's cultural heritage, it remains important to make data on archaeological collections in the Iraq Museum available—not only to ensure that stolen items can be retrieved but also to disseminate knowledge of these collections within and beyond the realm of scholarly communities.

Launched in 1992, the Oriental Institute's Diyala Project will provide a full publication of all artifacts and archival materials from the Diyala expedition in an on-line database. For more information visit the project's URL: diyala.uchicago.edu.

Exhibition Checklist

Institutional Abbreviations

BMAG:
Birmingham Museum and Art Gallery

BM:
The British Museum

TBM:
The Brooklyn Museum

Field:
The Field Museum of Natural History, Chicago

GF:
Fondation Alberto & Annette Giacometti, Paris

HMF:
The Henry Moore Foundation, Perry Green,
Much Hadham

ISAW:
Institute for the Study of the Ancient World

IWM:
Imperial War Museum, London

OIM:
Oriental Institute Museum, Oriental Institute of
the University of Chicago

MMA:
The Metropolitan Museum of Art, New York

Montserrat:
Father Bonaventura Ubach Photographic Archive,
Montserrat Abbey, Montserrat Monastery

Penn Museum:
University of Pennsylvania Museum of Archaeology and Anthropology

SCVA:
Sainsbury Center for Visual Arts, University of
East Anglia

UIC:
University of Illinois, Chicago

1.
Statues in situ, Locus: Q42:7, Sin Temple VIII.
Khafajah
Photograph, H. 13 cm; W. 18 cm
ca. 1930-37
Iraq Expedition of the Oriental Institute,
1930-1937
OIM: Kh. IV.135 (Fig. 1–1)

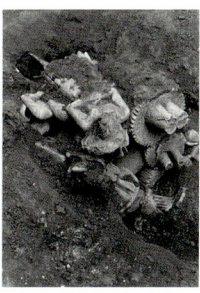

2.
Statues in situ, Locus D17: 9, Square Temple
(Shrine II), Tell Asmar
Photograph, H. 17.9 cm; W. 12.9 cm
ca. 1934
Courtesy of the Oriental Institute of the
University of Chicago
OIM: As. 1092 (P. 23289)

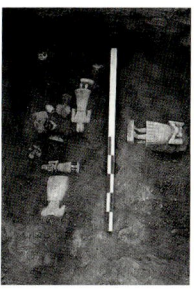

3.
Statues in situ, Khafajah
Photograph
H. 17.8 cm; W. 12.8 cm, ca. 1937
Iraq Expedition of the Oriental Institute,
1930-1937
OIM: Kh. VIII. 72

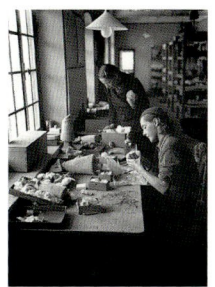

4.
Workroom in the Iraq Expedition House, Tell Asmar
Photograph, H. 17.9 cm; W. 13 cm
January 29, 1934
Courtesy of the Oriental Institute of the
University of Chicago
OIM: As. 1097

5.
Interior of the Iraq Expedition House, Tell Asmar
Photograph, H. 17.9 cm; W. 13 cm
January 29, 1934
Courtesy of the Oriental Institute of the
University of Chicago
OIM: As. 1098 (P. 24084) (Fig. 2–14)

6.
Group of figures from the Square Temple, Tell
Asmar
Photograph by Rigmor Jacobsen
H. 20.7 cm; W. 25.4 cm
1930s (?)
Courtesy of the Oriental Institute of the
University of Chicago
OIM: As. 1152 (Fig. 6–5)

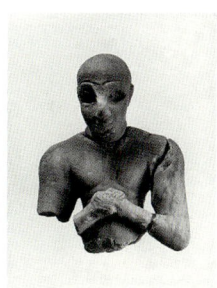

7.
Study photograph of top half of a male figure
(OIM: A12387)
Photograph, H. 25.4 cm; W. 19.8 cm
ca. 1933-34
Iraq Expedition of the Oriental Institute,
1930-1937
OIM: P. 23421

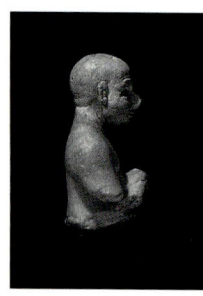

8.
Study photograph of top half of a male figure
(OIM: A12387)
Photograph, H. 22.5 cm; W. 15.3 cm
ca. 1933-34
Iraq expedition of the Oriental Institute,
1930-1937
OIM: P. 31685

9.
Study photograph of head of a male (OIM:
A18018)
Photograph, H. 17.8 cm; W. 12.8 cm
ca. 1935-37
Iraq Expedition of the Oriental Institute,
1930-1937
OIM: AG. 15 P. 28091 (Fig. 1–16)

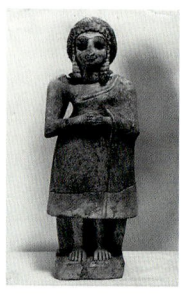

10.
Study photograph of standing female figure
(OIM: A12412)
Photograph, H. 25.2 cm; W. 17 cm
ca. 1933-34
Iraq Expedition of the Oriental Institute,
1930-1937
OIM: Kh. IV 181. P. 23378

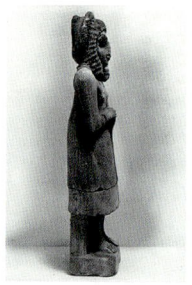

11.
Study photograph of a standing female figure
(OIM: A12412)
Photograph, H. 25.2 cm; W. 17 cm
ca. 1933-34
Iraq Expedition of the Oriental Institute,
1930-1937
OIM: Kh. IV 183. P. 23377

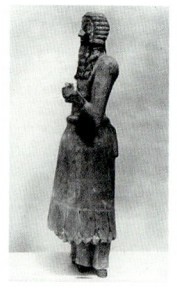

12.
Study photograph of a standing male figure
(OIM: A12434)
Photograph, H. 25.3 cm; W. 16 cm
ca. 1933-34
Iraq Expedition of the Oriental Institute,
1930-1937
OIM: P. 35724

13.
Study photograph of top half of a male figure
(OIM: A12340)
Photograph, H. 25.3 cm; W. 18.3 cm
ca. 1930-37
Iraq Expedition of the Oriental Institute,
1930-1937
OIM: Kh. IV. 193 (Fig. 1–16)

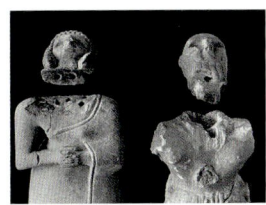

14.
Study photograph of a fragmented female figure
(OIM: A12412)
Photograph, H. 18.8 cm; W. 25.3 cm
ca. 1933-34
Iraq Expedition of the Oriental Institute,
1930-1937
OIM: Kh. IV. 206

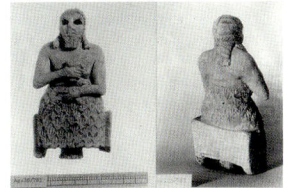

15.
Study photograph of a seated male figure
(OIM: A18108)
Photograph, H. 12.7 cm; W. 18.1 cm
ca. 1930-37
Courtesy of the Oriental Institute of the
University of Chicago
OIM: P. 21084, P. 28085

16.
Reconstruction of votive figurines from
Tell Asmar
Watercolor on paper by Rachel Levy
H. 38.4 cm; W. 32.4 cm
1934
Courtesy of the Oriental Institute of the
University of Chicago
OIM: D.017485 (Fig. 2–15)

17.
"Century of Progress" International Exposition,
Chicago, 1933-1934
Photograph, H. 9 cm; W. 11 cm
ca. 1933-34
Courtesy of the University of Illinois at Chicago
UIC: COP_17_0003_00087_002 (Fig. 6–12)

18.
"Century of Progress" International Exposition,
Chicago, 1933-1934
Photograph, H. 18.7 cm; W. 24.7 cm
1934
Courtesy of the Oriental Institute of the
University of Chicago
OIM: P. 24146 (Fig. 6–11)

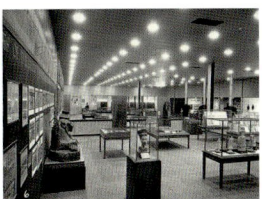

19.
"Century of Progress" International Exposition,
Chicago, 1933-1934
Photograph, H. 18.7 cm; W. 24.7 cm
1934
Courtesy of the Oriental Institute of the
University of Chicago
OIM: P. 24148

20.
Postcard of the installation of Diyala figurines at
the Oriental Institute, 1950–70.
Ektachrome on paper, H. 20.7 cm; W. 25.4 cm
ca. 1960-70
Courtesy of the Oriental Institute of the
University of Chicago Archives
(Fig. 6–13)

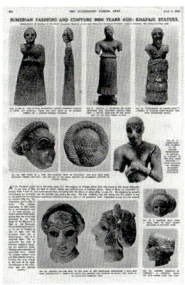

21.
"Sumerian Fashions and Coiffure 5000 Years
Ago: Khafaje Statues"
Illustrated London News, June 9, 1934
H. 37.5 cm; W. 26.5 cm
Courtesy of the Department of Ancient Near
Eastern Art, The Metropolitan Museum of Art
MMA: ANE.ILN.1

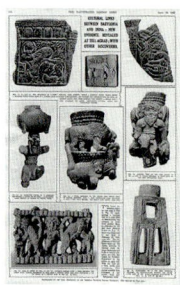

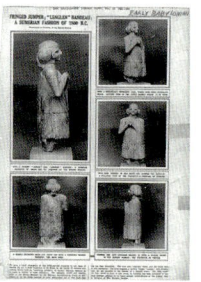

22.
"Cultural Links between Babylonia and India: New Evidence Revealed at Tell Agrab; With Other Discoveries"
Illustrated London News, September 12, 1936
H. 37.5 cm; W. 26.5 cm
Courtesy of the Department of Ancient Near Eastern Art, The Metropolitan Museum of Art
MMA: ANE.ILN.3

23.
"An Extraordinary Discoveryof Early Sumerian Sculpture"
Illustrated London News, May 19, 1934
H. 37.5 cm; W. 26.5 cm
Courtesy of the Department of Ancient Near Eastern Art, The Metropolitan Museum of Art.
MMA: ANE.ILN.4 (Fig. 1–3)

24.
"Home of the Kings 'Dated' from the Flood: A Palace of 3500 B.C."
Illustrated London News, May 9, 1925
H. 37.5 cm; W. 26.5 cm
Courtesy of the Department of Ancient Near Eastern Art, The Metropolitan Museum of Art.
MMA: ANE.ILN.7 (Fig. 2–8)

25.
"Fringed Jumper; 'Lenglen' Bandeau: A Sumerian Fashion of 2800 B.C."
Illustrated London News, November 15, 1924
H. 37.5 cm; W. 26.5 cm
Courtesy of the Department of Ancient Near Eastern Art, The Metropolitan Museum of Art
MMA: ANE.ILN.8

26.
"Khafaje Statuary—With a Revelatory 'Bearded Priest'"
Illustrated London News, October 8, 1932
H. 37.5 cm; W. 26.5 cm
Courtesy of the Department of Ancient Near Eastern Art, The Metropolitan Museum of Art
MMA: ANE.ILN.10 (Fig. 2–10)

27.
Field card: head of a statue
Paper, H. 15.4 cm; W. 12.7 cm
December 11, 1930
Courtesy of the Oriental Institute of the University of Chicago
OIM: 158 (Fig. 1–16)

28.
Field object card, Khafajah: for head of a statue
Paper
H. 15.4 cm; W. 12.7 cm
December 11, 1930
Courtesy of the Oriental Institute of the University of Chicago
OIM: Kh. I 158 (Fig. 1–16)

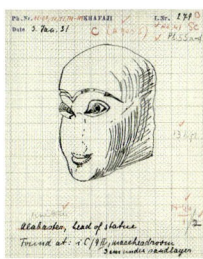

29.
29. Field object card, Khafajah: head of
a male figure
Paper, H. 15.4 cm; W. 12.7 cm
January 3, 1931
Courtesy of the Oriental Institute of the
University of Chicago
OIM: Kh. I 279

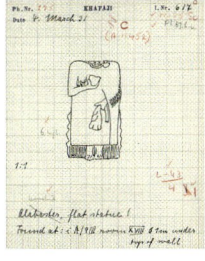

30.
Field object card, Khafajah: headless standing
female figure
Paper, H. 15.4 cm; W. 12.7 cm
March 4, 1931
Courtesy of the Oriental Institute of the
University of Chicago
OIM: Kh. I 617

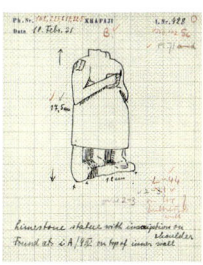

31.
Field object card, Khafajah: headless standing
female figure
Paper, H. 15.4 cm; W. 12.7 cm
February 10, 1931
Courtesy of the Oriental Institute of the
University of Chicago
OIM: Kh. I 428

32.
Field object card, Khafajah: top half of a
male figure
Paper, H. 15.4 cm; W. 12.7 cm
January 3, 1931
Courtesy of the Oriental Institute of the
University of Chicago
OIM: Kh. I 280 (Fig. 1– 15)

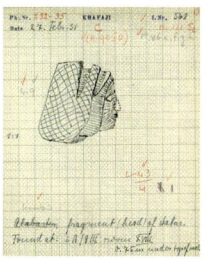

33.
Field card: head of a female figure
Paper, H. 15.4 cm; W. 12.7 cm
February 27, 1931
Courtesy of the Oriental Institute of the
University of Chicago
OIM: 562

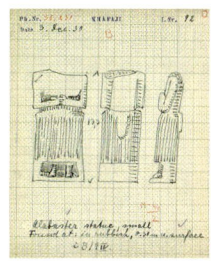

34.
Field object card, Khafajah: headless standing
male figure
Paper, H. 15.4 cm; W. 12.7 cm
December 3, 1930
Courtesy of the Oriental Institute of the
University of Chicago
OIM: Kh. I 92

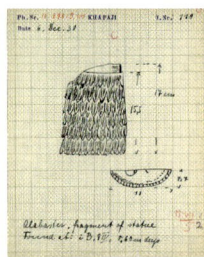

35.
Field object card, Khafajah: fragment of a standing figure
Paper, H. 15.4 cm; W. 12.7 cm
December 6, 1930
Courtesy of the Oriental Institute of the University of Chicago
OIM: Kh. I 110

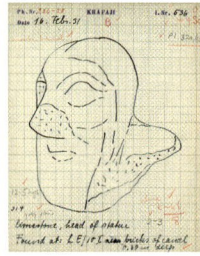

36.
Field object card, Khafajah: head of a male figure
Paper, H. 15.4 cm; W. 12.7 cm
February 16, 1931
Courtesy of the Oriental Institute of the University of Chicago
OIM: Kh. I 536

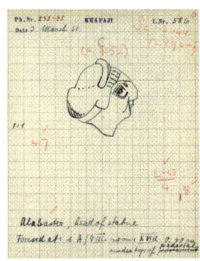

37.
Field object card, Khafajah: head of a female figure
Paper, H. 15.4 cm; W. 12.7 cm
March 3, 1931
Courtesy of the Oriental Institute of the University of Chicago
OIM: Kh. I 586

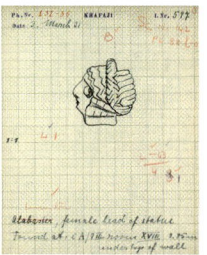

38.
Field object card, Khafajah: head of a female figure
Paper, H. 15.4 cm; W. 12.7 cm
March 3, 1931
Courtesy of the Oriental Institute of the University of Chicago
OIM: Kh. I 597

39.
Field register of objects, Khafajah
Paper, H. 35.5 cm; W. 50 cm (open)
November 1930–March 1932
Courtesy of the Oriental Institute Archive (Fig. 1–14 and Fig. 1–15)

40.
Field register of objects, Khafajah
Paper, H. 42 cm; W. 69 cm (open)
November 1931–February 1933
Courtesy of the Oriental Institute Archive

41.
Field register of objects, Tell Asmar
Paper, H. 41.5 cm; W. 79 cm (open)
February 1933–March 1934
Courtesy of the Oriental Institute Archive

42.
Field register of objects, Khafajah
Paper, H. 42 cm; W. 69 cm (open)
February 15, 1933–March 5, 1934
Courtesy of the Oriental Institute Archive

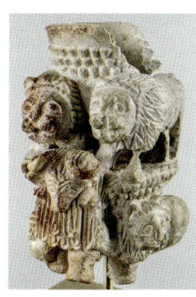

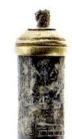 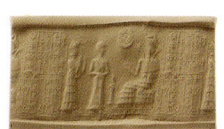

43.
Cup with Nude Hero, Bulls, and Lions
Gypsum, H. 16 cm; W. 12 cm
Tell Agrab (Shara Temple)
ca. 3000-2600 BCE
Iraq Expedition of the Oriental Institute,
1930–1937
OIM: A17948

46.
Cylinder Seal, with inscription to Bilalama and
modern impression
Gold, Lapis Lazuli, Bronze
H. 4.3 cm; Diam. 1.5 cm
Eshnunna, ca. 2000 BCE
Iraq Expedition of the Oriental Institute,
1930-1937
OIM: A7468

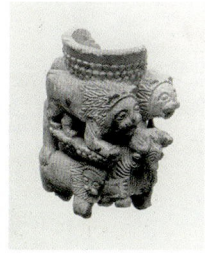

44.
Study photograph: cup with nude hero, bulls,
and lions (OIM: A17948)
Photograph, H. 13.2 cm; W. 9.4 cm
ca. 1935–1937
Iraq Expedition of the Oriental Institute,
1930-1937
OIM: Ag. 11

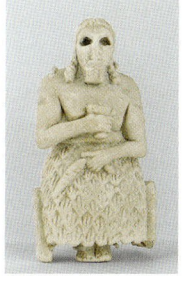

47.
Seated Male Figure Holding a Cup
Gypsum, H. 13 cm; W. 5.6 cm
Tell Agrab (Shara Temple),
ca. 2700-2500 BCE
Iraq Expedition of the Oriental Institute,
1930-1937
OIM: A18108

48.
Standing Female Figure
Gypsum, H. 36.2 cm
ca. 2700-2500 BCE
Private Collection, USA (Fig. 1–17)

49.
Standing Male Figure
Alabaster, Shell, Lapis Lazuli
H. 23 cm; W. 8 cm; D. 7 cm
Khafajah (Nintu Temple), Early Dynastic II
(ca. 2650-2550 BCE)
Khafaje Expedition
Penn: 37-15-28 (Figs. 1–13a, b)

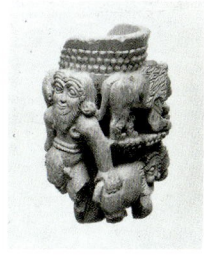

45.
Study photograph: cup with nude hero, bulls,
and lions (OIM: A17948)
Photograph, H. 13 cm; W. 9.5 cm
ca. 1935–1937
Iraq Expedition of the Oriental Institute,
1930-1937
OIM: Ag. 12

50.
Top Half of a Male Figure
Gypsum, H. 9 cm
Khafajah (Sin Temple IX), ca. 2700-2500 BCE
Iraq Expedition of the Oriental Institute,
1930-1937
OIM: A12387 (Fig. 6–7)

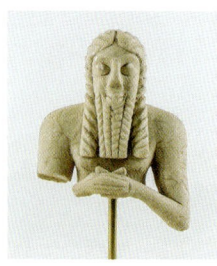

51.
Top Half of a Male Figure
Gypsum, H. 10.2 cm; W. 7.9 cm; D. 3.4 cm
Khafajah (Sin Temple IX), ca. 2700-2500 BCE
Iraq Expedition of the Oriental Institute,
1930-1937
OIM: A12340

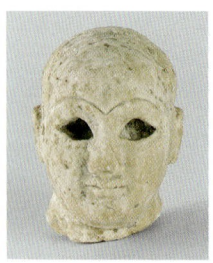

52.
Head of a Male Figure
Gypsum, Bitumen, H. 8.8 cm; W. 6.5 cm
Khafajah (Shara Temple), ca. 2700-2500 BCE
Iraq Expedition of the Oriental Institute,
1930-1937
OIM: A18018

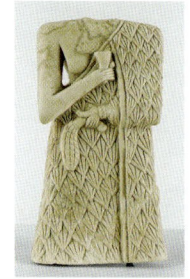

53.
Headless Standing Female Figure
Gypsum, H. 17 cm; W. 9.8 cm; D. 6.1 cm
Khafajah (Sin Temple VII), ca. 2700-2500 BCE
Iraq Expedition of the Oriental Institute,
1930-1937
OIM: A12334

54.
Standing Male Figure
Gypsum, Shell, Bitumen
H. 47 cm; W. 17.5 cm; D. 11.5 cm
Khafajah (Sin Temple IX), ca. 2700-2500 BCE
Iraq Expedition of the Oriental Institute,
1930-1937
OIM: A12434 (Fig. 6–6)

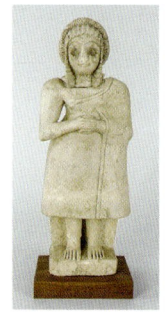

55.
Standing Female Figure
Gypsum, Shell, H. 36.1 cm; W. 13.5 cm; D. 7.1 cm
Khafajah (Sin Temple IX), ca. 2700-2500 BCE
Iraq Expedition of the Oriental Institute,
1930-1937
OIM: A12412

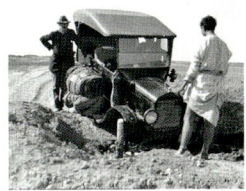

56.
Dudley Buxton on the way to Jamdat Nasr
Photograph
ca. 1924-25
Lent by the Field Museum of Natural History,
Chicago
Field: 58576

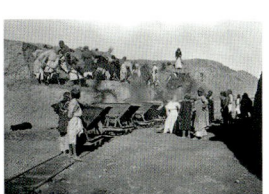

57.
Filling trucks at the excavation, Kish
Photograph
ca. 1928
Lent by the Field Museum of Natural History,
Chicago
Field: 66754

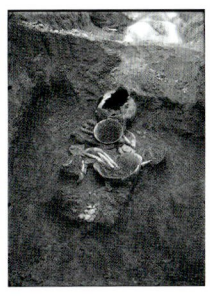

58.
Grave, south end of Y trench, Kish
Photograph
ca. 1928
Lent by the Field Museum of Natural History,
Chicago
Field: 60239

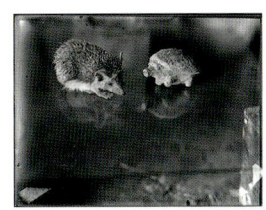

59.
Hedgehog with hedgehog figurine, Kish
Photograph
ca. 1928
Lent by the Field Museum of Natural History,
Chicago
Field: 6019

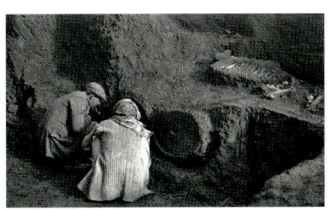

60.
Studying a burial, Kish
Photograph
ca. 1928
Lent by the Field Museum of Natural History,
Chicago
Field: 59632

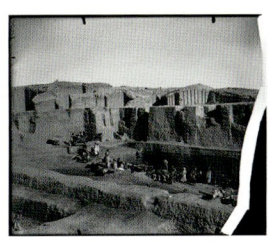

61.
Looking northeast over a Y trench, Kish
Photograph
ca. 1928
Lent by the Field Museum of Natural History,
Chicago
Field: 60218

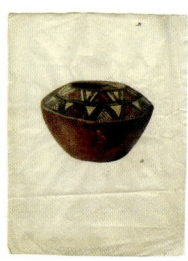

62.
Illustration of a polychrome vessel from Kish
Watercolor on Paper, H. 25.4 cm; W. 21.59 cm
1929
Lent by the Field Museum of Natural History,
Chicago

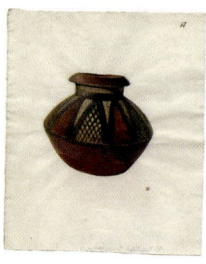

63.
Illustration of a polychrome vessel from Kish
Watercolor on Paper, H. 32.38 cm; W. 24.77 cm
ca. 1929
Lent by the Field Museum of Natural History,
Chicago

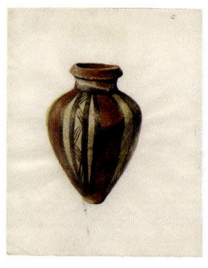

64.
Illustration of a polychrome vessel from Kish
Watercolor on Paper, H. 26.67 cm; W. 21.9 cm
ca. 1929
Lent by the Field Museum of Natural History

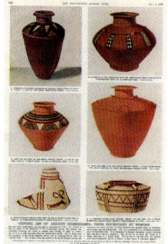

65.
"Early Mesopotamian Painted Pottery"
Illustrated London News, December 3, 1938
H. 37.5 cm; W. 26.5 cm
Courtesy of the Department of Ancient Near
Eastern Art, The Metropolitan Museum of Art
MMA: ANE.ILN.5

66.
"Relics of Sumer's First Capital After the Flood:
Discoveries at Kish. Chariots and oxen of
3500 B.C.; and a woman's splendid jewels"
Illustrated London News, June 2, 1928
H. 37.5 cm; W. 26.5 cm
Courtesy of the Department of Ancient Near
Eastern Art, The Metropolitan Museum of Art
MA: ANE.ILN.6
(Fig. 2–9)

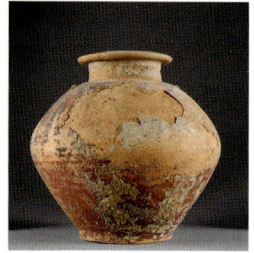

67.
Polychrome Vessel
Baked Clay, H. 26 cm; W. 27.3 cm; Diam. 27.3 cm
Jamdat Nasr, ca. 3100-2900 BCE
Lent by the Field Museum of Natural History
Field: 158355

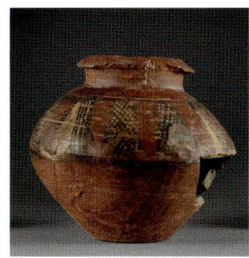

68.
Polychrome Vessel
Baked Clay, H. 20 cm; W. 23.5 cm; Diam. 23.5 cm
Jamdat Nasr, ca. 3100-2900 BCE
Lent by the Field Museum of Natural History
Field: 158312

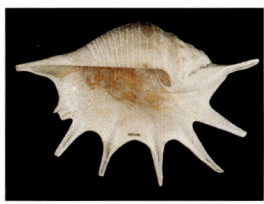

69.
Vessel
Shell, H. 9 cm; W. 28 cm; Diam. 19 cm
Kish, ca. 2900-2350 BCE
Lent by the Field Museum of Natural History
Field Museum: 236636

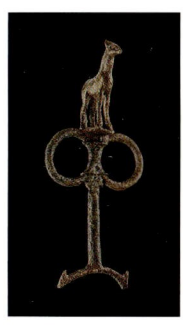

70.
Copper Rein Ring
Copper Alloy, H. 20.2 cm; W. 9 cm; D. 7 cm
Kish East, Ingharra, ca. 2900-2700 BCE
Lent by the Field Museum of Natural History
Field: 236528

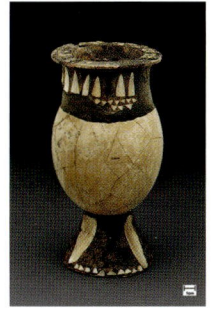

71.
Ostrich-Egg Vessel
Ostrich Egg, Bitumen, Mother-of-Pearl
H. 22.5 cm; W. 11 cm; D. 11 cm
Kish, ca. 2500-2350 BCE
Lent by the Field Museum of Natural History
Field: 156986

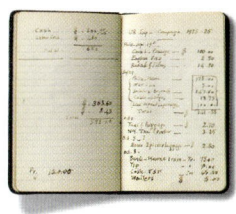

72.
Travel notebook of Leon Legrain
Paper, H. 13.4 cm; W. 16.6 cm (open)
1924-26
Courtesy of the University of Pennsylvania
Museum of Archaeology and Anthropology

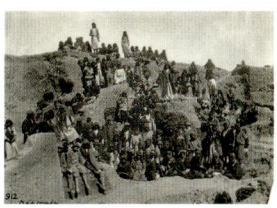

73.
Excavation team and workmen, Ur
Photograph, H. 11.5 cm; W. 15.3 cm
ca. 1922-35
Courtesy of the University of Pennsylvania
Museum of Archaeology and Anthropology
Penn Museum: 912

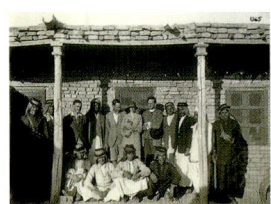

74.
Excavation team posing at the Expedition House, Ur
Photograph, H. 11.5 cm; W. 16 cm
ca. 1922-35
Courtesy of the University of Pennsylvania
Museum of Archaeology and Anthropology
Penn Museum: 1365

75.
Leonard Woolley brushing an artifact, Ur
Photograph, H. 11.5 cm; W. 15.3 cm
ca. 1925
Courtesy of the University of Pennsylvania
Museum of Archaeology and Anthropology
Penn Museum (Fig. 1–5)

76.
Excavation team packing pottery into boxes, Ur
Photograph, H. 11.5 cm; W. 15.3 cm
1929
Courtesy of the University of Pennsylvania
Museum of Archaeology and Anthropology
Penn Museum: 1328 (Fig. 2–4)

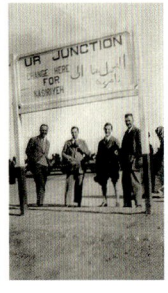

77.
Ur Junction with unidentified travelers
Photograph, H. 11.43 cm; W. 7.62 cm
ca. 1923-29
Courtesy of the University of Pennsylvania
Museum of Archaeology and Anthropology

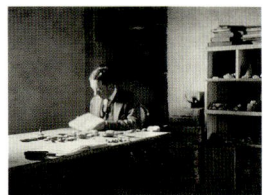

78.
Leon Legrain working in the "Tablet Room" of the
Expedition House, Ur
Photograph, H. 7.62 cm; W. 11.43 cm
1923-29
Courtesy of the University of Pennsylvania
Museum of Archaeology and Anthropology

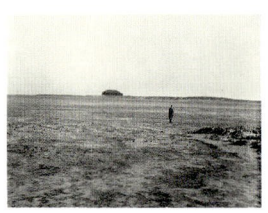

79.
Ziggurat at Ur
Photograph, H. 7.62 cm; W. 11.43 cm
ca. 1923-29
Courtesy of the University of Pennsylvania
Museum of Archaeology and Anthropology

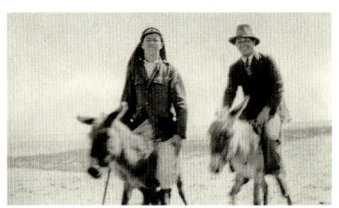

80.
Men on donkeys traveling to Ur
Photograph, H. 7.62 cm; W. 11.43 cm
ca. 1923-29
Courtesy of the University of Pennsylvania
Museum of Archaeology and Anthropology

81.
Telegram by Leonard Woolley from Basra,
January 4, 1928
H. 21.7 cm; W. 20 cm
Courtesy of the University of Pennsylvania
Museum of Archaeology and Anthropology
(Fig. 3–1)

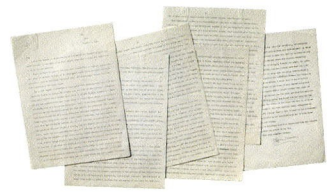

82.
Letter by Leonard Woolley from Ur, January 3, 1928
Paper, H. 25.7 cm; W. 20 cm
Courtesy of the University of Pennsylvania Museum of Archaeology and Anthropology

83.
Press Release from the Bureau of Publicity, University of Pennsylvania, Philadelphia
Paper
H. 27.9 cm; W. 21.5 cm
January 12, 1928
Courtesy of the University of Pennsylvania Museum of Archaeology and Anthropology
(Fig. 1–11)

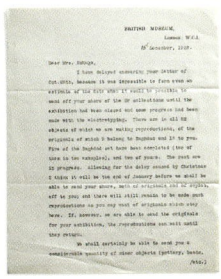

84.
Letter to Mrs. McHugh at the University of Pennsylvania from Sir Frederic Kenyon at the British Museum, London
Paper, H. 24 cm; W. 19.2 cm
December 15, 1928
Courtesy of the University of Pennsylvania Museum of Archaeology and Anthropology

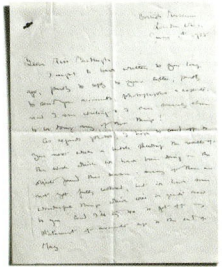

85.
Letter to Mrs. McHugh at the University of Pennsylvania from Sir Leonard Woolley at the British Museum
Paper, H. 23 cm; W. 17.5 cm
June 1, 1928
Courtesy of the University of Pennsylvania Museum of Archaeology and Anthropology

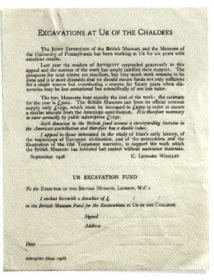

86.
Leonard Woolley's request for donation for excavation at Ur
Paper, H. 23 cm; W. 17.5 cm
September 1928
Courtesy of the University of Pennsylvania Museum of Archaeology and Anthropology

87.
Ur excavation field notes
Paper, H. 38.5 cm; W. 16 cm (open)
1927-28
Courtesy of the Trustees of the British Museum
BM: ME Archive 630

88.
Ur excavation catalogue
Paper, H. 38.5 cm; W. 16 cm (open)
1927-28
Courtesy of the Trustees of the British Museum
BM: ME Archive 766

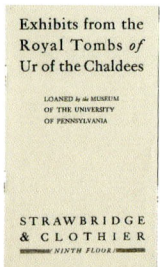

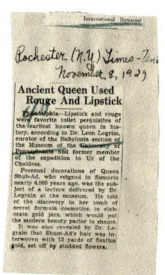

89.
"Exhibits from the Royal Tombs of Ur of the Chaldees"
Paper, H. 15 cm; W. 18 cm (open)
1934
Courtesy of the University of Pennsylvania Museum of Archaeology and Anthropology

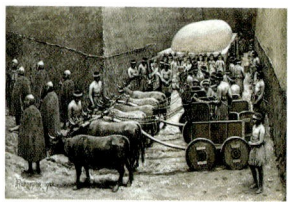

90.
Reconstruction of the scene in PG 789 just before the death of the royal retainers , by Amedée Forestier
Paper, H. 38.8; W. 56 cm; D. 4.5 cm (Framed)
1928
Courtesy of the Trustees of the British Museum
BM: 2008,6047.1

91.
"Queen Shub-ad's 5000-Year-Old Golden Head-Dress: An Ur Treasure"
Illustrated London News, August 11, 1928
H. 37.5 cm; W. 26.5 cm
Courtesy of the Department of Ancient Near Eastern Art, The Metropolitan Museum of Art
MMA: ANE.ILN.2 (Fig. 2–5)

92.
"Ancient Queen Used Rouge and Lipstick"
Rochester (NY) Times, November 8, 1929
H. 12 cm; W. 7.1 cm
Courtesy of the University of Pennsylvania Museum of Archaeology and Anthropology

93.
"Golden Treasures from Ur"
Seattle Post Intelligencer, November 24, 1929
H. 49 cm; W. 39 cm
Courtesy of the University of Pennsylvania Museum of Archaeology and Anthropology
(Fig. 2–6)

94.
"Ur of Chaldees"
Memphis (TN) Commercial Appeal, July 21, 1929
H. 60.5 cm; W. 45.5 cm
Courtesy of the University of Pennsylvania Museum of Archaeology and Anthropology
(Fig. 5–4)

95.
"A Princess of 3000 BC"
St. Louis Post-Dispatch Sunday Magazine, September 28, 1930
H. 59.3 cm; W. 45.6 cm
Courtesy of the University of Pennsylvania Museum of Archaeology and Anthropology
(Fig. 5–2)

96.
"Evidence that the Queen of Ancient Ur Was Clubbed to Death"
Washington (DC) Herald, November 25, 1928
H. 56 cm; W. 39 cm
Courtesy of the University of Pennsylvania Museum of Archaeology and Anthropology
(Fig. 1–12)

97.
"Grim Tragedy of Wicked Queen Shubad's 100
Poisoned Slaves"
Philadelphia Inquirer, May 20, 1934
H. 58.6 cm; W. 44 cm
Courtesy of the University of Pennsylvania
Museum of Archaeology and Anthropology
(Fig. 2–7)

98.
Jewelry in situ, Ur
Photograph, H. 13.3 cm; W. 15.5 cm
1929
Courtesy of the University of Pennsylvania
Museum of Archaeology and Anthropology
Penn Museum: 1363

99.
Early reconstruction of Puabi's headdress by
Katharine Woolley
Photograph, H. 19.2 cm; W. 14.2 cm
1930
Courtesy of the University of Pennsylvania
Museum of Archaeology and Anthropology
Penn: 1136A (Fig. 3–10)

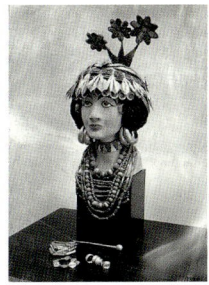

100.
Early reconstruction of Puabi's headdress by
Léon Legrain
Photograph, H. 20.5 cm; W. 15 cm
1930
Courtesy of the University of Pennsylvania
Museum of Archaeology and Anthropology
Penn: 1332

101.
Léon Legrain adjusting Puabi's headdress
Photograph, H. 11.5 cm; W. 15.3 cm
1929
Courtesy of the University of Pennsylvania
Museum of Archaeology and Anthropology
(Fig. 1–7)

102.
Illustration of Puabi and headdress,
by Mary Louise Baker
Watercolor on paper, H. 47 cm; W. 37 cm
1932
Birmingham Museums Trust
BMAG: 1964 A2626 (Fig. 5–5)

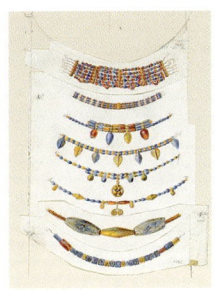

103.
Illustration of jewelry from Ur
Watercolor on paper, H. 47 cm; W. 37 cm
1932
Birmingham Museums Trust
BMAG: 1964 A2631-A2634

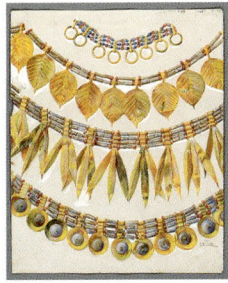

104.
Illustration of jewelry from Ur
Watercolor on paper, H. 47 cm; W. 37 cm
1932
Birmingham Museums Trust
BMAG: 1973A1261

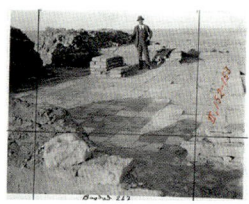

105.
Father Bonaventura Ubach and Leonard Woolley
at the Nebuchadnezzar Temple, Ur
Photograph, H. 8 cm; W. 11 cm
1922
Montserrat Monastery

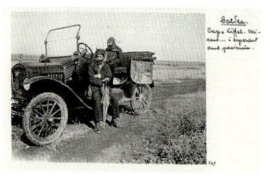

106.
Men waiting in a car on the road to Kiffel
Photograph, H. 8.4 cm; W. 13.5 cm
1922-23
Montserrat Monastery

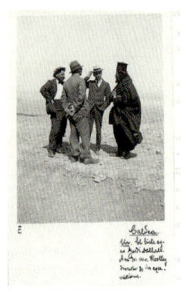

107.
The Syrian Bishop George Dallal and
Leonard Woolley
Photograph, H. 8.4 cm; W. 13.5 cm
1922-23
Montserrat Monastery

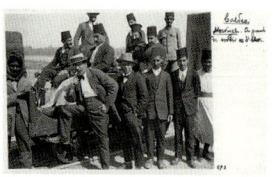

108.
Group of men at Nasiriyah, ready to leave Ur
Photograph, H. 8.4 cm; W. 13.5 cm
1922-23
Montserrat Monastery

109.
Headdress of Puabi
Gold
Ur
ca. 2500–2300 BCE
Joint Expedition of the British Museum and of
the Museum of the University of Pennsylvania,
6th season, 1927-1928
Penn: B16992A (Hair Ring), B17709 (Wreath),
B16693 (Decorative Comb), B17710 (Wreath),
B17711 (Wreath), B17711A (Hair Ribbon),
B17712A, B (Earrings), 98-9-9A, B (Hair Rings),
B17708 (Frontlet) (Figs. 5–1, 5–11, 5–12, 5–14
to 5–16, 5–21)

110.
Necklace
Gold, Lapis Lazuli, L. 43 cm; H. 0.3 cm; W. 3 cm
Ur, ca. 2500-2300 BCE
Joint Expedition of the British Museum and of
the Museum of the University of Pennsylvania,
6th season, 1927–1928
Penn: B16694 (Fig. 5–1)

111.
Cloak of Stringed Beads
Gold, Various Stones
Ur, ca. 2500-2300 BCE
Joint Expedition of the British Museum and of
the Museum of the University of Pennsylvania,
6th season, 1927–1928
Penn: 83-7-1.1–83-7-1.89 (Fig. 5–1)

112.
Belt
Gold, Lapis Lazuli, Carnelian
L. 62 cm; H. 0.5 cm; W. 12 cm
Ur, ca. 2500-2300 BCE
Joint Expedition of the British Museum and of
the Museum of the University of Pennsylvania,
6th season, 1927 –1928
Penn: B17063 (Fig. 5–1)

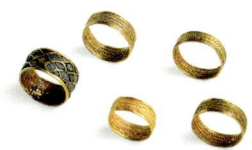

113–17. Five Finger Rings
Gold, Lapis Lazuli, D. 2.0 to 2.2 cm
Ur, ca. 2500–2300 bce
Joint Expedition of the British Museum and
of the Museum of the University of
Pennsylvania, 6th season, 1927–28
Penn: B16717, B16718, B16719, B16720,
B16721

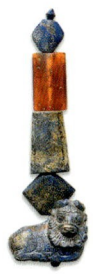

118.
Amulet and Beads
Gold, Lapis Lazuli, L. 12.3 cm; H. 2 cm; W. 4.2 cm
Ur, ca. 2500-2300 BCE
Joint Expedition of the British Museum and of
the Museum of the University of Pennsylvania,
6th season, 1927–1928
Penn: B16726

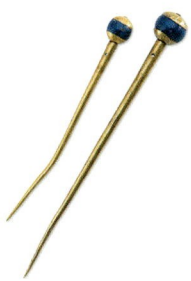

119–20. Two Garment Pins
Gold, Lapis Lazuli
L. 16 cm; W. 2 cm. L. 21.1 cm; D. 2.5 cm
Ur, ca. 2500-2300 BCE
Joint Expedition of the British Museum and of
the Museum of the University of Pennsylvania to
Mesopotamia, 6th and 7th seasons, 1927–29
Penn: 30-12-552; B16729

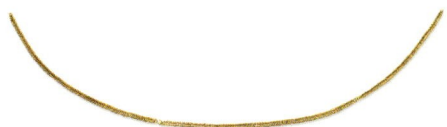

121.
Chain, Part of a Frontlet
Gold, L. 44 cm; H. 0.4 cm
Ur, ca. 2500-2300 BCE
Joint Expedition of the British Museum and of
the Museum of the University of Pennsylvania,
6th season, 1927–1928
Penn: B16761

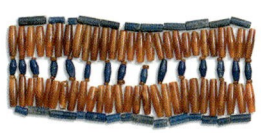

122.
Cuff
Lapis Lazuli, Carnelian
L. 14.5 cm; W. 5.9 cm; H. 0.4 cm
Ur, ca. 2500-2300 BCE
Joint Expedition of the British Museum and of
the Museum of the University of Pennsylvania,
6th season, 1927–28
Penn: B17292

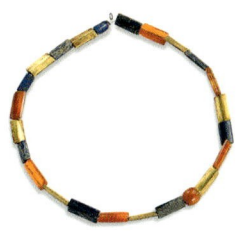

123.
Garter
Gold, Lapis Lazuli, Carnelian
L. 38 cm; H. 0.6 cm; W. 0.9 cm
Ur, ca. 2500-2300 BCE
Joint Expedition of the British Museum and of
the Museum of the University of Pennsylvania,
6th season, 1927–28
Penn: B16783

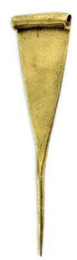

124.
Pin
Gold, L. 12.8 cm; W. 3.2 cm; H. 0.8 cm
Ur, ca. 2500-2300 BCE
Joint Expedition of the British Museum and of
the Museum of the University of Pennsylvania,
6th season, 1927–28
Penn: B16908

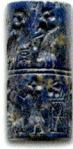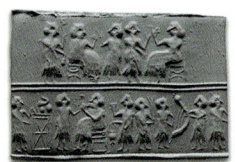

125.
Cylinder Seal Found with Puabi and modern
impression
Lapis Lazuli , W. 4 cm; D. 2 cm
Ur, ca. 2500-2300 BCE
Joint Expedition of the British Museum and of
the Museum of the University of Pennsylvania,
6th season, 1927–28
Penn: B16728

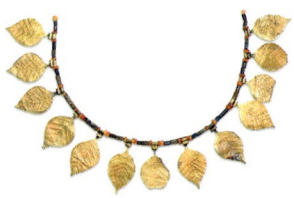

126.
Wreath
Gold, Lapis Lazuli, Carnelian, L. 40 cm
Ur, ca. 2500-2300 BCE
Joint Expedition of the British Museum and of
the Museum of the University of Pennsylvania to
Mesopotamia, 6th season, 1927–28
Penn: B16705

127.
String of Beads or Necklace, modern
interpretation
Gold, Lapis Lazuli, Carnelian, L. 36 cm
Ur, ca. 2500-2300 BCE
Joint Expedition of the British Museum and of
the Museum of the University of Pennsylvania to
Mesopotamia, 6th season, 1927–28
Penn: B17642 (Fig. 2–18)

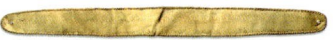

128.
Frontlet
Gold, L. 31.7 cm; W. 3 cm; D. 0.3 cm
ca. 2600-2450 BCE
Joint Expedition of the British Museum and of
the Museum of the University of Pennsylvania to
Mesopotamia, 7th season, 1928–29
Penn: 30-12-604

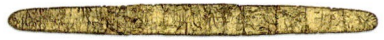

129.
Frontlet with engraved imagery
Gold, L. 32 cm; W. 2.8 cm; D. 0.3 cm
ca. 2600-2450 BCE
Joint Expedition of the British Museum and of
the Museum of the University of Pennsylvania to
Mesopotamia, 5th season, 1926–27
Penn: B16686

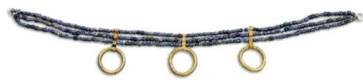

130.
Frontlet, modern interpretation
Gold, Lapis Lazuli, H. 02 cm; W. 2.5 cm; L. 21.5 cm
Ur, ca. 2500-2300 BCE
Joint Expedition of the British Museum and of
the Museum of the University of Pennsylvania to
Mesopotamia, 6th season, 1927–28
Penn: B17657

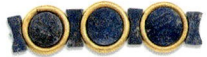

131.
Frontlet
Gold, Lapis Lazuli, Carnelian, L. 36.5 cm
Ur, ca. 2500-2300 BCE
Joint Expedition of the Baghdad School and the
University Museum to Mesopotamia, 1937
Penn: 30-12-619

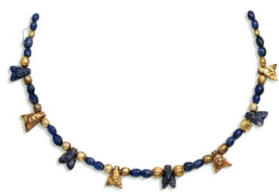

132.
String of Beads, modern interpretation
Gold, Lapis Lazuli, L. 22.7 cm
Ur, ca. 2500-2300 BCE
Joint Expedition of the British Museum and of
the Museum of the University of Pennsylvania to
Mesopotamia, 7th season, 1928–29
Penn: 30-12-570

133.
Belt
Gold, Lapis Lazuli, L. 10.8 cm
Ur, ca. 2500-2300 BCE
Joint Expedition of the British Museum and of
the Museum of the University of Pennsylvania to
Mesopotamia, 7th season, 1928–29
Penn: 30-12-559

134.
Frontlet
Gold, Lapis Lazuli, Carnelian, L. 40 cm; Diam. 1 cm
Ur, ca. 2500-2300 BCE
Joint Expedition of the British Museum and of
the Museum of the University of Pennsylvania to
Mesopotamia, 7th season, 1928 –29
Penn: 30-12-618

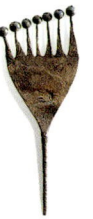

135.
Decorative Comb
Silver, Lapis Lazuli, L. 13 cm; W. 11 cm, D. 3 cm
Ur, ca. 2500-2300 BCE
Joint Expedition of the British Museum and of
the Museum of the University of Pennsylvania to
Mesopotamia, 8th season, 1929-1930
Penn: B17005

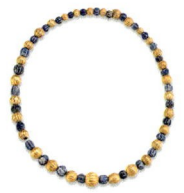

136.
Necklace
Gold, Lapis Lazuli, L. 28 cm; Diam. 1 cm
Ur, ca. 2600-2450 BCE
Joint Expedition of the British Museum and of
the Museum of the University of Pennsylvania to
Mesopotamia, 8th season, 1929-1930
Penn: B16715

137.
"Diadem"
Gold, Lapis Lazuli, Bitumen, L. 88 cm
Ur, ca. 2500-2300 BCE
Joint Expedition of the British Museum and of
the Museum of the University of Pennsylvania to
Mesopotamia, 8th season, 1929-1930
Penn: B16684.1 (Figs. 4-2 and 4-11 to 4-20)

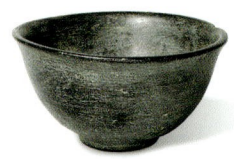

138.
Bowl
Steatite, H. 8.6 cm; Diam. 17.2 cm
Ur, ca. 2500-2300 BCE
Joint Expedition of the British Museum and of
the Museum of the University of Pennsylvania to
Mesopotamia, 7th season, 1928–29
Penn: 30-12-81

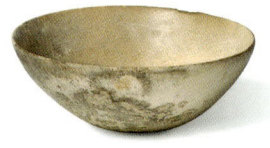

139.
Bowl
Gypsum, Diam. 16.7 cm
Ur, ca. 2600-2450 BCE
Joint Expedition of the British Museum and of
the Museum of the University of Pennsylvania to
Mesopotamia, 8th season, 1929–30
Penn: 31-16-418

140.
Standing Male Figure
Gypsum, Alabaster, Shell, Black Limestone,
Bitumen, H. 29.5 cm; W. 12.9 cm; D. 10 cm
Eshnunna (Tell Asmar), ca. 2900–2600 BCE
Fletcher Fund, 1940
MMA: 40.156 (Figs. 1-2, 6-2)

141.
Willem de Kooning, *Woman on a Sign*
Oil on Paper Mounted on Canvas
H. 142.24 cm; W. 105.41 cm
1967
The Fayez Sarofim Collection (Fig. 1–21)

142.
Willem de Kooning, *Woman*
Oil on Paper Board, H. 90.8 cm; W. 61.9 cm
1953-54
Gift of Mr. and Mrs. Alastair B. Martin, the
Guennol Collection
TBM: 57.124 (Fig. 1–20)

143.
Alberto Giacometti, *Seated Gudea: After a
Sumerian Sculpture*
Ink on paper, H. 26.9 cm; W. 21 cm
ca. 1935
Courtesy of the Alberto Giacometti Estate
GF: 1994-0704 (Fig. 1–19)

144.
Alberto Giacometti, *Seated Gudea: After a
Sumerian Sculpture*
Pencil on paper, H. 29.8 cm; W. 17.3 cm
ca. 1935
Courtesy of the Alberto Giacometti Estate
GF: 1994-1808 (Fig. 2–19)

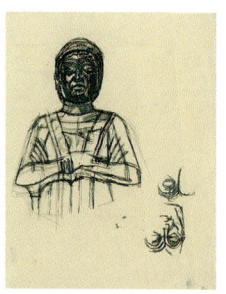

145.
Alberto Giacometti, *Female Figure: After a
Sumerian Sculpture*
Pen and black ink on paper, H. 26.9 cm; W. 20.9 cm
ca. 1935
Courtesy of the Alberto Giacometti Estate
GF: 1994-0703

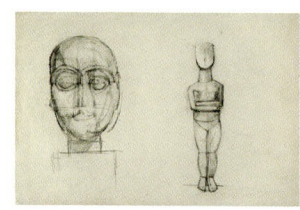

146.
Alberto Giacometti, *Head of Gudea and a Cycladic
Idol: After Sumerian and Cycladic Sculptures*
Pencil on paper, H. 31.9 cm; W. 48.2 cm
ca. 1935
Courtesy of the Alberto Giacometti Estate
GF: 1994-0741

147.
Henry Moore, *Seated Figure*
Cast concrete, H. 45 cm; W. 17.4 cm; D. 23.5 cm
1929
Gift of Irina Moore
HMF: LH 65 (Fig. 1–4)

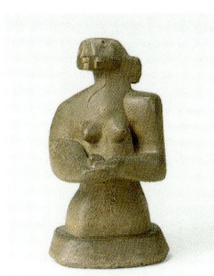

148.
Henry Moore, *Half Figure II*
Cast concrete, H. 39.4 cm, W. 23 cm; D. 17 cm
1929
The Robert and Lisa Sainsbury Collection, SCVA:
UEA 79

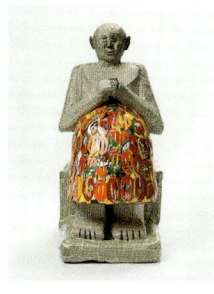

149.
Michael Rakowitz, *The Invisible Enemy Should Not
Exist: Seated statue of Scribe Dudu*
(IM55204)
Middle Eastern Packaging and Newspapers,
Glue, H. 54 cm; W. 24.5 cm; D. 34.5 cm
2014
Courtesy of the artist and Lombard Freid Gallery:
12183

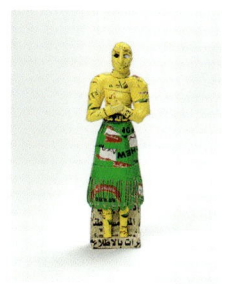

150.
Michael Rakowitz, *The Invisible Enemy Should Not
Exist: Standing male figure with one
unpierced eyeball of shell* (Kh. IV 261)
Middle Eastern Packaging and Newspapers,
Glue, H. 28.6 cm; W. 8.9 cm; D. 5.7 cm
2013
Courtesy of the artist and Lombard Freid Gallery:
11957

151.
Michael Rakowitz, *The Invisible Enemy Should
Not Exist: Bearded male with skirt holding vase*
(IM19753)
Middle Eastern Packaging and Newspapers,
Glue, H. 48 cm; W. 17.5 cm; D. 8.5 cm
2007
Courtesy of the artist and Lombard Freid Gallery:
8046 (Fig. 1–23)

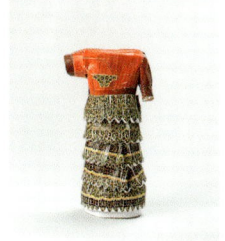

152.
Michael Rakowitz, *The Invisible Enemy Should Not
Exist: Statuette of male* (IM51145)
Middle Eastern Packaging and Newspapers,
Glue, H. 24 cm; W. 13.5 cm; D. 9 cm
2007
Courtesy of the artist and Lombard Freid Gallery:
8367

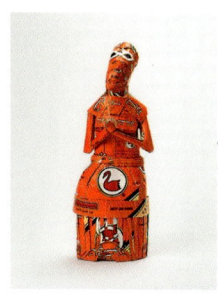

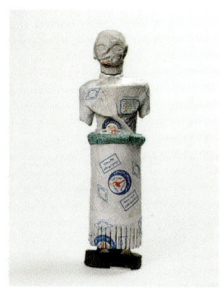

153.
Michael Rakowitz, *The Invisible Enemy Should Not Exist: Standing male figure* (Kh. IV 251)
Middle Eastern Packaging and Newspapers,
Glue, H. 46 cm; W. 15.5 cm; D. 11 cm
2007
Courtesy of the artist and Lombard Freid Gallery:
8370

155.
Michael Rakowitz, *The Invisible Enemy Should Not Exist: Large male figure with inscription*
(Kh. IV 126)
Middle Eastern Packaging and Newspapers,
Glue, H. 57.2 cm; W. 19 cm; D. 12 cm
2009
Courtesy of the artist and Lombard Freid Gallery:
10050

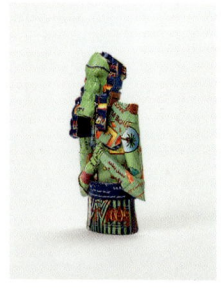

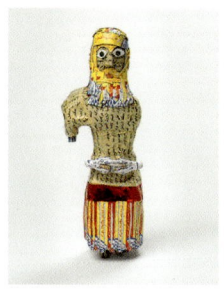

154.
Michael Rakowitz, *The Invisible Enemy Should Not Exist: Head and torso of male* (IM 41080)
Middle Eastern Packaging and Newspapers,
Glue, H. 21 cm; W. 11.5 cm; D. 5.5 cm
2007
Courtesy of the artist and Lombard Freid Gallery:
8434

156.
Michael Rakowitz, *The Invisible Enemy Should Not Exist: Standing male figure; feet, leg, and arms missing. Eyeballs of shell; traces of
bitumen in eyebrows, on hair and beard* (IM41081)
Middle Eastern Packaging and Newspapers,
Glue, H. 20 cm; W. 7.5 cm; D. 6.6 cm
2009
Courtesy of the artist and Lombard Freid Gallery:
11950

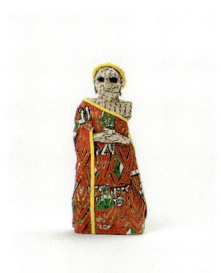

157.
Michael Rakowitz, *The Invisible Enemy Should Not Exist: Standing female statue; flat body; right arm missing. Eyeballs of shell set in bitumen; pupil of bitumen* (Kh. IV 303)
Middle Eastern Packaging and Newspapers, Glue, H. 15.5 cm; W. 7.5 cm; D. 4.3 cm
2013
Courtesy of the artist and Lombard Freid Gallery: 11951

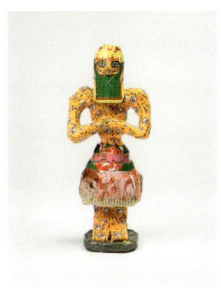

158.
Michael Rakowitz, *The Invisible Enemy Should Not Exist: Standing male figure*
Middle Eastern Packaging and Newspapers, Glue, H. 30 cm; W. 13.5 cm; D. 11 cm
2013
Courtesy of the artist and Lombard Freid Gallery: 11953

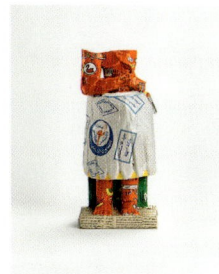

159.
Michael Rakowitz, *The Invisible Enemy Should Not Exist: Standing male figure; head, shoulders and most of arm missing* (IM41016)
Middle Eastern Packaging and Newspapers, Glue, H. 31 cm; W. 14 cm; D. 8.7 cm
2013
Courtesy of the artist and Lombard Freid Gallery: 11958

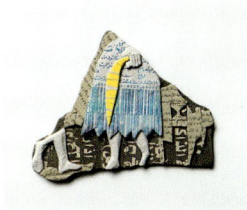

160.
Michael Rakowitz, *The Invisible Enemy Should Not Exist: Fragment of relief plaque* (IM41015)
Middle Eastern Packaging and Newspapers, Glue, H. 12.5 cm; W. 15 cm
2007
Courtesy of the artist and Lombard Freid Gallery: 11952

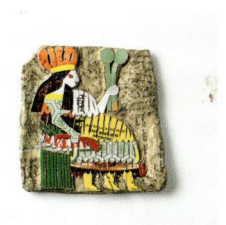

161.
Michael Rakowitz, *The Invisible Enemy Should Not Exist: Horned cap and garmented figure plaque* (IM42494)
Middle Eastern Packaging and Newspapers, Glue, H. 11 cm; W. 10.5 cm
2013
Courtesy of the artist and Lombard Freid Gallery: 8245

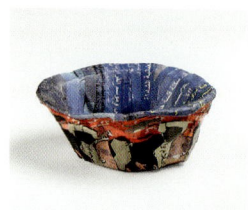

162.
Michael Rakowitz, *The Invisible Enemy Should Not Exist: Bowl with bull relief* (IM11959)
Middle Eastern Packaging and Newspapers, Glue, H. 6 cm; Diam. 14.7 cm
2007
Courtesy of the artist and Lombard Freid Gallery: 8649

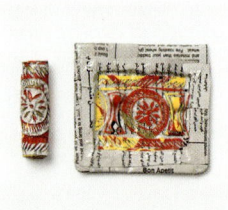

163.
Michael Rakowitz, *The Invisible Enemy Should Not Exist: Cylinder seal with geometric pattern* (Kh. V 95)
Middle Eastern Packaging and Newspapers, Glue, H. 7.6 cm; W. 8.1 cm (Impression)
H. 6 cm; Diam. 2.2 cm (Cylinder Seal)
2009
Courtesy of the artist and Lombard Freid Gallery: 10198

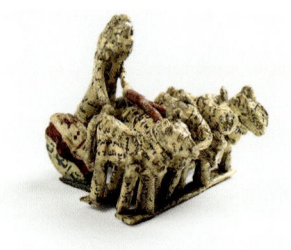

164.
Michael Rakowitz, *The Invisible Enemy Should Not Exist: Chariot* (IM31389)
Middle Eastern Packaging and Newspapers, Glue, H. 9.5 cm; W. 11 cm
2007
Courtesy of the artist and Lombard Freid Gallery: 8040

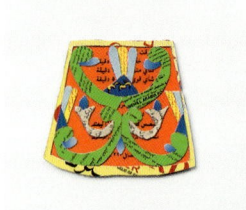

165.
Michael Rakowitz, *The Invisible Enemy Should Not Exist: Winged male facing left, holding a flower in his left hand a feather in the right below a floral design; wears short wig and ankle-length skirt* (IM65399)
Middle Eastern Packaging and Newspapers, Glue, H. 9.5 cm; W. 11 cm
2013
Courtesy of the artist and Lombard Freid Gallery: 11955

166.
Michael Rakowitz, *The Invisible Enemy Should Not Exist: Stylized tree with two curved branches acting as the trunk and supporting another curved branch* (IM65405)
Middle Eastern Packaging and Newspapers, Glue, H. 8.5 cm; W. 10 cm
2013
Courtesy of the artist and Lombard Freid Gallery: 11956

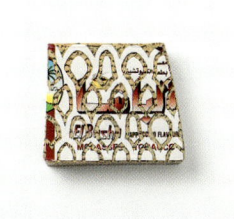

167.
Michael Rakowitz, *The Invisible Enemy Should Not Exist: Scale pattern relief* (IM69975)
Middle Eastern Packaging and Newspapers, Glue, H. 9.5 cm; W. 11 cm
2013
Courtesy of the artist and Lombard Freid Gallery: 8369

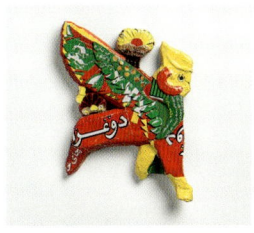

170.
Michael Rakowitz, *The Invisible Enemy Should Not Exist: Winged ram headed sphinx* (ND13305)
Middle Eastern Packaging and Newspapers, Glue, H. 10.5 cm; W. 12.5 cm
2009
Courtesy of the artist and Lombard Freid Gallery: 12109

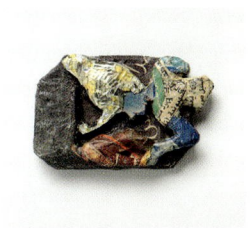

168.
Michael Rakowitz, *The Invisible Enemy Should Not Exist: Male figure with double crown* (ND13430)
Middle Eastern Packaging and Newspapers, Glue, H. 8 cm; W. 5.3 cm
2008
Courtesy of the artist and Lombard Freid Gallery: 8711

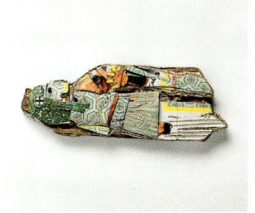

171.
Michael Rakowitz, *The Invisible Enemy Should Not Exist: Male facing right wearing wig* (ND13153)
Middle Eastern Packaging and Newspapers, Glue, H. 18.1 cm; W. 7 cm
2009
Courtesy of the artist and Lombard Freid Gallery: 12110

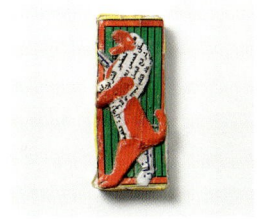

169.
Michael Rakowitz, *The Invisible Enemy Should Not Exist: Lion* (ND13646)
Middle Eastern Packaging and Newspapers, Glue, H. 6.1 cm; W. 3.1 cm
2009
Courtesy of the artist and Lombard Freid Gallery: 12108

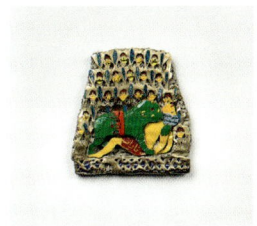

172.
Michael Rakowitz, *The Invisible Enemy Should Not Exist: Ivory plaque, lioness attacking a Nubian* (IM56642)
Middle Eastern Packaging and Newspapers, Glue, H. 10.5 cm; W. 10 cm
2024
Courtesy of the artist and Lombard Freid Gallery: 12304

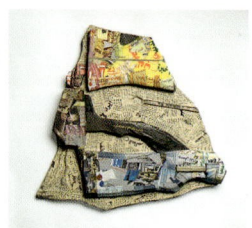

173.
Michael Rakowitz, *The Invisible Enemy Should Not Exist: Fragmented stela with legs of two figures* (Is. 35:36)
Middle Eastern Packaging and Newspapers, Glue, H. 44.5 cm; W. 39 cm
2009
Courtesy of the artist and Lombard Freid Gallery: 9330

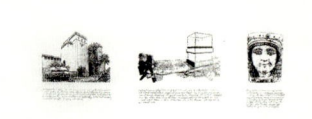

174.
Michael Rakowitz, *The Invisible Enemy Should Not Exist (Recovered, Missing, Stolen Series)*: *The Looting*
Pencil on Vellum, H. 28 cm; W. 53 cm
2007
Courtesy of the artist and Lombard Freid Gallery: 12307

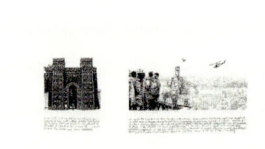

175.
Michael Rakowitz, *The Invisible Enemy Should Not Exist (Recovered, Missing, Stolen Series)*: *New Babylon*
Pencil on Vellum, H. 28 cm; W. 48 cm
2007
Courtesy of the artist and Lombard Freid Gallery: 12308

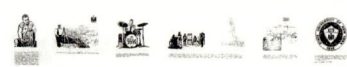

176.
Michael Rakowitz, *The Invisible Enemy Should Not Exist (Recovered, Missing, Stolen Series)*: *The Ballad of Donny George*
Pencil on Vellum, H. 28 cm; W. 90.5 cm
2007
Courtesy of the artist and Lombard Freid Gallery: 12305

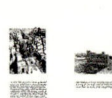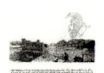

177.
Michael Rakowitz, *The Invisible Enemy Should Not Exist (Recovered, Missing, Stolen Series)*: *Excavation Extraction*
Pencil on Vellum, H. 28 cm; W. 49 cm
2007
Courtesy of the artist and Lombard Freid Gallery: 12306

178.
Jananne al-Ani, *Untitled May 1991 [Gulf War Work]*
Silver gelatin prints on paper, 20 units: H. 20 cm; W. 20 cm (each)
1991
Courtesy of the artist
IWM: ART 16417 (Fig. 1–22)

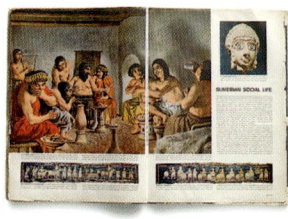

179.
"Sumerian Social Life"
Newspaper clipping, H. 37.5 cm; W. 53 cm
1955–57
Lent by Kim Benzel

180.
Charles Olson, *Archaeologist of Morning*
Paper, H. 27.69 cm; W. 20.32 cm
1970
Private Collection, USA (Fig. 1–18)

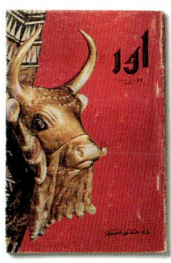

181.
Shah al-Siwani, *Ur*
Paper, H. 21.5 cm; W. 14.6 cm
1976
Private Collection

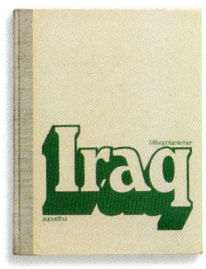

182.
Allan Breck, *Mésopotamie hier, Iraq aujourd'hui*
Paper, H. 30 cm; W. 23.9 cm
1977
Private Collection

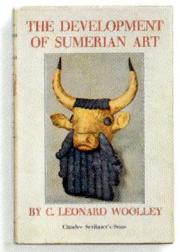

183. C. Leonard Woolley, *The Development of Sumerian Art*
Paper, H. 28.4 cm; W. 19.7 cm
1935
Private Collection

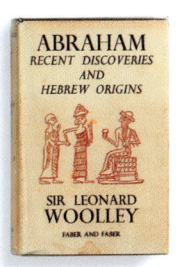

184.
C. Leonard Woolley, *Abraham: Recent Discoveries and Hebrew Origins*
Paper, H. 18.7 cm; W: 13 cm
1936
Private Collection

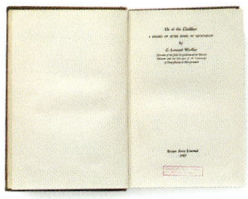

185.
C. Leonard Woolley, *Ur of the Chaldees, A Record of Seven Years of Excavation*
Paper, H. 18.7 cm; W: 13 cm
1929
Private Collection

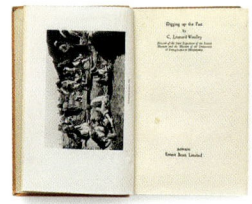

186.
C. Leonard Woolley, *Digging Up the Past*
Paper, H. 18.7 cm; W. 13 cm
1930
Private Collection

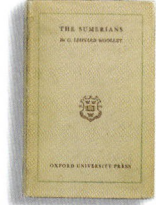

187.
C. Leonard Woolley, *The Sumerians*
Paper, H. 18.7 cm; W: 13 cm
1929
Private Collection

188.
Christian Zervos, *L'art de la Mésopotamie: De la fin du quatrième millénaire au XVe siècle avant notre ère*
Paper, H. 18.7 cm; W. 13 cm
1935
Private Collection (Fig. 2–17)

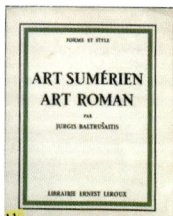

189.
Jurgis Baltrusaitis, *Art sumerien, art roman*
Paper, H. 23.5 cm; W. 19 cm
1934
Courtesy of ISAW
ISAW: N5370.B3 1934

Bibliography

Alpers, Svetlana

1991   "The Museum as a Way of Seeing." In *Exhibiting Cultures: The Poetics and Politics of Museum Display*, edited by Ivan Karp and Steven D. Lavine, 25–32. Washington: Smithsonian Institution Press.

Amiet, Pierre

1980   *La glyptique mésopotamienne archaïque*. Paris: Éditions du Centre national de la recherche scientifique.

Andrae, Walter

1922   *Die archaischen Ischtar-Tempel in Assur*. Leipzig: J. C. Hinrichs.

Aruz, Joan, and Ronald Wallenfels

2003   *Art of the First Cities: The Third Millennium B.C. from the Mediterranean to the Indus*. New York: Metropolitan Museum of Art; New Haven: Yale University Press.

Azara, Pedro (ed.)

2012   *Antes del diluvio: Mesopotamia, 3500–2100 A.C.* Barcelona: Polígrafa and Fundación "la Caixa."

Baadsgaard, Aubrey

2008   *Trends, Traditions and Transformations: Fashions in Dress in Early Mesopotamia*. PhD diss., University of Pennsylvania.

Baadsgaard, Aubrey, Janet Monge, and Richard L. Zettler

2012   "Bludgeoned, Burned, and Beautified: Reevaluating Mortuary Practices in the Royal Cemetery of Ur." In *Sacred Killing: The Archaeology of Sacrifice in the Near East*, edited by Anne Porter and Glenn M. Schwartz, 125–58. Winona Lake, IN: Eisenbrauns.

Baadsgaard, Aubrey, et al.

2011   "Human Sacrifice and Intentional Corpse Preservation in the Royal Cemetery of Ur." *Antiquity* 85, no. 327: 27–42.

Bahrani, Zainab

2014   *The Infinite Image: Art, Time and the Aesthetic Dimension in Antiquity*. London: Reaktion.

2011a   "Poseer Mesopotamia." In Azara 2011, 104–7.

2011b   "Untold Tales of Mesopotamian
         Discovery." In *Scramble for the Past:
         A Story of Archaeology in the Ottoman
         Empire, 1753–1914*, edited by Zainab
         Bahrani, Çelik Zeynep, and Edhem
         Eldem, 125–55. Istambul: SALT.

2008   *Rituals of War: The Body and Violence in
         Mesopotamia.* New York: Zone.

2006   "Race and Ethnicity in Mesopotamian
         Antiquity." *World Archaeology* 38, no. 1:
         52–53.

2003   *The Graven Image: Representation in
         Babylonia and Assyria.* Philadelphia:
         University of Pennsylvania Press.

2002   "Performativity and the Image:
         Narrative, Representation, and the Uruk
         Vase." In *Leaving No Stones Unturned:
         Essays on the Ancient Near East and
         Egypt in Honor of Donald P. Hansen*,
         edited by Erica Eherenberg, 15–22.
         Winona Lake, IN: Eisenbrauns.

1995   "Assault and Abduction: The Fate of the
         Royal Image in the Ancient Near East."
         Art History 18, no. 3 (Sept.): 363–82.

Barrett, Caítlin E.

2007   "Was Dust Their Food and Clay
         Their Bread? Grave Goods, the
         Mesopotamian Afterlife, and the
         Liminal Role of Inana/Ishtar." *Journal of
         Ancient Near Eastern Religions* 7, no. 1:
         7–64.

Basmachi, Faraj

1976   *Treasures of the Iraq Museum.* Baghdad:
         Ministry of Information, Directorate
         General of Antiquities.

Benzel, Kim

2013   "Pu-abi's Adornment for the Afterlife:
         Materials and Technologies of Jewelry
         at Ur in Mesopotamia." Ph.D. disserta-
         tion, Columbia University.

Bernhardsson, Magnus T.

2005   *Reclaiming a Plundered Past:
         Archaeology and Nation Building in
         Modern Iraq.* Austin: University of Texas
         Press.

Bimson, Mavis

1980   "Cosmetic Pigments from the 'Royal
         Cemetery' at Ur." *Iraq* 42, no. 1 (Spring):
         75–77.

Bowring, Joanna

2012   "Chronology of Temporary Exhibitions
         at the British Museum." *British Museum
         Research Publication* 189.

Braun-Holzinger, Eva Andrea

1991   *Mesopotamische Weihgaben der
         frühdynastischen bis altbabylonischen
         Zeit.* Heidelberger Studien zum alten
         Orient 3. Heidelberg: Heidelberger
         Orientverlag.

1977   *Frühdynastische Beterstatuetten.*
         Abhandlungen der Deutschen Orient-
         Gesellschaft 19. Berlin: Mann.

Brier, Bob

2013   *Egyptomania: Our Three Thousand
         Year Obsession with the Land of
         the Pharaohs.* New York: Palgrave
         Macmillan.

Bruschweiler, Françoise

1987   *Inanna: La déesse triomphante et vain-
         cue dans la cosmologie Sumérienne.* Les
         Cahiers du CEPOA 4. Leuven: Peeters.

Cassin, Elen

1968   *La splendeur divine.* Civilisations et
         Sociétés 8. Paris: Mouton.

Century of Progress

1934   Century of Progress International
         Exposition. *Official Guide Book of
         the World's Fair of 1934.* Chicago:
         the Exposition

Cohen, Andrew C.

2005   *Death Rituals, Ideology, and the
         Development of Early Mesopotamian
         Kingship: Toward a New Understanding
         of Iraq's Royal Cemetery of Ur.* Leiden
         Boston: Brill.

Collins, Paul, and Liam McNamara

2014   *Discovering Tutankhamun.* Exh. cat.
         Oxford: Ashmolean Museum of Art and
         Archaeology.

Connelly, Frances S.

1998   S.v., "Primitivism." In *Encyclopedia of
         Aesthetics*, edited by Michael Kelly.
         New York: Oxford University Press.

1995 *The Sleep of Reason: Primitivism in Modern European Art and Aesthetics, 1725–1907*. University Park: Pennsylvania State University Press.

Cooper, Jerrold
1993 "Sumerian and Aryan: Racial Theory, Academic Politics and Parisian Assyriology." In *Revue de l'histoire des religions* 210, no. 2: 169–205.

Córdoba, Joaquín Ma, Fernando Escribano, and Montserrat Mané
2006/7 "Viajeros y estudiosos en el redescubrimiento del Oriente Próximo antiguo: Otras consideraciones, vols. 1 y 2." *Isimu: Revista sobre el Oriente Próximo y Egipto en la Antigüedad* 9 (2006) and 10 (2007).

Danto, Arthur C.
1987 "Primitivism in 20th Century Art." In *The State of Art*, 23–27. New York: Prentice Hall.
1981 *The Transfiguration of the Commonplace: A Philosophy of Art*. Cambridge, MA: Harvard University Press.

Dick, Michael B.
2005 "The Mesopotamian Cult Statue: A Sacramental Encounter with Divinity." In *Cult Image and Divine Representation in the Ancient Near East*, edited by Neal H. Walls, pp. 43–67. Boston: American Schools of Oriental Research.

Didi-Huberman, George
2007 *L'image ouverte: Motifs de l'incarnation dans les arts visuels*. Paris: Gallimard.
1992 *Ce que nous voyons, ce qui nous regarde*. Paris: Minuit.

Directorate General of Antiquities [Iraq]
1942 *A Guide to the 'Iraq Museum Collections*. Baghdad: printed at the Government Press.

Dyson, Robert H., Jr.
1977 "Archival Glimpses of the Ur Expedition in the Years 1920 to 1926." *Expedition* 7, no. 1 (Fall): 5–23. http://www.penn.museum/documents/publications/expedition/PDFs/20-1/Archival.pdf.

Emberling, Geoff
2010 *Pioneers to the Past: American Archaeologists in the Middle East, 1919–1920*. Chicago: Oriental Institute of the University of Chicago.

2009 "Views of a Museum: The Extraordinary Collection of the Oriental Institute, University of Chicago." *Journal of the Canadian Society for Mesopotamian Studies* 4 (Fall): 29–35.

Emberling, Geoff, and Katharyn Hanson
2008 *Catastrophe! The Looting and Destruction of Iraq's Past*. Oriental Institute Museum Publication 28. Chicago: Oriental Institute of the University of Chicago.

Errington, Shelly
1994 "What Became Authentic Primitive Art?" *Cultural Anthropology* 9, no. 2: 201–26.

Evans, Jean M.
2014 "The Tell Asmar Hoard and Rituals of Early Dynastic Sculpture." In *Critical Approaches to Ancient Near Eastern Art*, edited by Brian A. Brown and Marian H. Feldman, 645–65. Boston: Walter de Gruyter.
2012a *The Lives of Sumerian Sculpture: An Archaeology of the Early Dynastic Temple*. Cambridge: Cambridge University Press.
2012b "Reconstruction of Statues and Statue from Tell Asmar, Iraq." In Green, Teeter, and Larson 2012, 141–42.

2007 "The Square Temple at Tell Asmar and the Construction of Early Dynastic Mesopotamia, ca. 2900–2350 B.C.E." *American Journal of Archaeology* 111, no. 4: 599–632.

Fabian, Johannes
1983 *Time and the Other: How Anthropology Makes Its Object*. New York: Columbia University Press.

Falk, John H.
2006 "An Identity-Centered Approach to Understanding Museum Learning." *Curator: The Museum Journal* 49, no. 2: 151–66.

Falk, John H., and Dierking, Lynn D.
2013   *The Museum Experience Revisited.*
        Walnut Creek, CA: Left Coast Press.

Förtsch, Wilhelm
1914   *Religionsgeschichtliche Unter-
        suchungen zu den ältesten babylo-
        nischen Inschriften.* Mitteilungen der
        Vorderasiatischen Gesellschaft 19.
        Leipzig: J. C. Hinrichs.

Franke, Judith A.
1977   "The Oriental Institute Museum." In
        *The Oriental Institute Annual Report,
        1976–77,* 56–59. Chicago: Oriental
        Institute of the University of Chicago.

Frankfort, Henri
1954   *The Art and Architecture of the Ancient
        Orient.* Harmondsworth: Penguin.
        Reprinted, New Haven: Yale University
        Press, 1995.
1943   *More Sculpture from the Diyala Region.*
        Oriental Institute Publications 60.
        Chicago: University of Chicago Press.
        http://oi.uchicago.edu/research/pub-
        lications/oip/oip-60-more-sculpture-
        diyala-region.
1939   *Sculpture of the Third Millennium B.C.
        from Tell Asmar and Khafājah.* Chicago:
        University of Chicago Press. http://
        oi.uchicago.edu/research/publications/
        oip/oip-44-sculpture-third-millennium-
        bc-tell-asmar-and-khafajah.
1936   *Progress of the Work of the Oriental
        Institute in Iraq, 1934/35: Fifth
        Preliminary Report of the Iraq Expedition.*
        Oriental Institute Communications 20.
        Chicago: University of Chicago Press.
1935a   *Oriental Institute Discoveries in Iraq,
        1933/34: Fourth Preliminary Report of
        the Iraq Expedition.* Oriental Institute
        Communications 19. Chicago:
        University of Chicago Press.
1935b   "Sumerian Sculpture." *Burlington
        Magazine* 66, no. 384 (Mar.): 110–21.
1935c   "New Works by Barbara Hepworth."
        *Axis: A Quarterly Review of
        Contemporary "Abstract" Painting and
        Sculpture* 3: 14–18.
1934a   "An Extraordinary Discovery of Early
        Sumerian Sculpture." *Illustrated London
        News,* May 19, 771–78, 802.
1934b   "Sumerian Sculpture about 3000
        B.C." *Illustrated London News,* June 9,
        910–13.

1932a   *Archaeology and the Sumerian Problem.*
        Chicago: University of Chicago Press.
1932b   "On Egyptian Art." *The Journal of
        Egyptian Archaeology* 18: 33–48.

**Frankfort, Henri, and
H. A. Groenewegen-Frankfort**
1946   "Myth and Reality." In *The Intellectual
        Adventure of Ancient Man: An Essay on
        Speculative Thought in the Ancient Near
        East,* by Henri Frankfort et al., 3–27.
        Chicago: University of Chicago Press.

Gansell, Amy Rebecca
2007   "Identity and Adornment in the
        Third-Millennium BC Mesopotamian
        'Royal Cemetery' at Ur." *Cambridge
        Archaeological Journal* 17, no. 1
        (Feb.): 29–46.

Ganz, Cheryl R.
2012   *The 1933 Chicago World's Fair: A
        Century of Progress.* Urbana: University
        of Illinois Press.

Gelb, Ignace J.
1957   *Glossary of Old Akkadian.* Materials for
        the Assyrian Dictionary 3. Chicago:
        University of Chicago Press.

Gell, Alfred
1998   *Art and Agency: An Anthropological
        Theory.* Oxford: Clarendon.
1992   "The Technology of Enchantment and
        the Enchantment of Technology." In
        Anthropology, Art, and Aesthetics, edited
        by Jeremy Coote and Anthony Shelton,
        40–66. Oxford: Clarendon.

Green, Jack, and Emily Teeter (eds.)
2013   *Our Work: Modern Jobs, Ancient
        Origins.* Portrait photography by Jason
        Reblando. Oriental Institute Museum
        Publications 36. Chicago: Oriental
        Institute of the University of Chicago.

**Green, Jack, Emily Teeter, and
John A. Larson**
2012   *Picturing the Past: Imaging and
        Imagining the Ancient Middle East.*
        Oriental Institute Museum Publications
        34. Chicago: Oriental Institute of the
        University of Chicago.

Green, Margaret W., and Hans J. Nisen
1987   *Zeichenliste der Archaischen Texte aus Uruk. Archäische Texte aus Uruk*, vol. 2. Ausgrabungen der deutschen Forschungsgemeinshaft in Uruk-Warka 11. Berlin: Gerb. Mann Verlag.

Hall, H. R.
1928   "The Excavations at Ur." *The British Museum Quarterly* 3, no. 3: 65–69.
1924   "Notes on the Excavations of 1919 at Muqayyar, el-ʿObeid, and Abu Shahrein." In *Centenary Supplement of the Journal of the Royal Asiatic Society.* London: The Society: 103–15.
1923   "Ur and Eridu: The British Excavations of 1919." *The Journal of Egyptian Archaeology* 9, nos. 1–4 (Apr.–Oct.): 176–95.
1922   "The Discoveries at Tell El-ʿObeid in Southern Babylonian, and Some Egyptian Comparisons." *The Journal of Egyptian Archaeology* 8: 241–57.

Hall, H. R., and C. Leonard Woolley
1927   *Ur Excavations*. Vol. 1, *Alʾ-Ubaid: A Report on the Work Carried out at Al-ʿUbaid for the British Museum in 1919 and for the Joint Expedition in 1922–23*. Publications of the Joint Expedition of the British Museum and of the Museum of the University of Pennsylvania to Mesopotamia 3. Oxford: Oxford University Press.

Jacobsen, Thorkild
1995   "Searching for Sumer and Akkad." In *Civilizations of the Ancient Near East*, edited by Jack M. Sasson, vol. 4, 2743–52. New York: Scribner.
1987   *The Harps That Once: Sumerian Poetry in Translation*. New Haven: Yale University Press.

Jones, Tom (ed.)
1969   *The Sumerian Problem*. New York: Wiley.

Katz, Dina
1995   Inanna's descent and undressing the dead as a divine law. ZA 85: 221–33.

Keith, Arthur
1934   "Report on the Human Remains." In Woolley 1934, 400–409.

Koerner, Joseph Leo
1999   "Factura." Editorial. *RES: Anthropology and Aesthetics* 36 (Autumn): 5–19.

Kopytoff, Igor
1986   "The Cultural Biography of Things: Commoditization as Process." In *The Social Life of Things: Commodities in Cultural Perspective*, edited by Arjun Appadurai, 64–91. Cambridge: Cambridge University Press.

Kramer, Samuel Noah
1960   "Death and Nether World According to the Sumerian Literary Texts." *Iraq* 22 (Spring/Autumn): 59–68.

Kuklick, Bruce
1996   *Puritans in Babylon: The Ancient Near East and American Intellectual Life, 1880–1930*. Princeton: Princeton University Press.

Laude, Jean
1981   "Art et mythe: Formes de la fonction signifiante dans l'Afrique sub-saharienne." In *Dictionnaire des mythologies et des religions des sociétés traditionnelles et du monde antique*, vol. 1, edited by Yves Bonnefoy, 74–78. Paris: Flammarion.

Lazaar, Lina (ed.)
2011   *The Future of a Promise [Contemporary Art from the Arab World]*. Tunis: Ibraaz.

Legrain, Léon
1931   "L'art sumérien au temps de la reine Shoubad." *Gazette des Beaux-Arts* 73, pt. 2 (July): 1–26.
1929   "The Boudoir of Queen Shubad." *Museum Journal* (University of Pennsylvania Museum) 20 (Sept./Dec.): 211–45.

Marchesi, Gianni
2004   "Who Was Buried in the Royal Tombs of Ur? The Epigraphic and Textual Data." *Orientalia* 73: 153–97.

Mackay, Ernest
1929   *A Sumerian Palace and the "A" Cemetery at Kish, Mesopotamia*. Anthropology, Memoirs, no. 2. Chicago: Field Museum of Natural History.

Maxwell-Hyslop, K. R.
1971   *Western Asiatic Jewellery, c. 300–612 B.C.*. London: Methuen.

Meskell, Lynn
2004   *Object Worlds in Ancient Egypt: Material Biographies Past and Present.* Oxford: Berg.

Michalowski, Piotr
2006   "Puabi." In *Reallexikon der Assyriologie*, vol. 11, fasc. 1/2, edited by Michael P. Streck, 105–6. Berlin: de Gruyter.

Miller, Daniel (ed.)
1998   *Material Cultures: Why Some Things Matter.* Chicago: University of Chicago Press.

Miller, Naomi F.
2013   "Symbols of Fertility and Abundance in the Royal Cemetery at Ur, Iraq." *American Journal of Archaeology* 117, no. 1 (Jan.): 127–33.
2000   "Plant Forms in Jewellery from the Royal Cemetery at Ur." *Iraq* 62: 149–55.
1999   "Date Sex in Mesopotamia!" *Expedition* 41, no. 1 (Mar.): 29–30.

Mitchell, W. J. T.
2005   *What Do Pictures Want? The Lives and Loves of Images.* Chicago: University of Chicago Press.
1994   *Picture Theory: Essays on Verbal and Visual Representation.* Chicago: University of Chicago Press.
1986   *Iconology: Image, Text, Ideology.* Chicago: University of Chicago Press.

Molleson, Theya, and Dawn Hodgson
2003   "The Human Remains from Woolley's Excavations at Ur." *Iraq* 65: 91–129.

Morphy, Howard, and Morgan Perkins (eds.)
2005   *The Anthropology of Art: A Reader.* Malden, MA: Wiley-Blackwell.

Moser, Stephanie
2006   *Wondrous Curiosities: Ancient Egypt at the British Museum.* Chicago: University of Chicago Press.

Müller-Scheessel, Nils
2001   "Fair Prehistory: Archaeological Exhibits at French Expositions Universelles." *Antiquity* 75, no. 288: 391–401.

Oriental Institute
1982   *A Guide to the Oriental Institute Museum.* Chicago: Oriental Institute of the University of Chicago.

Pallis, Svend Aage
1956   *The Antiquity of Iraq: A Handbook of Assyriology.* Copenhagen: E. Munksgaard.

Pittman, Holly
1998   "Jewelry." In *Treasures from the Royal Tombs of Ur*, edited by Richard L. Zettler and Lee Horne, 87–122. Philadelphia: University of Pennsylvania Museum of Archaeology and Anthropology.

Polonsky, Janice
2002   "The Rise of the Sun God and the Determination of Destiny in Ancient Mesopotamia." Ph.D. diss., University of Pennsylvania.

Rancière, Jacques
2011   *Aisthesis: Scènes du régime esthétique de l'art.* Paris: Galilée.

Reade, Julian
2003   "The Royal Tombs of Ur." In Aruz and Wallenfels 2003, 93–96.

Redman, Charles L.
1978   *The Rise of Civilization: From Early Farmers to Urban Society in the Ancient Near East.* San Francisco: W. H. Freeman.

Roelstraete, Dieter
2014   *The Way of the Shovel: On the Archaeological Imaginary in Art.* Exh. cat., Museum of Contemporary Art. Chicago: University of Chicago Press.

Rothschild, Edward F.
1929   "Ancient Sculpture." *The American Journal of Semitic Languages and Literature* 45, no. 3: 218.

Rubin, William
1984   *"Primitivism" in 20th Century Art: Affinity of the Tribal and the Modern.* New York: Museum of Modern Art.

Rubio, G.
1999   "On the Alleged 'Pre-Sumerian Substratum.'" *Journal of Cuneiform Studies* 51: 1–16.

Schauensee, Maude de
2002   *Two Lyres from Ur.* Philadelphia: University of Pennsylvania Museum of Archaeology and Anthropology.

Shaw, Wendy M. K.
2003   *Possessors and Possessed: Museums, Archaeology and the Visualization of History in the Late Ottoman Empire.* Berkeley: University of California Press.

Shrenk, Lisa D.
2007   *Building a Century of Progress: The Architecture of Chicago's 1933–34 World's Fair.* Minneapolis: University of Minnesota Press.

Sladek, William R.
1974   *Inanna's Descent to the Netherworld.* Ph.D. diss., Johns Hopkins University.

Sollberger, Edmond
1960   "Notes on the Early Inscriptions from Ur and El-'Obed." *Iraq* 22: 69–89.

Spycket, Agnès
1981   *La statuaire du proche-orient ancien.* Leiden: E. J. Brill.

Steiner, Christopher B.
2002   "The Taste of Angels in the Art of Darkness: Fashioning the Canon of African Art." In *Art History and Its Institutions: Foundations of a Discipline*, edited by Elizabeth Mansfield, 136–39. London: Routledge.

Suter, Claudia E.
2000   *Gudea's Temple Building: The Representation of an Early Mesopotamian Ruler in Text and Image.* Groningen: STYX.

Sweeney, James Johnson
1943   *Plastic Redirections in 20th Century Painting.* Chicago: University of Chicago Press.

Teeter, Emily
2012   "Copy of the Bust of Nefertiti." In Green et al. 2012, 165–66.

Tengberg, M., D. T. Potts, and H.-P. Francfort
2008   "The Golden Leaves of Ur." *Antiquity* 82: 925–36.

Vuure, T., van
2005   *Retracing the Aurochs: History, Morphology, and Ecology of an Extinct Wild Ox.* Sofia: Pensoft.

Walker, Christopher, and Michael B. Dick
1999   "The Induction of the Cult Image in Ancient Mesopotamia: The Mesopotamian *mūs pî* Ritual." In *Born in Heaven, Made on Earth: The Making of the Cult Image in the Ancient Near East*, edited by Michael B. Dick, 55–121. Winona Lake, IN: Eisenbrauns.

Winter, Irene J.
2012   "Gold! Divine Light, Lustre and in Ancient Mesopotamia." In *Ancient and Modern Issues in Cultural Heritage: Colour and Light in Architecture, Art and Material Culture; Islamic Archaeology. Proceedings of the Seventh International Congress on the Archaeology of the Ancient Near East, London, 12–16 April 2010, the British Museum and UCL, London*, edited by Roger Matthews and John Curtis, vol. 2, 153–72. Wiesbaden: Harrassowitz.
2009   "What/When Is a Portrait? Royal Images of the Ancient near East" In *Proceedings of the American Philosophical Society,* 153, no. 3 (Sept.), 354–70.
2008   "Sennacherib's Expert Knowledge: Skill and Mastery as Components of Royal Display." In *Classifying Knowledge: Proceedings of the 51st Rencontre Assyriologique Internationale* [SAOC 62], edited by R. D. Biggs, J. Meyers, and M. T. Roth, 333–40. Chicago: Oriental Institute of the University of Chicago.

2007 "Representing Abundance: the Visual Dimension of the Agrarian State." In Settlement and Society: Essays Dedicated to Robert McCormick Adams, edited by Elizabeth Caecilia Stone, 117–38. Los Angeles: Cotsen Institute of Archaeology,University of California; Chicago: Oriental Institute of the University of Chicago.

2003 "'Surpassing Work': Mastery of Materials and the Value of Skilled Production in Ancient Sumer." In Culture through Objects: Ancient Near Eastern Studies in Honour of P. R. S. Moorey, edited by Timothy Potts, Michael Roaf, and Diana Stein, 403–21. Oxford: Griffith Institute.

1999 "The Aesthetic Value of Lapis Lazuli in Mesopotamia." In Cornaline et pierres précieuses: La Méditerranée, de l'antiq-uité à l'Islam; Actes du colloque organisé au Musée du Louvre par le Service culturel les 24 et 25 novembre 1995, edited by Annie Caubet, 43–58. Paris: Documentation française.

1995 "Aesthetics in Ancient Mesopotamian Art." In Civilizations of the Ancient Near East, edited by Jack M. Sasson, vol. 4, 2569–80. New York: Scribner.

1989 "The Body of the Able Ruler: Toward an Understanding of the Statues of Gudea." In Dumu-e2-dub-ba-a: Studies in Honor of Åke W. Sjöberg, edited by Hermann Behrens, Darlene Loding, and Maria Tobi Roth, 573–83. Philadelphia: Samuel Noah Kramer Fund, University Museum.

Wood, Jon
2003 "Gods, Graves and Sculptors: Gudea, Sumerian Sculpture, and the Avant-Garde, c. 1930–1935." Sculpture Journal 10: 67–82.

Woolley, C. Leonard
1954 Excavations at Ur: A Record of Twelve Years Work. London: Benn.
1953 Spadework: Adventures in Archaeology. London: Lutterworth.
1935 Abraham: Recent Discoveries and Hebrew Origins. London: Faber and Faber.
1934 The Royal Cemetery. 2 vols. Ur Excavations 2. London: The Trustees of the British Museum and the Museum of the University of Pennsylvania.

1929 "Excavations at Ur, 1928–9." The Antiquaries Journal 9, no. 4: 305–43.
1928 "Excavations at Ur, 1927–8." The Antiquaries Journal 8, no. 4: 415–48.
1927–76 Ur Excavations. 10 vols. London: Oxford University Press. http://ancient-worldonline.blogspot.com.es/2014/09/open-access-monograph-series-ur.html.

Wronski, Torseten, et al.
2010 "Differences in Sexual Dimorphism among Four Gazelle Taxa (Gazella spp.) in the Middle East." Animal Biology 60, no. 4 (2010): 395–412.

Zervos, Christian
1935 L'Art de la Mésopotamie de la fin du quatrième millénaire au XVe siècle avant notre ère. Paris: Éditions "Cahiers d'art."

Zettler, Richard L.
1998 "Ur of Chaldees." In Zettler and Horne 1998, 10–21.

Zettler, Richard L., and Lee Horne (eds.)
1998 Treasures from the Royal Tombs of Ur. Philadelphia: University of Pennsylvania Museum of Archaeology and Anthropology.

Zimmerman, Paul C.
1998a "A Critical Reexamination of the Early Dynastic 'Royal Tomb': Architecture from Ur." Unpublished M.A. research paper, Department of Anthropology, University of Pennsylvania.
1998b "Two Tombs or Three?" In Zettler and Horne 1998, 39.

Zimmerman, Paul C., and Richard L. Zettler
Forthcoming "Two Tombs or Three? PG 789 and PG 800 Again!"

Maps

The base maps (page 20, Chapter 6: Fig. 1) have been supplied by the Ancient World Mapping Center, University of North Carolina, Chapel Hill. Terrain depiction calculated from "SRTM Shade Relief," on ESRI Data and Map, DVD-ROM (Redlands, CA: Environmental System Research Institute, 2008). All other map information and final design: Jennifer M. Babcock, Narges Bayani, and CoDe. New York Inc. © 2015 ISAW

Drawings

Andrae, W., *Die archaischen Ischtar-Tempel in Assur.* Ausgrabungen der Deutschen Orient-Gesellschaft in Assur 52 (Leipzig: J. C. Hinrichs, 1992), table 11a.
Chapter 6, Fig. 9

Delougaz, P., and S. Lloyd, *Pre-Sargonid Temples in the Diyala Region*, Oriental Institute Publications 58 (Chicago: University of Chicago Press, 1942), fig. 159.
Chapter 6, Fig. 16

Delougaz, P. *The Temple Oval at Khafaje.* Oriental Institute Publications 53 (Chicago: University of Chicago Press, 1940), pl. III.
Chapter 7: Fig. 1 Inset and Fig. 3 Inset

Reconstructions by William B. Hafford, Ur Digitization Project, University of Pennsylvania Museum of Archaeology and Anthropology.
Chapter 3: Figs. 2, 6

Woolley, C. L., *The Royal Cemetery*, Ur Excavations 2 (Oxford: Oxford University Press, 1934).
Chapter 3: Fig. 3: pls. 273, 274. Fig. 4: pl. 36. Fig. 5: pl. 29. Chapter 4: Fig. 1: pl. 146. Fig. 7: pl. 142

Zettler, R. L., and L. Horne, eds., *Treasures from the Royal Tombs of Ur* (Philadelphia: University of Pennsylvania Museum of Archaeology and Anthropology, 1998), 93, fig. 30.
Chapter 4: Fig. 9
Chapter 7: Figs. 1 (top), 4, 5 Inset
Unpublished field plans and drawings © Conrad Preusser and Hamilton Darby, 1930–31. Courtesy of Oriental Institute's Diyala Project. Chapter 7: Fig. 1 (bottom): © Hamilton Darby

Photography

Alinari Archives, Florence:
Chapter 6: Fig. 8

The Gertrude Bell Archive, Newcastle University
Chapter 2: Fig. 2

Birmingham Museums and Art Gallery: © Marie Louise Baker Estate. Photo © Birmingham Museums Trust
Chapter 5: Fig. 5. Checklist: Nos. 103, 104

The British Museum: © The Trustees of the British Museum
Chapter 3: Figs. 7–9. Chapter 4: Figs. 3, 5, 6, 8. Checklist: No. 90

The Brooklyn Museum: © The Willem de Kooning Foundation/Artists Rights Society (ARS), New York
Chapter 1: Fig. 20

Mary Evans Picture Library: © Illustrated London News Ltd/Mary Evans
Chapter 1: Fig. 3. Chapter 2: Figs. 5, 8–10, 16. Chapter 6: Fig. 10. Checklist: Nos. 21, 22, 25, 65

The Field Museum of Natural History, Chicago: © The Field Museum
Checklist: Nos. 56–61. Checklist: Nos. 62–64: Photo: Karen Bean. Checklist: Nos. 67, 68: 158355, 158312, Photo: Sarah Rivers. Checklist: Nos. 69–71: 236636, 236527, 156986, Photo: John Weinstein

Additional Photography